SOLO

THE MESSAGE//REMIX: SOLO

AN UNCOMMON DEVOTIONAL

THE MESSAGE TEXT BY EUGENE H. PETERSON

DEVOTIONAL CONTENT BY JAN JOHNSON, J.R. BRIGGS, AND KATIE PECKHAM

SOLO

NAVPRESS⬤

NavPress is the publishing ministry of The Navigators, an international Christian organization and leader in personal spiritual development. NavPress is committed to helping people grow spiritually and enjoy lives of meaning and hope through personal and group resources that are biblically rooted, culturally relevant, and highly practical.

For a free catalog go to www.NavPress.com
or call 1.800.366.7788 in the United States or 1.800.839.4769 in Canada.

ISBN-13: 978-1-60006-869-0

Cover design by Burnkit
Creative Team: Kent Wilson, Laura Wright, Amy Spencer, Lori Mitchell, Reagen Reed, Arvid Wallen, Pat Reinheimer

Some of the anecdotal illustrations in this book are true to life and are included with the permission of the persons involved. All other illustrations are composites of real situations, and any resemblance to people living or dead is coincidental.

Unless otherwise identified, all Scripture quotations in this publication are taken from *THE MESSAGE* (MSG). Copyright © 1993, 1994, 1995, 1996, 2000, 2001, 2002, 2005. Used by permission of NavPress Publishing Group. Also used is the HOLY BIBLE: NEW INTERNATIONAL VERSION® (NIV®). Copyright © 1973, 1978, 1984 by International Bible Society. Used by permission of Zondervan Publishing House. All rights reserved.

Devotional text by Jan Johnson, J. R. Briggs, and Katie Peckham.

Published in association with the literary agency of Alive Communications, Inc., 7680 Goddard Street, Suite 200, Colorado Springs, CO 80920, www.alivecommunications.com.

Printed in the United States of America

3 4 5 6 7 8 9 10 / 14 13 12 11 10 09

INTRODUCTION TO *SOLO*

The devotional you hold is unique. It isn't designed to teach you to study the Bible but rather to develop a conversation between you and God. The devotions found in *Solo* are based on the classical method of lectio divina: reading, thinking, praying, and living Scripture with the intention of inviting an infinite, omniscient God into your life — as it is, no gloss, no veneer. Lectio divina is more Bible basking than Bible study, as it teaches you to absorb and meditate on Scripture, to converse with God openly, and to live out what has become a part of you — his Word.

But it's not easy. Lectio divina takes practice, and lots of it. You will have to learn to be quiet, to silence the voices of responsibility, self, family, and even religion in order to hear what God has to say to you. Try not to view the elements of lectio divina as steps to be checked off your to-do list. Instead, allow them to meld together in the intentional process of listening to God, of focusing on him and learning what he would have from you and for you, his beloved. Don't worry if no lightning strikes or brilliant revelations come. Sometimes devotion means just sitting in the presence of God.

We know the four elements of lectio divina as Read, Think, Pray, and Live. Each element has a purpose, but don't be surprised if they overlap and weave into each other. Remember as you dive into this devotional that lectio divina is about wholeness: whole practice, whole Bible, whole God.

Read. Thoughtfully, leisurely, faithfully — read the epic love story that is the Bible. Yes, love story. The Bible is the chronicle of God's love for his people from the darkness before Eden to eternity with him in heaven. You are in it; I am in it. But most important, God is in it. Here you will meet him face-to-face.

Eugene Peterson called the Bible "a book that reads us even as we read it." That's an uncommon sort of book, and it requires an uncommon sort of read. Knowing facts about God doesn't change your relationship with him, so take the time to splash around in the Word, to absorb it, to discover what God has to say to you each day.

In each *Solo* devotion, you will find a Scripture passage, but also a reference to an expanded passage. I encourage you to read them both, slowly, attentively, and repeatedly. As Peterson said, "The Bible is given to us in the first place simply to invite us to make ourselves at home in the world of God . . . and become familiar with the way God speaks and the ways in which we answer him with our lives." No Scripture passage exists in a vacuum. Whenever you can, take the time to stretch beyond the passage put before you to understand the larger context in which it is found. The more you read, the more you will understand about yourself and this God who created you.

Think. Each subtle, significant, powerful word of Scripture is meant for you. One word may speak today and another tomorrow, but God sent each of them straight into your life. So listen. Go into your reading with a clean slate. Don't bring what you think you need to hear, what others have said, or what you've been taught about a particular passage. Don't bring fear that you'll misinterpret the text. This is about what God has to say to you.

Our lives are full of static. Whether it's our to-do list, our emotions, or just plain noise, it can be hard to sift God's voice from all the racket. By meditating on each word, by turning it over and over in your mind, you will discover that, as God himself is infinitely complex, so his thoughts have subtle meaning beyond the rote. The more you think about what you read, the more familiar you will become with his voice.

Pray. God yearns to converse with you. And he wants far more than just "thanks for this, can I please have that" prayer. Respond to him in dialogue. That means it's as much about listening as it is about speaking. Open your ears and your heart to hear his voice. Sing praises or laments; write your thoughts in a journal; dance or prostrate yourself before him. Pray.

Maybe God has challenged you. Tell him how you feel, but always remember that what he asks, he asks for your good. He is loving and merciful, not manipulative and harsh. If you come across something in your reading that you don't understand, tell him about it. Ask him about it. Fill your prayers with Scripture. Using the words you have read helps you ensure that your prayers line up with God's Word and intention for your life.

It's easy for us in our culture of doing to want to skim over this part. Don't. Even if you are quiet and he is quiet, you are learning to communicate with God.

Live. You can read, think, and pray all day, but unless you live in God's Word as well, you miss the point. The Bible says, "Isn't it obvious that

God-talk without God-acts is outrageous nonsense?" (James 2). If you have taken God's Word to heart and truly made it part of you, it will by its very nature change you. And when it does, you will find yourself called to act. There will come a time when God takes you to the end of yourself then asks you to go further. He wants you to put yourself at his disposal, to go and do what he asks, even the impossible. When that time comes, you will need the Word he has seared on your heart to give you comfort and strength. This is the "more and better life than they ever dreamed of" of which Jesus spoke (John 10).

III

Solo. One on one. Just you and God.

This book is designed to help you develop the habit of lectio divina. For those of you new to the discipline, several of the devotions are specifically intended to help you begin what may become a lifelong pursuit. You will find a list of these beginner devotions in the back of the book, and they are each marked with a ❂. Also, though lectio divina emphasizes becoming familiar with God's whole Word, rather than focusing on any particular part, there may be times when you need to hear God's voice on a specific issue. For those times we have provided an index of topics that will guide you to a devotion that may be just what you need.

The *Solo* devotions are tailored to help you learn to listen to what God may want to say to you through his Word. You will find that every seventh day is marked as a day of reflection, a time to sit back and let God guide your thoughts and prayers back to themes and Scripture from the previous week. Don't be afraid to reflect, and don't be afraid to go back. Each time you read these devotions, you may find that God has something new to say, for though he is the same always, you change a little each day as he shapes you into the person he designed you to be.

And so begins the journey.

TO THE READER

If there is anything distinctive about *The Message*, perhaps it is because the text is shaped by the hand of a working pastor. For most of my adult life I have been given a primary responsibility for getting the message of the Bible into the lives of the men and women with whom I worked. I did it from pulpit and lectern, in home Bible studies and at mountain retreats, through conversations in hospitals and nursing homes, over coffee in kitchens and while strolling on an ocean beach. *The Message* grew from the soil of forty years of pastoral work.

As I worked at this task, this Word of God, which forms and transforms human lives, did form and transform human lives. Planted in the soil of my congregation and community, the seed words of the Bible germinated and grew and matured. When it came time to do the work that is now *The Message*, I often felt that I was walking through an orchard at harvest time, plucking fully formed apples and peaches and plums from laden branches. There's hardly a page in the Bible I did not see lived in some way or other by the men and women, saints and sinners, to whom I was pastor — and then verified in my nation and culture.

I didn't start out as a pastor. I began my vocational life as a teacher and for several years taught the biblical languages of Hebrew and Greek in a theological seminary. I expected to live the rest of my life as a professor and scholar, teaching and writing and studying. But then my life took a sudden vocational turn to pastoring in a congregation.

I was now plunged into quite a different world. The first noticeable difference was that nobody seemed to care much about the Bible, which so recently people had been paying me to teach them. Many of the people I worked with now knew virtually nothing about it, had never read it, and weren't interested in learning. Many others had spent years reading it but for them it had gone flat through familiarity, reduced to clichés. Bored, they dropped it. And there weren't many people in between. Very few were interested in what I considered my primary work, getting the words of the Bible into their heads and hearts, getting the message lived. They found newspapers and magazines, videos and pulp fiction more to their taste.

Meanwhile I had taken on as my life work the responsibility of getting these very people to listen, really listen, to the message in this book. I knew I had my work cut out for me.

I lived in two language worlds, the world of the Bible and the world of Today. I had always assumed they were the same world. But these people didn't see it that way. So out of necessity I became a "translator" (although I wouldn't have called it that then), daily standing on the border between two worlds, getting the language of the Bible that God uses to create and save us, heal and bless us, judge and rule over us, into the language of Today that we use to gossip and tell stories, give directions and do business, sing songs and talk to our children.

And all the time those old biblical languages, those powerful and vivid Hebrew and Greek originals, kept working their way underground in my speech, giving energy and sharpness to words and phrases, expanding the imagination of the people with whom I was working to hear the language of the Bible in the language of Today and the language of Today in the language of the Bible.

I did that for thirty years in one congregation. And then one day (it was April 30, 1990) I got a letter from an editor asking me to work on a new version of the Bible along the lines of what I had been doing as a pastor. I agreed. The next ten years was harvest time. *The Message* is the result.

The Message is a reading Bible. It is not intended to replace the excellent study Bibles that are available. My intent here (as it was earlier in my congregation and community) is simply to get people reading it who don't know that the Bible is read-able at all, at least by them, and to get people who long ago lost interest in the Bible to read it again. But I haven't tried to make it easy — there is much in the Bible that is hard to understand. So at some point along the way, soon or late, it will be important to get a standard study Bible to facilitate further study. Meanwhile, read in order to live, praying as you read, "God, let it be with me just as you say."

— Eugene H. Peterson

✚ DESIRE FOR RECONCILIATION

GENESIS 3:1-10

1 The serpent was clever, more clever than any wild animal GOD had made. He spoke to the Woman: "Do I understand that God told you not to eat from any tree in the garden?"

2-3 The Woman said to the serpent, "Not at all. We can eat from the trees in the garden. It's only about the tree in the middle of the garden that God said, 'Don't eat from it; don't even touch it or you'll die.'"

4-5 The serpent told the Woman, "You won't die. God knows that the moment you eat from that tree, you'll see what's really going on. You'll be just like God, knowing everything, ranging all the way from good to evil."

6 When the Woman saw that the tree looked like good eating and realized what she would get out of it — she'd know everything! — she took and ate the fruit and then gave some to her husband, and he ate.

7 Immediately the two of them did "see what's really going on" — saw themselves naked! They sewed fig leaves together as makeshift clothes for themselves.

8 When they heard the sound of GOD strolling in the garden in the evening breeze, the Man and his Wife hid in the trees of the garden, hid from GOD.

9 GOD called to the Man: "Where are you?"

10 He said, "I heard you in the garden and I was afraid because I was naked. And I hid."

READ

Read the passage, Genesis 3:1-10, carefully.

THINK

For many of us, these are familiar verses. The first two chapters of Genesis speak of God's amazing Creation. Chapter 3 speaks of the rebellion of humankind. And the remainder of the Message details God's intricate and loving plan to redeem, restore, and reconcile creation back to himself after what happened in Genesis 3. God's plan hinges on what happened in the garden. How does this passage speak to your situation today?

PRAY

There is no better way to begin to understand God's Message than to grasp our separation from him because of sin and our desperate need for him to reconcile our relationship. Take some time to confess those areas where you have deliberately rebelled against God.

LIVE

Knowing that you and everyone else on earth have rebelled against God, what do you feel? In what ways does this knowledge affect the way you live your life?

Reread verse 9. If God knows everything, why did he call out to Adam asking, "Where are you?"

In verse 10, Adam responds to God's question by saying, "I heard you in the garden and I was afraid because I was naked. And I hid." When are you most tempted to hide?

WRESTLING IN THE NIGHT

GENESIS 32:22-32

22-23 But during the night he got up and took his two wives, his two maid-servants, and his eleven children and crossed the ford of the Jabbok. He got them safely across the brook along with all his possessions.

24-25 But Jacob stayed behind by himself, and a man wrestled with him until daybreak. When the man saw that he couldn't get the best of Jacob as they wrestled, he deliberately threw Jacob's hip out of joint.

26 The man said, "Let me go; it's daybreak."

Jacob said, "I'm not letting you go 'til you bless me."

27 The man said, "What's your name?"

He answered, "Jacob."

28 The man said, "But no longer. Your name is no longer Jacob. From now on it's Israel (God-Wrestler); you've wrestled with God and you've come through."

29 Jacob asked, "And what's your name?"

The man said, "Why do you want to know my name?" And then, right then and there, he blessed him.

30 Jacob named the place Peniel (God's Face) because, he said, "I saw God face-to-face and lived to tell the story!"

31-32 The sun came up as he left Peniel, limping because of his hip. (This is why Israelites to this day don't eat the hip muscle; because Jacob's hip was thrown out of joint.)

READ

Read the passage slowly. (To find out about Jacob's fear of meeting his brother, Esau, whom he had tricked many years before, read the expanded passage.)

THINK

Read the passage aloud this time and pause after each of the three questions in the text (verses 27,29). Jacob, whose name means "manipulator," had made elaborate plans to reconcile with Esau in a generous, peaceful way. Then he stayed behind, which was uncharacteristic of such a quintessential deal maker. There with the night sounds and the smell of the brook, Jacob encountered "a man." Was this man an angel, a God-man, Jesus? (It's okay that we don't know for sure.)

1. Picture yourself in this passage. Are you Jacob? Are you an invisible bystander watching it all?
2. What moment in this passage resonates with you most?

   ☐ wanting desperately to be blessed
   ☐ wanting desperately to know more of God
   ☐ other:

PRAY

Depending on what resonated with you, pray about what you desperately want from God. To avoid letting your mind wander, try writing down your prayer, listening for words from God in response.

LIVE

Sit quietly before God, imagining the night sounds and the smell of running water. Try to be comfortable with God in this wild atmosphere. What does it feel like to trust and to reveal the desires of your heart? Be honest if you feel uncomfortable. What would you like it to feel like? Rest in that.

A PICTURE OF FORGIVENESS

GENESIS 50:15-21

15   After the funeral, Joseph's brothers talked among themselves: "What if Joseph is carrying a grudge and decides to pay us back for all the wrong we did him?"

16-17   So they sent Joseph a message, "Before his death, your father gave this command: Tell Joseph, 'Forgive your brothers' sin — all that wrongdoing. They did treat you very badly.' Will you do it? Will you forgive the sins of the servants of your father's God?"

When Joseph received their message, he wept.

18   Then the brothers went in person to him, threw themselves on the ground before him and said, "We'll be your slaves."

19-21   Joseph replied, "Don't be afraid. Do I act for God? Don't you see, you planned evil against me but God used those same plans for my good, as you see all around you right now — life for many people. Easy now, you have nothing to fear; I'll take care of you and your children." He reassured them, speaking with them heart-to-heart.

READ

Take some time before you begin to rest in silence. Let your mind settle. Silently read the passage.

THINK

Read the passage again, this time aloud, listening specifically for a word or phrase that touches your heart. When you finish, close your eyes. Recall the word or phrase, taking it in and mulling it over. After a few moments, write it down. Don't write anything else.

PRAY

Read the passage aloud again, searching for how forgiveness is illustrated in the text. Think about what it feels like to be the forgiver, as well as what it feels like to be the forgiven. How is this expression of love meaningful to you? Briefly note your thoughts.

Read the text one last time, then stop and listen for what God is inviting you to do or become this week. Perhaps his invitation will have to do with a new perspective on who you are in his eyes, or maybe you sense an action he is calling you to take. After your prayer, write down what you feel invited to do.

LIVE

Take time to meditate on the following quote from the *Book of Common Prayer* (1979), and let it become your own: "Let not the needy, O Lord, be forgotten; nor the hope of the poor be taken away."[1]

✚ LEARNING TO PAY ATTENTION

EXODUS 3:1-6

1-2 Moses was shepherding the flock of Jethro, his father-in-law, the priest of Midian. He led the flock to the west end of the wilderness and came to the mountain of God, Horeb. The angel of GOD appeared to him in flames of fire blazing out of the middle of a bush. He looked. The bush was blazing away but it didn't burn up.

3   Moses said, "What's going on here? I can't believe this! Amazing! Why doesn't the bush burn up?"

4   GOD saw that he had stopped to look. God called to him from out of the bush, "Moses! Moses!"

    He said, "Yes? I'm right here!"

5   God said, "Don't come any closer. Remove your sandals from your feet. You're standing on holy ground."

6   Then he said, "I am the God of your father: The God of Abraham, the God of Isaac, the God of Jacob."

    Moses hid his face, afraid to look at God.

READ

Read the passage aloud.

THINK

Moses is shepherding his father-in-law's sheep. In the distance he sees a bush in flames, but the bush mysteriously doesn't burn up. He walks closer, perhaps expecting a miracle, only to have a more unique encounter than he ever imagined. He interacts with the living God.

When have you experienced a unique encounter with the living God? What was your burning bush like?

What do you think God meant when he said, "Remove your sandals from your feet. You're standing on holy ground"?

God is holy. What difference does that make in your life?

PRAY

Ask God to reveal himself to you today in a fresh way, a way that he has never revealed himself before.

LIVE

Moses heard from God when he paid attention. Like Moses, we often encounter God when we pay attention to what's going on around us. Find a quiet place and spend a few moments in utter silence, paying attention to those aspects of your life that you often neglect: people, situations, quiet moments, creation, and so on. As you do this, look for God waiting there to interact with you.

THE BREAD GOD HAS GIVEN

EXODUS 16:9-16

9 Moses instructed Aaron: "Tell the whole company of Israel: 'Come near to GOD. He's heard your complaints.'"

10 When Aaron gave out the instructions to the whole company of Israel, they turned to face the wilderness. And there it was: the Glory of GOD visible in the Cloud.

11-12 GOD spoke to Moses, "I've listened to the complaints of the Israelites. Now tell them: 'At dusk you will eat meat and at dawn you'll eat your fill of bread; and you'll realize that I am GOD, *your* God.'"

13-15 That evening quail flew in and covered the camp and in the morning there was a layer of dew all over the camp. When the layer of dew had lifted, there on the wilderness ground was a fine flaky something, fine as frost on the ground. The Israelites took one look and said to one another, *man-hu* (What is it?). They had no idea what it was.

15-16 So Moses told them, "It's the bread GOD has given you to eat. And these are GOD's instructions: 'Gather enough for each person, about two quarts per person; gather enough for everyone in your tent.'"

READ

Read the passage aloud. Have fun pronouncing *man-hu* in different ways. If you'd like, read the expanded passage to get a picture of the complaining that came before this and the obsessive hoarding that came after. Both give us a picture of the neediness of the Israelites at this time.

THINK

Read the passage again slowly, pausing to feel each emotion of the Israelites:

- the deep neediness of complaining
- the excitement of seeing the glory of God visible in the Cloud
- the perplexity of seeing this strange bread from heaven
- the satisfaction of having enough

Then consider: If you were to complain to God right now, what would your complaint be? (Don't choose this yourself; wait and let it come to you.) In what ways, if any, have you been perplexed by God's response to your complaining? How might God have truly provided enough but you didn't recognize it as God's bread from heaven — exactly what you needed?

PRAY

If you haven't formally complained to God about this matter, do so. Ask God to show you how he has provided you with enough, even though you still might wonder.

LIVE

Sit in the quiet and feel God's "enoughness" in your body. Where do you feel it? In arms that are full? In a quiet mind? In a stomach that feels full? In muscles that work well? If you can really mean it, try delighting in this enoughness.

GOD REVEALS HIMSELF

EXODUS 33:21–34:7

21-23 GOD said, "Look, here is a place right beside me. Put yourself on this rock. When my Glory passes by, I'll put you in the cleft of the rock and cover you with my hand until I've passed by. Then I'll take my hand away and you'll see my back. But you won't see my face."

1-3 GOD spoke to Moses: "Cut out two tablets of stone just like the originals and engrave on them the words that were on the original tablets you smashed. Be ready in the morning to climb Mount Sinai and get set to meet me on top of the mountain. Not a soul is to go with you; the whole mountain must be clear of people, even animals — not even sheep or oxen can be grazing in front of the mountain."

4-7 So Moses cut two tablets of stone just like the originals. He got up early in the morning and climbed Mount Sinai as GOD had commanded him, carrying the two tablets of stone. GOD descended in the cloud and took up his position there beside him and called out the name, GOD. GOD passed in front of him and called out, "GOD, GOD, a God of mercy and grace, endlessly patient — so much love, so deeply true — loyal in love for a thousand generations, forgiving iniquity, rebellion, and sin. Still, he doesn't ignore sin. He holds sons and grandsons responsible for a father's sins to the third and even fourth generation."

READ

Read the passage slowly. To get a broader feel for what's happening, quickly read the expanded passage.

THINK

During a second read, explore the nooks and crannies of God's communication with Moses, noticing words that embellish your mental picture of who God is or of the situation at hand. The third time, listen for one or two of God's words that especially impress you. Choose one word or phrase, then take time to repeat it to yourself, letting it interact with your thoughts, feelings, and desires.

PRAY

Deeply ponder the quality of God that the word or phrase portrays. Share with him what's striking to you about this aspect of his character. Explore what makes you desirous of someone with this trait. If more thoughts, feelings, or desires come to the surface, open up to them and ask God to clarify how they expand or even alter your understanding of this part of his personality. End your prayer by letting the word or words drift through your mind and heart again.

LIVE

Envision the ways God is present to you right now. What posture does he have (for example, standing tall, sitting near)? What expression is on his face? If he speaks to you, what tones does his voice hold? Ask him to enhance — and correct, if necessary — in the coming months this picture of how you see him, through the Bible passages you read and through your experiences.

DAY 7

GOD ENCOUNTERS

On this seventh day, review and reflect on all you have read this week. Take the time to revel in the ways you've encountered God in the past six days.

THE NECESSITY OF SACRIFICE

LEVITICUS 4:32-35

32-35 "If he brings a lamb for an Absolution-Offering, he shall present a female without any defect, lay his hand on the head of the Absolution-Offering, and slaughter it at the same place they slaughter the Whole-Burnt-Offering. The priest will take some of the blood of the Absolution-Offering with his finger, smear it on the horns of the Altar of Burnt-Offering, and pour the rest at the base of the Altar. He shall remove all the fat, the same as for the lamb of the Peace-Offering. Finally, the priest will burn it on the Altar on top of the gifts to God.

"In this way, the priest makes atonement for him on account of his sin and he's forgiven."

READ

Read the passage in a very soft voice, maybe even a whisper. Focus on each word as you read, listening intently to each word you are reading.

THINK

We might be tempted to believe that Leviticus is a confusing and irrelevant book, but it has some direct implications for our lives. In Leviticus we find specific rules and regulations from Yahweh, given to distinguish his people, the nation of Israel, from every other culture. God commanded the offering of many different types of sacrifices: burnt, grain, fellowship, sin, and guilt. Each of these served a specific purpose for interaction with God. For example, a sin offering was given for confession, forgiveness, and cleansing.

Why do you think God prescribed offerings to be done in such a unique way? Is he cruel to require that animals be killed to make offerings to him? Why or why not? Why don't we do these types of sacrifices today?

Why does God take sin so seriously? When we sin, what sort of sacrifices are we required to bring to God?

PRAY

Ask God to help you understand the severity of your own sin. Thank God that he sent Jesus, the Lamb of God, to come and be the sacrifice for your sins.

LIVE

Knowing that God has provided the ultimate sacrifice through his Son, Jesus, consider sharing this great truth with someone today. As you drive, walk, work, and relax, whisper under your breath, "Thank you, Jesus," each time you remember the sacrifice he made for your sins.

LETTING GO OF SIN

LEVITICUS 16:20-22

20-22 "When Aaron finishes making atonement for the Holy of Holies, the Tent of Meeting, and the Altar, he will bring up the live goat, lay both hands on the live goat's head, and confess all the iniquities of the People of Israel, all their acts of rebellion, all their sins. He will put all the sins on the goat's head and send it off into the wilderness, led out by a man standing by and ready. The goat will carry all their iniquities to an empty wasteland; the man will let him loose out there in the wilderness."

READ

Read the passage slowly. (Read the expanded passage to see how the scapegoat is sent off.)

THINK

The practice in this passage may seem odd today. It was also odd in those days because instead of killing a near-perfect animal, this animal would be allowed to live.

Read the passage again.

1. Picture yourself laying your hands on this precious animal's head. Even better, hold a stuffed animal, figurine, or even your pet, and put your hands on its head.
2. Confess to God your acts of rebellion, your bad attitudes, and your harsh thoughts about others.
3. Experience the feeling of transferring your sin to this animal. (Don't feel sorry for the animal. God didn't give it the capacity to take on hurt or guilt from your sin.)
4. See yourself sending it off as it takes your sin far away from you.

PRAY

What do you wish to say to God about having sent your sins off without you?

LIVE

Quiet your mind and wait on God to show you situations in which you need to remember what you just did. Practice resting assured of God's love in those situations as you are resting assured now.

MY HOLY NAME

LEVITICUS 22:1-8

1-2   GOD spoke to Moses: "Tell Aaron and his sons to treat the holy offerings that the Israelites consecrate to me with reverence so they won't desecrate my holy name. I am GOD.

3   "Tell them, From now on, if any of your descendants approaches in a state of ritual uncleanness the holy offerings that the Israelites consecrate to GOD, he will be cut off from my presence. I am GOD.

4-8   "Each and every one of Aaron's descendants who has an infectious skin disease or a discharge may not eat any of the holy offerings until he is clean. Also, if he touches anything defiled by a corpse, or has an emission of semen, or is contaminated by touching a crawling creature, or touches a person who is contaminated for whatever reason — a person who touches any such thing will be ritually unclean until evening and may not eat any of the holy offerings unless he has washed well with water. After the sun goes down he is clean and may go ahead and eat the holy offerings; they are his food. But he must not contaminate himself by eating anything found dead or torn by wild animals. I am GOD."

READ

Get comfortable. Take time to clear your mind, then focus only on this activity. Read the passage silently. Now read it once more, aloud.

THINK

As you read God's statements about himself and about the priests, what is your reaction? Notice whether you are drawn toward God as you read or repelled from God. Talk to him about this. Explore what might be causing your response. Ask him to show you more of yourself — the memories, opinions, and feelings you bring to him on this day.

PRAY

Silently pray the passage. Praying in your own words by responding to what you're reading is okay at first. But as you continue, use the words of the passage as your prayer. Perhaps you will repeat to your soul "he is God" or ask him to increase your belief that he is holy. Ask God to show you how this truth interacts with your first reaction.

LIVE

Use this silent time simply to rest in the presence of the holy God who has just made himself known to you. Let go of your own words and let yourself enjoy the experience.

DON'T FORGET

NUMBERS 9:4-5,9-12

4-5   Moses told the People of Israel to celebrate the Passover and they did —
in the Wilderness of Sinai at evening of the fourteenth day of the first
month. The People of Israel did it all just as GOD had commanded
Moses. . . .

9-12   GOD spoke to Moses: "Tell the People of Israel, If one or another of
you is ritually unclean because of a corpse, or you happen to be off on a
long trip, you may still celebrate GOD's Passover. But celebrate it on the
fourteenth day of the second month at evening. Eat the lamb together
with unraised bread and bitter herbs. Don't leave any of it until morning.
Don't break any of its bones. Follow all the procedures."

READ

Read the passage five times, each time focusing on a different aspect of it.

THINK

As humans, we are forgetful people, and as forgetful people we need tangible reminders — symbols — of who God is and what he's done. Therefore, as God commanded, many Jewish homes celebrate Passover around the time of Easter to remember all that God orchestrated to bring them out of bondage in Egypt and into the Promised Land. Under what circumstances are you most prone to forget who God is and what he's done for you?

PRAY

Take a stroll down memory lane. Think about the times when God was evident and at work. Allow your memories to guide your prayers of gratitude for all he has done.

LIVE

Create a symbol that will remind you of God's faithfulness in your life. Maybe it's a photograph of your close friends or a rock you picked up during a hike. Put this symbol in a place where you will see it often. When you look at it, be reminded and thank God for his blessings.

A DIFFERENT STORY

NUMBERS 14:17-24

17 "Now, please, let the power of the Master expand, enlarge itself greatly, along the lines you have laid out earlier when you said,

18 GOD, slow to get angry and huge in loyal love,
     forgiving iniquity and rebellion and sin;
  Still, never just whitewashing sin.
     But extending the fallout of parents' sins
  to children into the third,
     even the fourth generation.

19 "Please forgive the wrongdoing of this people out of the extravagance of your loyal love just as all along, from the time they left Egypt, you have been forgiving this people."

20-23 GOD said, "I forgive them, honoring your words. But as I live and as the Glory of GOD fills the whole Earth — not a single person of those who saw my Glory, saw the miracle signs I did in Egypt and the wilderness, and who have tested me over and over and over again, turning a deaf ear to me — not one of them will set eyes on the land I so solemnly promised to their ancestors. No one who has treated me with such repeated contempt will see it.

24 "But my servant Caleb — this is a different story. He has a different spirit; he follows me passionately. I'll bring him into the land that he scouted and his children will inherit it."

READ

Read the passage aloud slowly. Keep in mind that this is the prayer of Moses after ten of the twelve members of the Israelite scouting party to the Promised Land expressed doubt that they could make their home in that land, even with God's help. (Read the expanded passage to learn more about the depths of the Israelites' doubt.)

THINK

Read the passage again slowly, noting (a) qualities of God that stand out, (b) qualities of Caleb's response to God, and (c) whatever else comes to you.

What impresses you most about God? Why?

What impresses you most about Caleb? Why?

How do you respond to God's willingness to forgive so many Israelites even though he seems to think they do not have the capacity to be used by him?

PRAY

Ask God to show you where you fit in this passage. How might you be tempted to "[turn] a deaf ear"? How might God be calling you to live a different story — to be one who has "a different spirit" from others, who follows God passionately even though it might involve risks (for example, loving the unlovely, pursuing a career that makes less money, admitting to others the mistakes you've made)?

LIVE

Imagine what it would feel like to have such trust in God that you would be willing to take whatever next steps God presents to you. Imagine what it would be like to be so different from others that you might be excluded because of it.

GOD OF THE ASYLUM-CITY

NUMBERS 35:9-15

9-15 GOD spoke to Moses: "Speak to the People of Israel. Tell them, When you cross the River Jordan into the country of Canaan, designate your asylum-cities, towns to which a person who accidentally kills someone can flee for asylum. They will be places of refuge from the avenger so that the alleged murderer won't be killed until he can appear before the community in court. Provide six asylum-cities. Designate three of the towns to the east side of the Jordan, the other three in Canaan proper — asylum-cities for the People of Israel, for the foreigner, and for any occasional visitors or guests — six asylum-cities to run to for anyone who accidentally kills another."

READ

Read the passage without worrying about specifics; just try to understand its overall idea.

THINK

God wanted communities to try suspected murderers justly in court, but he also planned "asylum-cities" as a refuge from would-be avengers until the trial could be held. Spend time thinking about the God who is making himself known here. Jot down a few words to describe him.

PRAY

For a moment, set aside this passage. Check in with yourself — explore recent thoughts, feelings, and events in your life and how you've responded to them. What's primarily on your heart today? Is anything troubling you?

Bring your thoughts to the God who created asylum-cities. Read the verses again. As you do, picture God entering the room. How do you relate to his presence? Share with him what you've been thinking, if you can. Does doing so make you uncomfortable? Why or why not?

LIVE

Think about what it's been like for you to be with the God who is both a God of justice and a God of refuge. Has it left you with questions or with new thoughts on how you want to deal with your sin in the future? Make note of anything that seems significant.

DAY 14

GOD ENCOUNTERS

On this seventh day, review and reflect on all you have read this week. Take the time to revel in the ways you've encountered God in the past six days.

LISTEN!

DEUTERONOMY 6:1-9

1-2 This is the commandment, the rules and regulations, that GOD, your God, commanded me to teach you to live out in the land you're about to cross into to possess. This is so that you'll live in deep reverence before GOD lifelong, observing all his rules and regulations that I'm commanding you, you and your children and your grandchildren, living good long lives.

3 Listen obediently, Israel. Do what you're told so that you'll have a good life, a life of abundance and bounty, just as GOD promised, in a land abounding in milk and honey.

4 Attention, Israel!

GOD, our God! GOD the one and only!

5 Love GOD, your God, with your whole heart: love him with all that's in you, love him with all you've got!

6-9 Write these commandments that I've given you today on your hearts. Get them inside of you and then get them inside your children. Talk about them wherever you are, sitting at home or walking in the street; talk about them from the time you get up in the morning to when you fall into bed at night. Tie them on your hands and foreheads as a reminder; inscribe them on the doorposts of your homes and on your city gates.

READ

Stand in a posture signifying respect for and full attention to God's Word. Read the passage aloud.

THINK

This passage is extremely important among Jewish people. In Jesus' time, every good Jew would recite it as soon as he woke up in the morning and right before he went to bed at night. The passage is referred to as the *Shema,* which comes from the Hebrew "to listen" or "to hear." If you visit the Western Wall in Jerusalem today, you will see Jews fervently praying in front of it. They will have leather straps wrapped around their arms and tiny boxes (called phylacteries) containing Scriptures tied to their arms and foreheads.

How seriously do you take the words of God?

PRAY

Slowly and reverently, pray the words found in verses 4 and 5: "GOD, our God! GOD the one and only! Love GOD, your God with your whole heart: love him with all that's in you, love him with all you've got!" Repeat these words over and over again, letting what the words ask of you to sink into your heart.

LIVE

Memorize the words you just prayed, and pray them as often as you remember them.

LIVE IN HIS PRESENCE

DEUTERONOMY 10:12-21

12-13 So now Israel, what do you think GOD expects from you? Just this: Live in his presence in holy reverence, follow the road he sets out for you, love him, serve GOD, your God, with everything you have in you, obey the commandments and regulations of GOD that I'm commanding you today — live a good life.

14-18 Look around you: Everything you see is GOD's — the heavens above and beyond, the Earth, and everything on it. But it was your ancestors who GOD fell in love with; he picked their children — that's *you*! — out of all the other peoples. That's where we are right now. So cut away the thick calluses from your heart and stop being so willfully hardheaded. GOD, your God, is the God of all gods, he's the Master of all masters, a God immense and powerful and awesome. He doesn't play favorites, takes no bribes, makes sure orphans and widows are treated fairly, takes loving care of foreigners by seeing that they get food and clothing.

19-21 You must treat foreigners with the same loving care —
        remember, you were once foreigners in Egypt.
    Reverently respect GOD, your God, serve him, hold tight to him,
        back up your promises with the authority of his name.
    He's your praise! He's your God!
    He did all these tremendous, these staggering things
        that you saw with your own eyes.

READ

Read the passage aloud slowly.

THINK

Read it aloud slowly again.

1. What phrase is most memorable?
2. What quality of God stands out to you? Why?
3. What command stands out to you? Why?

PRAY

Here are some ways to pray back the passage. Use as many of these suggestions as you wish.

- Express to God your thoughts about living in his presence. Has living in his presence been important to you or not?
- Express to God those areas in which you would guess he considers you "hardheaded." (Pause and let this come to you. Don't necessarily go with the first thing that comes to mind.)
- Express to God your feelings about the have-nots you know (widows, orphans, foreigners). Talk to God honestly about how willing or unwilling you've been to include such people in your life.

LIVE

Experiment with living in God's presence while caring for the rest of the world. Relax. Quiet yourself. Just be.

YOU WERE ONCE SLAVES

DEUTERONOMY 24:10-15,17-22

10-13   When you make a loan of any kind to your neighbor, don't enter his house to claim his pledge. Wait outside. Let the man to whom you made the pledge bring the pledge to you outside. And if he is destitute, don't use his cloak as a bedroll; return it to him at nightfall so that he can sleep in his cloak and bless you. In the sight of GOD, your God, that will be viewed as a righteous act.

14-15   Don't abuse a laborer who is destitute and needy, whether he is a fellow Israelite living in your land and in your city. Pay him at the end of each workday; he's living from hand to mouth and needs it now. If you hold back his pay, he'll protest to GOD and you'll have sin on your books. . . .

17-18   Make sure foreigners and orphans get their just rights. Don't take the cloak of a widow as security for a loan. Don't ever forget that you were once slaves in Egypt and GOD, your God, got you out of there. I command you: Do what I'm telling you.

19-22   When you harvest your grain and forget a sheaf back in the field, don't go back and get it; leave it for the foreigner, the orphan, and the widow so that GOD, your God, will bless you in all your work. When you shake the olives off your trees, don't go back over the branches and strip them bare — what's left is for the foreigner, the orphan, and the widow. And when you cut the grapes in your vineyard, don't take every last grape — leave a few for the foreigner, the orphan, and the widow. Don't ever forget that you were a slave in Egypt. I command you: Do what I'm telling you.

READ

Read the passage, noting especially the three scenarios and God's instructions for how to respond to them.

THINK

What common theme links the three scenarios? Write it down in one sentence. Get a picture in your mind of what this God is like — One who would give such instructions to his people. What stands out to you about him? Jot that down too.

PRAY

Sit with your eyes closed. Think about a recent encounter with someone who might relate to you like the neighbor, laborer, foreigner, or orphan described in the passage. Perhaps you spoke a few words to a homeless beggar, or you listened to someone at school or work who was upset. When faced with the person's need, what did you feel? What thoughts popped into your head? What did you do? Take a few moments to explore with God what was going on in your heart during the encounter.

LIVE

Now look back at the theme you wrote down from the passage and at the traits you noticed about God. How do you picture this God responding to you as you think about the situation you faced? Do you sense him speaking a personal message to you? What is it? (If you have a tendency to assume what God's response would be, say, something similar to what an authority figure in your life might say, resist that.) If you feel clueless about what God might be saying to you, offer this up to him and ask him to show you in the coming weeks.

17

LEAVING A LEGACY

DEUTERONOMY 34:1-4

1-3   Moses climbed from the Plains of Moab to Mount Nebo, the peak of Pisgah facing Jericho. GOD showed him all the land from Gilead to Dan, all Naphtali, Ephraim, and Manasseh; all Judah reaching to the Mediterranean Sea; the Negev and the plains which encircle Jericho, City of Palms, as far south as Zoar.

4   Then and there GOD said to him, "This is the land I promised to your ancestors, to Abraham, Isaac, and Jacob with the words 'I will give it to your descendants.' I've let you see it with your own eyes. There it is. But you're not going to go in."

READ

Read the passage the way you might to a room full of children. Articulate your words. Use inflections. Sound excited as you read.

THINK

Moses was the leader of the nation of Israel for the latter part of his life. He was mostly obedient and faithful, but there were times of disobedience. Because of that, God told Moses that the Israelites would enter the Promised Land but that he would not. In chapter 34 Moses dies atop Mount Nebo, located in the modern-day country of Jordan, just to the east of the Dead Sea in Israel.

Why do you think God takes disobedience so seriously? What have been some consequences of your own disobedience?

Are you able to trust the promises of God, even if you never end up seeing them? Why or why not?

PRAY

Ask God to help you live a life of faith and obedience, the kind of life that honors him at all times.

LIVE

Think of Moses-like people you know — older, godly individuals living faithfully for God. Consider connecting with them and getting to know them and their stories.

COURAGEOUS WHEN IT COUNTS

JOSHUA 1:1-9

1-9   After the death of Moses the servant of GOD, GOD spoke to Joshua, Moses' assistant:

"Moses my servant is dead. Get going. Cross this Jordan River, you and all the people. Cross to the country I'm giving to the People of Israel. I'm giving you every square inch of the land you set your foot on — just as I promised Moses. From the wilderness and this Lebanon east to the Great River, the Euphrates River — all the Hittite country — and then west to the Great Sea. It's all yours. All your life, no one will be able to hold out against you. In the same way I was with Moses, I'll be with you. I won't give up on you; I won't leave you. Strength! Courage! You are going to lead this people to inherit the land that I promised to give their ancestors. Give it everything you have, heart and soul. Make sure you carry out The Revelation that Moses commanded you, every bit of it. Don't get off track, either left or right, so as to make sure you get to where you're going. And don't for a minute let this Book of The Revelation be out of mind. Ponder and meditate on it day and night, making sure you practice everything written in it. Then you'll get where you're going; then you'll succeed. Haven't I commanded you? Strength! Courage! Don't be timid; don't get discouraged. GOD, your God, is with you every step you take."

READ

As you read the passage, imagine that you wrote these words yourself and are now reflecting on what you wrote.

THINK

Israel is grieving the loss of its trusted leader, Moses. But with every ending comes a new beginning. In the midst of the mourning, God approaches Joshua and assures him that he is the man to lead the people into the Promised Land. God promises Joshua that he will be with him and that the land will be given to the nation of Israel. God commands Joshua to be courageous and tells him to remain committed to the study of his Word.

Read verse 9 again. Is embracing these words in your life hard or easy? At what times are you scared? Why? When you are fearful, what can you do about it?

PRAY

Be blatantly honest with God about your fears, worries, concerns, and anxieties. Tell him exactly why you are scared, and be assured that he hears you. Thank him for listening. Then reread the passage, personalizing the words by making God's words to Joshua your very own.

LIVE

When you find yourself in situations that expose your fears, remember the promises of God — his presence and his guidance for you into the future.

SLOW DOWN AND INQUIRE

JOSHUA 9:3-9,11,14-16

3-6 The people of Gibeon heard what Joshua had done to Jericho and Ai and cooked up a ruse. They posed as travelers: their donkeys loaded with patched sacks and mended wineskins, threadbare sandals on their feet, tattered clothes on their bodies, nothing but dry crusts and crumbs for food. They came to Joshua at Gilgal and spoke to the men of Israel, "We've come from a far-off country; make a covenant with us."

7 The men of Israel said to these Hivites, "How do we know you aren't local people? How could we then make a covenant with you?"

8 They said to Joshua, "We'll be your servants."

Joshua said, "Who are you now? Where did you come from?"

9,11 They said, "From a far-off country, very far away. Your servants came because we'd heard such great things about GOD, your God — all those things he did in Egypt! . . . Our leaders and everybody else in our country told us, 'Pack up some food for the road and go meet them. Tell them, We're your servants; make a covenant with us.' . . .

14 The men of Israel looked them over and accepted the evidence. But they didn't ask GOD about it.

15 So Joshua made peace with them and formalized it with a covenant to guarantee their lives. The leaders of the congregation swore to it.

16 And then, three days after making this covenant, they learned that they were next-door neighbors who had been living there all along!

READ

Read the passage slowly. Keep in mind that the people of Gibeon were afraid because Joshua had conquered Jericho and Ai.

THINK

Read the passage slowly again. The people of Gibeon repeatedly flattered Joshua in order to get their way. He accepted their evidence without inquiring after God. Is there a place in your life where you are susceptible to offers and flattery, so you form attachments without asking God for input? (*Attachments* refers to relationships and commitments to people, tasks, and organizations.)

PRAY

Ask God to help you go over your attachments by moving through the following questions as if God were sitting next to you with his arm around you.

What attachments, if any, have you formed because you think the people involved do something for you?

What attachments, if any, have you rushed into without investigating further, especially by asking God what you need to know about the situation?

Ask God to show you where, if at all, you need to back off from an attachment.

LIVE

Wait with an open heart for anything God might say to you. If nothing comes to you, ask God to make it apparent in the next few weeks if there's anything you need to know about your attachments.

DAY 21

GOD ENCOUNTERS

On this seventh day, review and reflect on all you have read this week. Take the time to revel in the ways you've encountered God in the past six days.

AN UNQUALIFIED YES

JOSHUA 24:16-24

16 The people answered, "We'd never forsake GOD! Never! We'd never leave GOD to worship other gods.

17-18 "GOD is our God! He brought up our ancestors from Egypt and from slave conditions. He did all those great signs while we watched. He has kept his eye on us all along the roads we've traveled and among the nations we've passed through. Just for us he drove out all the nations, Amorites and all, who lived in the land.

"Count us in: We too are going to worship GOD. He's our God."

19-20 Then Joshua told the people: "You can't do it; you're not able to worship GOD. He is a holy God. He is a jealous God. He won't put up with your fooling around and sinning. When you leave GOD and take up the worship of foreign gods, he'll turn right around and come down on you hard. He'll put an end to you — and after all the good he has done for you!"

21 But the people told Joshua: "No! No! We worship GOD!"

22 And so Joshua addressed the people: "You are witnesses against yourselves that you have chosen GOD for yourselves — to worship him."

And they said, "We are witnesses."

23 Joshua said, "Now get rid of all the foreign gods you have with you. Say an unqualified Yes to GOD, the God of Israel."

24 The people answered Joshua, "We will worship GOD. What he says, we'll do."

READ

Read the passage, paying special attention to what it shows you about the nature of the human heart.

PRAY

As you read of the Israelites' passionate desire to follow God ("We'd never forsake GOD!"), what is your reaction to them? When you take a bird's-eye view of the history of Israel, noticing their many rebellions against God and inability to stay committed, what does it make you think and feel? Do you relate to Israel at all — in their desire, in their failure, or both? Talk to God about your thoughts and feelings, eventually sitting quietly to listen for his response.

THINK/LIVE

Write about your prayer experience. What was it like for you? What stood out to you about the Israelites? About yourself? About God? If you contemplated your own fickleness or zeal, do you sense that God is leading or challenging you in some way regarding this? Make a note of anything that seems significant.

WHEN YOU CAN'T TAKE THE CREDIT

JUDGES 7:1-7

1 Jerub-Baal (Gideon) got up early the next morning, all his troops right there with him. They set up camp at Harod's Spring. The camp of Midian was in the plain, north of them near the Hill of Moreh.

2-3 GOD said to Gideon, "You have too large an army with you. I can't turn Midian over to them like this — they'll take all the credit, saying, 'I did it all myself,' and forget about me. Make a public announcement: 'Anyone afraid, anyone who has any qualms at all, may leave Mount Gilead now and go home.'" Twenty-two companies headed for home. Ten companies were left.

4-5 GOD said to Gideon: "There are still too many. Take them down to the stream and I'll make a final cut. When I say, 'This one goes with you,' he'll go. When I say, 'This one doesn't go,' he won't go." So Gideon took the troops down to the stream.

5-6 GOD said to Gideon: "Everyone who laps with his tongue, the way a dog laps, set on one side. And everyone who kneels to drink, drinking with his face to the water, set to the other side." Three hundred lapped with their tongues from their cupped hands. All the rest knelt to drink.

7 GOD said to Gideon: "I'll use the three hundred men who lapped at the stream to save you and give Midian into your hands. All the rest may go home."

READ

As you read the passage, underline the words that stick out to you or surprise you.

THINK

The book of Judges is filled with violence. Christians struggle to understand how God's redemptive plan can involve these events. Yet God's power is at work when the Israelites battle foreign, pagan armies. God uses Gideon to lead the nation into battle for his purposes. But as he guides Gideon, he asks much of him. God cuts Gideon's army down from thirty-two thousand men to ten thousand, and eventually to three hundred. God wants to show *his* power through Gideon. He wants Israel to credit him.

When have you accomplished things in your own strength and taken all the credit while forgetting about God? When have you accomplished things that seemed big and impossible, knowing you did so only because God intervened?

PRAY

Write a list of huge requests you have for God — things so large that if they came to fruition, you would know they did so only because God intervened. Spend time praying through this list.

LIVE

Review your list on a regular basis, watching for God's incredible — and at times subtle — intervention. As you see God's faithfulness, thank him often that he is a caring friend.

TALKING WITH GOD

JUDGES 13:2-3,6-9,17-20

2-3   At that time there was a man named Manoah from Zorah from the tribe of Dan. His wife was barren and childless. The angel of God appeared to her and told her, "I know that you are barren and childless, but you're going to become pregnant and bear a son." . . .

6-7   The woman went to her husband and said, "A man of God came to me. He looked like the angel of God — terror laced with glory! I didn't ask him where he was from and he didn't tell me his name, but he told me, 'You're pregnant. You're going to give birth to a son. Don't drink any wine or beer and eat nothing ritually unclean. The boy will be God's Nazirite from the moment of birth to the day of his death.'"

8   Manoah prayed to GOD: "Master, let the man of God you sent come to us again and teach us how to raise this boy who is to be born."

9   God listened to Manoah. God's angel came again to the woman. She was sitting in the field; her husband Manoah wasn't there with her. . . .

17   Then Manoah asked the angel of God, "What's your name? When your words come true, we'd like to honor you."

18   The angel of GOD said, "What's this? You ask for my name? You wouldn't understand — it's sheer wonder."

19-20   So Manoah took the kid and the Grain-Offering and sacrificed them on a rock altar to GOD who works wonders. As the flames leapt up from the altar to heaven, GOD's angel also ascended in the altar flames. When Manoah and his wife saw this, they fell facedown to the ground.

READ

Read the passage aloud slowly. Manoah and his wife will become Samson's parents, and so God prepares them for this task. (Read the expanded passage to hear even more of the story.)

THINK

Read the passage aloud slowly again, taking note of the back-and-forth conversation between God and this couple. It forms a picture of what an interactive life with God might be like.

Notice the conversational interaction: who listened; who asked questions.

Would you have asked the question Manoah asked ("What's your name?") or a different question?

How would it be to talk to God when lying facedown (see verse 20)?

PRAY

Try this: Lie facedown on the floor or the ground as Manoah and his wife did. Ask God for further instruction about something in your life. Notice what it's like to talk to God in this position. Don't get up too soon.

LIVE

Rest your forehead on the ground with your arms above you. Just "be" before God this way.

LET ME BE AVENGED

JUDGES 16:25-30

25-27 Then this: Everyone was feeling high and someone said, "Get Samson! Let him show us his stuff!" They got Samson from the prison and he put on a show for them.

They had him standing between the pillars. Samson said to the young man who was acting as his guide, "Put me where I can touch the pillars that hold up the temple so I can rest against them." The building was packed with men and women, including all the Philistine tyrants. And there were at least three thousand in the stands watching Samson's performance.

28 And Samson cried out to GOD:

Master, GOD!
　Oh, please, look on me again,
　Oh, please, give strength yet once more.

God!
　With one avenging blow let me be avenged
　On the Philistines for my two eyes!

29-30 Then Samson reached out to the two central pillars that held up the building and pushed against them, one with his right arm, the other with his left. Saying, "Let me die with the Philistines," Samson pushed hard with all his might. The building crashed on the tyrants and all the people in it. He killed more people in his death than he had killed in his life.

READ

Sit quietly and let your thoughts settle. Now read the passage silently. Let the events of the story filter into your heart and interact with your present state of mind.

THINK

What stands out to you about Samson's dramatic action and the ending of his life? Do you resonate with his deep desire for justice to be served? What do you observe about how he acted on that desire for revenge?

PRAY

Read the passage a second time, looking specifically for a word or phrase about Samson's desire for revenge or justice that is meaningful to you. Maybe his act angers you, or you feel a similar desire. When you finish reading, close your eyes. Recall the word or phrase and sit quietly, mulling it over. Let it stimulate you into a dialogue with God.

LIVE

Read the passage a third time, watching how God interacts with Samson and with the Philistines: Although God does not directly act or speak in the passage, he grants Samson's request to avenge himself, and he allows the Philistines to lose their lives. What stands out to you about God's involvement (or lack of involvement)? Talk with him about your perception of him in this passage. Be open to what he may be showing you through what you read.

WELCOMING THE STRANGER

RUTH 3:1-2,4,8-13,16-18

1-2 One day her mother-in-law Naomi said to Ruth, "My dear daughter, isn't it about time I arranged a good home for you so you can have a happy life? And isn't Boaz our close relative, the one with whose young women you've been working? Maybe it's time to make our move. Tonight is the night of Boaz's barley harvest at the threshing floor. . . .

4 "When you see him slipping off to sleep, watch where he lies down and then go there. Lie at his feet to let him know that you are available to him for marriage. Then wait and see what he says. He'll tell you what to do." . . .

8 In the middle of the night the man was suddenly startled and sat up. Surprise! This woman asleep at his feet!

9 He said, "And who are you?"

She said, "I am Ruth, your maiden; take me under your protecting wing. You're my close relative, you know, in the circle of covenant redeemers — you do have the right to marry me."

10-13 He said, "GOD bless you, my dear daughter! What a splendid expression of love! And when you could have had your pick of any of the young men around. And now, my dear daughter, don't you worry about a thing; I'll do all you could want or ask. Everybody in town knows what a courageous woman you are — a real prize! You're right, I am a close relative to you, but there is one even closer than I am. So stay the rest of the night. In the morning, if he wants to exercise his customary rights and responsibilities as the closest covenant redeemer, he'll have his chance. . . .

16-17 When she came to her mother-in-law, Naomi asked, "And how did things go, my dear daughter?"

Ruth told her everything that the man had done for her, adding, "And he gave me all this barley besides — six quarts! He told me, 'You can't go back empty-handed to your mother-in-law!'"

18 Naomi said, "Sit back and relax, my dear daughter, until we find out how things turn out; that man isn't going to fool around. Mark my words, he's going to get everything wrapped up today."

READ

Read the passage slowly. Naomi is Ruth's mother-in-law, the mother of Ruth's deceased husband.

THINK

Read the passage again slowly, this time keeping in mind that Ruth is a foreign Moabite woman while Naomi and Boaz are Israelites. Ruth is different from them in nationality, background, and age.

Who do you identify with most: Naomi or Boaz, the older, wiser Israelites, or Ruth, the younger, foreign woman?

Imagining you are the person you identified with, how does it feel to hear or say the term *daughter*? (Again, this was unusual because of their differences in nationality.)

What might God be saying to you about the "strangers" in your life?

What might God be telling you about the places in your life where you feel like a stranger?

PRAY

Thank God for how he provides for those who are strangers and aliens, that he isn't partial to just one group. Ask God how you might partner with him in this.

LIVE

In the quiet, consider God's attentiveness to all people. Is there someone specific he brings to mind? Today and in the next few days, look for opportunities to pay attention to the stranger in the same way God does.

DECIPHERING GOD'S VOICE

1 SAMUEL 3:8-10

8-9 GOD called again, "Samuel!" — the third time! Yet again Samuel got up and went to Eli, "Yes? I heard you call me. Here I am."

That's when it dawned on Eli that GOD was calling the boy. So Eli directed Samuel, "Go back and lie down. If the voice calls again, say, 'Speak, GOD. I'm your servant, ready to listen.'" Samuel returned to his bed.

10 Then GOD came and stood before him exactly as before, calling out, "Samuel! Samuel!"

Samuel answered, "Speak. I'm your servant, ready to listen."

READ

As you read the passage, imagine yourself in the story, watching the situation from the back of the room.

THINK

At the beginning of 1 Samuel, Hannah wanted to give birth to a son, but she was barren. She prayed earnestly, crying out to the Lord. God heard her prayer, and she gave birth to Samuel. She dedicated him to the temple, where he ministered under Eli the priest. Scholars believe Samuel was a teenager when the events of this passage occurred.

Does hearing God so clearly seem possible? How do you decipher between his voice and the other voices in your life? Samuel needed Eli's guidance for this. What people around you could help you discern when God is trying to communicate with you and what he's saying?

PRAY

Often the most effective way to hear God's voice is to still our minds and quiet our hearts for a considerable amount of time. Set aside twenty minutes in a quiet place and make yourself comfortable. Invite God to communicate with you. Don't read or pray. Just listen and be, bringing your mind back if it wanders.

LIVE

Sometime in the next week, schedule another twenty minutes of silence and once again listen and wait for God to speak to you. Don't give up. Your practice will pay off.

DAY 28

GOD ENCOUNTERS

On this seventh day, review and reflect on all you have read this week. Take the time to revel in the ways you've encountered God in the past six days.

IS GOD ENOUGH?

1 SAMUEL 8:1,3-7,9-10,19-22

1,3   When Samuel got to be an old man, he set his sons up as judges in Israel. . . . But his sons didn't take after him; they were out for what they could get for themselves, taking bribes, corrupting justice.

4-5   Fed up, all the elders of Israel got together and confronted Samuel at Ramah. They presented their case: "Look, you're an old man, and your sons aren't following in your footsteps. Here's what we want you to do: Appoint a king to rule us, just like everybody else."

6   When Samuel heard their demand — "Give us a king to rule us!" — he was crushed. How awful! Samuel prayed to GOD.

7,9   GOD answered Samuel, "Go ahead and do what they're asking. They are not rejecting you. They've rejected me as their King. . . . So let them have their own way. But warn them of what they're in for. Tell them the way kings operate, just what they're likely to get from a king."

10   So Samuel told them, delivered GOD's warning to the people who were asking him to give them a king. . . .

19-20   But the people wouldn't listen to Samuel. "No!" they said. "We will have a king to rule us! Then we'll be just like all the other nations. Our king will rule us and lead us and fight our battles."

21-22   Samuel took in what they said and rehearsed it with GOD. GOD told Samuel, "Do what they say. Make them a king."

Then Samuel dismissed the men of Israel: "Go home, each of you to your own city."

READ

Read the passage aloud slowly.

THINK

The Israelites wanted God, but they were afraid they'd miss out if they didn't have a king like the other nations. They wanted to fit in with the other nations by having a king lead them and fight their battles for them. Read the passage again, this time deeply feeling the determination of the Israelites and the disappointment of Samuel.

1. Who do you resemble most? (a) Samuel — being confronted by people asking him to make changes he believes are wrong, or (b) the Israelites — wanting to be like others?

2. If you chose *a*, converse with God about this as Samuel did: What would you like to say to God regarding these demands? If *b*, how would you finish this sentence: I want to be like _____. If you continue wanting to be like a certain person, how might it cheat you out of what God wants for *you*?

3. What would your life look like if you trusted God to give you what you need, regardless of how odd that may seem when compared to other people's lives?

PRAY

Be honest with God about any frustration of wanting to be like others or frustration with those who do. Ask God to show you the advantages of trusting him more with these things.

LIVE

While you sit in a quiet place, practice feeling okay being different from other people. If you can, view that difference as special or chosen. Relax with a sense of God's hand on you.

29

AND GOD HELP YOU!

1 SAMUEL 17:31-40

31 The things David was saying were picked up and reported to Saul. Saul sent for him.

32 "Master," said David, "don't give up hope. I'm ready to go and fight this Philistine."

33 Saul answered David, "You can't go and fight this Philistine. You're too young and inexperienced — and he's been at this fighting business since before you were born."

34-37 David said, "I've been a shepherd, tending sheep for my father. Whenever a lion or bear came and took a lamb from the flock, I'd go after it, knock it down, and rescue the lamb. If it turned on me, I'd grab it by the throat, wring its neck, and kill it. Lion or bear, it made no difference — I killed it. And I'll do the same to this Philistine pig who is taunting the troops of God-Alive. GOD, who delivered me from the teeth of the lion and the claws of the bear, will deliver me from this Philistine."

Saul said, "Go. And GOD help you!"

38-39 Then Saul outfitted David as a soldier in armor. He put his bronze helmet on his head and belted his sword on him over the armor. David tried to walk but he could hardly budge.

David told Saul, "I can't even move with all this stuff on me. I'm not used to this." And he took it all off.

40 Then David took his shepherd's staff, selected five smooth stones from the brook, and put them in the pocket of his shepherd's pack, and with his sling in his hand approached Goliath.

READ

While you read, let the scenario unfold in your mind. When David describes grabbing a bear by its throat, hear the roaring and grunting. Feel the ponderous weight of the bronze helmet, and then the light, smooth weight of the stones in your hand.

THINK

What one particular event, character, or feature of the story stands out to you? Take time to concentrate on that. Are you drawn to David's courage? Are you repulsed by Saul's disbelieving "GOD help you"? Maybe you're surprised when David rejects Saul's armor. Consider what your own reaction would be, and then consider how the characters in the story reacted. As you meditate, allow God to show you more about yourself, him, and the way life is.

PRAY/LIVE

Priest and author Henri Nouwen wrote, "Make the conscious choice to move the attention of your anxious heart away from [the] waves and direct it to the One who walks on them and says, 'It's me. Don't be afraid.' . . . Look at him and say, 'Lord, have mercy.' Say it again and again, not anxiously but with confidence that he is very close to you and will put your soul to rest.[2] (To read the rest of the story, see John 6:16-21.)

What do you feel anxious about, if anything? What might happen if you shifted your attention "away from [the] waves" and "to the One who walks on them"? What concrete thing could you do to help redirect your attention?

HONORING AND VALUING OTHERS

1 SAMUEL 26:7-11

7   So David and Abishai entered the encampment by night, and there he was — Saul, stretched out asleep at the center of the camp, his spear stuck in the ground near his head, with Abner and the troops sound asleep on all sides.

8   Abishai said, "This is the moment! God has put your enemy in your grasp. Let me nail him to the ground with his spear. One hit will do it, believe me; I won't need a second!"

9   But David said to Abishai, "Don't you dare hurt him! Who could lay a hand on GOD's anointed and even think of getting away with it?"

10-11   He went on, "As GOD lives, either GOD will strike him, or his time will come and he'll die in bed, or he'll fall in battle, but GOD forbid that I should lay a finger on GOD's anointed. Now, grab the spear at his head and the water jug and let's get out of here."

READ

Hold this book in your hands. As you read the passage, pace the room or walk outside. As you do, consider the speed at which you are reading. Take your time and find a rhythm of reading that matches your pace. (For example, if you are reading fast, walk fast.)

THINK

Earlier in 1 Samuel, God anointed David to be the future king of Israel, even though Saul was still on the throne. This man, overcome with cruelty, jealousy, evil, and insecurity, then repeatedly attempted to take David's life. For many years, David hid from Saul's army.

One night, David and Abishai sneak into Saul's camp, and there Abishai notices the perfect opportunity to kill Saul. But David refuses. David is so certain of God's sovereignty that he refuses to kill Saul.

We all have enemies, big or small, and desire for them to come to ruin. Yet ponder the interchange between Saul and David in verses 21-24.

PRAY

Think of the people you consider your enemies. Pray for them and ask God to help you honor them, even though doing so may seem impossible.

LIVE

Seek out intentional opportunities to honor those who dishonor you and to value the lives of those who do not value you.

PAIN, DISAPPOINTMENT, AND HEARTBREAK

2 SAMUEL 1:24-27

24-25   Women of Israel, weep for Saul.
         He dressed you in finest cottons and silks,
         spared no expense in making you elegant.
     The mighty warriors — fallen, fallen
         in the middle of the fight!
         Jonathan — struck down on your hills!

26   O my dear brother Jonathan,
         I'm crushed by your death.
     Your friendship was a miracle-wonder,
         love far exceeding anything I've known —
         or ever hope to know.

27   The mighty warriors — fallen, fallen.
         And the arms of war broken to bits.

READ

King Saul (who tried to kill David many times) and his son, Jonathan (David's best friend), are dead. If possible, read the expanded passage, the song of lament David wrote in response to the news of their death.

THINK

Sometimes pain and suffering are the central emotions of our hearts. We cannot avoid pain and suffering, but we can control how we respond to them. David's reaction is to be honest and open about the pain rather than avoid it or pretend it isn't there.

What is your response to heartbreak? Do you think David's response is healthy? Why or why not? What thoughts and feelings go through you as David honors the evil king in death?

PRAY

Think of the pain and heartbreak you have experienced in your lifetime. Maybe that pain is a current reality. Though doing so may be difficult, spend time expressing your pain in a lament to God. See him attentively listening to you and reaching out to comfort you. What does it feel like to be comforted?

LIVE

Live knowing that God is loving enough to listen to you and big enough to care for you in your pain.

GOD'S TRACK RECORD WITH ME

2 SAMUEL 7:18,20-23,28-29

18,20-21   King David went in, took his place before God, and prayed: "Who am I, my Master God, and what is my family, that you have brought me to this place in life? . . . What can I possibly say in the face of all this? You know me, Master God, just as I am. You've done all this not because of who I am but because of who you are — out of your very heart! — but you've let me in on it.

22-23   "This is what makes you so great, Master God! There is none like you, no God but you, nothing to compare with what we've heard with our own ears. And who is like your people, like Israel, a nation unique in the earth, whom God set out to redeem for himself (and became most famous for it), performing great and fearsome acts, throwing out nations and their gods left and right as you saved your people from Egypt? . . .

28-29   "And now, Master God, being the God you are, speaking sure words as you do, and having just said this wonderful thing to me, please, just one more thing: Bless my family; keep your eye on them always. You've already as much as said that you would, Master God! Oh, may your blessing be on my family permanently!"

READ

Read the passage aloud slowly.

THINK

Read the passage even more slowly and deliberately, considering every word. Listen for the line that resonates with you and read it again after you finish the passage. Pause. Consider any of the following issues, letting God nudge you.

- In what ways has God changed you that you can be grateful for?
- What has God brought you out of?
- How has God been heroic regarding you ("performing great and fearsome acts, throwing out nations and their gods left and right")?
- What would you like to ask God for regarding the future?

PRAY

Pray through the above passage, innovating and personalizing your prayer according to the questions in the Think section.

LIVE

Give this a try: Consider the line from the passage that caught your attention and put it to a tune from a song you already know (or make a tune up, if you wish). Sing that line and then sit in the quiet. Sing it again and sit in the quiet. Sing it one more time and sit in the quiet.

HONORING OTHERS

2 SAMUEL 9:8-13

8   Shuffling and stammering, not looking him in the eye, Mephibosheth said, "Who am I that you pay attention to a stray dog like me?"

9-10   David then called in Ziba, Saul's right-hand man, and told him, "Everything that belonged to Saul and his family, I've handed over to your master's grandson. You and your sons and your servants will work his land and bring in the produce, provisions for your master's grandson. Mephibosheth himself, your master's grandson, from now on will take all his meals at my table." Ziba had fifteen sons and twenty servants.

11-12 "All that my master the king has ordered his servant," answered Ziba, "your servant will surely do."

And Mephibosheth ate at David's table, just like one of the royal family. Mephibosheth also had a small son named Mica. All who were part of Ziba's household were now the servants of Mephibosheth.

13   Mephibosheth lived in Jerusalem, taking all his meals at the king's table. He was lame in both feet.

READ

Read the passage slowly, setting yourself inside the throne room. Look at David up close — the imposing crown, the rugged face that's seen countless wars, the lavish surroundings. Now see Mephibosheth, "a stray dog" hunched in fear, embarrassed and uncomfortable. How might he have come into the room, being "lame in both feet"? What feelings rise up in you as you see the story play out? What questions come to mind?

THINK

Pause to become aware of how you relate to what is unfolding here. Which character do you identify with, if any? Why?

PRAY

Read the story a second time, being aware of memories, thoughts, or ideas it triggers. Read it one last time, listening for how the story's message about honoring others relates to what is in you today. Spend time meditating on what you discover.

LIVE

Ask God if there is something he is specifically inviting you to do based on your reading today. Is there anything standing in your way of responding? Explore it with God. Talk to him about what holds you back from following him completely.

DAY 35

GOD ENCOUNTERS

On this seventh day, review and reflect on all you have read this week. Take the time to revel in the ways you've encountered God in the past six days.

AN ABSALOM MOMENT

2 SAMUEL 15:3-6

3-6 Then Absalom would say, "Look, you've got a strong case; but the king isn't going to listen to you." Then he'd say, "Why doesn't someone make me a judge for this country? Anybody with a case could bring it to me and I'd settle things fair and square." Whenever someone would treat him with special honor, he'd shrug it off and treat him like an equal, making him feel important. Absalom did this to everyone who came to do business with the king and stole the hearts of everyone in Israel.

READ

Read the passage five times.

THINK

There are points in our lives (more often than we would like to admit) when we attempt consciously and subconsciously to promote ourselves in unhealthy and selfish ways. We puff ourselves up, brag about our accomplishments, and embellish the truth.

Absalom, the son of King David, promotes himself for selfish gain in front of those who came to the city gate. The text says he "stole the hearts of everyone in Israel."

When are you most tempted to steal the hearts of everyone in _____? Think about your most recent Absalom moment. Consider the roots of your temptation and how you might avoid it in the future.

PRAY

Spend time inviting God to remind you that he loves you just the way you are, that you cannot earn his approval. Welcome God to show you your true identity as his child, an identity that is defined not by what you do, but by who you are and to whom you belong.

LIVE

Ask a good friend to gently keep you accountable when you begin to promote yourself in front of others. Be ready to accept your friend's input.

LOVING THOSE IN THE HERE AND NOW

2 SAMUEL 19:1-8

1-4 Joab was told that David was weeping and lamenting over Absalom. The day's victory turned into a day of mourning as word passed through the army, "David is grieving over his son." The army straggled back to the city that day demoralized, dragging their tails. And the king held his face in his hands and lamented loudly,

> O my son Absalom,
> Absalom my dear, dear son!

5-7 But in private Joab rebuked the king: "Now you've done it — knocked the wind out of your loyal servants who have just saved your life, to say nothing of the lives of your sons and daughters, wives and concubines. What is this — loving those who hate you and hating those who love you? Your actions give a clear message: officers and soldiers mean nothing to you. You know that if Absalom were alive right now, we'd all be dead — would that make you happy? Get hold of yourself; get out there and put some heart into your servants! I swear to GOD that if you don't go to them they'll desert; not a soldier will be left here by nightfall. And that will be the worst thing that has happened yet."

8 So the king came out and took his place at the city gate. Soon everyone knew: "Oh, look! The king has come out to receive us." And his whole army came and presented itself to the king. But the Israelites had fled the field of battle and gone home.

READ

Read the passage aloud slowly. Absalom had rebelled against his father, David, and took over Israel. As David mourns Absalom, the people who defended him and brought him back with honor are listening.

THINK

Read the passage aloud slowly again. David did what we often do. He lived in regret. He wanted what he used to have and what he couldn't now have. As a result, he undervalued and discouraged the people who had stood by him and helped him.

1. Who do you identify with more: David or the army?
2. Consider their feelings: David living in regret; the army feeling ignored and discarded.
3. Consider their next steps: David turning his heart to the people around him who loved him; the army speaking up and stating their needs to a hurting person.

PRAY

Pray for yourself and others, especially that they'll see and implement any possible next steps (for example, moving out of regret and valuing the people in front of them, or speaking up to someone who is devaluing others).

LIVE

Let your mind rest in glad appreciation for those who stand by you. Ask God for opportunities to bless them. Then in the dailiness of life, look for those opportunities.

GOD FEELS THE PAIN

2 SAMUEL 24:13-17,25

13 Gad came to deliver the message: "Do you want three years of famine in the land, or three months of running from your enemies while they chase you down, or three days of an epidemic on the country? Think it over and make up your mind. What shall I tell the one who sent me?"

14 David told Gad, "They're all terrible! But I'd rather be punished by GOD, whose mercy is great, than fall into human hands."

15-16 So GOD let loose an epidemic from morning until suppertime. From Dan to Beersheba seventy thousand people died. But when the angel reached out over Jerusalem to destroy it, GOD felt the pain of the terror and told the angel who was spreading death among the people, "Enough's enough! Pull back!"

The angel of GOD had just reached the threshing floor of Araunah the Jebusite. David looked up and saw the angel hovering between earth and sky, sword drawn and about to strike Jerusalem. David and the elders bowed in prayer and covered themselves with rough burlap.

17 When David saw the angel about to destroy the people, he prayed, "Please! I'm the one who sinned; I, the shepherd, did the wrong. But these sheep, what did they do wrong? Punish me and my family, not them." . . .

25 He built an altar to GOD there and sacrificed burnt offerings and peace offerings. GOD was moved by the prayers and that was the end of the disaster.

READ

Skim the expanded passage. Now read the excerpt three times carefully.

THINK/PRAY

Set the text aside and imaginatively replay the story, inserting yourself as a character in it. Perhaps you will be one of David's elders, or David himself.

What do you think and feel as you hear God's words of discipline? What do you experience as you walk through this tension-filled and tragic day? What do you see? Hear? Smell? What questions do you have for God? Are you angry? Afraid? Talk to him.

As the end of the day approaches and you see God's interaction with the angel, what is that like for you? When God's heart is changed by David's prayers, what thoughts and feelings bubble up in you? Express them to God.

LIVE

C. S. Lewis wrote, "[Each sinful act leaves a mark] on that tiny central self which no one sees in this life but which each of us will have to endure — or enjoy — for ever. One man may be so placed that his anger sheds the blood of thousands, and another so placed that, however angry he gets, he will only be laughed at. But the little mark on the soul may be much the same in both."[3] Are there any "little marks" on your soul that you haven't talked about with God? Explore recent experiences, reactions, thoughts, and feelings you've had. What do they tell you about what's inside your heart? Talk to God about this, and make note of any action you feel he is leading you to.

A DREAM FULFILLED

1 KINGS 5:1-5

1-4 Hiram king of Tyre sent ambassadors to Solomon when he heard that he had been crowned king in David's place. Hiram had loved David his whole life. Solomon responded, saying, "You know that David my father was not able to build a temple in honor of GOD because of the wars he had to fight on all sides, until GOD finally put them down. But now GOD has provided peace all around—no one against us, nothing at odds with us.

5 "Now here is what I want to do: Build a temple in honor of GOD, *my* God, following the promise that GOD gave to David my father, namely, 'Your son whom I will provide to succeed you as king, he will build a house in my honor.'"

READ

Read the passage aloud slowly.

THINK

Read the passage aloud slowly again, especially verses 3-5.

1. Listen for the words or phrases that stand out to you — perhaps one of these:

   - "build a temple in honor of GOD"
   - "wars he had to fight on all sides, until GOD finally put them down"
   - "GOD has provided peace all around — no one against us, nothing at odds with us"
   - "here is what I want to do . . . in honor of GOD, *my* God, following the promise that GOD gave"

   These phrases indicate that David lived an interactive life with God and that Solomon is attempting to do the same. They also refer to David and Solomon's dream coming true. David had wisely let go of his dream of building the temple, while Solomon was now taking the next step by implementing the dream.

2. What dreams have you had?
3. What dreams have you let go of or picked up?

PRAY

Talk to God about the phrases in the passage that hint at dreams you have. Ask God to give you wisdom about whether you need to let go of these dreams or pick them up. Ask God for vision and power to take your next step.

LIVE

Relish the peace that God gives, knowing that dreams don't have to be realized today. Maybe ponder and pursue your next step. Put on the idea of readiness and see if it fits.

PAY ATTENTION TO MY PRAYERS

1 KINGS 8:22-30

22-25 Before the entire congregation of Israel, Solomon took a position before the Altar, spread his hands out before heaven, and prayed,

> O GOD, God of Israel, there is no God like you in the skies above or on the earth below who unswervingly keeps covenant with his servants and relentlessly loves them as they sincerely live in obedience to your way. You kept your word to David my father, your personal word. You did exactly what you promised — every detail. The proof is before us today!
>
> Keep it up, GOD, O God of Israel! Continue to keep the promises you made to David my father when you said, "You'll always have a descendant to represent my rule on Israel's throne, on the condition that your sons are as careful to live obediently in my presence as you have."

26 > O God of Israel, let this all happen;
> confirm and establish it!

27-30 Can it be that God will actually move into our neighborhood? Why, the cosmos itself isn't large enough to give you breathing room, let alone this Temple I've built. Even so, I'm bold to ask: Pay attention to these my prayers, both intercessory and personal, O GOD, my God. Listen to my prayers, energetic and devout, that I'm setting before you right now. Keep your eyes open to this Temple night and day, this place of which you said, "My Name will be honored there," and listen to the prayers that I pray at this place.

READ

Read the passage.

THINK

What's your immediate reaction to Solomon's candid prayer to God? Think about the statements Solomon makes and the things he asks God to do. Are they things you could let yourself ask of God? Or do they indicate a belief in qualities of God that you have not encountered or experienced? Which qualities?

PRAY

Read Solomon's prayer again, this time listening for what stands out to you as representing the lack of belief you noticed in yourself when you read the passage the first time. Explore your reaction more deeply, paying attention to what it tells you about yourself. Maybe you feel that you can bring to God only desires that are completely selfless, or perhaps you don't trust that he "relentlessly loves" you. Share with God what you uncover.

LIVE

Ignatius of Loyola once said, "Everything that one turns in the direction of God is prayer." No matter what has arisen in you during this time — irritation, fear, desire, disinterest, lack of trust in God — it can all be prayer when shared with him; it's all part of your conversation with God. Notice how Solomon lets his anxiety and insecurity spill into his prayer to God, and allow yourself to do the same.

IDOL FACTORIES

1 KINGS 12:27-33

27 "As soon as these people resume worship at The Temple of GOD in Jerusalem, they'll start thinking of Rehoboam king of Judah as their ruler. They'll then kill me and go back to King Rehoboam."

28-30 So the king came up with a plan: He made two golden calves. Then he announced, "It's too much trouble for you to go to Jerusalem to worship. Look at these — the gods who brought you out of Egypt!" He put one calf in Bethel; the other he placed in Dan. This was blatant sin. Think of it — people traveling all the way to Dan to worship a calf!

31-33 And that wasn't the end of it. Jeroboam built forbidden shrines all over the place and recruited priests from wherever he could find them, regardless of whether they were fit for the job or not. To top it off, he created a holy New Year festival to be held on the fifteenth day of the eighth month to replace the one in Judah, complete with worship offered on the Altar at Bethel and sacrificing before the calves he had set up there. He staffed Bethel with priests from the local shrines he had made. This was strictly his own idea to compete with the feast in Judah; and he carried it off with flair, a festival exclusively for Israel, Jeroboam himself leading the worship at the Altar.

READ

Each time you read this passage, focus on the sentence "This was blatant sin."

THINK

Israel at this time was split into two sections: the northern and the southern kingdoms. Jeroboam was ruling in the northern kingdom. He erected two golden calves (as Aaron had at Sinai in Exodus). In addition to calves, he erected forbidden shrines and created a sacred holiday.

Instead of placing his entire trust in Yahweh, Jeroboam chose to erect idols to be the center of worship for the people in his kingdom. Under his leadership, the significance of worshiping the Lord God was lessened and eventually lost.

Sneering at such blatant disrespect of the living God is easy for us. But even though we don't erect golden calves, our focus on certain things eclipses our worship of God. John Calvin said that our hearts are idol factories.

Meditate on some of the golden calves in your life that eclipse your worship of God. These could be reputation, power, wealth, identity, fame, church, relationships — anything that takes your eyes off God.

PRAY

Spend time confessing your golden calves. Ask the Holy Spirit to pinch you each time you turn to them.

LIVE

Be aware that your heart is an idol factory. Recognize that idols come in all shapes and sizes. When you find yourself bowing a knee to them, return to the Lord in humility.

41

42

DAY 42

GOD ENCOUNTERS

On this seventh day, review and reflect on all you have read this week. Take the time to revel in the ways you've encountered God in the past six days.

WHEN TRUSTING GOD IS A HANDFUL

1 KINGS 17:7-16

7-9 Eventually the brook dried up because of the drought. Then GOD spoke to him: "Get up and go to Zarephath in Sidon and live there. I've instructed a woman who lives there, a widow, to feed you."

10-11 So he got up and went to Zarephath. As he came to the entrance of the village he met a woman, a widow, gathering firewood. He asked her, "Please, would you bring me a little water in a jug? I need a drink." As she went to get it, he called out, "And while you're at it, would you bring me something to eat?"

12 She said, "I swear, as surely as your GOD lives, I don't have so much as a biscuit. I have a handful of flour in a jar and a little oil in a bottle; you found me scratching together just enough firewood to make a last meal for my son and me. After we eat it, we'll die."

13-14 Elijah said to her, "Don't worry about a thing. Go ahead and do what you've said. But first make a small biscuit for me and bring it back here. Then go ahead and make a meal from what's left for you and your son. This is the word of the GOD of Israel: 'The jar of flour will not run out and the bottle of oil will not become empty before GOD sends rain on the land and ends this drought.'"

15-16 And she went right off and did it, did just as Elijah asked. And it turned out as he said — daily food for her and her family. The jar of meal didn't run out and the bottle of oil didn't become empty: GOD's promise fulfilled to the letter, exactly as Elijah had delivered it!

READ

Read the passage aloud slowly.

THINK

Read the passage slowly again. This time notice the repetitive phrases and words that seem to shimmer. Are there any in this passage that you sense God saying directly to you?

1. How do you resemble Elijah, the loner who was perhaps content by the solitary brook but now has to venture into Palestinian territory and ask a widow for her last dime?
2. How do you identify with the widow and feel that Elijah is asking too much? How difficult is it for you to give up the last handful of flour? Hold out your hand in front of you. Open and close it. Imagine that the amount of flour your hand could hold is all that stands between you and death.
3. How do you think the widow felt every time she put her hand in the jar and there was another handful of flour?

PRAY

Ask God what might be your jar of flour today — something that needs filling up. It's okay to tell God he's asking too much. At first, the widow did just that. Trusting God is a process.

LIVE

Consider how it would feel to trust God this much. How would your life be different if you trusted God with just a little more every single morning, as the widow did?

43

BECAUSE OF HIS REPENTANCE

1 KINGS 21:20-29

20-22   Ahab answered Elijah, "My enemy! So, you've run me down!"

"Yes, I've found you out," said Elijah. "And because you've bought into the business of evil, defying GOD. 'I will most certainly bring doom upon you, make mincemeat of your descendants, kill off every sorry male wretch who's even remotely connected with the name Ahab. And I'll bring down on you the same fate that fell on Jeroboam son of Nebat and Baasha son of Ahijah — you've made me *that* angry by making Israel sin.'"

23-24   As for Jezebel, GOD said, "Dogs will fight over the flesh of Jezebel all over Jezreel. Anyone tainted by Ahab who dies in the city will be eaten by stray dogs; corpses in the country will be eaten by carrion crows."

25-26   Ahab, pushed by his wife Jezebel and in open defiance of GOD, set an all-time record in making big business of evil. He indulged in outrageous obscenities in the world of idols, copying the Amorites whom GOD had earlier kicked out of Israelite territory.

27   When Ahab heard what Elijah had to say, he ripped his clothes to shreds, dressed in penitential rough burlap, and fasted. He even slept in coarse burlap pajamas. He tiptoed around, quiet as a mouse.

28-29   Then GOD spoke to Elijah the Tishbite: "Do you see how penitently submissive Ahab has become to me? Because of his repentance I'll not bring the doom during his lifetime; Ahab's son, though, will get it."

READ

Read the passage, putting yourself into the scene as much as you can.

THINK

Imagine yourself as Elijah, noticing what you think and feel throughout this tale. (See the expanded passage for more details.) Read the passage again until you reach God's words to Ahab and Jezebel, and the description of what they have done to defy him. Pause there.

PRAY

As you picture yourself speaking God's words of judgment to Ahab, listen to what you are saying. What does God's anger toward this enemy make you feel? Do you feel the same anger God does over the injustice? If not, what does Ahab's sin make you feel? When you picture the three of you there — Ahab, God, you — what position is your body inclined to take toward each of them? Talk to God about your response.

Now return to the passage, and continue reading where you left off. When you reach the part about Ahab's repentance, hear God tell you about his change of mind. What does this make you feel? Where do your thoughts go? Talk to God about your response.

LIVE

Meditate on the following prayer from the *Book of Common Prayer* (1979): "The Lord is full of compassion and mercy: O come, let us adore him."[4] Notice what your response is. If there is something you need to repent of today, go to God and receive his mercy. If you want to adore him for his compassion, spend time doing so. If you don't want to adore God, take time to open yourself to the reality that he is praiseworthy. Don't force yourself to feel things you don't feel or to say things you don't mean, but do consider the reality acknowledged in the prayer.

44

✚ FALSE HOPES?

2 KINGS 4:20,24-29

20   The servant took him in his arms and carried him to his mother. He lay on her lap until noon and died. . . .

24-25   She went ahead and saddled the donkey, ordering her servant, "Take the lead — and go as fast as you can; I'll tell you if you're going too fast." And so off she went. She came to the Holy Man at Mount Carmel.

25-26   The Holy Man, spotting her while she was still a long way off, said to his servant Gehazi, "Look out there; why, it's the Shunammite woman! Quickly now. Ask her, 'Is something wrong? Are you all right? Your husband? Your child?'"

She said, "Everything's fine."

27   But when she reached the Holy Man at the mountain, she threw herself at his feet and held tightly to him.

Gehazi came up to pull her away, but the Holy Man said, "Leave her alone — can't you see that she's in distress? But GOD hasn't let me in on why; I'm completely in the dark."

28   Then she spoke up: "Did I ask for a son, master? Didn't I tell you, 'Don't tease me with false hopes'?"

29   He ordered Gehazi, "Don't lose a minute — grab my staff and run as fast as you can. If you meet anyone, don't even take time to greet him, and if anyone greets you, don't even answer. Lay my staff across the boy's face."

READ

Read the passage, preferably including the expanded passage.

THINK

Have you ever felt the bitter sting of shattered hopes and desires? The barren woman from Shunem knows the sting intimately — her grief here seems to confirm the doubt she experienced earlier when the holy man, Elisha, prophesied that she would have a son. At the time of the prophecy, not wanting to get her hopes up, she wouldn't even let on that she desired a son. Now she seems to wish she'd never hoped at all.

Notice Elisha's response to the woman in her fear, grief, and regret. Take several minutes to think about this. How might Elisha's response reflect God's response to her? What might God have been feeling as he watched her struggle with her son's death?

PRAY

Explore your own heart to see if there are any deep desires there that you are afraid to trust God with. Can you tell him why you hold back? Ask him to show you his response to your desires and to help you trust him more, just as the Shunammite woman trusted Elisha enough to expose her anguish to him.

LIVE

Henri Nouwen wrote, "At every moment you have to decide to trust the voice that says, 'I love you. I knit you together in your mother's womb' (Ps. 139:13)."[5] Ponder this quote. What might your life look like if you were to take God at his word, believing that he knows all about you and cares for you as tenderly as Elisha cared for the Shunammite? How might you pray differently? Live differently?

45

INVESTING IN PEOPLE

2 KINGS 11:17–12:2

17   Jehoiada now made a covenant between GOD and the king and the people: They were GOD's people. Another covenant was made between the king and the people.

18-20   The people poured into the temple of Baal and tore it down, smashing altar and images to smithereens. They killed Mattan the priest in front of the altar.

    Jehoiada then stationed sentries in The Temple of GOD. He arranged for the officers of the bodyguard and the palace security, along with the people themselves, to escort the king down from The Temple of GOD through the Gate of the Guards and into the palace. There he sat on the royal throne. Everybody celebrated the event. And the city was safe and undisturbed — they had killed Athaliah with the royal sword.

21   Joash was seven years old when he became king.

1   In the seventh year of Jehu, Joash began his kingly rule. He was king for forty years in Jerusalem. His mother's name was Gazelle. She was from Beersheba.

2   Taught and trained by Jehoiada the priest, Joash did what pleased GOD for as long as he lived.

READ

Read the passage aloud slowly, keeping in mind that Jehoiada is a priest of Judah at a time when Judah has been worshiping Baal instead of God.

THINK

Read the passage again slowly, trying to picture the priest Jehoiada and his young pupil, Joash, who becomes one of the few good kings of Judah.

1. What about Jehoiada do you most admire or dislike?
2. How would you like, or not like, to resemble Jehoiada as a teacher and leader? (Think of a teacher as anyone from whom others learn, and think of a leader as anyone who finds others following him or her. Even in friendships, sometimes one friend is the teacher and the other is the student, although they may not realize it.)

PRAY

Pray for people who look up to you — either for good or bad. In that case, you are their teacher and leader. Ask God who he is asking you to reach out to as an informal teacher or leader. Or you may want to simply pray about what you pass on to others.

LIVE

Sit in the quiet with God, holding before him those who follow you or look up to you. You might wish to ask God, "What do I need to know about myself as a teacher or leader?" Ideas might not come to you right away. Note those that do, and keep watch for them in the coming days and weeks.

GOD'S WHITE-HOT ANGER

2 KINGS 22:11-17

11-13 When the king heard what was written in the book, God's Revelation, he ripped his robes in dismay. And then he called for Hilkiah the priest, Ahikam son of Shaphan, Acbor son of Micaiah, Shaphan the royal secretary, and Asaiah the king's personal aide. He ordered them all: "Go and pray to GOD for me and for this people — for all Judah! Find out what we must do in response to what is written in this book that has just been found! GOD's anger must be burning furiously against us — our ancestors haven't obeyed a thing written in this book, followed none of the instructions directed to us."

14-17 Hilkiah the priest, Ahikam, Acbor, Shaphan, and Asaiah went straight to Huldah the prophetess. She was the wife of Shallum son of Tikvah, the son of Harhas, who was in charge of the palace wardrobe. She lived in Jerusalem in the Second Quarter. The five men consulted with her. In response to them she said, "GOD's word, the God of Israel: Tell the man who sent you here that I'm on my way to bring the doom of judgment on this place and this people. Every word written in the book read by the king of Judah will happen. And why? Because they've deserted me and taken up with other gods, made me thoroughly angry by setting up their god-making businesses. My anger is raging white-hot against this place and nobody is going to put it out."

READ

Read the passage once aloud to get a feel for what's happening.

THINK

Read the passage again. As you do, listen for words or images that especially impact you, such as raging anger that "nobody is going to put . . . out," or the king ripping his robes "in dismay."

PRAY

Take time to silently repeat this word or phrase from the passage or to let the image play itself out in your mind. See how it meshes with your thoughts, feelings, and memories. Eventually let your contemplation lead you to consider whether there are any questionable or sinful areas of your life that you have been ignoring lately. Can you tell why you've been ignoring them? Bring them before God. What is your posture?

LIVE

Picture this God whose "anger is raging white-hot." What's it like to be before him? Now see Jesus, the mediator between the holy God pictured in this passage and the sinful people God loves. Turn to Jesus and together examine your heart. Watch his response to the sinful areas you noticed. What is he inviting you to do in response to what you see? Respond to his invitation. Watch God the Father accept Jesus' redemption of your sin — see God's white-hot anger cool — and experience being welcomed back into full fellowship with him once more.

LINKING ARMS

1 CHRONICLES 11:10-11

10-11 These are the chiefs of David's Mighty Men, the ones who linked arms with him as he took up his kingship, with all Israel joining in, helping him become king in just the way GOD had spoken regarding Israel. The list of David's Mighty Men:

Jashobeam son of Hacmoni was chief of the Thirty. Singlehandedly he killed three hundred men, killed them all in one skirmish.

READ

Read the passage and underline every verb or action word.

THINK

David's Mighty Men were willing to risk their lives by crossing the Philistine military camp in order to bring David water from the Bethlehem well. What incredible friendships!

Discuss this passage with a friend or spiritual mentor. What do you think about the idea of linking arms with others? Is it awkward? Is it worth the effort?

PRAY

Tell God about any worries or insecurities you have about linking up with others. Pray for the discernment to choose a few mature, like-minded people to link arms with you and the boldness to ask them for help.

LIVE

Approach these individuals and ask them to link arms with you.

DAY 49

GOD ENCOUNTERS

On this seventh day, review and reflect on all you have read this week. Take the time to revel in the ways you've encountered God in the past six days.

SHOUT FROM THE MOUNTAINTOPS

1 CHRONICLES 16:23-29

23-27   Sing to GOD, everyone and everything!
      Get out his salvation news every day!
    Publish his glory among the godless nations,
      his wonders to all races and religions.
    And why? Because GOD is great—well worth praising!
      No god or goddess comes close in honor.
    All the popular gods are stuff and nonsense,
      but GOD made the cosmos!
    Splendor and majesty flow out of him,
      strength and joy fill his place.

28-29   Shout Bravo! to GOD, families of the peoples,
      in awe of the Glory, in awe of the Strength: Bravo!
    Shout Bravo! to his famous Name,
      lift high an offering and enter his presence!
    Stand resplendent in his robes of holiness!

READ

Read the passage aloud slowly, keeping in mind that "Shout Bravo!" here means something like "give credit to."

Read the passage aloud again, but do it this time as if you are speaking convincingly, first to "everyone and everything" (verse 23 addresses the entire planet, including the vegetation and animals of the earth), then to all the "families of the peoples" (verse 28, all nations, all tribes, all classes of people).

THINK

Read the passage again silently and ponder the following:

1. Consider the words you most relish. What phrase did you particularly enjoy saying as you read the passage dramatically?
2. What would you most want the earth to know or understand about God?
3. What would you most want the families of the earth to know or understand about God?

PRAY

Begin by asking God to lead you in your prayer. Wait for him. Once you get started, you may wish to say something like, "O God, I'm so glad you are . . ." and finish with ideas from this psalm.

LIVE

If you could shout this psalm from anywhere in the world, where would that be? (It might be on a specific mountaintop or by a certain waterfall or even before an international group, such as the United Nations.) Picture yourself saying these verses from your heart in that setting, without embarrassment or any other reservation. Rest in your boldness.

OUR LIVES ARE MERE SHADOWS

1 CHRONICLES 29:12-19

12-13   Riches and glory come from you,
          you're ruler over all;
      You hold strength and power in the palm of your hand
          to build up and strengthen all.
      And here we are, O God, our God, giving thanks to you,
          praising your splendid Name.

14-19   "But me — who am I, and who are these my people, that we should presume to be giving something to you? Everything comes from you; all we're doing is giving back what we've been given from your generous hand. As far as you're concerned, we're homeless, shiftless wanderers like our ancestors, our lives mere shadows, hardly anything to us. GOD, our God, all these materials — these piles of stuff for building a house of worship for you, honoring your Holy Name — it all came from you! It was all yours in the first place! I know, dear God, that you care nothing for the surface — you want *us*, our true selves — and so I have given from the heart, honestly and happily. And now see all these people doing the same, giving freely, willingly — what a joy! O GOD, God of our fathers Abraham, Isaac, and Israel, keep this generous spirit alive forever in these people always, keep their hearts set firmly in you. And give my son Solomon an uncluttered and focused heart so that he can obey what you command, live by your directions and counsel, and carry through with building The Temple for which I have provided."

READ

David is blessing God in this passage. To see his entire prayer, read the expanded passage, seeing how he dedicates to God the money and materials generously given by him and all the Israelites for building the temple.

THINK

When David talks about our lives as "mere shadows" — that everything we have is actually only being borrowed from God — how does that strike you? What item do you own, or what relationship do you have, that you hold more tightly than you would a shadow? Be honest.

PRAY

As you approach God in prayer, picture yourself bringing with you the item that is hard to hold loosely. Talk to God about what keeps you attached to it. Don't try to navigate the prayer so that by the end you are letting go of your treasured thing. Don't try to force yourself to be less attached to it than you actually are. Simply talk to God while you imaginatively hold it tightly in your hands, and tell him about why it's so important to you. Keep in mind that if you are still in the same position internally at the end of your prayer time, that's okay.

LIVE

Take a few more minutes to reflect on what talking to God was like as you held on to the item you're unwilling to give up — at least not easily. Did you feel guilty or uncomfortable, or do you have trouble being honest with him? Why might that be?

EXPANDED PASSAGE: 2 CHRONICLES 6:12-42

DEDICATION CEREMONIES

2 CHRONICLES 6:12-18

12-16   Before the entire congregation of Israel, Solomon took his position at the Altar of GOD and stretched out his hands. Solomon had made a bronze dais seven and a half feet square and four and a half feet high and placed it inside the court; that's where he now stood. Then he knelt in full view of the whole congregation, stretched his hands to heaven, and prayed:

> GOD, O God of Israel, there is no God like you in the skies above or on the earth below, who unswervingly keeps covenant with his servants and unfailingly loves them while they sincerely live in obedience to your way. You kept your word to David my father, your promise. You did exactly what you promised — every detail. The proof is before us today!
>
> Keep it up, GOD, O God of Israel! Continue to keep the promises you made to David my father when you said, "You'll always have a descendant to represent my rule on Israel's throne, on the one condition that your sons are as careful to live obediently in my presence as you have."

17   O GOD, God of Israel, let this all happen —
     confirm and establish it!

18   Can it be that God will actually move into our neighborhood? Why, the cosmos itself isn't large enough to give you breathing room, let alone this Temple I've built.

READ

Read the passage, underlining words that stand out to you.

THINK

King Solomon, son of King David, built the famous temple to the Lord on Mount Zion in Jerusalem as a gathering place for the Jews to worship Yahweh. It took him years to build this temple, and at its completion he assembled all the people for a public dedication. To dedicate something is to set it aside for a special purpose. As you read the dedication prayer of Solomon, notice the gratitude and the humility of the king as he prays.

What precious aspects of your life (for example, people, positions, locations, important events, yourself) do you need to set solely aside for the Lord as a public reminder that all you have belongs to God? What would it take for you to do that . . . and with the attitude of Solomon?

PRAY

Write out a prayer of dedication to God for an individual, situation, event, or position.

LIVE

Keep your dedication prayer so you can occasionally refer to it. In fact, if you wish, make a note on your calendar a few weeks from today to reread your prayer. At that time, think about what's different in your life due to your dedication.

FROG:
FULLY RELY ON GOD

2 CHRONICLES 16:7-9

7-9   Just after that, Hanani the seer came to Asa king of Judah and said, "Because you went for help to the king of Aram and didn't ask GOD for help, you've lost a victory over the army of the king of Aram. Didn't the Ethiopians and Libyans come against you with superior forces, completely outclassing you with their chariots and cavalry? But you asked GOD for help and he gave you the victory. GOD is always on the alert, constantly on the lookout for people who are totally committed to him. You were foolish to go for human help when you could have had God's help. Now you're in trouble — one round of war after another."

READ

Read the passage aloud slowly.

THINK

Read the passage again slowly. Previously Asa had been a good king. After hearing convicting prophecy, he "took a deep breath, then rolled up his sleeves, and went to work" cleaning out the temples (15:8).

1. Which phrase or idea sticks with you?

   ☐ that Asa "went for help to the king of Aram and didn't ask GOD for help"
   ☐ that "GOD is always on the alert, constantly on the lookout for people who are totally committed to him."
   ☐ that not relying on God results in "one round of war after another"
   ☐ other:

2. Why does that idea stick with you?
3. The theme of this passage could be summed up in the acronym FROG, standing for Fully Rely on God. Consider your life — for what large or small issues might you FROG that you have not thought of before? (Don't use this passage to beat yourself up; that's not profitable. Use it instead as a springboard to ask God for guidance.)

PRAY

Thank God that you can fully rely on him. Admire God for his divine alertness and for how relying on him keeps you out of "trouble — one round of war after another." Take your time so that you fully explore your gratitude and admiration.

LIVE

Take some deep breaths and ponder what it would feel like in your gut to rely on God all the time, every day. Taste the sweetness of reliance so it's not a chore but the absolute best way to live.

OPEN ARMS

2 CHRONICLES 30:1,5-9

1,5   Then Hezekiah invited all of Israel and Judah, with personal letters to Ephraim and Manasseh, to come to The Temple of GOD in Jerusalem to celebrate the Passover to Israel's God. . . . And they sent out the invitation from one end of the country to the other, from Beersheba in the south to Dan in the north: "Come and celebrate the Passover to Israel's God in Jerusalem." No one living had ever celebrated it properly.

6-9   The king gave the orders, and the couriers delivered the invitations from the king and his leaders throughout Israel and Judah. The invitation read: "O Israelites! Come back to GOD, the God of Abraham, Isaac, and Israel, so that he can return to you who have survived the predations of the kings of Assyria. Don't repeat the sins of your ancestors who turned their backs on GOD, the God of their ancestors who then brought them to ruin — you can see the ruins all around you. Don't be pigheaded as your ancestors were. Clasp GOD's outstretched hand. Come to his Temple of holy worship, consecrated for all time. Serve GOD, *your* God. You'll no longer be in danger of his hot anger. If you come back to GOD, your captive relatives and children will be treated compassionately and allowed to come home. Your GOD is gracious and kind and won't snub you — come back and he'll welcome you with open arms."

READ

Read the passage several times.

THINK

As you read, listen for a new perspective on the way life is, or the way God is, that stands out to you today. Perhaps you will notice that God can have dangerously "hot anger," yet under other circumstances he is tender and open to a people who have walked far from intimacy with him. Maybe you'll be struck by the pigheadedness that kept some Israelites from taking "God's outstretched hand."

PRAY

Study the perspective you've absorbed, looking at it from different angles and holding it up against different experiences you've had. Do you ever fear approaching God because you worry he might snub you? Have you ever refused grace? Consider a specific situation. Then become aware of God's presence with you. Tell him what was going on during that time. How does the God of this passage (offering his "outstretched hand" to the Israelites) compare to your image of God in that situation?

LIVE

Close your time today by saying the Lord's Prayer. Speak the words aloud very slowly. Picture the righteous but compassionate God described in this passage, the One who is hearing your prayer now: "Our Father in heaven, reveal who you are. Set the world right; do what's best — as above, so below. Keep us alive with three square meals. Keep us forgiven with you and forgiving others. Keep us safe from ourselves and the Devil. You're in charge! You can do anything you want! You're ablaze in beauty! Yes. Yes. Yes" (Matthew 6:9-13).

WHAT CAN WE SAY FOR OURSELVES?

EZRA 9:10-15

10-12 "And now, our God, after all this what can we say for ourselves? For we have thrown your commands to the wind, the commands you gave us through your servants the prophets. They told us, 'The land you're taking over is a polluted land, polluted with the obscene vulgarities of the people who live there; they've filled it with their moral rot from one end to the other. Whatever you do, don't give your daughters in marriage to their sons nor marry your sons to their daughters. Don't cultivate their good opinion; don't make over them and get them to like you so you can make a lot of money and build up a tidy estate to hand down to your children.'

13-15 "And now this, on top of all we've already suffered because of our evil ways and accumulated guilt, even though you, dear God, punished us far less than we deserved and even went ahead and gave us this present escape. Yet here we are, at it again, breaking your commandments by intermarrying with the people who practice all these obscenities! Are you angry to the point of wiping us out completely, without even a few stragglers, with no way out at all? You are the righteous GOD of Israel. We are, right now, a small band of escapees. Look at us, openly standing here, guilty before you. No one can last long like this."

READ

Read this prayer, spoken by Ezra on behalf of all the exiled Israelites.

THINK

Think about how you relate to this prayer. Have you ever felt similar remorse to what Ezra expresses here? Maybe you feel frustration with the injustices of your community or nation, or maybe you experience guilt on a deep level — not for anything in particular, but just a general sense of not getting it right, ever. What have you done with that feeling? Stuffed it? Allowed it to constantly criticize what you do and say? Have you ever thought of sharing it with God?

PRAY

Ezra's raw confession of messing up before God indicates that he feels very secure in God's merciful love; otherwise, being this defenseless before anyone is hard.

Read Ezra's prayer again, looking for a word, a phrase, or even something about his tone that resonates with you. Take several minutes to mull this over, and listen for what it gives voice to in your heart. Allow yourself to make Ezra's prayer your own, repeating it and following him in prayer to God. Or perhaps you don't identify with what he says, yet beyond your words is a pain you want to share with God. Sit with him in this.

LIVE

When you mess up today, remember Ezra, and remember God's merciful love.

DAY 56

GOD ENCOUNTERS

On this seventh day, review and reflect on all you have read this week. Take the time to revel in the ways you've encountered God in the past six days.

BURDEN FOR THE POOR

NEHEMIAH 5:6-11

6-7 I got really angry when I heard their protest and complaints. After thinking it over, I called the nobles and officials on the carpet. I said, "Each one of you is gouging his brother."

7-8 Then I called a big meeting to deal with them. I told them, "We did everything we could to buy back our Jewish brothers who had to sell themselves as slaves to foreigners. And now you're selling these same brothers back into debt slavery! Does that mean that we have to buy them back again?"

They said nothing. What could they say?

9 "What you're doing is wrong. Is there no fear of God left in you? Don't you care what the nations around here, our enemies, think of you?

10-11 "I and my brothers and the people working for me have also loaned them money. But this gouging them with interest has to stop. Give them back their foreclosed fields, vineyards, olive groves, and homes right now. And forgive your claims on their money, grain, new wine, and olive oil."

LIVE

In preparation for this lesson, fast from one meal. (Use discernment regarding fasting; check with your doctor before doing it. If you can't do it for whatever reason, that's okay.) When you feel the pangs of hunger, use that discomfort as a catalyst for this devotion.

READ

Read the passage slowly.

THINK

While in Babylonian exile as a cupbearer to a foreign king, Nehemiah has a God-given burden: to rebuild the ransacked walls of the forgotten city of Jerusalem and, in the process, to restore the hope of his people. But in the midst of this massive architectural restoration project, the people are being abused by their own countrymen.

Nehemiah's burden grows larger. His burden now includes poverty and injustice. Imagine yourself in Nehemiah's shoes today. What does this burden feel like? Consider your empty stomach and write down how you feel.

PRAY

Begin praying by listening for God's heart regarding justice. Ask him to show you people who need your prayers. Then ask him to point out when you need to speak up on their behalf, and ask for the courage to actually follow through with it.

ZEAL FOR RIGHTEOUSNESS

NEHEMIAH 13:7-13

7-9   I arrived in Jerusalem and learned of the wrong that Eliashib had done in turning over to him a room in the courts of The Temple of God. I was angry, really angry, and threw everything in the room out into the street, all of Tobiah's stuff. Then I ordered that they ceremonially cleanse the room. Only then did I put back the worship vessels of The Temple of God, along with the Grain-Offerings and the incense.

10-13   And then I learned that the Levites hadn't been given their regular food allotments. So the Levites and singers who led the services of worship had all left and gone back to their farms. I called the officials on the carpet, "Why has The Temple of God been abandoned?" I got everyone back again and put them back on their jobs so that all Judah was again bringing in the tithe of grain, wine, and oil to the storerooms. I put Shelemiah the priest, Zadok the scribe, and a Levite named Pedaiah in charge of the storerooms. I made Hanan son of Zaccur, the son of Mattaniah, their right-hand man. These men had a reputation for honesty and hard work. They were responsible for distributing the rations to their brothers.

READ

Read the passage, including the expanded portion for background, if you can.

THINK

In these earlier days, what do you notice about the way of life God required his people to abide by? Why do you think this was important to him? What do you think their relationship with God was like? How might it be different from your relationship with him?

PRAY

Become aware of God's presence with you now. Share your thoughts with him, including what you noticed about your own relationship with him. Let this lead you into silent prayer, pondering what's happened in your life since you last talked with him and whether there is anything you need to clear up. Listen for what he might be saying in response to you. If you don't sense him saying anything directly, be open to other ways he might try to communicate with you (such as through other people or recent experiences).

LIVE

Think about the passion Nehemiah demonstrates for honoring God. What would your life look like with more passion? How might you honor God with your lifestyle the way Nehemiah desires to honor God? Jesus said, "Love the Lord your God with all your passion and prayer and intelligence. . . . Love others as well as you love yourself" (Matthew 22:37,39). With this command in mind, think of one small new habit you could cultivate that would honor God in a particular area of your life.

JUST SUCH A TIME

ESTHER 4:7-14

7-8   Mordecai told him everything that had happened to him. He also told him the exact amount of money that Haman had promised to deposit in the royal bank to finance the massacre of the Jews. Mordecai also gave him a copy of the bulletin that had been posted in Susa ordering the massacre so he could show it to Esther when he reported back with instructions to go to the king and intercede and plead with him for her people.

9-11   Hathach came back and told Esther everything Mordecai had said. Esther talked it over with Hathach and then sent him back to Mordecai with this message: "Everyone who works for the king here, and even the people out in the provinces, knows that there is a single fate for every man or woman who approaches the king without being invited: death. The one exception is if the king extends his gold scepter; then he or she may live. And it's been thirty days now since I've been invited to come to the king."

12-14   When Hathach told Mordecai what Esther had said, Mordecai sent her this message: "Don't think that just because you live in the king's house you're the one Jew who will get out of this alive. If you persist in staying silent at a time like this, help and deliverance will arrive for the Jews from someplace else; but you and your family will be wiped out. Who knows? Maybe you were made queen for just such a time as this."

READ

As you read this story, imagine how you might feel if you were Esther: You were chosen to be queen by a king who doesn't know of your ethnicity, and now you're hearing word of a political plot that will wipe out your people and your family.

THINK

Focus your attention on either Esther's fear of putting her life on the line for her people or Mordecai's challenge to her in the face of her fear. Meditatively read that part of the passage again. Picture the speaker, including the situation from which the words are spoken. Select one word or phrase to contemplate during your prayer time.

PRAY

Prayerfully ponder a word or phrase from Mordecai or Esther and identify a memory that relates. Maybe at one time you were called on to do something courageous — big or small — but couldn't bring yourself to do it. Or maybe you wonder why God would allow Esther to bear such a heavy responsibility. Perhaps you were recently helped because someone took a stand for you.

Invite God the Father into your meditation. Try not to analyze or push toward solutions. Just notice what comes up and show it to him, as a child might show Daddy a favorite toy that's broken or tell him about a fascinating discovery.

LIVE

Take some time now to rest with the Father. If you have more to say in your conversation with him about Esther's dilemma, continue it. If you have other subjects you'd like to talk to him about, do so. But if you want to just sit in the presence of your loving Father, go ahead.

59

PREOCCUPATIONS

ESTHER 5:9-13

9-13 Haman left the palace that day happy, beaming. And then he saw Mordecai sitting at the King's Gate ignoring him, oblivious to him. Haman was furious with Mordecai. But he held himself in and went on home. He got his friends together with his wife Zeresh and started bragging about how much money he had, his many sons, all the times the king had honored him, and his promotion to the highest position in the government. "On top of all that," Haman continued, "Queen Esther invited me to a private dinner she gave for the king, just the three of us. And she's invited me to another one tomorrow. But I can't enjoy any of it when I see Mordecai the Jew sitting at the King's Gate."

READ

Read the passage aloud slowly. Haman is upset because the king ordered all those at the King's Gate to bow to him, and Mordecai the Jew does not (see Esther 3:3-6).

THINK

Read the passage again slowly.

1. How did Haman's preoccupations affect him? What did those pre-occupations reveal about the kind of person he was inside?
2. What preoccupations have filled your mind for the past twenty-four hours? What do these preoccupations reveal about who you are inside?
3. What things would you like to be preoccupied with?

PRAY

Pray this verse in your own words: "Set your minds on things above" (Colossians 3:2, NIV). Ask God for guidance in what kind of person you want to be and what to focus on.

LIVE

Dream about becoming the kind of person whose mind is preoccupied with God. Contemplation is a time for receiving from God. Receive an image of yourself from him. Embrace the future you.

JUSTICE SERVED

ESTHER 7:3-10

3 Queen Esther answered, "If I have found favor in your eyes, O King, and if it please the king, give me my life, and give my people their lives.

4 "We've been sold, I and my people, to be destroyed — sold to be massacred, eliminated. If we had just been sold off into slavery, I wouldn't even have brought it up; our troubles wouldn't have been worth bothering the king over."

5 King Xerxes exploded, "Who? Where is he? This is monstrous!"

6 "An enemy. An adversary. This evil Haman," said Esther.

Haman was terror-stricken before the king and queen.

7-8 The king, raging, left his wine and stalked out into the palace garden.

Haman stood there pleading with Queen Esther for his life — he could see that the king was finished with him and that he was doomed. As the king came back from the palace garden into the banquet hall, Haman was groveling at the couch on which Esther reclined. The king roared out, "Will he even molest the queen while I'm just around the corner?"

When that word left the king's mouth, all the blood drained from Haman's face.

9 Harbona, one of the eunuchs attending the king, spoke up: "Look over there! There's the gallows that Haman had built for Mordecai, who saved the king's life. It's right next to Haman's house — seventy-five feet high!"

The king said, "Hang him on it!"

10 So Haman was hanged on the very gallows that he had built for Mordecai. And the king's hot anger cooled.

READ

Take some time before you begin to sit in silence. Let your thoughts settle. Now read the passage once silently.

THINK

Read this story of justice being served again, this time aloud. Listen specifically for a word or a phrase that touches your heart in some way. When you finish reading, close your eyes. Recall the word and sit quietly, mulling it over. After a few moments, write the word down. Don't explain it or say more about it; just note it.

PRAY

Read the passage aloud again, this time looking for a person or an action that accentuates your internal picture of God's justice or heightens your understanding of how he governs the world. Perhaps it will be Haman's response to his fate or King Xerxes' authoritative command. How is this depiction of God's justice meaningful to you today? Again sit in silence. Briefly note what comes to you.

LIVE

Read the text one final time. This time, listen for what God, through the text, is inviting you to do or become. Perhaps he is offering a new perspective on how he cares when unjust things happen to you, just as King Xerxes was outraged to discover the threat to Esther's people. Or maybe you sense that God is calling you to take a stand for justice in a particular situation, like Esther did. Write down what you are being invited to do.

GOD GIVES, GOD TAKES

JOB 1:1,8-11,21

1   Job was a man who lived in Uz. He was honest inside and out, a man of his word, who was totally devoted to God and hated evil with a passion. . . .

8   GOD said to Satan, "Have you noticed my friend Job? There's no one quite like him — honest and true to his word, totally devoted to God and hating evil."

9-10   Satan retorted, "So do you think Job does all that out of the sheer goodness of his heart? Why, no one ever had it so good! You pamper him like a pet, make sure nothing bad ever happens to him or his family or his possessions, bless everything he does — he can't lose!

11   "But what do you think would happen if you reached down and took away everything that is his? He'd curse you right to your face, that's what." . . .

21   Naked I came from my mother's womb,
       naked I'll return to the womb of the earth.
GOD gives, GOD takes.
       God's name be ever blessed.

READ

Read the passage, noticing God's involvement in the story and circling *God* each time he is mentioned.

THINK

Notice the interaction between God and Satan. Does it bother you that God is bartering with Satan with Job's life? Is this the God you know?

Notice the words of Job, "Naked I came from my mother's womb, naked I'll return to the womb of the earth. GOD gives, GOD takes. God's name be ever blessed." If you lost everything — family, fortune, and eventually your health — would you be able to say such a thing? Why or why not? What would have to happen for you to utter similar words — and actually mean them?

PRAY

Spend time meditating on the gut-honest yet God-honoring words of Job. Let your emotions serve as a backdrop to your prayers. Invite the Holy Spirit to speak to you in the silence.

LIVE

Today as you use different objects (your car, computer, TV, and so on) and as you enter different places (your home, school, workplace, and so on), consider how you might respond if God instantly removed an item without explanation.

DAY 63

GOD ENCOUNTERS

On this seventh day, review and reflect on all you have read this week. Take the time to revel in the ways you've encountered God in the past six days.

GIVING COMFORT

JOB 5:17-21

17-19 "So, what a blessing when God steps in and corrects you!
Mind you, don't despise the discipline of Almighty God!
True, he wounds, but he also dresses the wound;
the same hand that hurts you, heals you.
From one disaster after another he delivers you;
no matter what the calamity, the evil can't touch you —

20-21 "In famine, he'll keep you from starving,
in war, from being gutted by the sword.
You'll be protected from vicious gossip
and live fearless through any catastrophe."

READ

Read the passage aloud slowly, keeping in mind that Eliphaz from Teman is speaking to his friend Job, who has just experienced the death of his children and the loss of all he had.

THINK

Read the passage again and put yourself in the place of Job, who listened to these words. How do they fall on your ear?

Read the passage again and put yourself in the place of Eliphaz. What feelings and attitudes fill you as you speak these words?

1. What makes a comforter really helpful? Is telling the truth enough?
2. What did Job need from Eliphaz?
3. What might be in the heart of a person who preaches at someone who is so far down?

PRAY

Ask the Comforter, the Holy Spirit, to give you what is needed to truly comfort despairing people. If you want guidance for your prayer, ask the Comforter to give you tools to help people in trouble go to him. Ask him to give you tools to draw them out to say to him whatever they need to express. Plead with the Comforter to make you his messenger, to prevent you from moralizing and giving advice.

LIVE

Rest your mind on someone who is in deep trouble. Pray only the word *peace* for them — no suggestions, no fixing, no rescuing. Just trusting.

THE MYSTERY OF A MIGHTY GOD

JOB 9:2-4,14-23

2-4 "The question is, 'How can mere mortals get right with God?'
If we wanted to bring our case before him,
  what chance would we have? Not one in a thousand!
God's wisdom is so deep, God's power so immense,
  who could take him on and come out in one piece?

. . . .

14-20 "So how could I ever argue with him,
  construct a defense that would influence God?
Even though I'm innocent I could never prove it;
  I can only throw myself on the Judge's mercy.
If I called on God and he himself answered me,
  then, and only then, would I believe that he'd heard me.
As it is, he knocks me about from pillar to post,
  beating me up, black-and-blue, for no good reason.
He won't even let me catch my breath,
  piles bitterness upon bitterness.
If it's a question of who's stronger, he wins, hands down!
  If it's a question of justice, who'll serve him the subpoena?
Even though innocent, anything I say incriminates me;
  blameless as I am, my defense just makes me sound worse.

21-23 "Believe me, I'm blameless.
  I don't understand what's going on.
  I hate my life!
Since either way it ends up the same, I can only conclude
  that God destroys the good right along with the bad.
When calamity hits and brings sudden death,
  he folds his arms, aloof from the despair of the innocent."

READ

Read the passage. In Job's response to his recent tragedy, notice the powerful feelings that underlie his words: fear, anger, grief, and hope.

THINK

What phrase in Job's lament stands out to you? Spend time meditating on it. Mentally chew it the way you would chew a piece of gum — repeat it to yourself, pausing each time to see where it leads your mind and emotions.

PRAY

Keeping your phrase in mind, picture God in the room with you. How do you relate to his presence? Maybe you sit in reverence at his power, wisdom, and justice, realizing you've forgotten or minimized those qualities lately. Maybe you feel anguish like Job. Maybe you open up to your desire for a rescuer, for Christ's mercy.

At the end of this time, recall what this experience held for you. Write down for future reference anything that seemed significant.

LIVE

During the next week, before you begin your times of prayerful reading, recall your picture of God in the room. Recollect who he was to you and retain this image of him in your mind during each prayer time. Let that aspect of God mingle with the God you relate to during the week.

TALKING TRANSPARENTLY WITH GOD

JOB 19:13-27

13-20 "God alienated my family from me;
　　everyone who knows me avoids me.
My relatives and friends have all left;
　　houseguests forget I ever existed.
The servant girls treat me like a bum off the street,
　　look at me like they've never seen me before.
I call my attendant and he ignores me,
　　ignores me even though I plead with him.
My wife can't stand to be around me anymore.
　　I'm repulsive to my family.
Even street urchins despise me;
　　when I come out, they taunt and jeer.
Everyone I've ever been close to abhors me;
　　my dearest loved ones reject me.
I'm nothing but a bag of bones;
　　my life hangs by a thread.

21-22 "Oh, friends, dear friends, take pity on me.
　　God has come down hard on me!
Do you have to be hard on me, too?
　　Don't you ever tire of abusing me?

23-27 "If only my words were written in a book—
　　better yet, chiseled in stone!
Still, I know that God lives—the One who gives me back my life—
　　and eventually he'll take his stand on earth.
And I'll see him—even though I get skinned alive!—
　　see God myself, with my very own eyes.
　　Oh, how I long for that day!"

READ

Read the passage slowly, noticing the raw way Job communicates about God.

THINK

As you read Job's honest description of his situation — what it's really like — what word or phrase gives voice to some of your own thoughts, feelings, and desires? Perhaps one of Job's statements brings to mind something in your life that's weighing on you or confuses you.

PRAY

Talk to God about the feelings and thoughts that surface. Be as open as Job as you share them with him. You might write them out to him or just talk to him like a friend — one you're in conflict with, but one who wants to work through that conflict with you.

LIVE

As you go through the rest of your day, pay close attention to thoughts and feelings (similar to or different from those in your prayer time) that arise in relation to events, conversations, and experiences. Tell God about them as they come up, so you're carrying on an extended dialogue with him all day long.

At the end of the day, take a few moments to remember what happened, in particular what it was like to talk to God throughout the day's circumstances.

EMPTY COMFORT

JOB 22:1-11

1-11   Once again Eliphaz the Temanite took up his theme:

"Are any of us strong enough to give God a hand,
    or smart enough to give him advice?
So what if you were righteous — would God Almighty even notice?
    Even if you gave a perfect performance, do you think he'd applaud?
Do you think it's because he cares about your purity
    that he's disciplining you, putting you on the spot?
Hardly! It's because you're a first-class moral failure,
    because there's no end to your sins.
When people came to you for help,
    you took the shirts off their backs, exploited their helplessness.
You wouldn't so much as give a drink to the thirsty,
    or food, not even a scrap, to the hungry.
And there you sat, strong and honored by everyone,
    surrounded by immense wealth!
You turned poor widows away from your door;
    heartless, you crushed orphans.
Now *you're* the one trapped in terror, paralyzed by fear.
    Suddenly the tables have turned!
How do you like living in the dark, sightless,
    up to your neck in flood waters?"

READ

As you read the passage, consider what might have been comforting for Job and what might have left him more hurt than before.

THINK

Have there been times when you wished people would refrain from giving you perfectly packaged and Christian clichés in an attempt to console you? "Pray harder." "You'll have to persevere." "Oh, God's just working on you." "Search for the sin in your life and get rid of it." "Obey God." Maybe you didn't know what you wanted in your suffering, but that definitely wasn't it. Sometimes true comfort comes through silence and a hug.

Eliphaz, Bildad, and Zophar don't offer comfort, but instead attempt to convince Job of his sins. This time it's the social sin of neglecting the poor, the hungry, and the naked — none of which Job is guilty of.

Who are the people you interact with on a regular basis who are suffering emotional, mental, spiritual, or physical pain?

What are some ways you can appropriately comfort them in their pain?

PRAY

Who are hurting people in your life? Pray for them, submitting to God's guidance for how to best serve and minister to them.

LIVE

Consider a friend or acquaintance who needs comfort. Prayerfully approach the suffering individual, asking God to use you as a healing agent of comfort and hope. Also ask God to keep you from being someone who merely offers trite words that fall short.

THIRSTING FOR JUSTICE

JOB 24:1-10

1-10 "But if Judgment Day isn't hidden from the Almighty,
   why are we kept in the dark?
There are people out there getting by with murder —
   stealing and lying and cheating.
They rip off the poor
   and exploit the unfortunate,
Push the helpless into the ditch,
   bully the weak so that they fear for their lives.
The poor, like stray dogs and cats,
   scavenge for food in back alleys.
They sort through the garbage of the rich,
   eke out survival on handouts.
Homeless, they shiver through cold nights on the street;
   they've no place to lay their heads.
Exposed to the weather, wet and frozen,
   they huddle in makeshift shelters.
Nursing mothers have their babies snatched from them;
   the infants of the poor are kidnapped and sold.
They go about patched and threadbare;
   even the hard workers go hungry."

READ

Read the passage aloud slowly.

THINK

Read the passage again, noting the words or phrases that touch you.

1. Why do these phrases touch you?
2. What is the heart of God like for these situations?

Though God stays hidden in order to let human beings be the autonomous beings he created them to be, he delights in bringing justice. Slowly read aloud Isaiah 51:5 twice:

> My deliverance arrives on the run,
> my salvation right on time.
> I'll bring justice to the peoples.
> Even faraway islands will look to me
> and take hope in my saving power.

Ponder your heart's response to this.

PRAY

Ask God to intervene in situations you think are unjust, small or big. If nothing comes to you, look at a newspaper or watch a newscast. Then come before God and ask for people to be treated with fairness and goodness and kindness.

LIVE

While you pray, hold in front of you a symbol of the world's troubles, perhaps a newspaper or newsmagazine, a globe or map. Hold it up for God's light to permeate.

GOD'S SILENCE

JOB 30:15-20

15   "Terrors assault me —
    my dignity in shreds,
    salvation up in smoke.

16-19   "And now my life drains out,
    as suffering seizes and grips me hard.
Night gnaws at my bones;
    the pain never lets up.
I am tied hand and foot, my neck in a noose.
    I twist and turn.
Thrown facedown in the muck,
    I'm a muddy mess, inside and out.

20   "I shout for help, God, and get nothing, no answer!
    I stand to face you in protest, and you give me a blank stare!"

READ

Read the passage, attempting to identify in your own heart and mind with the expressions of the speaker.

THINK

Read the passage slowly again — until the words sink into your consciousness, becoming familiar to you and resonating with your present state of mind. Don't try to analyze Job's response or determine its validity. Simply open yourself to his experience.

PRAY

What goes on inside you when you hear Job talk about God's silence? Perhaps you feel irritated, or maybe you relate because you've experienced times when God seemed inaccessible. Talk to God about your reaction to this passage. To help clarify your reaction, write about it. Give yourself permission to be completely open and honest.

LIVE

Right now, practice resting in the knowledge that God is with you in both words and silence — whether you're doing things right or doing nothing at all, whether you feel he's near or you feel nothing. If this is especially tough for you to do, pray the prayer "Lord, I believe a little; help me believe more."

DAY 70

GOD ENCOUNTERS

On this seventh day, review and reflect on all you have read this week. Take the time to revel in the ways you've encountered God in the past six days.

CREATION MOVIE

JOB 38:4-11,24-27

4-11 "Where were you when I created the earth?
  Tell me, since you know so much!
Who decided on its size? Certainly you'll know that!
  Who came up with the blueprints and measurements?
How was its foundation poured,
  and who set the cornerstone,
While the morning stars sang in chorus
  and all the angels shouted praise?
And who took charge of the ocean
  when it gushed forth like a baby from the womb?
That was me! I wrapped it in soft clouds,
  and tucked it in safely at night.
Then I made a playpen for it,
  a strong playpen so it couldn't run loose,
And said, 'Stay here, this is your place.
  Your wild tantrums are confined to this place.'

.   .   .   .

24-27 "Can you find your way to where lightning is launched,
  or to the place from which the wind blows?
Who do you suppose carves canyons
  for the downpours of rain, and charts
  the route of thunderstorms
That bring water to unvisited fields,
  deserts no one ever lays eyes on,
Drenching the useless wastelands
  so they're carpeted with wildflowers and grass?"

READ

Read the passage aloud slowly.

THINK

Read the passage again aloud, noticing that this is a poetic account of the Creation of the world in contrast to Genesis 1, which is a narrative account. Think about the following questions, remembering to consider the "why" behind each one.

1. What is your favorite moment in this Creation story?
2. Are you more fascinated by God as a blueprints-and-measurements kind of being or as a tamer of ocean tantrums?
3. How do you respond to God as a lightning launcher or canyon carver?
4. For what part of God's creation would you have wanted a front-row seat (for example, a daisy, a zebra, or a waterfall)?

PRAY

Tell God your responses to these questions. What do you think might be God's response to you?

LIVE

Go for a walk or hike or run in a beautiful place. Notice every single detail of nature that you can, and take pleasure in thinking about how God created it.

GOD CAN HANDLE YOU

JOB 42:7-13

7-8   After GOD had finished addressing Job, he turned to Eliphaz the Temanite and said, "I've had it with you and your two friends. I'm fed up! You haven't been honest either with me or about me — not the way my friend Job has. So here's what you must do. Take seven bulls and seven rams, and go to my friend Job. Sacrifice a burnt offering on your own behalf. My friend Job will pray for you, and I will accept his prayer. He will ask me not to treat you as you deserve for talking nonsense about me, and for not being honest with me, as he has."

9   They did it. Eliphaz the Temanite, Bildad the Shuhite, and Zophar the Naamathite did what GOD commanded. And GOD accepted Job's prayer.

10-11   After Job had interceded for his friends, GOD restored his fortune — and then doubled it! All his brothers and sisters and friends came to his house and celebrated. They told him how sorry they were, and consoled him for all the trouble GOD had brought him. Each of them brought generous housewarming gifts.

12-13   GOD blessed Job's later life even more than his earlier life. He ended up with fourteen thousand sheep, six thousand camels, one thousand teams of oxen, and one thousand donkeys. He also had seven sons and three daughters.

READ

As you read this passage aloud, picture the events taking place.

THINK

In the silence that follows your reading, continue to mentally engage with the scene. Focus on the part of the story that affects you most, the one that provokes an internal response. How do you relate to God as he appears in this passage? Share that with him.

PRAY

What do you feel or think when you see God affirming Job's honesty, even though that included sharing strong negative feelings like anger and grief? Is it surprising? Are you apprehensive? Is it a relief? Tell God about what you find inside.

LIVE

Peter Kreeft writes, "[Job] is in a true relationship to God, as the three friends are not: a relationship of heart and soul, life-or-death passion. . . . God is infinite love, and the opposite of love is not hate but indifference. Job's love for God is infected with hate, but the three friends' love for God is infected with indifference. Job stays married to God and throws dishes at him; the three friends have a polite nonmarriage, with separate bedrooms and separate vacations. The family that fights together stays together."[6]

Ponder the idea that God can handle you, all of you, even your negative emotions. Do you really believe that God desires this honest intimacy with you? What would it look like for you to go one level deeper in intimacy with God?

A TREE REPLANTED IN EDEN

PSALM 1

1 How well God must like you —
    you don't hang out at Sin Saloon,
    you don't slink along Dead-End Road,
    you don't go to Smart-Mouth College.

2-3 Instead you thrill to GOD's Word,
    you chew on Scripture day and night.
You're a tree replanted in Eden,
    bearing fresh fruit every month,
Never dropping a leaf,
    always in blossom.

4-5 You're not at all like the wicked,
    who are mere windblown dust —
Without defense in court,
    unfit company for innocent people.

6 GOD charts the road you take.
The road *they* take is Skid Row.

READ

Go outside to your yard or a park. Once you find a healthy-looking tree, sit down and focus on it for a few moments. Look at the trunk and consider its strength. Focus on the leaves and admire their intricacies. Examine the roots that are above ground and consider the roots that are below ground.

After you do this, read the passage.

THINK

Contemplate the correlation between being in God's Word and the strength of a tree. Notice the difference between the wicked and the righteous in this psalm. What are the equivalents of "Sin Saloon," "Dead-End Road" and "Smart-Mouth College" in your life that should be avoided? Be specific. What would your life look like if it were "bearing fresh fruit every month"?

PRAY

With your eyes open and looking at the tree, ask God to guide you in such a way that you will always be in blossom and bearing fruit. Pray that your roots will go down deep and find their place in the healthy soil of God's Word.

LIVE

Thank God for the gift of his Word. Let the metaphor of a healthy tree guide your decisions today. Plan a time later to spend some additional minutes in *The Message,* living out the words of this psalm.

GOD, BRILLIANT LORD

PSALM 8

1   GOD, brilliant Lord,
    yours is a household name.

2   Nursing infants gurgle choruses about you;
    toddlers shout the songs
That drown out enemy talk,
    and silence atheist babble.

3-4   I look up at your macro-skies, dark and enormous,
    your handmade sky-jewelry,
Moon and stars mounted in their settings.
    Then I look at my micro-self and wonder,
Why do you bother with us?
    Why take a second look our way?

5-8   Yet we've so narrowly missed being gods,
    bright with Eden's dawn light.
You put us in charge of your handcrafted world,
    repeated to us your Genesis-charge,
Made us lords of sheep and cattle,
    even animals out in the wild,
Birds flying and fish swimming,
    whales singing in the ocean deeps.

9   GOD, brilliant Lord,
    your name echoes around the world.

READ

Read the passage aloud slowly.

THINK

Read the passage aloud again, letting your mouth play with the phrases, connections, and comparisons that appeal to you. Perhaps one of these does:

- "gurgle choruses" and "atheist babble"
- "macro-skies" and "micro-self"
- "handcrafted world" and "Genesis-charge"
- "household name" and "brilliant Lord"

One by one, hold in your mind the words that stood out to you. Imagine their physical representation, how they relate to each other. For example, hear the sounds of babies drowning out atheists, see God's name (and presence and power) as ordinary as something in your house yet so brilliantly magnificent as to echo around the world. What do these comparisons have to do with your life?

PRAY

Consider the exercise you just did. What does it make you want to say to God? Words of admiration? Requests to be a good caretaker of the earth? Offer it to him.

LIVE

In the evening or early morning when the sky is dark, take this book and a flashlight outside and read this psalm to God. Even if you have to whisper to avoid being heard, put your heart into it. Revel in the moment and enjoy God.

✚ TELL GOD YOUR DESIRE

PSALM 13

1-2   Long enough, GOD —
          you've ignored me long enough.
      I've looked at the back of your head
          long enough. Long enough
      I've carried this ton of trouble,
          lived with a stomach full of pain.
      Long enough my arrogant enemies
          have looked down their noses at me.

3-4   Take a good look at me, GOD, my God;
          I want to look life in the eye,
      So no enemy can get the best of me
          or laugh when I fall on my face.

5-6   I've thrown myself headlong into your arms —
          I'm celebrating your rescue.
      I'm singing at the top of my lungs,
          I'm so full of answered prayers.

READ

Read the passage with passion, experiencing for yourself the shift in emotion.

THINK

As you hear the psalmist's desire for God's attention, be aware of how you feel similarly. Search your awareness of what you want or need from God until you have a name for that desire. Desiring something practical, like a good grade on an exam, is fine. But pause to see what deeper desire might be behind it — perhaps a single word like *significance* or a phrase like "to know that you love me no matter what."

Now think about what name for God is most meaningful to you in light of the desire you just pinpointed. For example, if you desire a God who will radically alter a difficult circumstance, perhaps you will think of him as Powerful One. If you desire a God who will soothe your hurts and hold you close, perhaps you will think of him as Daddy.

PRAY

Consider that God is inviting you to express what you want. Tell him honestly and plainly. Combine your deeper desire with the name you chose for God. End up with a prayer that is six to nine syllables long, such as "Powerful One, give me justice." Use the next several minutes to pray this prayer to God, repeating it with each breath.

LIVE

Throughout the day, pray your phrase as often as possible — as you drive, as you wait in line, as you exercise. At times your prayer may be in the foreground of your thoughts; at others, in the background. At the end of the day, think about how God responded to your desire.

STAYING WITH GOD

PSALM 27:4-6

4   I'm asking GOD for one thing,
        only one thing:
To live with him in his house
        my whole life long.
I'll contemplate his beauty;
        I'll study at his feet.

5   That's the only quiet, secure place
        in a noisy world,
The perfect getaway,
        far from the buzz of traffic.

6   God holds me head and shoulders
        above all who try to pull me down.
I'm headed for his place to offer anthems
        that will raise the roof!
Already I'm singing God-songs;
        I'm making music to GOD.

READ

Read the passage rhythmically. Sing it, if you wish. See if you can find a pattern to the words. Pay attention to the syllables of the words in each line.

THINK

The psalms are some of the most honest words to God ever put on paper. David's expression, though raw, shows his confidence that God will protect him when his enemies are trying to harm or kill him. What would have to happen for you to speak to God in the same honest way?

David's desire is that God will be his guiding light and life source. He wrote, "With him on my side I'm fearless, afraid of no one and nothing" (verse 1). What would have to happen for you to say this same line . . . and mean it?

David sang, "I'm sure now I'll see God's goodness in the exuberant earth. Stay with GOD! Take heart. Don't quit. I'll say it again: Stay with GOD" (verses 13-14). When are you tempted to quit on God? What keeps you from running from him?

PRAY/LIVE

Find an atlas or compass. Look at it and ponder the words of this psalm: "Point me down your highway, GOD; direct me along a well-lighted street" (verse 11).

Ask God to guide you down his highway and help you live the life he wants you to live.

DAY 77

GOD ENCOUNTERS

On this seventh day, review and reflect on all you have read this week. Take the time to revel in the ways you've encountered God in the past six days.

RESCUED FROM THE PIT

PSALM 28:1-2,6-9

1   Don't turn a deaf ear
         when I call you, GOD.
     If all I get from you is
         deafening silence,
     I'd be better off
         in the Black Hole.

2   I'm letting you know what I need,
         calling out for help
     And lifting my arms
         toward your inner sanctum.

     .   .   .   .

6-7 Blessed be GOD —
         he heard me praying.
     He proved he's on my side;
         I've thrown my lot in with him.

     Now I'm jumping for joy,
         and shouting and singing my thanks to him.

8-9 GOD is all strength for his people,
         ample refuge for his chosen leader;
     Save your people
         and bless your heritage.
     Care for them;
         carry them like a good shepherd.

READ

Read the passage aloud slowly.

THINK

Read the passage again, whispering verses 1-2 as if in fear and then reading verses 6-9 in a louder, confident voice.

Put yourself in the "Black Hole," a cold, tar-black pit, silent except for the dripping of water. You call out to God and lift your arms to him, but at first there is no answer. Stay in this place for a few minutes. Imagine what you would do and think. What would you think about God? What would you say to him?

Feel in your body the moment when God shows up, when he takes your arms and pulls you out of the hole into the warm, bright light. You shiver and blink. Stay in this moment for a few minutes.

PRAY

Speak to God about what is most powerful for you in these verses. You might ask God to help you call out to him, to count on him, whenever you're close to the Black Hole of life. If you are now in a black hole, ask God to help you raise your hands in prayer and bless him. If you are not now in a black hole, offer a prayer that someone "jumping for joy" might pray.

LIVE

Try it. Jump for joy and shout and sing.

CELEBRATING GOD

PSALM 34:1-9

1   I bless GOD every chance I get;
my lungs expand with his praise.

2   I live and breathe GOD;
if things aren't going well, hear this and be happy:

3   Join me in spreading the news;
together let's get the word out.

4   GOD met me more than halfway,
he freed me from my anxious fears.

5   Look at him; give him your warmest smile.
Never hide your feelings from him.

6   When I was desperate, I called out,
and GOD got me out of a tight spot.

7   GOD's angel sets up a circle
of protection around us while we pray.

8   Open your mouth and taste, open your eyes and see —
how good GOD is.
Blessed are you who run to him.

9   Worship GOD if you want the best;
worship opens doors to all his goodness.

READ

Read the passage aloud as many times as it takes for the words and thoughts to become familiar to you.

THINK/PRAY

Imagine the face and posture of the psalmist expressing this worship. Maybe you'd like to join him, or maybe you're annoyed. What posture does your body take on when you hear the speaker's enthusiasm? When you imagine the God he's speaking about? Move your body into this posture — be it bowing on the floor, clenching your fists, hugging your knees, folding your arms across your chest, dancing, or something else.

Now set aside your physical response and return to the text. Mull the words until you can determine your mental reaction to them. Can you put clear words to your thoughts? Tell God, and write them down.

Now return to the text one last time. Read it silently, listening for God's response to your posture and your words.

LIVE

In his book *Prayer,* Richard Foster speaks of stepping-stones along the path of learning to adore God. Ultimately, adoring God involves gratitude, magnifying him, and "foot-stomping celebration," but these must be grown into, and our hearts must be taught. A good first step is simply to make a habit of watching small things in nature: ducks, butterflies, fluttering leaves. This does not mean analyzing but rather discovering the pleasure in simply observing and participating in nature.[7]

Find a small part of God's creation and spend a few minutes enjoying and engaging with it.

A SAFE PLACE TO HIDE

PSALM 46:3-11

3   Jacob-wrestling God fights for us,
     God-of-Angel-Armies protects us.

4-6 River fountains splash joy, cooling God's city,
     this sacred haunt of the Most High.
  God lives here, the streets are safe,
     God at your service from crack of dawn.
  Godless nations rant and rave, kings and kingdoms threaten,
     but Earth does anything he says.

7   Jacob-wrestling God fights for us,
     God-of-Angel-Armies protects us.

8-10 Attention, all! See the marvels of God!
     He plants flowers and trees all over the earth,
  Bans war from pole to pole,
     breaks all the weapons across his knee.
  "Step out of the traffic! Take a long,
     loving look at me, your High God,
     above politics, above everything."

11   Jacob-wrestling God fights for us,
     God-of-Angel-Armies protects us.

READ

Read the passage aloud.

THINK

When have you felt the safest in your lifetime? Why? Circle or underline every word in this passage that deals with the concept of safety and security. Consider your emotions that rise up in response to the words of this passage.

Why do you think the psalmist repeats this phrase three times: "Jacob-wrestling God fights for us, GOD-of-Angel-Armies protects us"?

What would your life look like if you lived this out: "Step out of the traffic! Take a long, loving look at me, your High God, above politics, above everything"?

PRAY

Take several minutes to free your mind of every anxious thought, concern, or stress that you have. Ask God to release you from these thoughts that hold you captive and paralyze you.

After this time, ask God to fill you with the promises from this psalm concerning the safety and security found only in him.

LIVE

In the midst of your busy schedule today, live in the safety of God.

SOAK OUT MY SINS

PSALM 51:1-12

1-3   Generous in love — God, give grace!
      Huge in mercy — wipe out my bad record.
Scrub away my guilt,
      soak out my sins in your laundry.
I know how bad I've been;
      my sins are staring me down.

4-6   You're the One I've violated, and you've seen
      it all, seen the full extent of my evil.
You have all the facts before you;
      whatever you decide about me is fair.
I've been out of step with you for a long time,
      in the wrong since before I was born.
What you're after is truth from the inside out.
      Enter me, then; conceive a new, true life.

7-12   Soak me in your laundry and I'll come out clean,
      scrub me and I'll have a snow-white life.
Tune me in to foot-tapping songs,
      set these once-broken bones to dancing.
Don't look too close for blemishes,
      give me a clean bill of health.
God, make a fresh start in me,
      shape a Genesis week from the chaos of my life.
Don't throw me out with the trash,
      or fail to breathe holiness in me.
Bring me back from gray exile,
      put a fresh wind in my sails!

READ

Read the passage aloud slowly.

THINK

Read the passage again, noting these items:

- the wrongs the psalmist confesses
- what the psalmist asks for from God

1. This psalm is an ideal psalm of confession because the psalmist not only confesses sins but also focuses on the way forward, noting the next positive steps to take. He asks for good things from God and does not get stuck in the past. Find where he does that.
2. The psalmist also understands that his sin is not just something he did, but a sin against God personally. Find the words *you* and *your.*
3. The biggest issue is not that he sinned but that he loves God. Why do you think we often make our sin the biggest issue instead?

PRAY

Pray the passage aloud, paraphrasing and embellishing the lines that fit your life today.

LIVE

Sit with your hands open in front of you with palms turned upward as a way of letting your confession bring you healing, cleansing, and renewal.

GOD, PAY THEM BACK!

PSALM 53:1-6

1-2   Bilious and bloated, they gas,
      "God is gone."

. . . .

God sticks his head out of heaven.
    He looks around.
He's looking for someone not stupid —
    one man, even, God-expectant,
    just one God-ready woman.

3   He comes up empty. A string
      of zeros. Useless, unshepherded
Sheep, taking turns pretending
    to be Shepherd.
The ninety and nine
    follow the one.

4   Don't they know anything,
      all these impostors?
Don't they know
    they can't get away with this,
Treating people like a fast-food meal
    over which they're too busy to pray?

5   Night is coming for them, and nightmare —
    a nightmare they'll never wake up from.
God will make hash of these squatters,
    send them packing for good.

6   Is there anyone around to save Israel?
      God turns life around.
Turned-around Jacob skips rope,
    turned-around Israel sings laughter.

PRAY

Spend several minutes in silence, examining your heart. What's in it today? Note what you find, but don't get too engrossed or sidetracked by any single thought or feeling. Simply acknowledge each item, as though you're gathering all your concerns and feelings into a basket.

READ

When you finish examining your heart, temporarily set aside the basket. Read the passage slowly and thoroughly, taking in the psalmist's experience. His energy is rising in response to a tough situation, and he is letting it drive him toward God.

THINK

What one aspect of the passage draws your attention? Maybe it is the psalmist's desire for justice, rather than a passive tolerance of wrongs. Or maybe it is his deep belief in God's concern for his welfare. Spend time pondering this.

Now return to your basket. Pick up each item and look at it through the filter of this passage. Again, don't get too absorbed in any one concern, but stay attuned to the psalm's message to you. How does it meet up with the items in your basket?

LIVE

Read the passage slowly again. To what action — whether emotional, mental, or physical — might God be calling you through these verses?

SOLID ROCK UNDER MY FEET

PSALM 62:1-2

1-2 God, the one and only —
  I'll wait as long as he says.
Everything I need comes from him,
  so why not?
He's solid rock under my feet,
  breathing room for my soul,
An impregnable castle:
  I'm set for life.

READ

Take this book outside and read the passage.

THINK

In our Western mind-set, we describe God with intangible ideas, such as God is love, God is peace, or God is compassionate. But in the Eastern mind-set, thoughts are described in vivid imagery and word pictures. The Psalms in particular describe God with tangible ideas: God is Father, God is the wind, God is an eagle. In this psalm David describes God as a rock.

Outdoors, find a few rocks and look at them. Take a few moments to reflect on the specific characteristics of rocks and how they describe God's character. Write down your reflections.

PRAY

Thank God that he is like a rock, referring to your list to offer specific details. Thank him for what each of these aspects of his character means to you.

LIVE

Find a small stone and carry it with you today in your pocket or purse. Every time your hand closes on it, reflect on the fact that God is your rock.

DAY 84

GOD ENCOUNTERS

On this seventh day, review and reflect on all you have read this week. Take the time to revel in the ways you've encountered God in the past six days.

CAN'T GET ENOUGH

PSALM 63:1-8

1 God — you're my God!
      I can't get enough of you!
   I've worked up such hunger and thirst for God,
      traveling across dry and weary deserts.

2-4 So here I am in the place of worship, eyes open,
      drinking in your strength and glory.
   In your generous love I am really living at last!
      My lips brim praises like fountains.
   I bless you every time I take a breath;
      My arms wave like banners of praise to you.

5-8 I eat my fill of prime rib and gravy;
      I smack my lips. It's time to shout praises!
   If I'm sleepless at midnight,
      I spend the hours in grateful reflection.
   Because you've always stood up for me,
      I'm free to run and play.
   I hold on to you for dear life,
      and you hold me steady as a post.

READ

Read the passage silently and slowly.

PRAY

Tell God how you honestly respond to this psalm.

Perhaps you don't have this drooling, lip-smacking desire for God. Maybe the idea even embarrasses you. Or maybe you'd like to be this way, but it sounds far too spiritual. Reveal your honest feelings to God.

Perhaps you do have these intense feelings for God. If so, which words in the psalm best describe that?

THINK

Read the passage again.

If one word or phrase describes your present state, say it aloud.

If one word or phrase describes how you would like to be, say it aloud.

LIVE

Consider this quotation from *The Cloud of Unknowing*: "Nourish in your heart a lively longing for God."[8] Bask in that idea, and try to see yourself doing it.

THE POSTURE OF GRATITUDE

PSALM 75:1-4

1   We thank you, God, we thank you —
        your Name is our favorite word;
        your mighty works are all we talk about.

2-4   You say, "I'm calling this meeting to order,
        I'm ready to set things right.
     When the earth goes topsy-turvy
        And nobody knows which end is up,
     I nail it all down,
        I put everything in place again.
     I say to the smart alecks, 'That's enough,'
        to the bullies, 'Not so fast.' "

LIVE

Take a clean sheet of paper and fill the page with all the things you are thankful for, big and small. Include items like names of people, elements of creation, God-orchestrated events and timing, and small things you often overlook. When you're finished, thank God for those blessings he is giving you today as well as those blessings he gave you months or even years ago.

READ/THINK

Now read the expanded passage. Notice the psalmist's reasons for thanking God. Make a list of these reasons on the back of your sheet of paper. This psalm highlights the fact that God is in complete and total control of the entire earth. Stop and ponder: Does that make you thankful or anxious or . . . ? Why?

PRAY

Based on the general outline of the expanded passage, take the list you made and prayerfully write your own psalm (poem) to God. Be creative and personal. (Nobody has to read what you write.) When you are finished, use your psalm to worship God. Read it aloud at least once.

I'LL WORSHIP YOU UNDIVIDED

PSALM 86:14-17

14-17   God, these bullies have reared their heads!
        A gang of thugs is after me —
        and they don't care a thing about you.
    But you, O God, are both tender and kind,
        not easily angered, immense in love,
        and you never, never quit.
    So look me in the eye and show kindness,
        give your servant the strength to go on,
        save your dear, dear child!
    Make a show of how much you love me
        so the bullies who hate me will stand there slack-jawed,
    As you, GOD, gently and powerfully
        put me back on my feet.

READ

Stand up and read aloud the psalmist's proclamation of God's trust-worthiness. As you read the phrase "God, these bullies have reared their heads," kneel. Remain on your knees until you finish the passage, as the psalmist expresses the depth of his trust in God amid danger. Repeat slowly and attentively three times.

THINK

What do you notice about yourself as you do this exercise? In what ways do you experience the passage differently than you normally would? Perhaps your body's position helps your mind focus. Or perhaps you protest the position because it doesn't fit your mood or energy level. Meditate on the reasons for your reaction.

PRAY

Now read the passage again, this time silently, keeping in mind what you just learned about yourself. Let the Holy Spirit show you a word or phrase that touches what has arisen in you. Spend a few minutes repeating the word or phrase prayerfully. How is God speaking to you?

LIVE

Consider what it was like for you to let your body take the lead in prayer. In what ways did your body help or hinder you in engaging with God?

WHEN THE ROCKS CRY OUT

PSALM 96:7-10

7   Bravo, GOD, Bravo!
    Everyone join in the great shout: Encore!
    In awe before the beauty, in awe before the might.

8-9 Bring gifts and celebrate,
    Bow before the beauty of GOD,
    Then to your knees — everyone worship!

10 Get out the message — GOD Rules!
    He put the world on a firm foundation;
    He treats everyone fair and square.

READ

Get in a comfortable position on your knees. As you are in this posture of submission, ask God to help your body be a symbolic expression of your heart during the next few moments. Admit to God that you want to be submissive to him — even if doing so is difficult — as you engage with his Word.

Keeping this position, read the passage.

THINK

The psalmist invites other people to join him in the praise of God. "Get out the message — GOD Rules!" In what specific ways can we get the message out in our praise of God?

Consider this picture of worship: "Bring gifts and celebrate, bow before the beauty of GOD, then to your knees — everyone worship!" Is it hard to imagine that God likes it when his people celebrate? Why or why not?

What is one attribute of God that you could celebrate right now? Why do you think that attribute comes to mind?

PRAY

While still on your knees, invite the Holy Spirit to come in and guide your prayers. Praise him for whatever comes to mind. If you feel comfortable, speak your praise aloud.

LIVE

Find a worship album or Christian radio station and spend the next several minutes listening to worship music. If you know the words to a song, join in and sing along, or invite friends to join you. If you know how to play an instrument, spend a few minutes playing it while singing praises to God.

BLESSING GOD

PSALM 103:1-14

1-2   O my soul, bless GOD.
       From head to toe, I'll bless his holy name!
    O my soul, bless GOD,
       don't forget a single blessing!

3-5   He forgives your sins — every one.
    He heals your diseases — every one.
    He redeems you from hell — saves your life!
    He crowns you with love and mercy — a paradise crown.
    He wraps you in goodness — beauty eternal.
    He renews your youth — you're always young in his presence.

6-14   GOD makes everything come out right;
       he puts victims back on their feet.
    He showed Moses how he went about his work,
       opened up his plans to all Israel.
    GOD is sheer mercy and grace;
       not easily angered, he's rich in love.
    He doesn't endlessly nag and scold,
       nor hold grudges forever.
    He doesn't treat us as our sins deserve,
       nor pay us back in full for our wrongs.
    As high as heaven is over the earth,
       so strong is his love to those who fear him.
    And as far as sunrise is from sunset,
       he has separated us from our sins.
    As parents feel for their children,
       GOD feels for those who fear him.
    He knows us inside and out,
       keeps in mind that we're made of mud.

READ

Read the passage quietly to yourself.

THINK

The idea of blessing God may sound odd to us. We might think, *Who am I to bless God? Isn't God the only one to bless people?* But the literal meaning of the Hebrew word *bless* is "to kneel."[9] So when we bless God, our souls kneel to him, usually in worship or gratitude.

Read the passage again with your heart kneeling before God. If possible, physically kneel where you are and read aloud. As you do, notice the phrases that reflect what you are most eager to praise God for — perhaps that he isn't easily angered or doesn't endlessly nag.

PRAY

Stay kneeling and pray aloud those phrases about God that touched you most. As you pray, add to them other ideas about God that come to mind. Raise your hands if you wish.

LIVE

Quietly kneel before God in whatever posture and mood this psalm has brought you:

- resting peacefully on your heels with your hands in your lap
- rising onto your knees with your hands raised
- kneeling before a chair or bed and bringing your whole self forward onto it

Be with God this way for a few minutes.

SPIRITUAL HISTORY LESSONS

PSALM 106:1-4,6-12

1-3   Hallelujah!
Thank GOD! And why?
   Because he's good, because his love lasts.
But who on earth can do it —
   declaim GOD's mighty acts, broadcast all his praises?
You're one happy man when you do what's right,
   one happy woman when you form the habit of justice.

4   Remember me, GOD, when you enjoy your people;
   include me when you save them;

   .   .   .   .

6-12   We've sinned a lot, both we and our parents;
   We've fallen short, hurt a lot of people.
After our parents left Egypt,
   they took your wonders for granted,
   forgot your great and wonderful love.
They were barely beyond the Red Sea
   when they defied the High God
   — the very place he saved them!
   — the place he revealed his amazing power!
He rebuked the Red Sea so that it dried up on the spot
   — he paraded them right through!
   — no one so much as got wet feet!
He saved them from a life of oppression,
   pried them loose from the grip of the enemy.
Then the waters flowed back on their oppressors;
   there wasn't a single survivor.
Then they believed his words were true
   and broke out in songs of praise.

READ

As you read this passage, listen for a word or phrase that says in some small way, "I am for you today."

THINK/PRAY

Let this word or phrase sink deeply into you by repeating it slowly to yourself several times. Bring your worries, thoughts, and memories to it, and see how it casts light on them. Talk to God about what's going through your mind and heart. Do you feel like he is "for you"?

LIVE

Ebenezer literally means "stone of help" in Hebrew. It can be used to refer to anything that reminds us of something spiritually significant. Today, create an Ebenezer for yourself.

First, think about how God spoke to you or what he did for you through today's passage. Second, write one sentence or a few words on a small piece of paper to describe that. Third, pick a symbol for it: Find a pebble from your yard, buy an inexpensive cross, or cut out a picture from a magazine. Fourth, fold up your note and attach it to the object. Fifth, put your Ebenezer somewhere you will see it often, as a visible reminder of what God said and did.

In the future, periodically reflect on your life (maybe two to four times a year) and create more Ebenezers, keeping them in a box, bowl, or bucket. Whenever you see them, recall who God has been to you.

DAY 91

GOD ENCOUNTERS

On this seventh day, review and reflect on all you have read this week. Take the time to revel in the ways you've encountered God in the past six days.

THE GIFT OF SCRIPTURE

PSALM 119:89-101,105

89-96
What you say goes, GOD,
 and *stays*, as permanent as the heavens.
Your truth never goes out of fashion;
 it's as up-to-date as the earth when the sun comes up.
Your Word and truth are dependable as ever;
 that's what you ordered — you set the earth going.
If your revelation hadn't delighted me so,
 I would have given up when the hard times came.
But I'll never forget the advice you gave me;
 you saved my life with those wise words.
Save me! I'm all yours.
 I look high and low for your words of wisdom.
The wicked lie in ambush to destroy me,
 but I'm only concerned with your plans for me.
I see the limits to everything human,
 but the horizons can't contain your commands!

97-101
Oh, how I love all you've revealed;
 I reverently ponder it all the day long.
Your commands give me an edge on my enemies;
 they never become obsolete.
I've even become smarter than my teachers
 since I've pondered and absorbed your counsel.
I've become wiser than the wise old sages
 simply by doing what you tell me.
I watch my step, avoiding the ditches and ruts of evil
 so I can spend all my time keeping your Word.

. . . .

105
By your words I can see where I'm going;
 they throw a beam of light on my dark path.

READ

Read the passage very slowly. Then read it again, this time even slower.

THINK

You've probably heard people say, "The Lord spoke to me," or "God told me x-y-z," and then been left feeling disbelief, confusion, frustration, or guilt. God does speak to us but not in a booming voice that sounds like actor James Earl Jones. God speaks to us through different means: creation, other people's words of guidance, promptings of the Holy Spirit, and "a gentle and quiet whisper" (1 Kings 19:12). But he also speaks to us through his Message.

Explore your attitudes or preconceived ideas about God's Message. Be brutally honest with yourself and God. Think of ways you could value God's Message more and find yourself more attentive to what it has to say.

Spend several minutes considering how God might be speaking to you through this passage concerning his Message.

PRAY

Pray through this passage of Scripture. Simply make the passage your very own, turning the words back to God (rephrased in your own words, if you wish) as a way to converse with him. Be assured that he is listening to you.

LIVE

Invite God to reveal general and specific elements of Scripture to guide your words, thoughts, and actions today.

CONFIDENCE IN GOD

PSALM 121

1-2   I look up to the mountains;
          does my strength come from mountains?
      No, my strength comes from GOD,
          who made heaven, and earth, and mountains.

3-4   _____, he won't let you stumble,
          your Guardian God won't fall asleep.
      Not on your life! Israel's
          Guardian will never doze or sleep.

5-6   GOD's your Guardian, _____,
          right at your side to protect you —
      Shielding you from sunstroke, _____,
          sheltering you from moonstroke.

7-8   GOD guards you, _____, from every evil,
          he guards your very life.
      He guards you when you leave and when you return, _____,
          he guards you now, he guards you always.

READ

Read the passage aloud slowly.

THINK

This psalm ranks as one of the greatest psalms of trust and confidence. As you read it aloud a second time, do something different from verse 3 on. Address yourself by name in the places where a blank appears.

As you read the passage a third time, notice the word or phrase that stands out most to you. Use that to create a mind-picture of yourself in a situation where you need to remember to trust. For example, picture yourself desperate for protection, and reread a phrase from verse 7 or 8. Or picture yourself in a situation where you need to know that God doesn't overlook or forget you, and reread a phrase from verse 3 or 4.

PRAY

Speak with God about how much you do or don't trust him. Tell him about your confidence level and ask him to give you grace to grow in it.

LIVE

Have a little fun here. Keep these ideas about confidence in mind and stand as confidently as you can. You might even want to gesture — put your hands on your hips or hold out your fists in front of you. Stay in this pose for several seconds, going over your selected phrase.

Now do this in front of a mirror. Imagine God standing next to you, protecting you in some way. For example, he could be shielding you from the side or standing behind you with arms wrapped around you.

✚ MY SOUL IS A BABY CONTENT

PSALM 131

1 GOD, I'm not trying to rule the roost,
    I don't want to be king of the mountain.
I haven't meddled where I have no business
    or fantasized grandiose plans.

2 I've kept my feet on the ground,
    I've cultivated a quiet heart.
Like a baby content in its mother's arms,
    my soul is a baby content.

3 Wait, Israel, for GOD. Wait with hope.
    Hope now; hope always!

READ

After you read this psalm, wait patiently for your response to the material.

THINK/PRAY

How does the message of the psalm resonate with you? Maybe the reality of your life is different from the speaker's, but he gives voice to your desire. Or maybe his message challenges your attitude or perspective.

Read it a second time, then share your response with God through prayer. At first it will feel natural to pray in your own words, responding to what you're reading, but as you keep going, stretch beyond this and pray using the words of the passage. Although doing so might feel awkward at first, give yourself time to get used to it. You'll likely hear yourself praying statements you don't genuinely mean and then feel your heart protesting. But stay honest with God by acknowledging this to him. Don't be hard on yourself. Just recall that God accepts you and loves you, then continue.

When you read this psalm one more time, let your meditation go a bit deeper. Wait for deeper memories and thoughts. These mirror more about you and your life. Bring these insights into your prayer.

LIVE

Spend time in silence. Imagine your soul as "a baby content in its mother's arms." Even if you find your thoughts continuously running, practice silence. Achieving silence doesn't mean you have to focus on stopping your thoughts. Just let them pass through, then bring your mind back to the image of resting. Just enjoy being in the presence of God.

94

CHEWING ON THE CUD

PSALM 139:1-12

1-6   GOD, investigate my life;
      get all the facts firsthand.
I'm an open book to you;
      even from a distance, you know what I'm thinking.
You know when I leave and when I get back;
      I'm never out of your sight.
You know everything I'm going to say
      before I start the first sentence.
I look behind me and you're there,
      then up ahead and you're there, too —
      your reassuring presence, coming and going.
This is too much, too wonderful —
      I can't take it all in!

7-12   Is there anyplace I can go to avoid your Spirit?
      to be out of your sight?
If I climb to the sky, you're there!
      If I go underground, you're there!
If I flew on morning's wings
      to the far western horizon,
You'd find me in a minute —
      you're already there waiting!
Then I said to myself, "Oh, he even sees me in the dark!
      At night I'm immersed in the light!"
It's a fact: darkness isn't dark to you;
      night and day, darkness and light, they're all the same to you.

THINK

To ruminate literally means "to chew the cud." A cow will chew on one particular wad of cud for hours at a time, over and over again, swallowing it and bringing it back up from its stomach. Consider the metaphor of the cud as you think about the phrases "investigate my life," "I'm an open book," and "you're there."

READ

Read the passage three times slowly, ruminating on it. Don't skim or speed-read; chew on each word. Hold the words in your mind until you feel you've considered every aspect of them.

PRAY

Spend time in silence, meditating on these phrases. Let them bounce around in your brain. Look at them from every direction. As you do that, explore the emotions and thoughts you are having. Specifically ask God, "Why am I feeling this way, God?" and put your heart in a posture of listening. Expect to hear from God.

LIVE

Spend a few more minutes listening to God and ask him, "What do you want me to do with what you have given to me?"

NO ONE IS LEFT OUT

PSALM 145:7-9,15-21

7   The fame of your goodness spreads across the country;
      your righteousness is on everyone's lips.

8   GOD is all mercy and grace —
      not quick to anger, is rich in love.

9   GOD is good to one and all;
      everything he does is suffused with grace.

      . . . .

15   All eyes are on you, expectant;
      you give them their meals on time.

16   Generous to a fault,
      you lavish your favor on all creatures.

17   Everything GOD does is right —
      the trademark on all his works is love.

18   GOD's there, listening for all who pray,
      for all who pray and mean it.

19   He does what's best for those who fear him —
      hears them call out, and saves them.

20   GOD sticks by all who love him,
      but it's all over for those who don't.

21   My mouth is filled with GOD's praise.
      Let everything living bless him,
      bless his holy name from now to eternity!

READ

Read the passage aloud slowly.

THINK

This psalm celebrates God's goodness to all and his goodness through everything. Notice how often the words *all* and *every* appear. While many psalms emphasize God as "my God," this one shows God's mercy to all.

Read it again, either emphasizing or pausing after the words *all* and *every*.

1. Who might *all* include that you may not have thought about before? Maybe people you know, people far away, or objects foreign to you. As you do this, what pictures come to mind?
2. Notice the many phrases about God's goodness. Which ones resonate most with you?

PRAY

Thank God for his deep goodness toward all. Use phrases from the psalm that best express this theme from your point of view.

LIVE

Go for a walk or hike, taking this book with you. As you walk, stop at certain points and read a verse or two aloud. Listen to the echo of your voice. Enjoy God, who is enjoying hearing you pour forth these words.

PRAISE HIM, SUN AND MOON

PSALM 148:2-12

2-5   Praise him, all you his angels,
    praise him, all you his warriors,
Praise him, sun and moon,
    praise him, you morning stars;
Praise him, high heaven,
    praise him, heavenly rain clouds;
Praise, oh let them praise the name of GOD —
    he spoke the word, and there they were!

6   He set them in place
    from all time to eternity;
He gave his orders,
    and that's it!

7-12   Praise GOD from earth,
    you sea dragons, you fathomless ocean deeps;
Fire and hail, snow and ice,
    hurricanes obeying his orders;
Mountains and all hills,
    apple orchards and cedar forests;
Wild beasts and herds of cattle,
    snakes, and birds in flight;
Earth's kings and all races,
    leaders and important people,
Robust men and women in their prime,
    and yes, graybeards and little children.

READ

Read the passage a few times aloud, zeroing in on each image. Allow the words to wash over you in their vividness: See specific birds or wild beasts, sense the chill of the ice, hear the roaring of the ocean. Watch every action of the characters. Compare the way each created thing uniquely praises its Maker.

THINK

In the silence that follows the reading, meditate on what you've seen and heard. With all these pieces of creation in the background, praising God, how do you see him? What is he like? Spend time thinking about him.

PRAY

Pick the character attribute of God that seems the most powerful after your meditation. Envision God in this role, then see yourself entering his presence. How do you respond to him? How does he treat you? Rest in God's presence or talk to him or adore him — whatever fits the scene.

LIVE

As you go through your day, pay special attention to natural objects around you (rocks, trees, animals, hills) as well as people (individuals, crowds). Observe how they glorify their Creator by their existence. Don't be overcritical or get caught up in evaluating — just notice.

DAY 98

GOD ENCOUNTERS

On this seventh day, review and reflect on all you have read this week. Take the time to revel in the ways you've encountered God in the past six days.

WORTH FAR MORE THAN MONEY

PROVERBS 2:2-5

2-5
Tune your ears to the world of Wisdom;
    set your heart on a life of Understanding.
That's right — if you make Insight your priority,
    and won't take no for an answer,
Searching for it like a prospector panning for gold,
    like an adventurer on a treasure hunt,
Believe me, before you know it Fear-of-God will be yours;
    you'll have come upon the Knowledge of God.

READ

Read the passage, imagining a grandparent or an older, wiser friend saying these words to you.

THINK

Our culture rarely considers or values wisdom. People want many things, but wisdom isn't usually one of them, or it's not high on the priority list. And there seems to be a widespread assumption that a person simply grows into wisdom as he or she gets older. This is a passive approach to obtaining wisdom. But the writer of this proverb tells us not only that wisdom is worth pursuing but also that it should be pursued with much time and energy. This is a proactive approach to obtaining wisdom.

Read the passage again. What would pursuing wisdom with all your might look like? Do you believe that wisdom is "better than a big salary" (3:14)? Is that hard to believe? Why or why not?

PRAY

Pause and ask God to give you wisdom. Ask him to help you raise the value and preciousness of wisdom in your life. Ask him to show you how to actively pursue wisdom. Listen for anything he might say now in response to your requests.

LIVE

Live wisely today, asking God to give you a spirit of discernment as you work, play, rest, eat, read, and sleep.

KEEP WATCH OVER YOUR HEART

PROVERBS 4:20-23; 5:8-14

20-22   Dear friend, listen well to my words;
      tune your ears to my voice.
  Keep my message in plain view at all times.
      Concentrate! Learn it by heart!
  Those who discover these words live, really live;
      body and soul, they're bursting with health.

23   Keep vigilant watch over your heart;
      that's where life starts.

. . . .

8-14   Keep your distance from such a woman;
      absolutely stay out of her neighborhood.
  You don't want to squander your wonderful life,
      to waste your precious life among the hardhearted.
  Why should you allow strangers to take advantage of you?
      Why be exploited by those who care nothing for you?
  You don't want to end your life full of regrets,
      nothing but sin and bones,
  Saying, "Oh, why didn't I do what they told me?
      Why did I reject a disciplined life?
  Why didn't I listen to my mentors,
      or take my teachers seriously?
  My life is ruined!
      I haven't one blessed thing to show for my life!"

READ

Read the passage aloud slowly, keeping in mind that "such a woman" refers to the things in your life that seduce you, meaning anything that sucks you in, lures you, misleads you, or even corrupts you.

THINK

1. Consider what has caused you to squander days of your life and leave you full of regret. It might be patterns of relating to people, patterns of spending your time, or patterns of making decisions. Then read verses 8-14 again and wait for thoughts to rise to the surface of your mind.
2. Read verses 20-23 and see what comes to you about the ways you need to avoid such patterns. Do you need to listen? Keep God's message in plain view? Keep a vigilant heart?
3. What would keeping watch over your heart look like? Keeping watch might be different for you than for others. Avoid grabbing at the first thing that comes to mind. Wait in that.

PRAY

Begin by confessing your regrets about time and energy you've squandered. Don't rush through this. Allow enough time to fully describe these things and let them go. Then ask God to help you listen to him and keep a watchful heart.

LIVE

Leave this book open to this passage and underline the phrase in verses 20-23 that stands out to you. As you move through your day, allow this to remind you to listen and keep an alert heart.

LURED INTO AMBUSH

PROVERBS 7:7-8,13-23

7 Watching the mindless crowd stroll by,
     I spotted a young man without any sense
8 Arriving at the corner of the street where she lived,
     then turning up the path to her house.
     . . . .

13-20 She threw her arms around him and kissed him,
     boldly took his arm and said,
   "I've got all the makings for a feast —
     today I made my offerings, my vows are all paid,
   So now I've come to find you,
     hoping to catch sight of your face — and here you are!
   I've spread fresh, clean sheets on my bed,
     colorful imported linens.
   My bed is aromatic with spices
     and exotic fragrances.
   Come, let's make love all night,
     spend the night in ecstatic lovemaking!
   My husband's not home; he's away on business,
     and he won't be back for a month."

21-23 Soon she has him eating out of her hand,
     bewitched by her honeyed speech.
   Before you know it, he's trotting behind her,
     like a calf led to the butcher shop,
   Like a stag lured into ambush
     and then shot with an arrow,
   Like a bird flying into a net
     not knowing that its flying life is over.

PRAY

Before you begin, ask the Holy Spirit to make his presence palpable as you pray. Ask him to make you open to whatever he gives, rather than taking charge of this time or trying to fix yourself. Even if a part of you disagrees, present yourself with the truth that opening to him is all you can really do.

READ/THINK

Read the passage once, slowly. Allow the story of the foolish man and the seductress to sink in until you understand its message. How do the words relate to your life? In what areas are you tempted — "lured into ambush" — to live foolishly? What are some things you know are right to do, but you drag your feet and don't do them? Don't try to fix yourself or be down on yourself. Instead, just let the reality settle in that this is who you are: someone very much in need of God's grace and mercy.

LIVE

Finish your devotion today by picturing God sitting with you. Tell him, "God, this is who I am." Remain open to whatever this might be, and if necessary, remind yourself that you don't want to fix yourself. If this seems difficult or if relaxing in his presence is challenging, take a few minutes to consider this truth: "The Lord is full of compassion and mercy" (James 5:11, NIV). Then return to relaxing in God's presence. Write down anything significant from this time that you can refer to.

SELF-EXAMINATION

PROVERBS 10:22-32

22 GOD's blessing makes life rich;
    nothing we do can improve on God.

23 An empty-head thinks mischief is fun,
    but a mindful person relishes wisdom.

24 The nightmares of the wicked come true;
    what the good people desire, they get.

25 When the storm is over, there's nothing left of the wicked;
    good people, firm on their rock foundation, aren't even fazed.

26 A lazy employee will give you nothing but trouble;
    it's vinegar in the mouth, smoke in the eyes.

27 The Fear-of-GOD expands your life;
    a wicked life is a puny life.

28 The aspirations of good people end in celebration;
    the ambitions of bad people crash.

29 GOD is solid backing to a well-lived life,
    but he calls into question a shabby performance.

30 Good people *last* — they can't be moved;
    the wicked are here today, gone tomorrow.

31 A good person's mouth is a clear fountain of wisdom;
    a foul mouth is a stagnant swamp.

32 The speech of a good person clears the air;
    the words of the wicked pollute it.

READ

Stand in front of a mirror and read the passage. When you're finished, stand motionless. Stare at yourself in the mirror.

THINK

When we read passages of God's Message that speak about the unrighteous or the evil or foolish person, we are often reminded of other individuals and think to ourselves, *That certainly isn't talking about me.* But we must be careful not to be blinded by the sin and pride in our own lives. Take a few minutes to perform a thorough self-examination. (This might be a difficult exercise for you; being willing to see our true selves is not easy.)

PRAY

Reread the passage. After each verse, pause, look in the mirror, and whisper, "God, is this me?" Allow time for God to prompt truths in your heart. Some of these thoughts may be hard to hear. If God brings to mind specific areas where you have failed, ask him to forgive you. If God brings to mind areas where you can grow, ask him to help you mature as you follow him. If God brings to mind ways in which you are living faithfully, thank him for his grace in your life.

LIVE

Whatever God-honoring quality was revealed to you today as you asked the question, "God, is this me?" go and live in that manner.

WISDOM ON YOUR DOORSTEP

PROVERBS 14:2-13

2 An honest life shows respect for GOD;
a degenerate life is a slap in his face.

3 Frivolous talk provokes a derisive smile;
wise speech evokes nothing but respect.

4 No cattle, no crops;
a good harvest requires a strong ox for the plow.

5 A true witness never lies;
a false witness makes a business of it.

6 Cynics look high and low for wisdom — and never find it;
the open-minded find it right on their doorstep!

7 Escape quickly from the company of fools;
they're a waste of your time, a waste of your words.

8 The wisdom of the wise keeps life on track;
the foolishness of fools lands them in the ditch.

9 The stupid ridicule right and wrong,
but a moral life is a favored life.

10 The person who shuns the bitter moments of friends
will be an outsider at their celebrations.

11 Lives of careless wrongdoing are tumbledown shacks;
holy living builds soaring cathedrals.

12-13 There's a way of life that looks harmless enough;
look again — it leads straight to hell.
Sure, those people appear to be having a good time,
but all that laughter will end in heartbreak.

READ

Read through these wise observations about life, pausing after each to consider what it says. Pick the statement that seems particularly vivid to you today, and read through it several more times, silently and aloud, until you become familiar with its message.

THINK

Where do you see yourself and the way you act fitting into this observation about life's realities? Maybe the image of the ox makes you recognize the laziness you've been lounging in, or perhaps you're struck by how much energy you expend trying to fit in with people. As you absorb this reality check, what are you feeling?

PRAY

Allow your inner exploration to take you into dialogue with God. Tell him about your discoveries. Let yourself be led into thankfulness, humility, or need. Maybe you're grateful to see the danger of your laziness before you get burned, or maybe you want to tell God how much you desire validation, even when you understand the folly of measuring your worth by the acceptance of others. Whatever this passage offers you personally, continue exploring it with God. Return to the passage if you find yourself stuck.

LIVE

Maybe the words "an honest life," "wise speech," or "respect" mean something new to you after pondering this passage. In what area is God inviting you to turn your life around — with his help? Write down in a short statement what you sense God inviting you to do.

THE IMPORTANCE OF WORDS

PROVERBS 16:21-32

21 A wise person gets known for insight;
  gracious words add to one's reputation.

22 True intelligence is a spring of fresh water,
  while fools sweat it out the hard way.

23 They make a lot of sense, these wise folks;
  whenever they speak, their reputation increases.

24 Gracious speech is like clover honey—
  good taste to the soul, quick energy for the body.

25 There's a way that looks harmless enough;
  look again—it leads straight to hell.

26 Appetite is an incentive to work;
  hunger makes you work all the harder.

27 Mean people spread mean gossip;
  their words smart and burn.

28 Troublemakers start fights;
  gossips break up friendships.

29 Calloused climbers betray their very own friends;
  they'd stab their own grandmothers in the back.

30 A shifty eye betrays an evil intention;
  a clenched jaw signals trouble ahead.

31 Gray hair is a mark of distinction,
  the award for a God-loyal life.

32 Moderation is better than muscle,
  self-control better than political power.

READ

Read the passage. Underline the word or phrase that stands out to you the most. Read the passage again. Underline a different word or phrase that stands out to you.

THINK

You may have heard the saying that only two things cannot be taken back: time and our words. Think back over all the words you have said in conversation over the past twenty-four hours (conversations you have had with friends, comments you have made in passing, phone calls, jokes you have told, and so on). What percentage of your conversation would you say was positive, encouraging, and uplifting? What percentage was negative, discouraging, and sarcastic?

Consider the words you are glad you said. Consider the words you regret saying.

PRAY

For the words you regret, ask for forgiveness. For the positive words you spoke, thank God they were words that built up rather than tore down.

Ask God to bring to mind words of truth and healing that you could speak to others. Ask him to bring to mind specific people to whom you could speak these words in the next few days.

LIVE

Have the courage to seek out opportunities to speak words of truth and healing to people who need to hear them. Hold your tongue when you are upset or frustrated — when you are about to speak words you'll regret. Above all else, ask God to help you guard your mouth by thinking before speaking.

DAY 105

GOD ENCOUNTERS

On this seventh day, review and reflect on all you have read this week. Take the time to revel in the ways you've encountered God in the past six days.

HUMILITY

PROVERBS 18:10-15

10   GOD's name is a place of protection —
      good people can run there and be safe.

11   The rich think their wealth protects them;
      they imagine themselves safe behind it.

12   Pride first, then the crash,
      but humility is precursor to honor.

13   Answering before listening
      is both stupid and rude.

14   A healthy spirit conquers adversity,
      but what can you do when the spirit is crushed?

15   Wise men and women are always learning,
      always listening for fresh insights.

READ

Read the passage aloud slowly.

THINK

Read the passage again slowly. Notice the different ways humility is expressed.

1. Which phrases describe who you have been and who you'd like to be?
2. What fears do you have about what might happen to you if you were humble? How might these fears be addressed by living in God's name, God's power, and God's presence as your place of protection?

Read the passage again.

3. What touches you most about this passage?
4. What is occurring in your life right now that this passage addresses?

PRAY

Ask God to show you more about living a richly humble life. Tell God what you need to learn from him about being his devoted, constant, listening student.

LIVE

Soak in the protection of God's name, presence, and power. Notice how this makes being humble easier.

✚ WAIT FOR GOD

PROVERBS 20:22-30

22   Don't ever say, "I'll get you for that!"
        Wait for GOD; he'll settle the score.

23   GOD hates cheating in the marketplace;
        rigged scales are an outrage.

24   The very steps we take come from GOD;
        otherwise how would we know where we're going?

25   An impulsive vow is a trap;
        later you'll wish you could get out of it.

26   After careful scrutiny, a wise leader
        makes a clean sweep of rebels and dolts.

27   GOD is in charge of human life,
        watching and examining us inside and out.

28   Love and truth form a good leader;
        sound leadership is founded on loving integrity.

29   Youth may be admired for vigor,
        but gray hair gives prestige to old age.

30   A good thrashing purges evil;
        punishment goes deep within us.

READ

Read this list of statements and instructions, pausing after each one to consider what it says. Does one stand out to you? Memorize it.

THINK

Why does this stand out to you? Let it lead you to ponder your own life. Try to avoid thinking about other people's actions or motives; think instead about only your own. Maybe you'll be reminded of making an impulsive promise, or perhaps you'll check your attitude toward "gray hair [giving] prestige" versus "youth . . . admired for vigor."

PRAY

Invite God into your thoughts. Tell him what you have been discovering. Be aware of your feelings while you pray — maybe fear of emptiness at the thought of getting older, joy that God will "settle the score" someday, or sadness over a foolish decision and its consequences. Be yourself in God's presence.

LIVE

Explore your overall experience with this text so far. Why did you respond the way you did to the wise instruction God is communicating in this passage? If you didn't care much, this might tell you that you don't care much about doing the right thing. If you anxiously tried to think of ways to improve yourself, perhaps you feel uncomfortable exposing your weakness to God. Honestly recognize what's in your heart today — and what that tells you about how you see yourself and how you see God.

Remember that God knows all about you — even the parts of you that are rebellious and don't care about what's right — and yet he loves you deeply. If you struggle to believe this, read Isaiah 43:1-7.

DOLLARS AND CENTS

PROVERBS 22:22-23,26-27; 23:4-8

22-23   Don't walk on the poor just because they're poor,
             and don't use your position to crush the weak,
         Because GOD will come to their defense;
             the life you took, he'll take from you and give back to them.

         . . . .

26-27   Don't gamble on the pot of gold at the end of the rainbow,
             hocking your house against a lucky chance.
         The time will come when you have to pay up;
             you'll be left with nothing but the shirt on your back.

         . . . .

4-5   Don't wear yourself out trying to get rich;
             restrain yourself!
         Riches disappear in the blink of an eye;
             wealth sprouts wings
             and flies off into the wild blue yonder.

6-8   Don't accept a meal from a tightwad;
             don't expect anything special.
         He'll be as stingy with you as he is with himself;
             he'll say, "Eat! Drink!" but won't mean a word of it.
         His miserly serving will turn your stomach
             when you realize the meal's a sham.

READ

Read the passage. Make a note of every implication to finances and wealth that you find.

THINK

Scripture has a lot to say about how we deal with our finances. Wisdom will determine a lot about how we deal with money, and money will determine a lot about how we deal with wisdom. Proverbs speaks often of the importance of dealing with money, because it's not simply about dollars and cents. It's a deeper issue that involves what our heart is attached to.

Think back over the purchases you have made in the past week, big and small. What was your motive in making those purchases (practical purposes, reputation, comfort and pleasure, necessity)?

Which of those would you categorize as being wise purchases? Which would you categorize as being unwise?

As you think about the purchases you have made in the past week, what emotions are you feeling? Are they positive or negative? Full of freedom and joy or guilt and frustration? Why do you think you are feeling that way?

PRAY

Take out your wallet, purse, money clip, credit cards, checkbook, and key chain, and hold them in your hands. As you look at the pile in your hands, keep your eyes open and pray. Ask your heavenly Father to help you be a wise steward of all the money and possessions he has entrusted to you.

LIVE

Every time you pull out your wallet or purse to make a purchase, ask yourself the question, *Will this purchase be a wise one, and will it honor God?*

WISDOM WITH FEET ON IT

PROVERBS 24:3-4,15-21,28-29

3-4   It takes wisdom to build a house,
      and understanding to set it on a firm foundation;
    It takes knowledge to furnish its rooms
      with fine furniture and beautiful draperies.

. . . .

15-16   Don't interfere with good people's lives;
      don't try to get the best of them.
    No matter how many times you trip them up,
      God-loyal people don't stay down long;
    Soon they're up on their feet,
      while the wicked end up flat on their faces.

17-18   Don't laugh when your enemy falls;
      don't crow over his collapse.
    God might see, and become very provoked,
      and then take pity on his plight.

19-20   Don't bother your head with braggarts
      or wish you could succeed like the wicked.
    Those people have no future at all;
      they're headed down a dead-end street.

21   Fear GOD, dear child — respect your leaders;
      don't be defiant or mutinous.

. . . .

28-29   Don't talk about your neighbors behind their backs —
      no slander or gossip, please.
    Don't say to anyone, "I'll get back at you for what you did to me.
      I'll make you pay for what you did!"

READ

Read the passage slowly. Now read the expanded passage.

THINK

Read the passage again, noticing that the first two verses introduce the importance of wisdom.

1. If you're wondering what wisdom is, notice the way the other verses describe how you can live out wisdom. Underline the practical descriptions of wisdom you find there.
2. Now read aloud the phrases you underlined. Which one resonates with you? Which one sounds like guidance you've been hearing God say to you for a while?
3. How does that phrase connect with you?

PRAY

Talk to God about what's been going on in your life and how the wise ideas in this passage shed light on your situation. Tell God why you would find it difficult or easy to do the wise thing. Thank God that he never finds it difficult — and that he can help you.

LIVE

Play with the idea that you're a truly wise person. Doodle a little in a journal, drawing a representation of yourself as wise. Consider why you drew what you did. Being wise doesn't mean you're a know-it-all or superior to other people so they don't want to hang out with you. Jesus was wise, but plenty of people liked to hang out with him.

WORD TO THE WISE

PROVERBS 28:4-12

4   If you desert God's law, you're free to embrace depravity;
        if you love God's law, you fight for it tooth and nail.

5   Justice makes no sense to the evilminded;
        those who seek GOD know it inside and out.

6   It's better to be poor and direct
        than rich and crooked.

7   Practice God's law — get a reputation for wisdom;
        hang out with a loose crowd — embarrass your family.

8   Get as rich as you want
        through cheating and extortion,
But eventually some friend of the poor
        is going to give it all back to them.

9   God has no use for the prayers
        of the people who won't listen to him.

10   Lead good people down a wrong path
        and you'll come to a bad end;
        do good and you'll be rewarded for it.

11   The rich think they know it all,
        but the poor can see right through them.

12   When good people are promoted, everything is great,
        but when the bad are in charge, watch out!

READ

Read the passage slowly, pausing for about thirty seconds after each verse to think about it.

THINK

There are many parts of Proverbs that carry a specific theme. But other parts of Proverbs deliver wise advice like machine-gun fire into the sky — wise sayings about various subjects in no particular order. Chapter 28 is one of these machine-gun-into-the-sky chapters. Yet no matter how they're fired, every bullet is precious.

This time, read the expanded passage, inviting the Holy Spirit to help you pick out two proverbs that speak to your specific condition this week.

PRAY

Ask the Holy Spirit to mold you and shape you so you become more and more like the two verses you have written down, so your life shows evidence of the change. Share these two verses with a close friend or family member, and invite him or her to help you work on these areas of your life.

LIVE

Write on an index card these verses the Holy Spirit brought to your attention. Carry the card with you. When you're sitting in traffic or have a few minutes between meetings or classes, pull out the card and consider the wise ways in which to live.

NOTICING THE NEEDY

PROVERBS 29:7,13-14,23,27

7   The good-hearted understand what it's like to be poor;
       the hardhearted haven't the faintest idea.

· · · · · · · · ·

13   The poor and their abusers have at least something in common:
       they can both *see* — their sight, GOD's gift!

14   Leadership gains authority and respect
       when the voiceless poor are treated fairly.

· · · · · · · · ·

23   Pride lands you flat on your face;
       humility prepares you for honors.

· · · · · · · · ·

27   Good people can't stand the sight of deliberate evil;
       the wicked can't stand the sight of well-chosen goodness.

READ

Read the verses aloud slowly.

THINK

God is the "powerful Advocate" of the needy (see Proverbs 23:11). The biblical categories of the needy (the widow, the fatherless, and the alien or stranger) are "voiceless." Because their voices are not valued or heard, God commissions his people to become modern-day public defenders, so to speak, defending the causes of the needy, maintaining their rights and pleading their cases (see Deuteronomy 27:19; Psalm 82:3; Proverbs 23:10-11; Isaiah 1:17).

1. Read the verses again, noticing what God asks of you regarding the poor.
2. Read the verses one more time, asking God to show you what you need to know about your relationship to the have-nots in your society and neighborhood.

PRAY

Ask God to help you find ways to "understand what it's like to be poor," to treat fairly those who are overlooked, and to participate in "well-chosen goodness" regarding the needy.

LIVE

Start seeing the have-nots in your world. You might find them riding buses, standing outside convenience stores, or riding their bikes. These people are present, but we usually overlook them. Really look at each person, especially his or her face. Acknowledge the person with a nod or a smile. Breathe in the deep good-heartedness of God, who asks you to "understand what it's like to be poor."

DAY 112

GOD ENCOUNTERS

On this seventh day, review and reflect on all you have read this week. Take the time to revel in the ways you've encountered God in the past six days.

THE SKEPTIC AND THE BELIEVER

PROVERBS 30:1-9

1-2   The skeptic swore, "There is no God!
    No God! — I can do anything I want!
I'm more animal than human;
    so-called human intelligence escapes me.

3-4   "I flunked 'wisdom.'
    I see no evidence of a holy God.
Has anyone ever seen Anyone
    climb into Heaven and take charge?
    grab the winds and control them?
    gather the rains in his bucket?
    stake out the ends of the earth?
Just tell me his name, tell me the names of his sons.
    Come on now — tell me!"

5-6   The believer replied, "Every promise of God proves true;
    he protects everyone who runs to him for help.
So don't second-guess him;
    he might take you to task and show up your lies."

7-9   And then he prayed, "God, I'm asking for two things
    before I die; don't refuse me —
Banish lies from my lips
    and liars from my presence.
Give me enough food to live on,
    neither too much nor too little.
If I'm too full, I might get independent,
    saying, 'God? Who needs him?'
If I'm poor, I might steal
    and dishonor the name of my God."

READ

As you read the words of this passage, be aware of the parts of your heart that are represented by the words. Perhaps under certain circumstances, you have intentionally ignored God's rules, while at other times you have run to God for protection, knowing he would help you.

THINK/PRAY

Read the passage a few more times. Each time you read, narrow your focus to the part that most deeply touches the reality of your life. Mull that over. Explore with God what he is saying to you through it, how he may want to lead, challenge, or refresh you.

LIVE

The prayer of verse 9 acknowledges the relationship between our physical and spiritual selves: When full of food, we may feel a false sense of security and disregard our need for God. When hungry, we may feel our need yet doubt that God will meet it.

Consider fasting today, for part or all of the day. Give up food or drink, or perhaps something you enjoy, such as reading or watching television. (Be sure to do this when you'll have time to replace your fasted activity with prayer. Also, check with your doctor before fasting from food or drink.) Let your fast help you get in touch with your heart's reaction to God.

When you would normally engage in the activity you're fasting from or when you feel an emptiness that you normally wouldn't notice, prayerfully read verse 9. In what ways does your fasting experience show you your need for God? Can you trust him to provide for your needs, or is your impulse to try to provide for yourself?

GIVING IN TO EVERY IMPULSE

ECCLESIASTES 2:4-10

4-8
Oh, I did great things:
 built houses,
 planted vineyards,
 designed gardens and parks
  and planted a variety of fruit trees in them,
 made pools of water
  to irrigate the groves of trees.
I bought slaves, male and female,
  who had children, giving me even more slaves;
 then I acquired large herds and flocks,
  larger than any before me in Jerusalem.
I piled up silver and gold,
  loot from kings and kingdoms.
I gathered a chorus of singers to entertain me with song,
 and — most exquisite of all pleasures —
 voluptuous maidens for my bed.

9-10
Oh, how I prospered! I left all my predecessors in Jerusalem far behind, left them behind in the dust. What's more, I kept a clear head through it all. Everything I wanted I took — I never said no to myself. I gave in to every impulse, held back nothing. I sucked the marrow of pleasure out of every task — my reward to myself for a hard day's work!

READ

Read the passage.

THINK

Nobody knows for certain who wrote Ecclesiastes — some have suggested King Solomon — but one thing is certain: The writer communicates with piercing honesty and urgent desperation about the condition of life. The writer has pursued every possible pleasure and has still come away empty.

Write down your prayerful answers to these questions:

1. What pleasures — big and small, evil and seemingly innocent — have you pursued in the past week?
2. What were your motives — good or bad — for pursuing and engaging in those pleasures? Dig deep and be honest: What meaning were you attempting to get?
3. What does it mean that you pursue pleasure? In other words, what lies does pleasure whisper in your ear?

PRAY

Choose the one pleasure you sought with the most effort. Write out a prayer to God that involves this pursuit and the pleasure itself. Maybe you need to ask God to forgive you because you sought the pleasure ultimately for meaning and significance. Now pray about the bigger picture. Take a hard look at the lifestyle you lead and the amount of pleasure you engage in on a regular basis. Lay everything before God and ask, "God, are these worth pursuing?"

LIVE

This week, with every pleasure you pursue, big and miniscule, consider what your motive is in approaching it.

114

DON'T GO IT ALONE

ECCLESIASTES 4:9-12

9-10
It's better to have a partner than go it alone.
Share the work, share the wealth.
And if one falls down, the other helps,
But if there's no one to help, tough!

11
Two in a bed warm each other.
Alone, you shiver all night.

12
By yourself you're unprotected.
With a friend you can face the worst.
Can you round up a third?
A three-stranded rope isn't easily snapped.

READ

Read the passage aloud slowly.

THINK

Community is an important spiritual practice. The Trinity itself is a community of love. Here on earth we get to try that out! We were built for relationship — to help others and be helped by them. Read the passage again aloud, remembering that it's poetry and trying to read it with rhythm, emphasis, and pauses.

1. What words or phrases speak to you? Why?
2. What do these words or phrases tell you about how you've been helped? About how you're built to help others?

PRAY

Ask God to show you clearly how people have shared their work and their wealth with you, how they've picked you up when you've fallen down, how they've warmed you when you were alone, how they've protected you when you faced the worst. Take as long as you need.

LIVE

Hold a rope or anything braided in your hand. (If you don't have something braided, you can do this in a hardware store or by sketching a braid on a piece of paper.) Run your finger along one of the strands and identify that strand as yourself. Ponder who the other two strands might be in your life — perhaps people you have overlooked. Keep your eyes open for your other two strands today.

⊕ WHAT'S THE POINT?

ECCLESIASTES 6:1-9

1-2   I looked long and hard at what goes on around here, and let me tell you, things are bad. And people feel it. There are people, for instance, on whom God showers everything — money, property, reputation — all they ever wanted or dreamed of. And then God doesn't let them enjoy it. Some stranger comes along and has all the fun. It's more of what I'm calling *smoke*. A bad business.

3-5   Say a couple have scores of children and live a long, long life but never enjoy themselves — even though they end up with a big funeral! I'd say that a stillborn baby gets the better deal. It gets its start in a mist and ends up in the dark — unnamed. It sees nothing and knows nothing, but is better off by far than anyone living.

6   Even if someone lived a thousand years — make it two thousand! — but didn't enjoy anything, what's the point? Doesn't everyone end up in the same place?

7   We work to feed our appetites;
Meanwhile our souls go hungry.

8-9   So what advantage has a sage over a fool, or over some poor wretch who barely gets by? Just grab whatever you can while you can; don't assume something better might turn up by and by. All it amounts to anyway is smoke. And spitting into the wind.

READ

Read the passage slowly.

THINK

In what ways do you relate to this point of view? Maybe you feel disillusioned with the promises of happiness made by each "new and improved" object, program, or adventure. Maybe you've felt so much pain you wish you'd never been born. Maybe you've been showered with good stuff that leaves you secure and comfortable, and you're left unsettled by the reality check in this passage. Look deep inside yourself and find out what's being stirred up there. What one image in the passage best encapsulates your thoughts?

PRAY

Sit with that image in your mind, and become aware of Jesus in the room with you now. Allow yourself to think more deeply about what he is saying through this passage about you and your life. Respond to him with an honest heart. Share with him exactly what you're feeling — the discontent and longing, the pain, the unsettling doubt, whatever it is. If you feel uncomfortable because you wish you could be doing something else, tell him that.

LIVE

Were you able to connect with Jesus in this time? If so, what was it like for you to relate to him? How would you describe the way Jesus was toward you during this time? If you weren't able to connect with him, what was that like for you? What would you have wanted from this time? Share your thoughts and feelings with Jesus.

PAIN

ECCLESIASTES 7:2-3

2 You learn more at a funeral than at a feast —
 After all, that's where we'll end up. We might discover
  something from it.

3 Crying is better than laughing.
 It blotches the face but it scours the heart.

READ

Spend five minutes slowly reading and rereading these two verses.

THINK

Why would the author of these words say such things? Do you relate to these verses? What feelings arise in response to them? Do you agree or disagree that "you learn more at a funeral than at a feast"? Why?

Consider a time when you experienced extreme sorrow. Looking back, what did you learn?

"Crying is better than laughing. It blotches the face but it scours the heart." Do you agree or disagree with this statement? Why?

PRAY

If you are currently experiencing sorrow, request that the Lord give you a teachable spirit to learn valuable lessons during this time. If you are not experiencing sorrow, invite the Lord to prepare your heart for those times when you will.

LIVE

C. S. Lewis wrote, "God whispers to us in our joy and shouts to us in our pain."[10] Next time you hear about the death of someone you know or attend a funeral, journal your thoughts or process with a friend what you observed and what you learned. In the meantime, live a life that is teachable and moldable, especially during difficult times.

DO ALL TO THE GLORY OF GOD

ECCLESIASTES 9:7-10

7-10   Seize life! Eat bread with gusto,
Drink wine with a robust heart.
Oh yes — God takes pleasure in *your* pleasure!
Dress festively every morning.
Don't skimp on colors and scarves.
Relish life with the spouse you love
Each and every day of your precarious life.
Each day is God's gift. It's all you get in exchange
For the hard work of staying alive.
Make the most of each one!
Whatever turns up, grab it and do it. And heartily!
This is your last and only chance at it,
For there's neither work to do nor thoughts to think
In the company of the dead, where you're most certainly headed.

READ

Read the passage aloud slowly.

THINK

This passage pictures what it looks like to do everything to the glory of God: "Let every detail in your lives — words, actions, whatever — be done in the name of the Master, Jesus, thanking God the Father every step of the way" (Colossians 3:17).

1. In what ways does God "seize" or "drink" or "relish"?
2. What pleasures do you enjoy that you think God might enjoy with you?

Read the passage aloud slowly again, noting the words or phrases that stand out to you.

3. What about life do you need to seize, drink, or relish?

PRAY

Respond to God regarding this idea of seizing, drinking, and relishing. Tell God if you're surprised to think of him this way. Talk to God about whether you need to do what this text says or cut back on doing too much of it. Be willing to hear from God about these things rather than coming up with your own answers, which might be based on what others have told you.

LIVE

Take a walk, preferably a hike. Move mentally and physically in the style of this passage. Seize on every view open to you. Drink in the colors you see, the sounds you hear, and the aromas you smell. Relish a leaf or flower by rubbing it against your cheek.

DAY 119

GOD ENCOUNTERS

On this seventh day, review and reflect on all you have read this week. Take the time to revel in the ways you've encountered God in the past six days.

MAKE THE MOST OF YOUR YOUTH

ECCLESIASTES 11:9; 12:1-7

9   You who are young, make the most of your youth.
      Relish your youthful vigor.
      Follow the impulses of your heart.
      If something looks good to you, pursue it.
      But know also that not just anything goes;
      You have to answer to God for every last bit of it.

      . . . .

1-2   Honor and enjoy your Creator while you're still young,
      Before the years take their toll and your vigor wanes,
      Before your vision dims and the world blurs
      And the winter years keep you close to the fire.

3-5   In old age, your body no longer serves you so well.
      Muscles slacken, grip weakens, joints stiffen.
      The shades are pulled down on the world.
      You can't come and go at will. Things grind to a halt.
      The hum of the household fades away.
      You are wakened now by bird-song.
      Hikes to the mountains are a thing of the past.
      Even a stroll down the road has its terrors.
      Your hair turns apple-blossom white,
      Adorning a fragile and impotent matchstick body.
      Yes, you're well on your way to eternal rest,
      While your friends make plans for your funeral.

6-7   Life, lovely while it lasts, is soon over.
      Life as we know it, precious and beautiful, ends.
      The body is put back in the same ground it came from.
      The spirit returns to God, who first breathed it.

READ

Read the passage.

THINK/LIVE

You are likely young, strong, healthy, and full of potential. But as you read this passage again, look deeply at the perspective it presents: old age. Mull over the images, putting yourself in that place as best you can. Think of the contact you've had with elderly people: the physical aspects, such as sights, sounds, textures, and smells; and the mental aspects, such as attitude, knowledge, and experience.

Now return to the present. Look down at your body. Examine your hands; feel your legs and stretch them out. Touch your hair and some of the muscles in your body. Look in a mirror at your eyes and face. Forget your standard checklist when you evaluate yourself. Instead see your youth, health, and strength. What does that feel like? What do you notice?

PRAY

Now read the first few lines of the passage again. When you are told to "make the most of your youth" and "relish" it, what does that mean to you? What would being present to your life and enjoying it right now mean? Does being aware that you won't always be young change your view? Talk with God about what you think of youth and old age, and write down anything significant from this time.

ACCEPTED JUST AS YOU ARE

SONG OF SONGS 1:5-10

5-6 I am weathered but still elegant,
    oh, dear sisters in Jerusalem,
Weather-darkened like Kedar desert tents,
    time-softened like Solomon's Temple hangings.
Don't look down on me because I'm dark,
    darkened by the sun's harsh rays.
My brothers ridiculed me and sent me to work in the fields.
    They made me care for the face of the earth,
    but I had no time to care for my own face.

7 Tell me where you're working
    — I love you so much —
Tell me where you're tending your flocks,
    where you let them rest at noontime.
Why should I be the one left out,
    outside the orbit of your tender care?

THE MAN

8 If you can't find me, loveliest of all women,
    it's all right. Stay with your flocks.
Lead your lambs to good pasture.
    Stay with your shepherd neighbors.

9-10 You remind me of Pharaoh's
    well-groomed and satiny mares.
Pendant earrings line the elegance of your cheeks;
    strands of jewels illumine the curve of your throat.

READ

Read the passage slowly.

THINK

Ask some questions of the text. Who are the speakers? What is the situation? What do you notice about the woman's fears? Do you have similar insecurities about your appearance or about what others think of you? Consider these questions, but don't let information gathering steal too much time from prayer.

PRAY

Read the passage again. As you listen to this couple's dialogue, watch for the quiet voice of a word or the subtle quality of an image through which God seems to be expressing his acceptance of you today. Mull this word or phrase over, letting it interplay with your concerns, ideas, and feelings. Remember not to be afraid of distracting memories or thoughts; they're part of the "you" that you bring to this experience.

Allow your mulling to turn into a conversation with this accepting God. If deeper memories or feelings arise, share them with him. Be open to how he may want to use the word or phrase he's given you as a means of blessing in the midst of your insecurities and fears.

LIVE

Take a while to let yourself relax in God's acceptance. If thoughts or feelings come, share them. If they do not, just enjoy the quietness, and experience what it's like to be accepted by God just as you are, without having to do anything or be anyone else.

GOD HAS EYES FOR YOU

SONG OF SONGS 4:9-15

9-15 You've captured my heart, dear friend.
>   You looked at me, and I fell in love.
>   One look my way and I was hopelessly in love!
How beautiful your love, dear, dear friend —
>   far more pleasing than a fine, rare wine,
>   your fragrance more exotic than select spices.
The kisses of your lips are honey, my love,
>   every syllable you speak a delicacy to savor.
Your clothes smell like the wild outdoors,
>   the ozone scent of high mountains.
Dear lover and friend, you're a secret garden,
>   a private and pure fountain.
Body and soul, you are paradise,
>   a whole orchard of succulent fruits —
Ripe apricots and peaches,
>   oranges and pears;
Nut trees and cinnamon,
>   and all scented woods;
Mint and lavender,
>   and all herbs aromatic;
A garden fountain, sparkling and splashing,
>   fed by spring waters from the Lebanon mountains.

READ

Read the passage slowly.

THINK

Read the passage again, but aloud this time. Consider this as God's love poem to you. Song of Songs illustrates how God treasures us — he can't take his eyes off us.

Which image do you prefer to be in God's sight?

- ☐ a dear friend
- ☐ one who looks God's way
- ☐ as pleasing as fine, rare wine
- ☐ as fragrant as an exotic spice
- ☐ one with kisses like honey
- ☐ one who speaks each syllable with sensitivity to God
- ☐ one whose clothes smell like the wild outdoors
- ☐ a lover and friend
- ☐ a private and pure fountain
- ☐ a sparkling, splashing fountain

PRAY

Pray what you most need to pray — perhaps that:

- you would grasp how loved and treasured you are by God
- you would define your relationship with God in the way of this passage rather than seeing yourself as _____ (maybe "God's slave")
- you would begin to grasp what it means to treasure God

LIVE

Put yourself near one of the objects mentioned in this poem: a pleasing drink, an exotic spice, the wild outdoors, a fountain. Gaze at it and smell it, cherishing the idea that this is how God cherishes you.

LOVE IS INVINCIBLE

SONG OF SONGS 8:6-7,11-12

THE WOMAN

6-7
Hang my locket around your neck,
  wear my ring on your finger.
Love is invincible facing danger and death.
  Passion laughs at the terrors of hell.
The fire of love stops at nothing —
  it sweeps everything before it.
Flood waters can't drown love,
  torrents of rain can't put it out.
  Love can't be bought, love can't be sold —
  it's not to be found in the marketplace.

. . . .

THE MAN

11-12
King Solomon may have vast vineyards
  in lush, fertile country,
Where he hires others to work the ground.
  People pay anything to get in on that bounty.
But *my* vineyard is all mine,
  and I'm keeping it to myself.
You can have your vast vineyards, Solomon,
  you and your greedy guests!

READ

Read the passage twice.

THINK

Direct your attention to the part of the text where you have the strongest reaction, either positive or negative. Maybe you'll consider the woman's statements about love. Do you agree or disagree with them? Or maybe you'll consider the man's promise to protect what is his. How do you respond to that promise?

PRAY

Start your prayer time by examining your feelings and beliefs about love — and not necessarily *romantic* love. Sift through these to see what in you is truly feeling and what is belief. For example, a feeling might be "I feel rejected." And a related belief might be "I believe no one could truly love me." Ask God what he thinks about your feelings and beliefs.

LIVE

Read the passage again, this time asking the Holy Spirit to show you a word or concept summing up something God is saying about love that you don't fully grasp or believe or that you don't yet accept or live out naturally. Ask God to teach you in the coming days and weeks, perhaps through further meditation, more about what he created love to be like.

BURNING OFF SIN

ISAIAH 6:1-8

1-8   In the year that King Uzziah died, I saw the Master sitting on a throne — high, exalted! — and the train of his robes filled the Temple. Angel-seraphs hovered above him, each with six wings. With two wings they covered their faces, with two their feet, and with two they flew. And they called back and forth one to the other,

> Holy, Holy, Holy is GOD-of-the-Angel-Armies.
> His bright glory fills the whole earth.

The foundations trembled at the sound of the angel voices, and then the whole house filled with smoke. I said,

> "Doom! It's Doomsday!
>   I'm as good as dead!
> Every word I've ever spoken is tainted —
>   blasphemous even!
> And the people I live with talk the same way,
>   using words that corrupt and desecrate.
> And here I've looked God in the face!
>   The King! GOD-of-the-Angel-Armies!"

Then one of the angel-seraphs flew to me. He held a live coal that he had taken with tongs from the altar. He touched my mouth with the coal and said,

> "Look. This coal has touched your lips.
>   Gone your guilt,
>   your sins wiped out."
> And then I heard the voice of the Master:
>   "Whom shall I send?
>   Who will go for us?"
> I spoke up,
>   "I'll go.
>   Send me!"

READ

Read the passage, making special note of the dialogue between the angels and Isaiah.

THINK

As the Lord God's mouthpiece to the nations, Isaiah experiences this unforgettable encounter with the Master at the outset of his ministry. An angel-seraph flies down to Isaiah and touches his mouth with a burning coal.

The mouth is one of the most sensitive parts of the body. Explore your spiritual life to identify sensitive areas that would hurt deeply at God's touch. Why are these areas the most sensitive? Consider what your relationship with God might look like, now and in the long term, if he purified these areas of your life.

PRAY

Invite God to burn these sensitive areas of your life so you can serve him more effectively. This is a scary prayer when offered sincerely and earnestly, but be encouraged by what happened in Isaiah's life as a result of his burned lips.

LIVE

Ask two people who are close to you what they believe to be areas of your life in need of refining by God's touch. Be prepared to consider answers that may be hard to hear but are beneficial.

THE PEACEABLE KINGDOM OF GOD

ISAIAH 11:6-9

6-9   The wolf will romp with the lamb,
            the leopard sleep with the kid.
        Calf and lion will eat from the same trough,
            and a little child will tend them.
        Cow and bear will graze the same pasture,
            their calves and cubs grow up together,
            and the lion eat straw like the ox.
        The nursing child will crawl over rattlesnake dens,
            the toddler stick his hand down the hole of a serpent.
        Neither animal nor human will hurt or kill
            on my holy mountain.
        The whole earth will be brimming with knowing God-Alive,
            a living knowledge of God ocean-deep, ocean-wide.

READ

Read the passage aloud slowly, noting how natural enemies are coexisting side by side (wolf and lamb, cow and bear, toddler and serpent).

THINK

Read the passage again, noting which images are most powerful or amazing to you.

This passage gives us a vivid picture of the kingdom of God as it will exist in the future. What a different place it will be! Interact with this passage in one of these ways, depending on what stood out to you:

- Ponder what you would like best about such a peaceable world — one that is "brimming with knowing God-Alive, a living knowledge of God ocean-deep, ocean-wide."
- Ponder what feelings would be present for these creatures to exist this way (for example, serenity).
- Name your own natural enemies and imagine them standing beside you, with you, for you. You might choose political enemies (for example, parties, opponents, countries, regions); family members, coworkers, or acquaintances you're at odds with; or an animal or a natural element that's difficult for you (for example, spiders, if you hate spiders).

PRAY

Share with God how you feel about such a peaceable world. Share with him what you think such a world shows you about him.

LIVE

Ponder the idea that this passage describes your future reality. You *will* experience this. This is what God is creating for you.

DAY 126

GOD ENCOUNTERS

On this seventh day, review and reflect on all you have read this week. Take the time to revel in the ways you've encountered God in the past six days.

A STRONG GOD

ISAIAH 27:1-5

1   At that time GOD will unsheathe his sword,
        his merciless, massive, mighty sword.
    He'll punish the serpent Leviathan as it flees,
        the serpent Leviathan thrashing in flight.
    He'll kill that old dragon
        that lives in the sea.

2-5   "At that same time, a fine vineyard will appear.
        There's something to sing about!
    I, GOD, tend it.
        I keep it well-watered.
    I keep careful watch over it
        so that no one can damage it.
    I'm not angry. I care.
        Even if it gives me thistles and thornbushes,
    I'll just pull them out
        and burn them up.
    Let that vine cling to me for safety,
        let it find a good and whole life with me,
        let it hold on for a good and whole life."

READ

Read the passage slowly, letting your imagination play with the imagery. Picture everything vividly, as if you were a child reading a story with beautiful, lifelike illustrations.

THINK

Read the passage again. What do you notice about the way God interacts with "that old dragon"? With "that vine"? What is he like? Now put yourself in the scene. What part do you play? How do you feel?

PRAY

Picture God turning to you and inviting you to talk with him about what you are feeling and thinking. Does he ever seem angry to you, or uncaring? What's it like for you to hear him say otherwise? Share with him your thoughts and feelings, and allow the conversation to unfold.

LIVE

Write about your experience of encountering the God who mercilessly kills the dragon, meanwhile mercifully letting the vine cling to him as it grows. Be sure to include what dialoging with him was like for you. What will you take away from this time?

THINKING THAT HORSES CAN HELP

ISAIAH 31:1-3

1-3   Doom to those who go off to Egypt
      thinking that horses can help them,
Impressed by military mathematics,
      awed by sheer numbers of chariots and riders —
And to The Holy of Israel, not even a glance,
      not so much as a prayer to GOD.
Still, he must be reckoned with,
      a most wise God who knows what he's doing.
He can call down catastrophe.
      He's a God who does what he says.
He intervenes in the work of those who do wrong,
      stands up against interfering evildoers.
Egyptians are mortal, not God,
      and their horses are flesh, not Spirit.
When GOD gives the signal, helpers and helped alike
      will fall in a heap and share the same dirt grave.

READ

Read the passage at least six times. Don't rush through it. Get familiar with it.

THINK

In ancient times, Egypt was a prosperous and powerful nation. Horses and chariots were crucial for ensuring security, especially in times of war. We don't rely on horses and chariots to protect us today, but there are countless things we put our trust in.

Consider the circumstances in your life when you have depended on something or someone other than God. If God and God alone provides ultimate security and comfort, why do you think we turn to him for help only as a last resort? If we truly understood God's power and control — his sovereignty — how might that change how we live?

PRAY

Spend a few minutes in quiet and solitude. Use the time to seek out the dark corners of your life. Whisper, "What do I put my trust in?" Allow the Spirit to do his work. Don't rush the process, but simply wait for him to reveal the horses and chariots you depend on. When you see them clearly, confess them to God immediately. Be assured that he hears your prayers and forgives you graciously.

LIVE

Be constantly aware of the horses and chariots that seek your trust. Remind yourself of their lies — that they offer complete security and comfort — and the futility in believing those lies.

PICTURES OF RESTORATION

ISAIAH 35:4-9

4
   Tell fearful souls,
      "Courage! Take heart!
   GOD is here, right here,
      on his way to put things right
   And redress all wrongs.
      He's on his way! He'll save you!"

5-7
   Blind eyes will be opened,
      deaf ears unstopped,
   Lame men and women will leap like deer,
      the voiceless break into song.
   Springs of water will burst out in the wilderness,
      streams flow in the desert.
   Hot sands will become a cool oasis,
      thirsty ground a splashing fountain.
   Even lowly jackals will have water to drink,
      and barren grasslands flourish richly.

8-9
   There will be a highway
      called the Holy Road.
   No one rude or rebellious
      is permitted on this road.
   It's for GOD's people exclusively—
      impossible to get lost on this road.
      Not even fools can get lost on it.
   No lions on this road,
      no dangerous wild animals—
   Nothing and no one dangerous or threatening.
      Only the redeemed will walk on it.

READ

Read the first verse aloud and then read the rest silently.

THINK

Read the passage again, watching for its emphasis on restoration and healing.

1. What pictures of healing speak to you?

   ☐ God putting things right
   ☐ blind eyes opening
   ☐ deaf ears hearing
   ☐ disabled people leaping
   ☐ voiceless people singing
   ☐ water flowing in the desert
   ☐ hot sands suddenly becoming cool

2. What do you like best about the "Holy Road"?

   ☐ no rude or rebellious drivers
   ☐ can't get lost on it
   ☐ no dangerous animals to stop you in your tracks

3. What one phrase speaks to you most? Why do you think that is? What does your choice tell you about what you want from God?

PRAY

Tell God about the images you most resonate with. Tell him why. Ask God for the restoration or healing that you or others need.

LIVE

Choose a color that symbolizes you as a fully restored or healed person. Why did you choose it? Pick up something of that color and be glad you're holding it.

THE ONLY GOD THERE IS

ISAIAH 37:9-11,14-20

9-11 Just then the Assyrian king received an intelligence report on King Tirhakah of Ethiopia: "He is on his way to make war on you."

On hearing that, he sent messengers to Hezekiah with instructions to deliver this message: "Don't let your GOD, on whom you so naively lean, deceive you, promising that Jerusalem won't fall to the king of Assyria. Use your head! Look around at what the kings of Assyria have done all over the world — one country after another devastated! And do you think you're going to get off? . . .

14 Hezekiah took the letter from the hands of the messengers and read it. Then he went into the sanctuary of GOD and spread the letter out before GOD.

15-20 Then Hezekiah prayed to GOD: "GOD-of-the-Angel-Armies, enthroned over the cherubim-angels, you are God, the only God there is, God of all kingdoms on earth. You *made* heaven and earth. Listen, O GOD, and hear. Look, O GOD, and see. Mark all these words of Sennacherib that he sent to mock the living God. It's quite true, O GOD, that the kings of Assyria have devastated all the nations and their lands. They've thrown their gods into the trash and burned them — no great achievement since they were no-gods anyway, gods made in workshops, carved from wood and chiseled from rock. An end to the no-gods! But now step in, O GOD, our God. Save us from him. Let all the kingdoms of earth know that you and you alone are GOD."

READ

Read this passage a few times slowly. Picture what's going on, and imagine what Hezekiah, the king of Judah, might be feeling in this situation.

THINK

Notice the Assyrian king's reaction to the news that he's about to be attacked by an enemy: He tries to puff himself up by scoffing at Judah. What might have motivated him to do this at this specific time? In contrast, how does Hezekiah react to the message his enemy sends him? What stands out to you about these different attitudes? How do they relate to you?

PRAY

Think about an area in which you hold responsibility, such as being a group leader at school or a manager at work — or having responsibility to uphold your end of a friendship. What are some recent problems that you are responsible to help resolve? In what ways are you dealing (or not dealing) with them? Have a conversation with God about what it's like for you to have responsibility in this area; share your heart and mind with him.

LIVE

Now read the passage again, keeping in mind the specific situation. Try to bring the problem to God the way Hezekiah did. For help, write a description of the dilemma on a piece of paper and then follow Hezekiah's example, spreading it out before God and asking for his help. Ask him to guide you in how to resolve it. Be aware that God is your leader, even as you are a leader to others.

YOU'RE MINE

ISAIAH 43:1-4

1-4 But now, GOD's Message,
>   the God who made you in the first place, Jacob,
>   the One who got you started, Israel:
"Don't be afraid, I've redeemed you.
>   I've called your name. You're mine.
When you're in over your head, I'll be there with you.
>   When you're in rough waters, you will not go down.
When you're between a rock and a hard place,
>   it won't be a dead end—
Because I am GOD, your personal God,
>   The Holy of Israel, your Savior.
I paid a huge price for you:
>   all of Egypt, with rich Cush and Seba thrown in!
That's how much you mean to me!
>   *That's* how much I love you!
I'd sell off the whole world to get you back,
>   trade the creation just for you."

READ

Read the passage aloud slowly, keeping in mind that God is the speaker.

THINK

Read the passage aloud again even more slowly, pausing between verses. Read it with the idea that God is saying these words directly to you.

1. Of God's words to you in this passage, what is your favorite?
2. Which phrase do you most need to hear from God?

Read the passage one more time. Rest in silence. Wait on God and hear him speaking directly to you.

PRAY

Respond to what God has said to you, perhaps with amazement or gratitude.

LIVE

Read the passage aloud one more time, and hear the echo of the words lingering in the air. Make up a song using a line from these verses. If you wish, use a tune you already know.

DEPENDABLE GODS?

ISAIAH 46:1-7

1-2   The god Bel falls down, god Nebo slumps.
       The no-god hunks of wood are loaded on mules
    And have to be hauled off,
       wearing out the poor mules —
    Dead weight, burdens who can't bear burdens,
       hauled off to captivity.

3-4   "Listen to me, family of Jacob,
       everyone that's left of the family of Israel.
    I've been carrying you on my back
       from the day you were born,
    And I'll keep on carrying you when you're old.
       I'll be there, bearing you when you're old and gray.
    I've done it and will keep on doing it,
       carrying you on my back, saving you.

5-7   "So to whom will you compare me, the Incomparable?
       Can you picture me without reducing me?
    People with a lot of money
       hire craftsmen to make them gods.
    The artisan delivers the god,
       and they kneel and worship it!
    They carry it around in holy parades,
       then take it home and put it on a shelf.
    And there it sits, day in and day out,
       a dependable god, always right where you put it.
    Say anything you want to it, it never talks back.
       Of course, it never *does* anything either!"

READ

Read the passage. Bel and Nebo were ancient false gods of the Israelites' neighbors. People would orient their lives around what they believed these gods were demanding or promising.

THINK

After you read how God addresses Israel's tendency to act like its neighbors — rather than trusting and obeying him — consider what gods might be in your culture and in your life. These don't have to be people or objects. They could be principles or beliefs that shape how we live, think, and feel every day. For example, "Having more money makes a person secure," or "If people just lost weight and worked out more, the opposite sex would be attracted to them."

Identify a god that tempts you personally. Are there aspects of the true God that you find difficult to accept (such as his holiness or the facts that he is invisible and sometimes silent)? In what ways do these "no-god hunks of wood" capitalize on those doubts and make themselves appear more appealing than God? What do they promise you? Now consider: What do they really bring you?

PRAY/LIVE

Read God's plea to Israel once more. Tell him what you see in yourself and in this god you've identified. Be real. Now hear him ask you, "To whom will you compare me, the Incomparable?" Don't answer immediately, but ponder the question. Ask him to help you stay committed to him and to working through the struggles you have with him. Watch today for when your "no-god hunks of wood" are the most appealing to you, for when you are most likely to "worship" them or believe their message.

DAY 133

GOD ENCOUNTERS

On this seventh day, review and reflect on all you have read this week. Take the time to revel in the ways you've encountered God in the past six days.

THE (UN)FORGETFUL GOD OF HEAVEN

ISAIAH 49:13-18

13   Heavens, raise the roof! Earth, wake the dead!
     Mountains, send up cheers!
GOD has comforted his people.
     He has tenderly nursed his beaten-up, beaten-down people.

14   But Zion said, "I don't get it. GOD has left me.
     My Master has forgotten I even exist."

15-18   "Can a mother forget the infant at her breast,
     walk away from the baby she bore?
But even if mothers forget,
     I'd never forget you — never.
Look, I've written your names on the backs of my hands.
     The walls you're rebuilding are never out of my sight.
Your builders are faster than your wreckers.
     The demolition crews are gone for good.
Look up, look around, look well!
     See them all gathering, coming to you?
As sure as I am the living God" — GOD's Decree —
     "you're going to put them on like so much jewelry,
     you're going to use them to dress up like a bride."

READ

Read the passage, underlining or mentally noting each time the word *forget* is present.

THINK

Can you think of a specific moment when you were forgotten — either intentionally or unintentionally? How did that make you feel? Why?

What times in your life do you most desire to be remembered? Be specific. How does it feel for you to know that there is a God who will never forget you under any circumstance?

PRAY

Pour out your heart in gratitude before God for the fact that he will "never forget you — never."

LIVE

"Look, I've written your names on the backs of my hands." Take a pen and make a small mark on the back of each of your hands. Every time you glance at one of the marks, remember God's character and rejoice in knowing that you are his child who will never be forgotten. If someone asks you about the marks, tell them about The God Who Remembers.

THE SUFFERING SERVANT

ISAIAH 53:2-5,11-12

2-5 The servant grew up before God — a scrawny seedling,
    a scrubby plant in a parched field.
There was nothing attractive about him,
    nothing to cause us to take a second look.
He was looked down on and passed over,
    a man who suffered, who knew pain firsthand.
One look at him and people turned away.
    We looked down on him, thought he was scum.
But the fact is, it was *our* pains he carried —
    our disfigurements, all the things wrong with *us*.
We thought he brought it on himself,
    that God was punishing him for his own failures.
But it was our sins that did that to him,
    that ripped and tore and crushed him — *our sins*!
He took the punishment, and that made us whole.
    Through his bruises we get healed.

. . . .

11-12 Out of that terrible travail of soul,
    he'll see that it's worth it and be glad he did it.
Through what he experienced, my righteous one, my servant,
    will make many "righteous ones,"
    as he himself carries the burden of their sins.
Therefore I'll reward him extravagantly —
    the best of everything, the highest honors —
Because he looked death in the face and didn't flinch,
    because he embraced the company of the lowest.
He took on his own shoulders the sin of the many,
    he took up the cause of all the black sheep.

READ

Read the passage aloud slowly, knowing that this "suffering servant" passage is a prophecy about Jesus. If possible, read the expanded passage as well.

THINK

Read the passage again. This time, consider who is speaking.

1. *We, our,* and *us* (verses 2-5) indicate that the speaker is Israel as a nation or a prophet of Israel (Isaiah). In this section, what words, phrases, or ideas are most personal for you?
2. *I* and *my* (verses 11-12) indicate God is the speaker. In this section, what most touches you about God's words about Jesus?
3. How will Jesus "make many 'righteous ones'" "through what he experienced"?

   ☐ his sacrifice of his life?
   ☐ his actions inspiring others?
   ☐ his person calling you?
   ☐ his praying for you? (see Romans 8:34)
   ☐ other:

PRAY

Respond to God about the words that touched you most. Talk also to God about how Jesus can make you righteous.

LIVE

Move through your day with this idea: Jesus "died without a thought for his own welfare." If he died that way, how much more must he have lived that way? Try living that selflessly a few minutes at a time.

MY LOVE WON'T WALK AWAY

ISAIAH 54:4-10

4-6 "Don't be afraid — you're not going to be embarrassed.
　　Don't hold back — you're not going to come up short.
You'll forget all about the humiliations of your youth,
　　and the indignities of being a widow will fade from memory.
For your Maker is your bridegroom,
　　his name, GOD-of-the-Angel-Armies!
Your Redeemer is The Holy of Israel,
　　known as God of the whole earth.
You were like an abandoned wife, devastated with grief,
　　and GOD welcomed you back,
Like a woman married young
　　and then left," says your God.

7-8　　Your Redeemer GOD says:

"I left you, but only for a moment.
　　Now, with enormous compassion, I'm bringing you back.
In an outburst of anger I turned my back on you —
　　but only for a moment.
It's with lasting love
　　that I'm tenderly caring for you.

9-10 "This exile is just like the days of Noah for me:
　　I promised then that the waters of Noah
　　would never again flood the earth.
I'm promising now no more anger,
　　no more dressing you down.
For even if the mountains walk away
　　and the hills fall to pieces,
My love won't walk away from you,
　　my covenant commitment of peace won't fall apart."
　　The GOD who has compassion on you says so.

READ

Read this passage picturing God speaking to Israel after yet another problem in their relationship.

THINK/PRAY

When you hear God saying that he turned his back in anger only for a moment but was not giving up on the relationship, what is your reaction? When you try to picture a commitment that won't fall apart, what does this evoke in you? Share your response with God. Maybe you've never experienced a relationship like that, so you don't know what it would look like. Maybe you've had similar promises made to you but were betrayed. If this reminds you of someone in your life (past or present), talk with God about what you might be incorrectly assuming to be true of God based on your experience with that person. Recognize that God knows your past, and he knows the baggage you bring into your relationship with him. Trust that he is "tenderly caring for you" and will help you deal with that baggage.

LIVE

Make a note of the themes that emerged during your prayer time. Ask God to help you grow in trust that he is completely committed to you as one whose "love won't walk away" and one who "has compassion on you." Spend a few minutes sitting quietly in his presence, enjoying the tranquillity of that space before you move on to the rest of your day.

OUR WRONGDOING

ISAIAH 59:9-15

9-11 Which means that we're a far cry from fair dealing,
 and we're not even close to right living.
We long for light but sink into darkness,
 long for brightness but stumble through the night.
Like the blind, we inch along a wall,
 groping eyeless in the dark.
We shuffle our way in broad daylight,
 like the dead, but somehow walking.
We're no better off than bears, groaning,
 and no worse off than doves, moaning.
We look for justice — not a sign of it;
 for salvation — not so much as a hint.

12-15 Our wrongdoings pile up before you, God,
 our sins stand up and accuse us.
Our wrongdoings stare us down;
 we know in detail what we've done:
Mocking and denying GOD,
 not following our God,
Spreading false rumors, inciting sedition,
 pregnant with lies, muttering malice.
Justice is beaten back,
 Righteousness is banished to the sidelines,
Truth staggers down the street,
 Honesty is nowhere to be found,
Good is missing in action.
 Anyone renouncing evil is beaten and robbed.

READ

Read the passage aloud. Reflect the nature of the words by your tone and inflection. (That is, if these were your words, how might you sound if you said them?)

THINK

The subject of this passage may seem like a depressing one to explore. But so is our sin. We often attempt to live our lives with God while forgetting to acknowledge our wrongdoings before him. Yet confession of wrongdoing is a normal and expected part of life for followers of God. We regularly fall short of God's desires for us, and he wants to hear us acknowledge this and depend on him in every area of our lives.

Read the passage again aloud, but make it more personal. When you come to the word *we,* replace it with *I,* and when you come to the word *our,* replace it with *my.* What might God be thinking as he hears you read this?

PRAY

Now, make a list of sins — big and small — that you've committed in the past seven days. Perhaps include things you felt you were supposed to do but did not. In prayer, go through your list and, with each item, admit to God that you should not have participated in such wrongdoing. Do this with a humble and repentant heart.

LIVE

As you walk to class or drive to work or whenever you are between tasks, confess your sins to God. As you do this, be as specific as you can about your sins, acknowledging your desperation and futility in attempting to live apart from him.

RESCUE AND RELEASE

ISAIAH 61:1-3,10-11

1-3   The Spirit of GOD, the Master, is on me
        because GOD anointed me.
He sent me to preach good news to the poor,
        heal the heartbroken,
Announce freedom to all captives,
        pardon all prisoners.
GOD sent me to announce the year of his grace —
        a celebration of God's destruction of our enemies —
        and to comfort all who mourn,
To care for the needs of all who mourn in Zion,
        give them bouquets of roses instead of ashes,
Messages of joy instead of news of doom,
        a praising heart instead of a languid spirit.
Rename them "Oaks of Righteousness"
        planted by GOD to display his glory.

    . . . .

10-11   I will sing for joy in GOD,
        explode in praise from deep in my soul!
He dressed me up in a suit of salvation,
        he outfitted me in a robe of righteousness,
As a bridegroom who puts on a tuxedo
        and a bride a jeweled tiara.
For as the earth bursts with spring wildflowers,
        and as a garden cascades with blossoms,
So the Master, GOD, brings righteousness into full bloom
        and puts praise on display before the nations.

READ

Read the passage aloud slowly.

THINK

Read verses 1-3 aloud slowly.

1. What roles of deliverance, rescue, and release do you most admire in God (which Jesus also claimed)?
2. Consider what words or phrases in verses 1-3 stand out to you. What do they tell you about the work God is calling you to do alongside him?

Read verses 10-11 aloud slowly, keeping in mind that those who rescue and release others this way find great joy in it. When they work alongside God, they do not burn out.

3. Consider what words or phrases in verses 10-11 stand out to you. What "joy in GOD" are you being called to, especially as it comes through serving under God, partnering with him in what he is doing on this earth?

PRAY

Ask God for guidance in how you serve. You might pray about the avenues of service you are choosing. Or pray about serving with great "joy in GOD" instead of serving with joy in results or feelings of success.

LIVE

As you serve someone today, be present to the reality that you are doing this with God's hand, under his power. This is his work and you get to be a part of it!

JESUS COMES TO YOU

ISAIAH 62:2-5

2-5   Foreign countries will see your righteousness,
       and world leaders your glory.
You'll get a brand-new name
       straight from the mouth of GOD.
You'll be a stunning crown in the palm of GOD's hand,
       a jeweled gold cup held high in the hand of your God.
No more will anyone call you Rejected,
       and your country will no more be called Ruined.
You'll be called Hephzibah (My Delight),
       and your land Beulah (Married),
Because GOD delights in you
       and your land will be like a wedding celebration.
For as a young man marries his virgin bride,
       so your builder marries you,
And as a bridegroom is happy in his bride,
       so your God is happy with you.

READ

Read the passage aloud slowly.

THINK

Read the passage again. This time reverse all the *you* pronouns to *I* and *me* pronouns. For example, change

- "you'll get a brand-new name" to "I'll get a brand-new name"
- "Because GOD delights in you" to "Because GOD delights in me"
- "so your God is happy with you" to "so my God is happy with me.

Have fun reading it this way a few times.

1. If you were to ask God for a new name, what would it be?
2. Set aside the idea that these verses are fantasy, and ponder the idea that they describe reality — a reality of our universe that most people don't understand.

PRAY

Tell God how it makes you feel to know that he delights in you and is happy with you. Tell God what you would like your new name to be. Wait in this moment and see if other names come to you.

LIVE

Rest for a few minutes in the truth that God delights in you. If you wish, imagine situations in which you feel anything but special (for example, when you are hard on yourself, when someone puts you down, or when you get back a test, paper, or work review that isn't so great). See yourself responding to the situation by saying, "Yes, this is true, but God delights in me."

DAY 140

GOD ENCOUNTERS

On this seventh day, review and reflect on all you have read this week. Take the time to revel in the ways you've encountered God in the past six days.

ANTICIPATING THE WORKINGS OF GOD

ISAIAH 65:17-22

17-22 "Pay close attention now:
　　I'm creating new heavens and a new earth.
All the earlier troubles, chaos, and pain
　　are things of the past, to be forgotten.
Look ahead with joy.
　　Anticipate what I'm creating:
I'll create Jerusalem as sheer joy,
　　create my people as pure delight.
I'll take joy in Jerusalem,
　　take delight in my people:
No more sounds of weeping in the city,
　　no cries of anguish;
No more babies dying in the cradle,
　　or old people who don't enjoy a full lifetime;
One-hundredth birthdays will be considered normal—
　　anything less will seem like a cheat.
They'll build houses
　　and move in.
They'll plant fields
　　and eat what they grow.
No more building a house
　　that some outsider takes over,
No more planting fields
　　that some enemy confiscates,
For my people will be as long-lived as trees,
　　my chosen ones will have satisfaction in their work."

READ

Read the passage.

THINK

In this passage God speaks with great joy, and the people feel great excitement. Here we find, in the midst of judgment and sorrow, the promise of a bright future for those who love and trust the Lord. God makes statements about the future peace that will be among his people. He is sending out the old and bringing in the new. For followers of God, there is intense anticipation.

Think about your own future. What are those things, general and specific, that you believe God will use to bring hope into your life? Joy? Peace? How does God promise this will happen? How does the promise of hope and joy and peace influence the way you live?

PRAY

Pick some specific elements of how God will bring hope and joy and peace into your life. Share the details with him, including your excitement and anticipation.

LIVE

Live with the deep assurance of God's desire for you to possess hope and joy and peace today.

GOD'S KNOWLEDGE OF US

JEREMIAH 1:5

5   "Before I shaped you in the womb,
       I knew all about you.
Before you saw the light of day,
       I had holy plans for you:
A prophet to the nations —
       that's what I had in mind for you."

READ

Write out Jeremiah 1:5 on an index card. Meditate on this verse.

THINK

God told Jeremiah that he had plans for Jeremiah's life before Jeremiah was even given his name. What a claim from God! Can you believe that God had plans for your life and knew everything about you before you were even conceived? Why or why not?

What emotions bubble to the surface when you consider that God knows you intimately? Are you excited? Comforted? Scared? Anxious? Indifferent? Why?

If God already knows everything about us, why does he desire that we pray to him?

PRAY

Meditate on this thought: The Creator of the universe, the living God, knows every possible thing about you. As you do so, tell God what you are feeling and why.

LIVE

Take the index card and put it where you will see it often (for example, on your bedside table, taped to the mirror in the bathroom, taped to the dashboard of your car, or in your purse or wallet). Whenever you look at it, read it and be reminded that God marked out a plan for your life long before you were born.

A TIME TO GRIEVE

JEREMIAH 8:18-21; 9:1-3

18-21   I drown in grief.
  I'm heartsick.
Oh, listen! Please listen! It's the cry of my dear people
  reverberating through the country.
Is GOD no longer in Zion?
  Has the King gone away?
Can you tell me why they flaunt their plaything-gods,
  their silly, imported no-gods before me?
The crops are in, the summer is over,
  but for us nothing's changed.
  We're still waiting to be rescued.
For my dear broken people, I'm heartbroken.
  I weep, seized by grief.

   .   .   .   .

1-2   I wish my head were a well of water
  and my eyes fountains of tears
So I could weep day and night
  for casualties among my dear, dear people.
At times I wish I had a wilderness hut,
  a backwoods cabin,
Where I could get away from my people
  and never see them again.
They're a faithless, feckless bunch,
  a congregation of degenerates.

3   "Their tongues shoot out lies
  like a bow shoots arrows—
A mighty army of liars,
  the sworn enemies of truth.
They advance from one evil to the next,
  ignorant of me."

READ

Read the passage aloud slowly. Most of it describes Jeremiah's grieving over the way Judah ignores God. In 9:3, God interrupts and agrees.

THINK

What makes God grieve that also makes you grieve? What breaks your heart that breaks the heart of God? Perhaps it resembles the following: the wickedness of people (such as genocide or sex trafficking in the world), the lack of desire — even among professed believers — to know God, the diseases that terrorize people's bodies.

Read the passage aloud again, reflecting on the tragic circumstance that breaks your heart and also breaks the heart of God. What words or phrases in the passage best express your grief? What does it feel like to grieve over the things that grieve God? How do you respond to the idea that God often weeps throughout the prophetic portion of the Bible and that we need to honor that grief and join him?

PRAY

Grieve with God in prayer as a prophet (like Jeremiah), using the phrases in the passage that stood out to you. Don't feel that you have to tidy up your prayer with a positive ending, although "God, help!" would be appropriate.

LIVE

Read the newspaper, listening to the news for the evil and suffering in the world that God surely grieves over. Notice how different such listening is from detached curiosity. Hear about these events with the listening ears of God.

ROTTEN AS OLD SHORTS

JEREMIAH 13:1-11

1-2   God told me, "Go and buy yourself some linen shorts. Put them on and keep them on. Don't even take them off to wash them." So I bought the shorts as God directed and put them on.

3-5   Then God told me, "Take the shorts that you bought and go straight to Perath and hide them there in a crack in the rock." So I did what God told me and hid them at Perath.

6-7   Next, after quite a long time, God told me, "Go back to Perath and get the linen shorts I told you to hide there." So I went back to Perath and dug them out of the place where I had hidden them. The shorts by then had rotted and were worthless.

8-11   God explained, "This is the way I am going to ruin the pride of Judah and the great pride of Jerusalem — a wicked bunch of people who won't obey me, who do only what they want to do, who chase after all kinds of no-gods and worship them. They're going to turn out as rotten as these old shorts. Just as shorts clothe and protect, so I kept the whole family of Israel under my care" — God's Decree — "so that everyone could see they were my people, a people I could show off to the world and be proud of. But they refused to do a thing I said."

READ

As you read the passage, imaginatively put yourself in Jeremiah's place.

THINK

In your mind's eye, look down and see the linen shorts you've been wearing for days or weeks. Set out on the journey to Perath. Discover the crack in the rock. Envision the long time that passes — what you do in the meantime, any particular events, the seasons that pass.

Now return to the rock and feel your own sweat as you dig out the shorts again. How do you first detect them? By touch? Smell? Sight? As you unearth them, what thoughts go through your head? What is the smell like? What do they look like?

Next think about God's metaphor. Listen to his explanation of the Israelites' rotted hearts illustrated by these decaying shorts. As you hear God's words, what are you thinking? What are you feeling?

PRAY

Set the text aside and explore your own heart honestly with God. When you think of God the Father rebuking you for something, what is your internal reaction? Do you perceive it as a positive thing, done in love? Or does his rebuke seem to say he is against you, doesn't care for you, or wants you to fix yourself? Talk this over with him.

LIVE

Read the passage again, listening for what God might be saying to you through Jeremiah. In what way is your Father challenging you? Make note of any action you feel he is leading you to.

TELLING GOD WHAT WE REALLY THINK

JEREMIAH 20:7-10

7-10 You pushed me into this, GOD, and I let you do it.
　　You were too much for me.
And now I'm a public joke.
　　They all poke fun at me.
Every time I open my mouth
　　I'm shouting, "Murder!" or "Rape!"
And all I get for my GOD-warnings
　　are insults and contempt.
But if I say, "Forget it!
　　No more GOD-Messages from me!"
The words are fire in my belly,
　　a burning in my bones.
I'm worn out trying to hold it in.
　　I can't do it any longer!
Then I hear whispering behind my back:
　　"There goes old 'Danger-Everywhere.' Shut him up! Report him!"
Old friends watch, hoping I'll fall flat on my face:
　　"One misstep and we'll have him. We'll get rid of him for good!"

READ

Read the passage twice very slowly.

THINK

Jeremiah was called by God to be a mouthpiece to the nation of Israel, but they rejected his message, scorning and mocking him. They even made death threats against him. And in this passage we read Jeremiah's complaint. He is not shy about telling God exactly what he feels. In fact, he has some choice words for the Creator concerning his situation.

Is it easy or hard for you to tell God exactly what you're thinking? Why? Do you think it's hard for God to hear our prayers when we are completely and blatantly honest with him?

LIVE

Write a letter to God, telling him what you think about him and how he is operating in the world. Include the good, the bad, and the ugly. Be thoughtful and honest and even raw if you need to be.

PRAY

After you finish writing the letter, find a room where you can shut the door and be alone. Read the letter aloud to God, speaking confidently because you know he hears your prayers.

CONSEQUENCES THAT BURN

JEREMIAH 28:10-17

10-11 At that, Hananiah grabbed the yoke from Jeremiah's shoulders and smashed it. And then he addressed the people: "This is GOD's Message: In just this way I will smash the yoke of the king of Babylon and get him off the neck of all the nations — and within two years."

Jeremiah walked out.

12-14 Later, sometime after Hananiah had smashed the yoke from off his shoulders, Jeremiah received this Message from GOD: "Go back to Hananiah and tell him, 'This is GOD's Message: You smashed the wooden yoke-bars; now you've got iron yoke-bars. This is a Message from GOD-of-the-Angel-Armies, Israel's own God: I've put an iron yoke on all these nations. They're harnessed to Nebuchadnezzar king of Babylon. They'll do just what he tells them. Why, I'm even putting him in charge of the wild animals.'"

15-16 So prophet Jeremiah told prophet Hananiah, "Hold it, Hananiah! GOD never sent you. You've talked the whole country into believing a pack of lies! And so GOD says, 'You claim to be sent? I'll send you all right — right off the face of the earth! Before the year is out, you'll be dead because you fomented sedition against GOD.'"

17 Prophet Hananiah died that very year, in the seventh month.

READ

Read the passage twice. (For more background, include the expanded passage.)

THINK

What does God seem to be addressing in Hananiah's underlying message or motive? Summarize in a sentence what you notice. What do you think about how God dealt with him? What do you, having read this story, feel toward God?

PRAY/LIVE

Take several minutes to think through your current situation. Where is God allowing you to feel the ache and consequence for something you've recently done (or not done)? Bring this openly before God and tell him how you feel about it. Ask him to help you see your heart clearly, to understand what drew you toward that action (or nonaction).

If you haven't let go of what you're doing wrong — despite the burning consequences — think about what rejecting this path might look like for you. What really keeps you from turning around? God is inviting you to live in a certain way in this area of your life. What are some small steps you could take toward receiving that invitation?

Take them.

DAY 147

GOD ENCOUNTERS

On this seventh day, review and reflect on all you have read this week. Take the time to revel in the ways you've encountered God in the past six days.

I WILL ANSWER YOU

JEREMIAH 33:2-3

2-3 "This is God's Message, the God who made earth, made it livable and lasting, known everywhere as God: 'Call to me and I will answer you. I'll tell you marvelous and wondrous things that you could never figure out on your own.'"

READ

Find a quiet place and read this passage slowly. Pause in the silence. Let these words wash over you. Make them personal. Claim them as God speaking specifically to you.

THINK

What sticks out to you? What word or phrase settles deeply in your soul? Why?

Deep down, do you really believe that God will answer you when you call to him? Why or why not? What does this passage say about his character?

As you hear God's personal message, spoken straight from his being, what do you feel? What words from this passage can you make your own?

PRAY

Ask God what he wants you to do with the word or phrase he has given you. Ask him how you can best live out this gift that the Holy Spirit has placed before you. Listen patiently in the silence for the response. You may be tempted to move on to some other thought or task, but resist, simply resting in the silence yet listening actively.

LIVE

Go and live out the answer of what the Holy Spirit instructed you to do today.

BAD THINGS HAPPEN TO VERY GOOD PEOPLE

JEREMIAH 38:1-6

1 Shaphatiah son of Mattan, Gedaliah son of Pashur, Jehucal son of Shelemiah, and Pashur son of Malkijah heard what Jeremiah was telling the people, namely:

2 "This is GOD's Message: 'Whoever stays in this town will die — will be killed or starve to death or get sick and die. But those who go over to the Babylonians will save their necks and live.'

3 "And, GOD's sure Word: 'This city is destined to fall to the army of the king of Babylon. He's going to take it over.'"

4 These officials told the king, "Please, kill this man. He's got to go! He's ruining the resolve of the soldiers who are still left in the city, as well as the people themselves, by spreading these words. This man isn't looking after the good of this people. He's trying to ruin us!"

5 King Zedekiah caved in: "If you say so. Go ahead, handle it your way. You're too much for me."

6 So they took Jeremiah and threw him into the cistern of Malkijah the king's son that was in the courtyard of the palace guard. They lowered him down with ropes. There wasn't any water in the cistern, only mud. Jeremiah sank into the mud.

READ

Read the passage aloud slowly.

THINK

Even though Jeremiah was a faithful servant of God, circumstances weren't turning out well for him. Read the passage again and experience for yourself the feelings Jeremiah probably had. Feel yourself sinking in the mud.

1. How difficult is it for you to accept that bad things happen to people who love God and do good?
2. Pretend once again that you are Jeremiah sinking in the mud. All you have now is the companionship of God. How does that feel? How close is that to being enough for you? What do you (as Jeremiah) want to pray?
3. What does it mean to hope in God's own being instead of simply hoping God will rescue you?

PRAY

Talk to God about a situation in which you've been left behind in the mud. (This may be happening now or in the past, or it may be something you foresee happening in the future.)

LIVE

Sit with your palms open and turned upward toward God. Rest in the idea that some days we have the companionship of God when it appears we have nothing else. Is that enough?

Be on the lookout for people sinking in the mud whom you might be called to love and help.

GOD'S DEEP COMMITMENT

JEREMIAH 51:1-5

1-5   There's more. GOD says more:

"Watch this:
    I'm whipping up
A death-dealing hurricane against Babylon — 'Hurricane Persia' —
    against all who live in that perverse land.
I'm sending a cleanup crew into Babylon.
    They'll clean the place out from top to bottom.
When they get through there'll be nothing left of her
    worth taking or talking about.
They won't miss a thing.
    A total and final Doomsday!
Fighters will fight with everything they've got.
    It's no-holds-barred.
They will spare nothing and no one.
    It's final and wholesale destruction — the end!
Babylon littered with the wounded,
    streets piled with corpses.
It turns out that Israel and Judah
    are not widowed after all.
As their God, GOD-of-the-Angel-Armies, I am still alive and well,
    committed to them even though
They filled their land with sin
    against Israel's most Holy God."

READ

Read the passage, including the expanded passage, if possible.

THINK

Sense for yourself God's vigor and aggression in going after his enemy Babylon. Take a few minutes to imagine the images God uses to describe how he will treat them. What is your reaction?

Now focus your attention on God's final statement, regarding his commitment to Israel. What does this tell you about God's motives for the destruction he's planning for Babylon? Think about his regard for Israel: What does he feel toward them? What does he feel about their sin?

PRAY

Look back on what you noticed about God — both his aggression and his commitment. Is there a phrase from the passage that stands out to you? As you think about this phrase and repeat it to yourself a few times, meditate on this picture of who God is. If in doing so you feel drawn into dialogue with him, go ahead and enter in.

LIVE

Hold in your mind God's qualities of aggression and commitment, then consider your own life. Maybe you'll think about your relationships, your attitude at work or school, your hobbies, or what you enjoy doing on the weekends. What is God saying about an area of your life right now?

WHEN DISAPPOINTMENT COMES

LAMENTATIONS 3:19-30

19-21   I'll never forget the trouble, the utter lostness,
     the taste of ashes, the poison I've swallowed.
I remember it all — oh, how well I remember —
     the feeling of hitting the bottom.
But there's one other thing I remember,
     and remembering, I keep a grip on hope:

22-24   GOD's loyal love couldn't have run out,
     his merciful love couldn't have dried up.
They're created new every morning.
     How great your faithfulness!
I'm sticking with GOD (I say it over and over).
     He's all I've got left.

25-27   GOD proves to be good to the man who passionately waits,
     to the woman who diligently seeks.
It's a good thing to quietly hope,
     quietly hope for help from GOD.
It's a good thing when you're young
     to stick it out through the hard times.

28-30   When life is heavy and hard to take,
     go off by yourself. Enter the silence.
Bow in prayer. Don't ask questions:
     Wait for hope to appear.
Don't run from trouble. Take it full-face.
     The "worst" is never the worst.

THINK

Lamentations is one of the saddest books in the Bible, but just because it's chock-full of disappointment doesn't mean it's absent of hope. Jeremiah, writing this book as he mourns the utter destruction of the famous and once-splendid city of Jerusalem, speaks of pain and sadness and disappointment. But he also reflects on the undying goodness and faithfulness of God.

READ

Read the passage carefully. As you do so, note Jeremiah's complete honesty before God. Also note the change in Jeremiah's attitude toward the end of the chapter from extreme disappointment to an embrace of hope because of God's faithfulness.

PRAY

Take a few minutes to consider the disappointments you have experienced or are experiencing. Then follow the guidance of Jeremiah's words, starting with "When life is heavy and hard to take." Just as he advises, "wait for hope to appear."

LIVE

Don't ever forget that despite disappointment and pain, God always remains faithful.

IN THE PIT

LAMENTATIONS 3:52-58

52-54 "Enemies with no reason to be enemies
hunted me down like a bird.
They threw me into a pit,
then pelted me with stones.
Then the rains came and filled the pit.
The water rose over my head. I said, 'It's all over.'

55-57 "I called out your name, O GOD,
called from the bottom of the pit.
You listened when I called out, 'Don't shut your ears!
Get me out of here! Save me!'
You came close when I called out.
You said, 'It's going to be all right.'

58 "You took my side, Master;
you brought me back alive!"

READ

Read the passage aloud slowly. Jeremiah had been thrown into a cistern, where he sank in the mud (see Jeremiah 38:1-6). Here he may be telling us what he thought while he was down there.

THINK

Read verses 52-54 again and pause. Sit in that despair. Read verses 55-58. Grin with joy.

1. What words or phrases in each section resonate for you?
2. In what ways do you call out to God — or not? Do you numb out or shut yourself up instead? Why?
3. Have you ever sensed the closeness of God? If so, how? If not, what do you think it would be like?

PRAY

Talk to God about the times he has come close when you have called out. Or if this hasn't happened, talk with God about what you think it would be like.

LIVE

Be open to the closeness of God coming to you now — even if you're not in a pit. Store that closeness for the times when you'll need it.

REMEMBER, GOD, ALL WE'VE BEEN THROUGH

LAMENTATIONS 5:1-12,17

1-12,17   "Remember, GOD, all we've been through.
   Study our plight, the black mark we've made in history.
Our precious land has been given to outsiders,
   our homes to strangers.
Orphans we are, not a father in sight,
   and our mothers no better than widows.
We have to pay to drink our own water.
   Even our firewood comes at a price.
We're nothing but slaves, bullied and bowed,
   worn out and without any rest.
We sold ourselves to Assyria and Egypt
   just to get something to eat.
Our parents sinned and are no more,
   and now we're paying for the wrongs they did.
Slaves rule over us;
   there's no escape from their grip.
We risk our lives to gather food
   in the bandit-infested desert.
Our skin has turned black as an oven,
   dried out like old leather from the famine.
Our wives were raped in the streets in Zion,
   and our virgins in the cities of Judah.
They hanged our princes by their hands,
   dishonored our elders.

. . . .

Because of all this we're heartsick;
   we can't see through the tears."

READ

Read the passage twice, keeping in mind other stories you've read about the Israelites' unreliable commitment to God and the times they walked away from him.

THINK

When you hold side by side this expression of Israel's humility with stories of their pride and hardheartedness, what is your response to their prayer in this passage? If you were God, how would you respond to them? Jot down some words that summarize your reaction.

PRAY

Read and absorb the following words spoken by Jesus many years later to the same people, when he came to give his life for them: "Jerusalem, Jerusalem, killer of prophets, abuser of the messengers of God! How often I've longed to gather your children, gather your children like a hen, her brood safe under her wings — but you refused and turned away!" (Luke 13:34). Set this book aside and sit with your eyes closed. Meditate on Jesus' words.

When you see this openhearted love that God continued to have for his people, despite their turning away, what do you feel? Ponder the reality that this is the God who rules the universe.

LIVE

What are the differences between your response to Israel and God's response? In what ways might your responses to yourself or others cloud your perception of how God responds? Ask him to help you learn to distinguish your reaction from his, so that you might know more clearly what he's like.

DAY 154

GOD ENCOUNTERS

On this seventh day, review and reflect on all you have read this week. Take the time to revel in the ways you've encountered God in the past six days.

A MOUTHFUL

EZEKIEL 3:1-11

1   He told me, "Son of man, eat what you see. Eat this book. Then go and speak to the family of Israel."

2-3   As I opened my mouth, he gave me the scroll to eat, saying, "Son of man, eat this book that I am giving you. Make a full meal of it!"

   So I ate it. It tasted so good — just like honey.

4-6   Then he told me, "Son of man, go to the family of Israel and speak my Message. Look, I'm not sending you to a people who speak a hard-to-learn language with words you can hardly pronounce. If I had sent you to such people, their ears would have perked up and they would have listened immediately.

7-9   "But it won't work that way with the family of Israel. They won't listen to you because they won't listen to me. They are, as I said, a hard case, hardened in their sin. But I'll make you as hard in your way as they are in theirs. I'll make your face as hard as rock, harder than granite. Don't let them intimidate you. Don't be afraid of them, even though they're a bunch of rebels."

10-11   Then he said, "Son of man, get all these words that I'm giving you inside you. Listen to them obediently. Make them your own. And now go. Go to the exiles, your people, and speak. Tell them, 'This is the Message of God, the Master.' Speak your piece, whether they listen or not."

READ

Read the passage. Try to read as though you are far from God, have no understanding of who Jesus is, and have never read a Bible before.

THINK

In this book, God has many unique lessons to communicate to Ezekiel, which he desires Ezekiel to pass on to others. He gives him visions of spinning wheels, he has Ezekiel lie on his side for several days, he has him shave his beard and divide the hair into three parts — all in order to communicate an important message to others.

One of God's unique lessons has Ezekiel eating the sacred scroll of the Scriptures — literally eating the word-filled pages. And we read that Ezekiel says the Scriptures taste good, like honey.

Read the passage again, meditating particularly on the final portion that starts with "Get all these words . . . inside you." Metaphorically speaking, what is the taste of God's word in your mouth?

PRAY/LIVE

What are two or three elements of Scripture that you are having a hard time digesting right now? Why? Tell God about it. Ask God to guide you in making the words your very own.

If you have honey, place a drop on your finger. Taste the honey slowly and attentively. Savor the sweetness in your mouth. As you do this, pray that God will give you such a desire for Scripture that it will taste like honey on your lips.

LEARN FROM THE WORST

EZEKIEL 18:14-17

14-17 "Now look: Suppose that this child has a child who sees all the sins done by his parent. The child sees them, but doesn't follow in the parent's footsteps —

> doesn't eat at the pagan shrines,
> doesn't worship the popular idols of Israel,
> doesn't seduce his neighbor's spouse,
> doesn't bully anyone,
> doesn't refuse to loan money,
> doesn't steal,
> doesn't refuse food to the hungry,
> doesn't refuse to give clothes to the ill-clad,
> doesn't live by impulse and greed,
> doesn't exploit the poor.

He does what I say;
> he performs my laws and lives by my statutes.

"This person will not die for the sins of the parent; he will live truly and well."

READ

Read the passage aloud slowly.

THINK

Read the passage aloud again, noting all the things the child learned from the negative example of the parent.

1. What words or phases or ideas particularly speak to you?
2. When have you learned important truths from watching someone else's negative example and then chosen to do otherwise?
3. Consider whether there is someone in your life now whose negative example can teach you something. (This could be someone you are close to and love deeply.)

PRAY

Ask God for wisdom to learn from the negative examples of people around you. Also ask God to help you avoid feeling morally superior to them — but instead be grateful for what you can learn. Pray for that person who is or was a negative example.

LIVE

Look at yourself in a mirror. See yourself as wholly different from the person who is a negative example — particularly if this person is a parent. Thank God that being wholly different is possible through him.

THE SHEPHERD AND ME

EZEKIEL 34:10-16

10 "'Watch out! I'm coming down on the shepherds and taking my sheep back. They're fired as shepherds of my sheep. No more shepherds who just feed themselves! I'll rescue my sheep from their greed. They're not going to feed off my sheep any longer!

11-16 "'God, the Master, says: From now on, *I myself* am the shepherd. I'm going looking for them. As shepherds go after their flocks when they get scattered, I'm going after my sheep. I'll rescue them from all the places they've been scattered to in the storms. I'll bring them back from foreign peoples, gather them from foreign countries, and bring them back to their home country. I'll feed them on the mountains of Israel, along the streams, among their own people. I'll lead them into lush pasture so they can roam the mountain pastures of Israel, graze at leisure, feed in the rich pastures on the mountains of Israel. And I myself will be the shepherd of my sheep. I myself will make sure they get plenty of rest. I'll go after the lost, I'll collect the strays, I'll doctor the injured, I'll build up the weak ones and oversee the strong ones so they're not exploited.'"

READ

Get a clean sheet of paper and something to draw with. Read the passage slowly, imagining the scene.

THINK

Read the passage again. As you do, let the images take vivid shape in your mind. You might read it a few times to get really familiar with the relationships, the experiences, the settings. In your mind, picture the pastures for grazing, the weak sheep and the strong, the way the shepherd interacts with them. Pick one thing that stands out to you and think about what it would look like or smell like or sound like and what it makes you feel.

PRAY

Consider whatever stood out to you and take several minutes to sketch whatever comes to mind. Avoid hurrying yourself or thinking that you can't draw. Just go with it. You might sketch many different things, or you might focus on one thing. As you draw, be aware of God's presence there with you. Don't force yourself to talk or think about anything in particular. Simply enjoy drawing with God.

LIVE

Think about approaching God as your Shepherd. What do you want to bring to him today? Are you injured or struggling? Are you feeling strong? Are you needing rest? Bring him your need and tell him about it. Receive the comfort he gives.

NOT A SCORCH MARK

DANIEL 3:19-27

19-23 Nebuchadnezzar, his face purple with anger, cut off Shadrach, Meshach, and Abednego. He ordered the furnace fired up seven times hotter than usual. He ordered some strong men from the army to tie them up, hands and feet, and throw them into the roaring furnace. Shadrach, Meshach, and Abednego, bound hand and foot, fully dressed from head to toe, were pitched into the roaring fire. Because the king was in such a hurry and the furnace was so hot, flames from the furnace killed the men who carried Shadrach, Meshach, and Abednego to it, while the fire raged around Shadrach, Meshach, and Abednego.

24 Suddenly King Nebuchadnezzar jumped up in alarm and said, "Didn't we throw three men, bound hand and foot, into the fire?"

"That's right, O king," they said.

25 "But look!" he said. "I see four men, walking around freely in the fire, completely unharmed! And the fourth man looks like a son of the gods!"

26 Nebuchadnezzar went to the door of the roaring furnace and called in, "Shadrach, Meshach, and Abednego, servants of the High God, come out here!"

Shadrach, Meshach, and Abednego walked out of the fire.

27 All the important people, the government leaders and king's counselors, gathered around to examine them and discovered that the fire hadn't so much as touched the three men — not a hair singed, not a scorch mark on their clothes, not even the smell of fire on them!

READ

Read the passage aloud slowly.

THINK

Read the passage aloud again, but this time read the dialogue as theatrically as possible. Catch the incredulous tones of the king in verses 24-25. And in verse 26, call out loudly as the king did.

Now read the passage silently and let yourself become someone in the passage: a bystander watching it all, the king, one of the three men, or even the mysterious fourth man. Imagine the thoughts and feelings of the person whose role you have assumed. If you had been this person, how would this experience have affected your relationship with God?

PRAY

Respond to God from what has come to you in this passage — particularly about trusting in him.

LIVE

Sit quietly before God with the palms of your hands open and turned upward. Receive from God. Be particularly open to receiving guidance, just as Shadrach, Meshach, and Abednego received from God. Receive the courage he gave them. Receive the power he gave them.

WHEN DOING THE RIGHT THING IS AGAINST THE LAW

DANIEL 6:6-10

6-7   The vice-regents and governors conspired together and then went to the king and said, "King Darius, live forever! We've convened your vice-regents, governors, and all your leading officials, and have agreed that the king should issue the following decree:

> For the next thirty days no one is to pray to any god or mortal except you, O king. Anyone who disobeys will be thrown into the lions' den.

8   "Issue this decree, O king, and make it unconditional, as if written in stone like all the laws of the Medes and the Persians."

9   King Darius signed the decree.

10   When Daniel learned that the decree had been signed and posted, he continued to pray just as he had always done. His house had windows in the upstairs that opened toward Jerusalem. Three times a day he knelt there in prayer, thanking and praising his God.

READ

The story of Daniel 6 is a familiar one, which means we often focus on Daniel inside the den of lions while missing what got him there in the first place. So before you read, pause and ask God to help you see this story with fresh eyes.

THINK

King Darius signs a deceptive decree that puts God-fearing Daniel in an interesting (to say the least) situation. But despite the new law and at great risk, Daniel maintains his routine of prayer. What does this story make you feel? Why?

Imagine yourself in the situation with Daniel. What do you see? What do you hear? If you were Daniel's friend, what would you say to him? What would you do? Would you kneel with him by the window? Would you kneel quietly in the corner so nobody could see you? Would you kneel at all? Would you stop praying to God?

Would these be difficult decisions for you? In what ways does this story speak to you about obedience?

PRAY

Allow the natural rhythm of your thoughts concerning Daniel's obedience to prompt you into conversation with God. (For example, you could pray after each category of thought or you could pray after your meditation is finished — whatever comes most naturally.)

Consider praying in a kneeling position by a window. As you pray, remember Daniel.

LIVE

Remember that God is worthy of your costly obedience.

✦ KING OF THE UNIVERSE

DANIEL 7:11-14

11-13 "I kept watching. The little horn was speaking arrogantly. Then, as I watched, the monster was killed and its body cremated in a roaring fire. The other animals lived on for a limited time, but they didn't really do anything, had no power to rule. My dream continued.

13-14 "I saw a human form, a son of man,
   arriving in a whirl of clouds.
He came to The Old One
   and was presented to him.
He was given power to rule — all the glory of royalty.
   Everyone — race, color, and creed — had to serve him.
His rule would be forever, never ending.
   His kingly rule would never be replaced."

READ

Read the passage as fast as you can. Then read it again at a normal pace. Finally read it aloud very slowly, focusing on and articulating each word.

THINK

The book of Daniel is full of radical stories of obedience, but it is also filled with strange and sensational dreams and visions. Chapter 7 includes a vision with four animals, plus the prophetic words found in verses 13-14.

Is God's kingly rule in the world evident to you? Do you believe he's really in charge? Think about God reigning as King over his people. Does that make you feel fear and dread or excitement and hope? Why?

If God is in control, we don't have to be. Does that thought induce anxiety or comfort? Why? Catastrophes, devastation, and suffering happen every day, yet God is ruling at this very moment. Do you believe that? How does believing that make you feel?

Not only is God in control today, but his reign lasts forever. In what ways does that fact impact your life?

PRAY

What are you worried about? Offer your concerns right now to the God who reigns over everything at this very moment and will continue to reign forever.

LIVE

Live freely and without worry as you focus on God's reign today.

DAY 161

GOD ENCOUNTERS

On this seventh day, review and reflect on all you have read this week. Take the time to revel in the ways you've encountered God in the past six days.

EXPANDED PASSAGE: DANIEL 9:1-19

CONFESSING FOR YOUR GROUP

DANIEL 9:4-9,18

4-8   "'O Master, great and august God. You never waver in your covenant commitment, never give up on those who love you and do what you say. Yet we have sinned in every way imaginable. We've done evil things, rebelled, dodged and taken detours around your clearly marked paths. We've turned a deaf ear to your servants the prophets, who preached your Word to our kings and leaders, our parents, and all the people in the land. You have done everything right, Master, but all we have to show for our lives is guilt and shame, the whole lot of us — people of Judah, citizens of Jerusalem, Israel at home and Israel in exile in all the places we've been banished to because of our betrayal of you. Oh yes, GOD, we've been exposed in our shame, all of us — our kings, leaders, parents — before the whole world. And deservedly so, because of our sin.

9   "'Compassion is our only hope, the compassion of you, the Master, our God, since in our rebellion we've forfeited our rights. . . .

18   "'Turn your ears our way, God, and listen. Open your eyes and take a long look at our ruined city, this city named after you. We know that we don't deserve a hearing from you. Our appeal is to your compassion. This prayer is our last and only hope.'"

READ
Read the passage aloud slowly.

THINK
Consider a group you belong to for which you could confess. This might be your family, your church, your nation, or a circle of friends or colleagues.

Read the passage again silently, noting if certain words or phrases apply to your group situation. Notice these phrases especially:

- "dodged and taken detours around [God's] clearly marked paths"
- "all we have to show for our lives is guilt and shame"
- "turned a deaf ear to your servants"

Read the passage again silently, noting the qualities of God that are mentioned. Which qualities does your group most need? Perhaps:

- never wavering, never giving up
- doing the right things
- compassion

PRAY
Paraphrase verse 18 in a way that makes sense to your situation.

LIVE
Check your feelings regarding confession. Are you letting it be a time of release and rest in the presence of your Father or a time of beating yourself up? Rest in the release of it all.

THE RIGHT PATH TO LIFE

DANIEL 12:1-3

1-2 "'That's when Michael, the great angel-prince, champion of your people, will step in. It will be a time of trouble, the worst trouble the world has ever seen. But your people will be saved from the trouble, every last one found written in the Book. Many who have been long dead and buried will wake up, some to eternal life, others to eternal shame.

3 "'Men and women who have lived wisely and well will shine brilliantly, like the cloudless, star-strewn night skies. And those who put others on the right path to life will glow like stars forever.'"

READ

Read the passage, including the complete chapter 12, if possible. Lay your watch or a clock next to your Bible. As you read, consider how this passages affects time, both right now and in the future.

THINK

A great deal has been said and written about the end times — in radio talk shows, best-selling novels, Hollywood blockbusters, and conversations over coffee.

In light of these verses, what are you thinking about the end times? What are you feeling? Does talk like this about the future excite you or scare you?

Focus for a few minutes specifically on 12:1-3. How do we know if we "lived wisely"? What does it mean to "put others on the right path to life"? What are the implications of these words in your life? Who do you have the opportunity to help get on the right path to life?

Do you think it's fair that God gives some people eternal life and banishes others to eternal shame? Is he being just when he does that? Why or why not?

PRAY

Tell God how you feel about the future — both your immediate future and the end of the world. Ask him to help you live wisely. Invite God to guide you in helping put others on the right path to life.

LIVE

Live with confidence today, knowing that God has already secured the future and will be victorious.

GOD AS LOVER

HOSEA 2:14-20

14-15   "And now, here's what I'm going to do:
        I'm going to start all over again.
  I'm taking her back out into the wilderness
        where we had our first date, and I'll court her.
  I'll give her bouquets of roses.
        I'll turn Heartbreak Valley into Acres of Hope.
  She'll respond like she did as a young girl,
        those days when she was fresh out of Egypt.

16-20   "At that time" — this is GOD's Message still —
        "you'll address me, 'Dear husband!'
  Never again will you address me,
        'My slave-master!'
  I'll wash your mouth out with soap,
        get rid of all the dirty false-god names,
        not so much as a whisper of those names again.
  At the same time I'll make a peace treaty between you
        and wild animals and birds and reptiles,
  And get rid of all weapons of war.
        Think of it! Safe from beasts and bullies!
  And then I'll marry you for good — forever!
        I'll marry you true and proper, in love and tenderness.
  Yes, I'll marry you and neither leave you nor let you go.
        You'll know me, GOD, for who I really am."

READ

Meditate on this passage.

THINK

When we think of love stories in the Bible, we usually think of the one narrated in Song of Songs, with all its steamy unpredictability. But Hosea offers us a love story too, one that's no less steamy, yet one that jolts us in a different way. In it Hosea actually lives out the heartbreaking metaphor of God's love for us . . . and our rejection of his love.

God commands Hosea to marry a prostitute named Gomer. Then God says that he is going to "start all over again." Hosea had to pursue the woman again and again as a symbolic act of how God runs after us when we've been unfaithful.

We are the prostitute in this story. What does that feel like?

We are also God's beloved in this story. What does it feel like to be courted by such a lover, one who cares deeply about you despite your past? Is thinking of God as a lover — *your* lover — easy or difficult? Consider the possible reasons for your answer.

Read again the final words of this passage (starting with the line "And then I'll marry you for good — forever!"). What is your reaction?

PRAY

Make these words your prayer as you desire to know God intimately: "You'll know me, GOD, for who I am really am."

LIVE

Carry the image of God as lover in your mind today.

LOVE AGAIN

HOSEA 3:1-3

1   Then GOD ordered me, "Start all over: Love your wife again,
      your wife who's in bed with her latest boyfriend, your cheating wife.
    Love her the way I, GOD, love the Israelite people,
      even as they flirt and party with every god that takes their fancy."

2-3   I did it. I paid good money to get her back.
      It cost me the price of a slave.
    Then I told her, "From now on you're living with me.
      No more whoring, no more sleeping around.
      You're living with me and I'm living with you."

READ

Read the passage slowly, whispering it.

THINK

Read the passage again slowly. Pause after verse 1 to consider how Hosea may have felt about doing what God instructed. Then read verses 2-3, noticing Hosea's firm resolution in restoring his wife.

1. What verses are most startling to you in this passage? Why?
2. How would you describe the way God loved the Israelite people (considering that they flirted and partied with other gods)?
3. Is there someone you need to love again? Reach out to? Simply stop criticizing and give that person a break?

PRAY

Ask God to help you love the person who came to mind in question 3 the way he loved the Israelites. (If this seems too difficult, include in your prayer your paraphrase of Romans 5:5: "God has poured out his love into our hearts by the Holy Spirit, whom he has given us" (NIV).

Ask God what that love might look like; it may look different from what you might automatically assume. Consider what this might cost you if you to love this person the way God shows you.

LIVE

Sit quietly before God, trying to sense what it was like for him to love the wayward Israelites no matter what.

EXPANDED PASSAGE: HOSEA 7–8

LIP SERVICE

HOSEA 8:1-3

1-3   "Blow the trumpet! Sound the alarm!
         Vultures are circling over God's people
    Who have broken my covenant
         and defied my revelation.
    Predictably, Israel cries out, 'My God! We know you!'
         But they don't act like it.
    Israel will have nothing to do with what's good,
         and now the enemy is after them."

READ

Read the passage, focusing on the words *me* and *my*.

THINK

Despite our lover God pursuing us tenderly, we continue to reject his love. We treat him not with tenderness but with contempt, discarding all he has done with us. And we continue to live like whores.

Read the passage again. Israel claims to know God, but its actions don't match its words. When have you experienced a similar situation — family members, friends, significant others, or your spouse saying one thing to you but doing just the opposite? How does that feel?

Consider your actions over the past week, the times when you have been the one to say something and then do the opposite. Is your love for God displayed in your actions, or do your actions fly in the face of everything you say to him?

PRAY

Tell God your desire to fall deeper and deeper in love with him, praying and asking him to help your actions communicate that to him.

Confess recent circumstances when your actions toward God and people did not match your profession of love for God.

LIVE

Note whether your actions align with the love for God that you profess.

DIGGING IN WITH GOD

HOSEA 10:11-12

11-12   Ephraim was a trained heifer
       that loved to thresh.
Passing by and seeing her strong, sleek neck,
       I wanted to harness Ephraim,
Put Ephraim to work in the fields —
       Judah plowing, Jacob harrowing:
Sow righteousness,
       reap love.
It's time to till the ready earth,
       it's time to dig in with GOD,
Until he arrives
       with righteousness ripe for harvest.

READ

Read the passage aloud slowly.

THINK

Read the passage aloud again. As you do, understand this to be God's dream for the northern tribes of Israel. Instead of doing these things, however, they rebelled.

Think of a time God used you to love someone or do something special for someone. In doing so, you were a well-trained heifer!

1. What does this passage tell you about what a well-trained heifer does?
2. Why is it a joy for a well-trained heifer to "dig in with God"?

Read the passage one more time. What words are attractive to your ears?

PRAY

Thank God for the times he has used you to do kingdom work — offering mercy, doing justice, or acting in faithfulness. Ask God to show you ways he wants to use you that you might not have noticed.

LIVE

Sit in the joy and satisfaction of digging in with God. If you have not experienced being used by God, imagine what that might feel like.

DAY 168

GOD ENCOUNTERS

On this seventh day, review and reflect on all you have read this week. Take the time to revel in the ways you've encountered God in the past six days.

HOW CAN I GIVE UP ON YOU?

HOSEA 11:1-5,7-9

1-5,7-9 "When Israel was only a child, I loved him.
　　I called out, 'My son!' — called him out of Egypt.
But when others called him,
　　he ran off and left me.
He worshiped the popular sex gods,
　　he played at religion with toy gods.
Still, I stuck with him. I led Ephraim.
　　I rescued him from human bondage,
But he never acknowledged my help,
　　never admitted that I was the one pulling his wagon,
That I lifted him, like a baby, to my cheek,
　　that I bent down to feed him.
Now he wants to go *back* to Egypt or go over to Assyria —
　　anything but return to me!
. . . .

"My people are hell-bent on leaving me.
　　They pray to god Baal for help.
　　He doesn't lift a finger to help them.
But how can I give up on you, Ephraim?
　　How can I turn you loose, Israel?
How can I leave you to be ruined like Admah,
　　devastated like luckless Zeboim?
I can't bear to even think such thoughts.
　　My insides churn in protest.
And so I'm not going to act on my anger.
　　I'm not going to destroy Ephraim.
And why? Because I am God and not a human.
　　I'm The Holy One and I'm here — in your very midst."

READ

Read the passage once to understand the situation. (Include the expanded passage for further information.) Read it again, but this time pause at each phrase or idea and linger there for a moment to really catch what is being said.

THINK

Quiet your mind. Read the passage a third time, aloud. This time notice the word or phrase that most vividly speaks to you of God's unrelenting faithfulness. Pause at this phrase, and hear yourself speak it. Then finish reading the passage.

PRAY

Spend time absorbing the word or phrase into yourself, as though your heart were a sponge slowly soaking up water. Memorize it. Let it intermingle with your concerns, memories, and feelings. Allow your meditation to grow into conversation with God. Notice God pointing out, through this illustration, how his devotedness frees you to experience life differently than you have before.

LIVE

Between now and your next time of prayer, plan at least three occasions throughout your day when you will pause and spend a few minutes mulling over the phrase that showed you the tenacity of God's love. Each time, you'll probably bring different emotions, attitudes, and experiences with you, and that's okay. Let them challenge God's message of commitment to you. Find out how his steadfast love responds to each challenge.

✛ CORPORATE CONFESSION

JOEL 1:8-10

8-10   Weep like a young virgin dressed in black,
        mourning the loss of her fiancé.
Without grain and grapes,
        worship has been brought to a standstill
        in the Sanctuary of GOD.
The priests are at a loss.
        GOD's ministers don't know what to do.
The fields are sterile.
        The very ground grieves.
The wheat fields are lifeless,
        vineyards dried up, olive oil gone.

READ

Read the passage and, if possible, the expanded passage.

THINK

In the first chapter of Joel, the prophet speaks of a famine that has significance far beyond mere physical consequences. There are certain passages of Scripture that we love to read, passages of comfort and rest, hope and promise. But there are others — like this one — that confront us with the truth, as hard as it may be to hear.

American Christianity often emphasizes the importance of personal confession of sin. But the concept of corporate sin is rarely discussed. In contrast, confession of corporate sin was a regular occurrence in the ancient Jewish world. National sin grieved the heart of the God-fearing Hebrew, and confessing it was desired and expected.

Take out a piece of paper and write down the corporate sins that our communities, our government, our country, and even our churches need to confess. (Include what wrongdoing has been done and what good-doing has been left undone.)

PRAY

Spend time specifically acknowledging and confessing these corporate sins against God and others. Ask God for forgiveness.

LIVE

Live with the awareness of our collective sins, knowing that God desires repentance for us as a community, a country, and his people. Ask often for corporate forgiveness.

COME BACK TO ME

JOEL 2:12-14

12 But there's also this, it's not too late—
  GOD's personal Message!—
"Come back to me and really mean it!
  Come fasting and weeping, sorry for your sins!"

13-14 Change your life, not just your clothes.
  Come back to GOD, *your* God.
And here's why: God is kind and merciful.
  He takes a deep breath, puts up with a lot,
This most patient God, extravagant in love,
  always ready to cancel catastrophe.
Who knows? Maybe he'll do it now,
  maybe he'll turn around and show pity.
Maybe, when all's said and done,
  there'll be blessings full and robust for your GOD!

READ

Read the passage aloud slowly, noting that verse 12 includes words from God himself.

THINK

Read the passage aloud again, repeating God's words in verse 12 in the tone you think he would have said them.

God says the phrase "Come back to me" many times through the prophets. God really does want his people, and he wants them back.

1. What does this passage tell you about what God is like?
2. How surprised are you that God wants his people (including you) back? (Keep in mind that turning back doesn't have to mean you ever dramatically turned away; it might mean you've just been distracted.)

   ☐ Very surprised: You thought God would scold people who wander away or ignore him.
   ☐ Somewhat surprised: You figured God wouldn't turn away someone who returns, but he would never plead with them.
   ☐ Not surprised: You frequently sense God calling you back and know he's not mad at you.
   ☐ Other:

PRAY

Tell God how you feel about being (or becoming) someone who always comes back to him. Do you always want to? Would you like to always want to? Talk to God about the "blessings full and robust" that come to you when you turn back to him.

171

LIVE

Picture this: If God had a body, how would he stand before people and plead for them to come back to him? What would he do with his hands? His arms? What would his face look like?

A GRANITE SAFE HOUSE

JOEL 3:14-19

14   "Mass confusion, mob uproar —
       in Decision Valley!
   GOD's Judgment Day has arrived
       in Decision Valley.

15-17   "The sky turns black,
       sun and moon go dark, stars burn out.
   GOD roars from Zion, shouts from Jerusalem.
       Earth and sky quake in terror.
   But GOD is a safe hiding place,
       a granite safe house for the children of Israel.
   Then you'll know for sure
       that I'm *your* GOD,
   Living in Zion,
       my sacred mountain.
   Jerusalem will be a sacred city,
       posted: 'NO TRESPASSING.'

18-19   "What a day!
       Wine streaming off the mountains,
   Milk rivering out of the hills,
       water flowing everywhere in Judah,
   A fountain pouring out of GOD's Sanctuary,
       watering all the parks and gardens!
   But Egypt will be reduced to weeds in a vacant lot,
       Edom turned into barren badlands,
   All because of brutalities to the Judean people,
       the atrocities and murders of helpless innocents."

READ

Read the passage, opening yourself up to the situation Joel is prophetically describing here. You might read it a few more times, allowing the words and images to become familiar.

THINK

Ponder the contrast between God as the terrifying roar amid chaos and God as a "granite safe house." Which words or images in particular catch your attention? Mull them over. Become aware of specific questions these verses raise for you.

PRAY

Let your questions and meditation lead you into conversation with God. You might think about facets of his character, like his terrifying might or his solid trustworthiness, or you might consider the reality of this future, even though we don't know exactly what it'll be like.

If your primary questions about the passage are intellectual, place them before God and ask him what he has for you. Stay honest with what you do and don't understand, sharing with God how this passage touches your life. Avoid getting lost in academic speculation or trying to force meaning out of the passage. Just ask God how he would like to use this experience of your limitedness today.

LIVE

As you look once more at the two vastly different perspectives on God presented in this passage, which side of God are you most in need of today: his fierce ability to bring justice or his safe protection from harm? Spend time now quietly resting in the presence of this God.

THE GOD OF JUSTICE

AMOS 2:6-8

6-8   GOD's Message:

"Because of the three great sins of Israel
   — make that four — I'm not putting up with them any longer.
They buy and sell upstanding people.
   People for them are only *things* — ways of making money.
They'd sell a poor man for a pair of shoes.
   They'd sell their own grandmother!
They grind the penniless into the dirt,
   shove the luckless into the ditch.
Everyone and his brother sleeps with the 'sacred whore' —
   a sacrilege against my Holy Name.
Stuff they've extorted from the poor
   is piled up at the shrine of their god,
While they sit around drinking wine
   they've conned from their victims."

READ

Read the words of God in these verses with the tone of voice you think God might have had when speaking these words.

THINK

The book of Amos communicates clearly and compellingly that God cares deeply about social justice — and he dislikes it when his people turn their heads from doing right. God is truly a God of mercy, yet he is also a God of justice. That means he treats injustice harshly.

What injustices exist around you — among your friends and in your city, state, country, and the entire world? What are we to do about injustice specifically?

Thinking *I'm not a part of an injustice* is easy. But take a hard look around you. In what ways might you be contributing — directly or indirectly — to injustice in the world? In what ways might you get involved — directly or indirectly — to facilitate justice that would reveal the heart of God?

If injustice makes God sick to his stomach, what should the presence of injustice do to you? Does it?

PRAY

Ask God to make injustice in the world as repulsive to you as it is to him. Ask him for wisdom to address injustice in a way that honors him with a godly balance of boldness and tenderness.

LIVE

Read some of the news articles in today's newspaper. As you absorb the accounts of atrocity, war, and corruption, pray for each situation. Pray that the God of justice will intervene.

SEEKING GOOD

AMOS 5:7,11-15

7   Woe to you who turn justice to vinegar
         and stomp righteousness into the mud.

      . . . .

11-12   But here it is, bluntly spoken:
         Because you run roughshod over the poor
         and take the bread right out of their mouths,
      You're never going to move into
         the luxury homes you have built.
      You're never going to drink wine
         from the expensive vineyards you've planted.
      I know precisely the extent of your violations,
         the enormity of your sins. Appalling!
      You bully right-living people,
         taking bribes right and left and kicking the poor when they're down.

13   Justice is a lost cause. Evil is epidemic.
         Decent people throw up their hands.
      Protest and rebuke are useless,
         a waste of breath.

14   Seek good and not evil—
         and live!
      You talk about God, the God-of-the-Angel-Armies,
         being your best friend.
      Well, *live* like it,
         and maybe it will happen.

15   Hate evil and love good,
         then work it out in the public square.
      Maybe God, the God-of-the-Angel-Armies,
         will notice your remnant and be gracious.

READ

Read the passage aloud slowly.

THINK

Read the passage again silently, noticing the pictures in the passage. Which do you find most dreadful?

Pictures of how those who have enough treat those who don't:	
stomping righteousness in the mud	running roughshod over the poor
yanking bread out of people's mouths	bullying people
taking bribes day in and day out	kicking poor people when they have nothing
Pictures of the consequences to those who have enough but don't share:	
luxury homes standing empty	exquisite wine going to waste unused

Read verses 14-15 again aloud. What is God saying to you about seeking good and helping others live?

PRAY

Talk to the Lord about what it would look like for you to seek good.

LIVE

Be alert for situations of injustice in which you can speak up or help someone. If you don't find any, ask someone else to give you ideas.

DAY 175

GOD ENCOUNTERS

On this seventh day, review and reflect on all you have read this week. Take the time to revel in the ways you've encountered God in the past six days.

PLUMB LINE

AMOS 7:1-9

1-2   GOD, my Master, showed me this vision: He was preparing a locust swarm. The first cutting, which went to the king, was complete, and the second crop was just sprouting. The locusts ate everything green. Not even a blade of grass was left.

    I called out, "GOD, my Master! Excuse me, but what's going to come of Jacob? He's so small."

3   GOD gave in.

    "It won't happen," he said.

4   GOD showed me this vision: Oh! GOD, my Master GOD was calling up a firestorm. It burned up the ocean. Then it burned up the Promised Land.

5   I said, "GOD, my Master! Hold it — please! What's going to come of Jacob? He's so small."

6   GOD gave in.

    "All right, this won't happen either," GOD, my Master, said.

7   GOD showed me this vision: My Master was standing beside a wall. In his hand he held a plumb line.

8-9   GOD said to me, "What do you see, Amos?"

    I said, "A plumb line."

    Then my Master said, "Look what I've done. I've hung a plumb line in the midst of my people Israel. I've spared them for the last time. This is it!

    "Isaac's sex-and-religion shrines will be smashed,
    Israel's unholy shrines will be knocked to pieces.
    I'm raising my sword against the royal family of Jeroboam."

READ

Read the passage carefully.

THINK

What theme do you see emerging? Write it down in one sentence. Be aware of what thinking might have motivated God to use the plumb line.

LIVE

Take a small, heavy object, like a key, a ring, or a pendant, and hang it from a string. As the object hangs straight toward the ground, the string is your plumb line by which you can measure the uprightness of other items. Take time to ponder this. Play with your plumb line and observe how it works. What do you notice?

PRAY

Setting the text and your plumb line aside, sit with your eyes closed. What are you feeling? What are your concerns and needs? Who are you as the person who is approaching this text today?

Now read the passage again. In what ways do you see the theme you already noted intersecting with your life today? Is there a message God is speaking to you? How does the plumb line hang in the midst of your own life? If you have trouble seeing a connection, read the passage again, pausing in the place that affects you most and leads you into prayer. Write down anything that seems significant.

GOD, THE RADICAL POLITICIAN

OBADIAH 12-14

12-14
You shouldn't have talked so big
    when everything was so bad.
You shouldn't have taken advantage of my people
    when their lives had fallen apart.
You of all people should not have been amused
    by their troubles, their wrecked nation.
You shouldn't have taken the shirt off their back
    when they were knocked flat, defenseless.
And you shouldn't have stood waiting at the outskirts
    and cut off refugees,
And traitorously turned in helpless survivors
    who had lost everything.

READ

Read the passage aloud slowly. Understand that the prophet Obadiah is speaking to the nation of Edom who enjoyed watching the nation of Judah experience troubles.

THINK

Put yourself in the place of the nation of Edom. You've had an ancient feud with the Israelites, and they are your bitter enemies. Politics are politics — enemy nations do *not* help each other. Right? Now read the passage again, with its very different viewpoint. Hear God's radical response to Edom's very normal behavior.

God's odd stance has been stated another way in 1 Corinthians 13:6: "[Love] doesn't revel when others grovel, [it] takes pleasure in the flowering of truth." What role does the love of God play in political affairs? What role does the love of God play in how nations treat the peoples of the world whom God loves?

PRAY

Ask God to help the nations of the world consider how they treat one another, especially nations who are ancient enemies. Pray for Christians who are active in inserting God's radical love into international politics (for example, Christian Peacemaker Teams).

LIVE

Stand in front of a world map or globe. Put your hand on a nation who has been an enemy of your nation. Pray for the people of that country. Pray for its leaders.

RESISTANT OR OBEDIENT?

JONAH 1:1-3

1-2   One day long ago, GOD's Word came to Jonah, Amittai's son: "Up on your feet and on your way to the big city of Nineveh! Preach to them. They're in a bad way and I can't ignore it any longer."

3   But Jonah got up and went the other direction to Tarshish, running away from GOD. He went down to the port of Joppa and found a ship headed for Tarshish. He paid the fare and went on board, joining those going to Tarshish — as far away from GOD as he could get.

READ

Pray and ask God to give you fresh eyes to see this familiar story in a new way. Then read the passage and chapters 1–2, if possible.

THINK

We might summarize this familiar story by saying that Jonah's resistance to being obedient to God's ways meant his learning a lesson the hard way. But there's more to it than that. In fact, the text tells us that Jonah was "running away from GOD." We run away from God too, even if only in subtle ways. When do you run from God?

PRAY

Try praying while holding out your hands, palms up, in front of you. Use this posture as a way to release your desires to God, to receive what he has for you, and to communicate your openness and willingness to obey him.

Ask the Holy Spirit to search your heart and reveal areas of your life where you resist what God desires. Invite him to illuminate your unwillingness to obey, and give him permission to do whatever it takes to show you that he cares deeply for you.

Request forgiveness for those times you have run from God, for your rebellion.

When you are finished, keeping your hands out, listen carefully in the silence.

LIVE

Go and live courageously and obediently in God's purposes for your life.

IN A SULK

JONAH 4:5-11

5   But Jonah just left. He went out of the city to the east and sat down in a sulk. He put together a makeshift shelter of leafy branches and sat there in the shade to see what would happen to the city.

6   GOD arranged for a broad-leafed tree to spring up. It grew over Jonah to cool him off and get him out of his angry sulk. Jonah was pleased and enjoyed the shade. Life was looking up.

7-8   But then God sent a worm. By dawn of the next day, the worm had bored into the shade tree and it withered away. The sun came up and God sent a hot, blistering wind from the east. The sun beat down on Jonah's head and he started to faint. He prayed to die: "I'm better off dead!"

9   Then God said to Jonah, "What right do you have to get angry about this shade tree?"

Jonah said, "Plenty of right. It's made me angry enough to die!"

10-11 GOD said, "What's this? How is it that you can change your feelings from pleasure to anger overnight about a mere shade tree that you did nothing to get? You neither planted nor watered it. It grew up one night and died the next night. So, why can't I likewise change what I feel about Nineveh from anger to pleasure, this big city of more than 120,000 child-like people who don't yet know right from wrong, to say nothing of all the innocent animals?"

READ

Allow the words and events of this passage to become familiar to you as you read. Let yourself sink into the scene described.

THINK

As you hear God's conversation with Jonah, think about how you would describe his reaction to Jonah's anger. Now read God's words again, and pay attention to the tone of voice you imagine God using. Is it condemning? Mocking? How might your perception of God shift if the same words were said in a tender but firm voice?

PRAY

What do you feel when you hear Jonah express his anger? When you see him walk away? Perhaps it makes you nervous or uncomfortable, or maybe there are times when you, too, want to yell at God. Talk to God about what you notice in your response, or write about it in a journal. Give yourself permission to be open and honest.

LIVE

Take some time to consider this statement: "God will love you [even] if you never pray."[11] Do you believe it? Talk to God about your reaction.

Recall your first, instinctive perception of God's response to Jonah. What does this show what you believe to be God's feelings toward you when you are resentful or disobedient? Ask him to help you understand over the coming months what his love for you is like and to help you take it in and receive it.

✚ IDOL-MAKING

MICAH 1:3-7

3-5   Look, here he comes! GOD, from his place!
           He comes down and strides across mountains and hills.
       Mountains sink under his feet,
           valleys split apart;
       The rock mountains crumble into gravel,
           the river valleys leak like sieves.
           All this because of Jacob's sin,
           because Israel's family did wrong.
       You ask, "So what is Jacob's sin?"
           Just look at Samaria — isn't it obvious?
       And all the sex-and-religion shrines in Judah —
           isn't Jerusalem responsible?

6-7   "I'm turning Samaria into a heap of rubble,
           a vacant lot littered with garbage.
       I'll dump the stones from her buildings in the valley
           and leave her abandoned foundations exposed.
       All her carved and cast gods and goddesses
           will be sold for stove wood and scrap metal,
       All her sacred fertility groves
           burned to the ground,
       All the sticks and stones she worshiped as gods,
           destroyed.
       These were her earnings from her life as a whore.
           This is what happens to the fees of a whore."

READ

Pause and request that God give you an open heart for what you are about to read. Give him permission to speak to you specifically about what he wants you to hear. Acknowledge that you desire to hear him speak to you and will listen attentively.

Now read the passage with listening ears and an open heart.

THINK

Sometimes we let ourselves believe that idols are mere physical objects that people made hundreds, even thousands, of years ago. But theologically speaking, an idol is anything that eclipses our worship of God. And with this definition, *everybody* makes idols today, whether material or immaterial.

What gets between you and a heartfelt, humble, and thankful response to God? To what shrines and idols, gods and goddesses are you tempted to give your allegiance? Make a mental list (or write it on paper, if it helps.)

Why do you think you are drawn to believe that certain things will give you more significance, purpose, and meaning than God himself? Why does God hate those things that take your worship, attention, and devotion? Is God's jealousy selfish? Why or why not?

PRAY

Bring your list of idols before God. Be utterly transparent with him, acknowledging and confessing the people, places, thoughts, ideas, emotions, and so on that have come between you and God. Invite him to fight alongside you against these temptations that divert your soul from the truth.

LIVE

When an idol lures you, simply whisper, "God, help me worship you and you alone."

TEACH US HOW TO LIVE

MICAH 4:1-4

1-4   But when all is said and done,
　　GOD's Temple on the mountain,
Firmly fixed, will dominate all mountains,
　　towering above surrounding hills.
People will stream to it
　　and many nations set out for it,
Saying, "Come, let's climb GOD's mountain.
　　Let's go to the Temple of Jacob's God.
He will teach us how to live.
　　We'll know how to live God's way."
True teaching will issue from Zion,
　　GOD's revelation from Jerusalem.
He'll establish justice in the rabble of nations
　　and settle disputes in faraway places.
They'll trade in their swords for shovels,
　　their spears for rakes and hoes.
Nations will quit fighting each other,
　　quit learning how to kill one another.
Each man will sit under his own shade tree,
　　each woman in safety will tend her own garden.
GOD-of-the-Angel-Armies says so,
　　and he means what he says.

READ

Read the passage aloud slowly.

THINK

Read the passage again, noting what it says about "true teaching" — how it's found, what it says, and what it results in.

1. What words or ideas touch you in the passage? Perhaps

   - nations streaming to hear God,
   - people wanting to live God's way
   - people giving up weapons to do their work quietly
   - other:

2. Why do you think those words or ideas touch you? How does this connect with what you want in life?

PRAY

Pray for God's true teaching to prevail in troubled places — within troubled people, within troubled relationships, within troubled groups, between troubled nations.

LIVE

Sit quietly before God, mentally rehearsing the sort of person you need to be to bring true teaching that results in such peace.

DAY 182

GOD ENCOUNTERS

On this seventh day, review and reflect on all you have read this week. Take the time to revel in the ways you've encountered God in the past six days.

OUR GOD

MICAH 7:15-20

15-17   Reproduce the miracle-wonders
      of our exodus from Egypt.
And the godless nations: Put them in their place —
      humiliated in their arrogance, speechless and clueless.
Make them slink like snakes, crawl like cockroaches,
      come out of their holes from under their rocks
And face our GOD.
      Fill them with holy fear and trembling.

18-20   Where is the god who can compare with you —
      wiping the slate clean of guilt,
Turning a blind eye, a deaf ear,
      to the past sins of your purged and precious people?
You don't nurse your anger and don't stay angry long,
      for mercy is your specialty. That's what you love most.
And compassion is on its way to us.
      You'll stamp out our wrongdoing.
You'll sink our sins
      to the bottom of the ocean.
You'll stay true to your word to Father Jacob
      and continue the compassion you showed Grandfather Abraham —
Everything you promised our ancestors
      from a long time ago.

PRAY

Before you read, pray about what's on your heart today. Is there something you want to talk to God about? Maybe it's a vague sense of shame or irritation, or maybe something specific is happening. Whatever it is, share your heart with God. Try writing your prayer in a journal. Ask God to speak to you right where you are through today's excerpt.

READ/THINK

As much as you can, set aside what you've been thinking about for a few minutes, trusting that God will hold it for you. Read today's passage, noticing what's happening in Micah's situation and the kinds of problems that God, through him, is addressing in Israel. If you have time, read the expanded passage too, observing in particular what God is like.

Write down what you notice about God and the attributes he displays in this passage.

LIVE

Look at what you wrote about yourself and about God. How do you think God is responding to you and the issues you shared earlier through this passage from Micah? What angers God? What touches his heart? When does he show tenderness, and when does he show firmness?

How do these traits compare to the way you normally perceive God? Where do you think your idea of him came from? Can you identify elements of your perception that are not of God but are rather reflections of you or other people you know?

Talk to God about what you notice.

PATIENT POWER

NAHUM 1:1-6

1   A report on the problem of Nineveh, the way God gave Nahum of Elkosh
to see it:

2-6   GOD is serious business.
     He won't be trifled with.
   He avenges his foes.
     He stands up against his enemies, fierce and raging.
   But GOD doesn't lose his temper.
     He's powerful, but it's a patient power.
   Still, no one gets by with anything.
     Sooner or later, everyone pays.
   Tornadoes and hurricanes
     are the wake of his passage,
   Storm clouds are the dust
     he shakes off his feet.
   He yells at the sea: It dries up.
     All the rivers run dry.
   The Bashan and Carmel mountains shrivel,
     the Lebanon orchards shrivel.
   Mountains quake in their roots,
     hills dissolve into mud flats.
   Earth shakes in fear of GOD.
     The whole world's in a panic.
   Who can face such towering anger?
     Who can stand up to this fierce rage?
   His anger spills out like a river of lava,
     his fury shatters boulders.

READ

Read the passage.

THINK

Ponder this passage: "But God doesn't lose his temper. He's powerful, but it's a patient power."

When you consider the word *power,* what comes to mind? Do you think of *power* as a positive or negative concept? Why?

When you consider God as powerful, is that positive or negative to you? Why? What's the difference between his being powerful and his being patiently powerful? Does the "patient" factor change your feelings about his power? If so, in what way? What would the world be like if God were powerful and *impatient*?

Why is it important that God is patiently powerful?

PRAY

Spend a few minutes letting the idea of a God who is patient yet powerful rest in your mind. Then ask God what he wants you to know about his power today, right now.

Thank him for his patience.

Thank him for his power.

LIVE

Rest today in the midst of your schedule, comforted that the God you serve is both powerful and patient.

WHAT ARE YOU COUNTING ON?

NAHUM 3:14-17

14-15   Store up water for the siege.
   Shore up your defenses.
Get down to basics: Work the clay
   and make bricks.
Sorry. Too late.
   Enemy fire will burn you up.
Swords will cut you to pieces.
   You'll be chewed up as if by locusts.

15-17   Yes, as if by locusts — a fitting fate,
   for you yourselves are a locust plague.
You've multiplied shops and shopkeepers —
   more buyers and sellers than stars in the sky!
A plague of locusts, cleaning out the neighborhood
   and then flying off.
Your bureaucrats are locusts,
   your brokers and bankers are locusts.
Early on, they're all at your service,
   full of smiles and promises,
But later when you return with questions or complaints,
   you'll find they've flown off and are nowhere to be found.

READ

Read the passage slowly to yourself. Be aware that this sad passage describes the ancient city of Nineveh, which is doomed. Everything Nineveh counted on has fallen through.

THINK

Read the passage again, noting what Nineveh counted on to keep itself out of trouble.

Why is it so tempting to rely on economic prosperity (shopkeepers, brokers, and bankers) and the government (bureaucrats)? (We even use phrases such as "having faith in" the stock market or "having faith in" government officials.)

What would your life look like if you relied on God for your future and your safety instead of on the economy or the government?

PRAY

Examine what you have that comes from the economy or the government, such as a job, streetlights, or a public library. Ask God to show you how much you count on these things and what counting on him in a deeper way would mean.

LIVE

Imagine yourself living in a place where the economy and the government have fallen apart. What might you feel like if you relied totally on God?

SPEAKING OUR MINDS AND HEARTS

HABAKKUK 1:12-17

12-13   GOD, you're from eternity, aren't you?
    Holy God, we aren't going to die, are we?
GOD, you chose *Babylonians* for your judgment work?
    Rock-Solid God, you gave *them* the job of discipline?
But you can't be serious!
    You can't condone evil!
So why don't you do something about this?
    Why are you silent *now*?
This outrage! Evil men swallow up the righteous
    and you stand around and *watch*!

14-16   You're treating men and women
    as so many fish in the ocean,
Swimming without direction,
    swimming but not getting anywhere.
Then this evil Babylonian arrives and goes fishing.
    He pulls in a good catch.
He catches his limit and fills his creel —
    a good day of fishing! He's happy!
He praises his rod and reel,
    piles his fishing gear on an altar and worships it!
It's made his day,
    and he's going to eat well tonight!

17   Are you going to let this go on and on?
    Will you let this Babylonian fisherman
Fish like a weekend angler,
    killing people as if they're nothing but fish?

READ
Read Habakkuk 1:12-17.

THINK

Sometimes we have a hard time being completely honest with God. But when we read certain passages of Scripture, such as in the Psalms and here in Habakkuk, we are encouraged to know that not only is God okay with our honesty, but he even invites it. Most prophets speak on behalf of God to us; Habakkuk speaks on behalf of us to God — and he does it with honesty that might make some people blush.

When you read Habakkuk's bold words — "This outrage! Evil men swallow up the righteous and you stand around and *watch*!" — how do you feel?

Does the same level of honesty in Habakkuk's words show up in you when you talk to God? Why or why not? Is that good or bad? What might happen in your life if you could speak to God with such honesty?

PRAY

Consider your life — your friendships, place in life, expectations, dreams, goals, hopes, job, school situation, and so on. About which of these areas do you wish you could speak honestly with God?

Take the risk and tell God exactly what's on your mind. Resist censoring yourself. Speak honestly and openly, assured that God is capable enough to handle your honesty.

LIVE

Know that God invites your honest communication with him at all times because, above all, he wants your heart.

186

FULLY ALIVE

HABAKKUK 2:1-4

1   What's God going to say to my questions? I'm braced for the worst.
     I'll climb to the lookout tower and scan the horizon.
  I'll wait to see what God says,
     how he'll answer my complaint.

2-3 And then GOD answered: "Write this.
     Write what you see.
  Write it out in big block letters
     so that it can be read on the run.
  This vision-message is a witness
     pointing to what's coming.
  It aches for the coming — it can hardly wait!
     And it doesn't lie.
  If it seems slow in coming, wait.
     It's on its way. It will come right on time.

4   "Look at that man, bloated by self-importance —
     full of himself but soul-empty.
  But the person in right standing before God
     through loyal and steady believing
     is fully alive, *really* alive."

READ

Read the passage aloud slowly, noting that this is a conversation between God and the prophet Habakkuk.

THINK

Habakkuk has just complained to God about the degraded life of Judah and asked God when he will act. In verse 1, Habakkuk insists on an answer, and verses 2-4 are the core of God's answer. Read the passage again with all this in mind.

1. What do you think of Habakkuk's questioning attitude? What does God seem to think of it?
2. In verses 2-4, God speaks to Habakkuk. What does God want Habakkuk to know or do?
3. Which of the words in this passage resonate most with you? Why do you think that is?
4. The second part of verse 4 is most often translated "the just shall live by faith." Take each phrase and rest in it:

   - "the just": "the person in right standing before God"
   - "shall live": "is fully alive, *really* alive"
   - "by faith": "through loyal and steady believing"

   What does all this tell you that you need to know today?

PRAY

Respond to God's statement "The person in right standing before God through loyal and steady believing is fully alive, *really* alive." What does this make you want to say to God? To ask God?

LIVE

Rest in Habakkuk 2:20: "But oh! GOD is in his holy Temple! Quiet everyone — a holy silence. Listen!"

HOLY JUDGE, REMEMBER MERCY

HABAKKUK 3:1-6

1-2   A prayer of the prophet Habakkuk, with orchestra:

GOD, I've heard what our ancestors say about you,
   and I'm stopped in my tracks, down on my knees.
Do among us what you did among them.
   Work among us as you worked among them.
And as you bring judgment, as you surely must,
   remember mercy.

3-6   God's on his way again,
   retracing the old salvation route,
Coming up from the south through Teman,
   the Holy One from Mount Paran.
Skies are blazing with his splendor,
   his praises sounding through the earth,
His cloud-brightness like dawn, exploding, spreading,
   forked-lightning shooting from his hand —
   what power hidden in that fist!
Plague marches before him,
   pestilence at his heels!
He stops. He shakes Earth.
   He looks around. Nations tremble.
The age-old mountains fall to pieces;
   ancient hills collapse like a spent balloon.
The paths God takes are older
   than the oldest mountains and hills.

READ

Read Habakkuk's description of God's activities. As you do, let them remind you of actions and characteristics of God that have stood out to you as you've read stories of the Israelites in his Message.

THINK

Think about what it means to ask God to "do among us what you did among [Israel]." What was he like with them? How did he deal with them? What characterized his relationship with them?

PRAY

Picture Habakkuk inviting you to join him in his prayer that God would act toward you as he did toward Israel. What rises up in you when you consider this? Fear? Frustration? Hope? Explore this with God. What does it show you about your internal picture of him? Of yourself?

LIVE

Sit silently with God and slowly reexamine what has taken place during your time with him today. Close with the following prayer: *Merciful God, shine your light of truth into me in the coming weeks and months, that I might more clearly understand what you're like and how you see me. Let my fears and pride be exposed for what they are, and keep them from distorting my picture of who you are. Give me courage, that I might face my true self, and hope, that I might face you. Help me see in you what Habakkuk saw, that "as you bring judgment, as you surely must, remember mercy." Amen.*

DAY 189

GOD ENCOUNTERS

On this seventh day, review and reflect on all you have read this week. Take the time to revel in the ways you've encountered God in the past six days.

THE BALANCE BETWEEN BEING JUST AND BEING MERCIFUL

ZEPHANIAH 1:7-11

7-11   "Quiet now!
   Reverent silence before me, GOD, the Master!
Time's up. My Judgment Day is near:
   The Holy Day is all set, the invited guests made holy.
On the Holy Day, GOD's Judgment Day,
   I will punish the leaders and the royal sons;
I will punish those who dress up like foreign priests and priestesses,
   Who introduce pagan prayers and practices;
And I'll punish all who import pagan superstitions
   that turn holy places into hellholes.
Judgment Day!" GOD's Decree!
   "Cries of panic from the city's Fish Gate,
Cries of terror from the city's Second Quarter,
   sounds of great crashing from the hills!
Wail, you shopkeepers on Market Street!
   Moneymaking has had its day. The god Money is dead."

READ

Read these verses in a place that is absolutely quiet.

THINK

Many people see God as a God of comfort, guidance, and love. This image is not wrong, but it is incomplete. God is also a God of justice, one who becomes angry with our complacent and arrogant sin when we dump him altogether.

How does the fact that God is a God of justice balance in your mind with the fact that God is also a God of mercy (as we know from other places of Scripture)?

Pause and consider areas of complacency and rebellion in your life. Wait and listen for the Holy Spirit to show you. In light of these areas, what do you feel about this God who says he loves you?

PRAY

In the midst of silence, continue searching your heart for recent thoughts and actions that have gone in a direct opposition to what God desires for your life. Tell God how you are feeling deep within. He wants to hear from you. Verbalize specifically your rebellion against him. Ask for his mercy. Ask him to give you the proper understanding of the balance between his justice and his mercy in the world.

LIVE

When you are tempted to sin today, be aware of how your rebellion angers the heart of God.

GOD SHOWS UP

ZEPHANIAH 2:3,6-10

3   Seek God, all you quietly disciplined people
      who live by God's justice.
Seek God's right ways. Seek a quiet and disciplined life.
      Perhaps you'll be hidden on the Day of God's anger.

. . . .

6-7   The lands of the seafarers
      will become pastureland,
A country for shepherds and sheep.
      What's left of the family of Judah will get it.
Day after day they'll pasture by the sea,
      and go home in the evening to Ashkelon to sleep.
Their very own God will look out for them.
      He'll make things as good as before.

8-10   "I've heard the crude taunts of Moab,
      the mockeries flung by Ammon,
The cruel talk they've used to put down my people,
      their self-important strutting along Israel's borders.
Therefore, as sure as I am the living God," says
      God-of-the-Angel-Armies,
      Israel's personal God,
"Moab will become a ruin like Sodom,
      Ammon a ghost town like Gomorrah,
One a field of rocks, the other a sterile salt flat,
      a moonscape forever.
What's left of my people will finish them off,
      will pick them clean and take over.
This is what they get for their bloated pride,
      Their taunts and mockeries of the people
      of God-of-the-Angel-Armies."

READ

Read the passage aloud slowly and silently.

You've probably experienced the wrath of a bully. The nation of Moab had been bullying the nation of Judah. In this passage God says that he plans to sweep in and save Judah. The encouraging words in verses 6-7 are spoken of Judah; verses 8-10 are indictments of Moab to defend Judah.

THINK

Read the passage again, noting the primary sins of Moab. As you read, grieve over them:

- cruelty, mockery, and taunts
- put-downs, self-importance, and pride

In what ways do these two sets of sins feed off each other?

When have you experienced such treatment? In what way did God intervene to rescue you? If you don't feel that God did so, take this rescue of Judah and appropriate it for yourself. This isn't fantasy — God did rescue you in some way, even if you didn't realize it.

PRAY

Thank God for rescuing you and providing moments of pastureland in your life. Ask God if he wants to use you to rescue someone. Listen for his guidance in doing so.

LIVE

Sit quietly before God. Feel in your gut the sensation of humiliation at someone else's self-importance. Then feel in your gut the sensations of safety and rescue. Understand that you are reliving Judah's experience.

AT HOME IN GOD

ZEPHANIAH 3:9-13

9-13   "In the end I will turn things around for the people.
        I'll give them a language undistorted, unpolluted,
    Words to address GOD in worship
        and, united, to serve me with their shoulders to the wheel.
    They'll come from beyond the Ethiopian rivers,
        they'll come praying —
    All my scattered, exiled people
        will come home with offerings for worship.
    You'll no longer have to be ashamed
        of all those acts of rebellion.
    I'll have gotten rid of your arrogant leaders.
        No more pious strutting on my holy hill!
    I'll leave a core of people among you
        who are poor in spirit —
    What's left of Israel that's really Israel.
        They'll make their home in GOD.
    This core holy people
        will not do wrong.
    They won't lie,
        won't use words to flatter or seduce.
    Content with who they are and where they are,
        unanxious, they'll live at peace."

READ

Read this passage, carefully listening for what it tells you about sin's impact on our lives.

THINK

How does this passage fill out your perspective on sin — what it's like to live with it, and what it's like to live without it? How does our sin affect us? From Zephaniah's point of view, why does God want us not to sin?

PRAY

Reread Zephaniah's description of a life that is cleared of sin. How does it make you feel? Timid? Hopeful? Sad? Does it feel foreign and unfamiliar? Become aware of God's presence with you now, and expose to him your response to this vision of life. Explore with him why the passage makes you feel the way you do.

LIVE

Consider how God is responding to what you just shared with him. Return to the question, Why does God want us not to sin? Again ponder Zephaniah's answer to this, and let it form your understanding of God's response to you now. What does God desire for you? What kind of life does he want you to have?

TURNAROUND NEEDED

HAGGAI 1:3-6,8-11

3-4 Shortly after that, GOD said more and Haggai spoke it: "How is it that it's the 'right time' for you to live in your fine new homes while the Home, GOD's Temple, is in ruins?"

5-6 And then a little later, GOD-of-the-Angel-Armies spoke out again:

"Take a good, hard look at your life.
    Think it over.
You have spent a lot of money,
    but you haven't much to show for it.
You keep filling your plates,
    but you never get filled up."

. . . .

8-9 Then GOD said:

"Here's what I want you to do:
    Climb into the hills and cut some timber.
Bring it down and rebuild the Temple.
    Do it just for me. Honor me.
You've had great ambitions for yourselves,
    but nothing has come of it.
The little you have brought to my Temple
    I've blown away—there was nothing to it.

9-11 "And why?" (This is a Message from GOD-of-the-Angel-Armies, remember.) "Because while you've run around, caught up with taking care of your own houses, my Home is in ruins. That's why. Because of your stinginess. And so I've given you a dry summer and a skimpy crop. I've matched your tight-fisted stinginess by decreeing a season of drought, drying up fields and hills, withering gardens and orchards, stunting vegetables and fruit. Nothing—not man or woman, not animal or crop—is going to thrive."

READ

Read the passage aloud slowly. God isn't demanding that the returned exiles (the Jews) change a thing or two. Their entire lives need a turnaround.

THINK

Read the passage aloud again.

1. How would you describe the turnaround God wants from the returned exiles?
2. How does stinginess affect one's mind so that a life of misery is inevitable?
3. How does this passage speak to you today?

PRAY

Talk to God about any stinginess in your soul. If you find none, look at any misery in your life and ask God to show you if it relates to a stingy, grudging attitude.

LIVE

Sit in the feeling of generosity. Imagine yourself joyously cutting timber, building walls, and honoring God. See yourself living your life this way.

HANDING OUT WHOLENESS AND HOLINESS

HAGGAI 2:1-9

1-3   On the twenty-first day of the seventh month, the Word of GOD came through the prophet Haggai: "Tell Governor Zerubbabel son of Shealtiel and High Priest Joshua son of Jehozadak and all the people:

'Is there anyone here who saw the Temple the way it used to be, all glorious? And what do you see now? Not much, right?

4-5   "'So get to work, Zerubbabel!' — GOD is speaking.

"'Get to work, Joshua son of Jehozadak — high priest!'

"'Get to work, all you people!' — GOD is speaking.

"'Yes, get to work! For I am with you.' The GOD-of-the-Angel-Armies is speaking! 'Put into action the word I covenanted with you when you left Egypt. I'm living and breathing among you right now. Don't be timid. Don't hold back.'

6-7   "This is what GOD-of-the-Angel-Armies said: 'Before you know it, I will shake up sky and earth, ocean and fields. And I'll shake down all the godless nations. They'll bring bushels of wealth and I will fill this Temple with splendor.' GOD-of-the-Angel-Armies says so.

8   'I own the silver,
I own the gold.'
     Decree of GOD-of-the-Angel-Armies.

9   "'This Temple is going to end up far better than it started out, a glorious beginning but an even more glorious finish: a place in which I will hand out wholeness and holiness.' Decree of GOD-of-the-Angel-Armies."

READ

Read the passage aloud, injecting the emotion of the characters as much as possible.

THINK

What stands out to you from the words of GOD-of-the-Angel-Armies? Perhaps it's God shaking down bushels of wealth like apples from a tree, the word *timid,* or the recurring "Get to work!" What does this draw your attention to about yourself, about God, and about the "wholeness and holiness" God desires his people to have?

PRAY/LIVE

Let your heart get caught up in pondering this insight for a while, as though you are playing with Play-Doh. Reshape two or three experiences (past or current) by the mold of this perspective, and see what they look like. Specifically, what in your life might be helped by this "wholeness and holiness"?

Now listen for God's input on your current situation(s), remaining in the mold of wholeness and holiness. In what areas might he want you to change your mind-set or take a particular action?

THE PROACTIVE NATURE OF GOD

ZECHARIAH 2:1-5,10-13

1-5   I looked up and was surprised to see
     a man holding a tape measure in his hand.
   I said, "What are you up to?"
     "I'm on my way," he said, "to survey Jerusalem,
     to measure its width and length."
   Just then the Messenger-Angel on his way out
     met another angel coming in and said,
   "Run! Tell the Surveyor, 'Jerusalem will burst its walls —
     bursting with people, bursting with animals.
   And I'll be right there with her' — GOD's Decree — 'a wall of fire
     around unwalled Jerusalem and a radiant presence within.'"

10   "Shout and celebrate, Daughter of Zion!
   I'm on my way. I'm moving into your neighborhood!"
     GOD's Decree.

11-12   Many godless nations will be linked up with GOD at that time. ("They will become my family! I'll live in their homes!") And then you'll know for sure that GOD-of-the-Angel-Armies sent me on this mission. GOD will reclaim his Judah inheritance in the Holy Land. He'll again make clear that Jerusalem is his choice.

13   Quiet, everyone! Shh! Silence before GOD. Something's afoot in his holy house. He's on the move!

READ

Read the passage, noticing all the exclamation points.

THINK

The prophet Zechariah receives several visions from God and writes about them in detail at the beginning of his book. Take the next several minutes to ponder this vision. In the interaction God says, "Shout and celebrate, Daughter of Zion! I'm on my way. I'm moving into your neighborhood!" (verse 10). Consider God's incredible plan to send his Son, Jesus, to live among us. What comes to mind as you think about God's pursuing his people enough to move literally into their neighborhood?

"Quiet, everyone! Shh! Silence before GOD. Something's afoot in his holy house. He's on the move!" (verse 13). What fills your mind as you consider that God is active in human history? How is that reality different from what other people, the media, and our culture say about God's involvement in the world?

What does God's activity say about his character? How do you respond to this type of God?

PRAY

Allow the reality of a loving God pursuing his people, on the move and moving into your neighborhood, guide your prayers right now.

What would your world be like if God moved into the house, apartment, or building next door to you? Allow your communication with God to flow out of your thoughts.

LIVE

As you walk or drive in your neighborhood, consider the implications for your life of having God residing in your — our! — midst. And thank God for the fact that he actively pursues you.

195
196

DAY 196

GOD ENCOUNTERS

On this seventh day, review and reflect on all you have read this week. Take the time to revel in the ways you've encountered God in the past six days.

INTERESTED IN PEOPLE

ZECHARIAH 7:4-10

4-6 GOD-of-the-Angel-Armies gave me this Message for them, for all the people and for the priests: "When you held days of fasting every fifth and seventh month all these seventy years, were you doing it for me? And when you held feasts, was that for me? Hardly. You're interested in religion, I'm interested in people.

7-10 "There's nothing new to say on the subject. Don't you still have the message of the earlier prophets from the time when Jerusalem was still a thriving, bustling city and the outlying countryside, the Negev and Shephelah, was populated? [This is the message that GOD gave Zechariah.] Well, the message hasn't changed. GOD-of-the-Angel-Armies said then and says now:

"'Treat one another justly.
Love your neighbors.
Be compassionate with each other.
Don't take advantage of widows, orphans, visitors, and the poor.
Don't plot and scheme against one another — that's evil.'"

READ

Read the passage aloud slowly.

THINK

Read the passage aloud again.

1. If God were looking directly at you and saying these verses, what would he mean by the phrase, "You're interested in religion, I'm interested in people"?
2. Who do you know needing justice, love, and compassion?
3. Which of your religious activities do you think might merely be meeting your own selfish needs? Examine them.

PRAY

Thank God for being interested in people. Admit any ideas you have that God is mostly interested in church programs and what church people are supposed to do.

LIVE

Imagine God being interested in you just because you're you. Now imagine God being interested in someone you don't find interesting. Wonder at that.

BREAKING THE BEAUTIFUL COVENANT

ZECHARIAH 11:4-11

4-5 GOD commanded me, "Shepherd the sheep that are soon to be slaughtered. The people who buy them will butcher them for quick and easy money. What's worse, they'll get away with it. The people who sell them will say, 'Lucky me! God's on my side; I've got it made!' They have shepherds who couldn't care less about them."

6 GOD's Decree: "I'm washing my hands of the people of this land. From now on they're all on their own. It's dog-eat-dog, survival of the fittest, and the devil take the hindmost. Don't look for help from me."

7-8 So I took over from the crass, money-grubbing owners, and shepherded the sheep marked for slaughter. I got myself two shepherd staffs. I named one Lovely and the other Harmony. Then I went to work shepherding the sheep. Within a month I got rid of the corrupt shepherds. I got tired of putting up with them — and they couldn't stand me.

9 And then I got tired of the sheep and said, "I've had it with you — no more shepherding from me. If you die, you die; if you're attacked, you're attacked. Whoever survives can eat what's left."

10-11 Then I took the staff named Lovely and broke it across my knee, breaking the beautiful covenant I had made with all the peoples. In one stroke, both staff and covenant were broken. The money-hungry owners saw me do it and knew GOD was behind it.

READ

Read the passage several times slowly, until you begin to grasp the symbolism and what's going on.

THINK

When you consider the consequences God allows to come to Israel for their continual disobedience to him, what stands out to you? Why do you think God would allow such horrible things to happen to them? What does this have to do with you?

PRAY

Read the passage again, prayerfully. What about God does it highlight? What words or actions especially draw your attention when you consider your life in light of this passage?

LIVE

Consider the following extract from Jan Karon's *These High, Green Hills:*

> "There's something I've been wanting to ask you, Father," said Nurse Kennedy, walking with him along the hall.
>
> "Shoot."
>
> "Why is it God so often breaks our hearts?"
>
> "Well, sometimes He does it to increase our faith. That's the way He stretches us. But there's another reason, I think, why our hearts get broken."
>
> She looked at him.
>
> "Usually," he said, "what breaks is what's brittle."[12]

In what area has your heart become brittle toward God? Have you been trying to protect your heart from him? If so, why? Don't put pressure on yourself to change this: There is probably some reason you have felt the need to protect yourself. But today, with God's help, become aware of it, and explore with him what might happen if you trust him with that area of your heart.

A REMINDER OF GOD'S MESSAGE OF LOVE

MALACHI 1:1-5

1 A Message. GOD's Word to Israel through Malachi:

2-3 GOD said, "I love you."

You replied, "Really? How have you loved us?"

"Look at history" (this is GOD's answer). "Look at how differently I've treated you, Jacob, from Esau: I loved Jacob and hated Esau. I reduced pretentious Esau to a molehill, turned his whole country into a ghost town."

4 When Edom (Esau) said, "We've been knocked down, but we'll get up and start over, good as new," GOD-of-the-Angel-Armies said, "Just try it and see how far you get. When I knock you down, you stay down. People will take one look at you and say, 'Land of Evil!' and 'the GOD-cursed tribe!'

5 "Yes, take a good look. Then you'll see how faithfully I've loved you and you'll want even more, saying, 'May GOD be even greater, beyond the borders of Israel!'"

READ

Before reading, close your eyes and pay attention to your breathing. After a few minutes of this silence, whisper, "God, I'm ready to hear from you now. Speak and I will listen."

Then turn to the book of Malachi and read the first five verses.

THINK

God's overriding Message to his people, evident throughout all the books of Scripture, is this: "I love you." But our muddled and complex lives blur that Message, and we forget the power of it. We need constant reminders of what's important in life, and history is an important reminder of God's incredible love for us. Looking back on the past can help provide the clarity and focus we've lost and give us back a God-minded perspective.

LIVE

Write out the ways God has been faithful to you in the past — big and small — through your relationships, your circumstances, your family, the blessings he has provided, important events, and so on.

Take as much time as you need.

PRAY

Reread verse 5: "Yes, take a good look. Then you'll see how faithfully I've loved you and you'll want even more, saying, 'May GOD be even greater, beyond the borders of Israel!'" Follow these instructions. Pray through your list line by line. Pour out your heart to God in unabashed gratefulness. Thank him for his faithfulness throughout your life and throughout the lives of many others.

GIVE LIFE AND PEACE

MALACHI 2:5-10

5-6 "My covenant with Levi was to give life and peace. I kept my covenant with him, and he honored me. He stood in reverent awe before me. He taught the truth and did not lie. He walked with me in peace and uprightness. He kept many out of the ditch, kept them on the road.

7-9 "It's the job of priests to teach the truth. People are supposed to look to them for guidance. The priest is the messenger of GOD-of-the-Angel-Armies. But you priests have abandoned the way of priests. Your teaching has messed up many lives. You have corrupted the covenant of priest Levi. GOD-of-the-Angel-Armies says so. And so I am showing you up for who you are. Everyone will be disgusted with you and avoid you because you don't live the way I told you to live, and you don't teach my revelation truly and impartially."

10 Don't we all come from one Father? Aren't we all created by the same God? So why can't we get along? Why do we desecrate the covenant of our ancestors that binds us together?

READ

Read the passage aloud slowly.

THINK

Read the passage aloud again, but this time substitute the word *Christian* everywhere the word *priest* appears, because Peter said, as he spoke to Christians, "But you are the ones chosen by God, chosen for the high calling of priestly work, chosen to be a holy people, God's instruments to do his work and speak out for him, to tell others of the night-and-day difference he made for you — from nothing to something, from rejected to accepted" (1 Peter 2:9-10).

1. In what ways do you enjoy the work of a priest?

   ☐ giving life and peace
   ☐ keeping covenant with God
   ☐ honoring God and standing in reverent awe before God
   ☐ teaching truth and not lies
   ☐ walking with God in peace and uprightness
   ☐ keeping people out of the ditch and on the right road
   ☐ other:

2. In what ways do Christians mess up many lives and make people disgusted, not living as God says and not teaching God's truth impartially?

3. In what areas of your life do you need more of God's help to be a priest for him?

PRAY

Tell God how you feel about being "chosen for the high calling of priestly work." Admit your faults and doubts. Feel the joy of being used by God — even if you don't do it perfectly.

LIVE

Imagine God anointing you anew as a priest "to give [others] life and peace" from God.

FIT FOR GOD

MALACHI 3:1-5

1 "Look! I'm sending my messenger on ahead to clear the way for me. Suddenly, out of the blue, the Leader you've been looking for will enter his Temple — yes, the Messenger of the Covenant, the one you've been waiting for. Look! He's on his way!" A Message from the mouth of God-of-the-Angel-Armies.

2-4 But who will be able to stand up to that coming? Who can survive his appearance?

He'll be like white-hot fire from the smelter's furnace. He'll be like the strongest lye soap at the laundry. He'll take his place as a refiner of silver, as a cleanser of dirty clothes. He'll scrub the Levite priests clean, refine them like gold and silver, until they're fit for God, fit to present offerings of righteousness. Then, and only then, will Judah and Jerusalem be fit and pleasing to God, as they used to be in the years long ago.

5 "Yes, I'm on my way to visit you with Judgment. I'll present compelling evidence against sorcerers, adulterers, liars, those who exploit workers, those who take advantage of widows and orphans, those who are inhospitable to the homeless — anyone and everyone who doesn't honor me." A Message from God-of-the-Angel-Armies.

THINK

Saint Irenaeus once said, "The glory of God is man fully alive." For a few minutes, isolate the second half of this statement and think about what it means to be "fully alive." Have you ever felt this way? When? What were you doing?

READ

Now read the passage (including the expanded passage for background). Do the words *clean* and *pleasing* have positive or negative implications to you? How do they intermingle with your idea of being fully alive? Do they act like pins to a balloon? Or do they mesh organically into the bigger picture?

PRAY

With your understanding of being fully alive in one hand and your awareness of God's desire for your purity in the other, explore how much you do or do not see the two connecting. Maybe you can easily see God's presence with you in your picture of yourself fully alive, or maybe that's hard to do; maybe you think living fully must be done behind God's back. Be honest — even if you recognize that your beliefs are not true, tell the truth of what's in your heart.

LIVE

Sit quietly with God, opening yourself to what he might want to say in response to what you've shared with him today. You might look back at the passage or reconsider Irenaeus's words. Wonder at the freedom intrinsic in someone who is fully alive *and* pure before God.

THE TESTAMENTS, OLD AND NEW

MATTHEW 2:1-6

1-2 After Jesus was born in Bethlehem village, Judah territory — this was during Herod's kingship — a band of scholars arrived in Jerusalem from the East. They asked around, "Where can we find and pay homage to the newborn King of the Jews? We observed a star in the eastern sky that signaled his birth. We're on pilgrimage to worship him."

3-4 When word of their inquiry got to Herod, he was terrified — and not Herod alone, but most of Jerusalem as well. Herod lost no time. He gathered all the high priests and religion scholars in the city together and asked, "Where is the Messiah supposed to be born?"

5-6 They told him, "Bethlehem, Judah territory. The prophet Micah wrote it plainly:

> It's you, Bethlehem, in Judah's land,
>> no longer bringing up the rear.
> From you will come the leader
>> who will shepherd-rule my people, my Israel."

READ

Read the passage, trying to absorb the words from the perspective of a Jew who has never heard of Jesus before.

THINK

In his gospel, Matthew emphasizes the number of Old Testament prophecies fulfilled in the person of Jesus. The Jewish people longed to see the Messiah, the Anointed One, whom they had been expecting for several hundred years. Jesus, Matthew writes, is the one they had been waiting for.

Read the passage again, and note the Old Testament quotation. How do you feel, knowing that God orchestrated these happenings to point to Jesus?

What promises has God made to you, in Scripture or personally, that have yet to come to fruition? Do you wonder if they will ever be fulfilled?

How does Matthew's focus on Old Testament prophecies affect your situation? What implication does it have on your daily life?

PRAY

Take time to thank God for the promises he has kept in your life. Ask God to give you an extra measure of faith to trust him when you feel he may never keep his other promises to you. Admit the specific areas where you have a hard time trusting that he will be faithful.

LIVE

God keeps his promises. Live in the truth that he is a promise keeper.

DAY 203

GOD ENCOUNTERS

On this seventh day, review and reflect on all you have read this week. Take the time to revel in the ways you've encountered God in the past six days.

LIVE BEFORE GOD

MATTHEW 5:27-29,33-37

27-28 "You know the next commandment pretty well, too: 'Don't go to bed with another's spouse.' But don't think you've preserved your virtue simply by staying out of bed. Your *heart* can be corrupted by lust even quicker than your *body*. Those leering looks you think nobody notices — they also corrupt.

29 "Let's not pretend this is easier than it really is. If you want to live a morally pure life, here's what you have to do: You have to blind your right eye the moment you catch it in a lustful leer. You have to choose to live one-eyed or else be dumped on a moral trash pile. . . .

33-37 "And don't say anything you don't mean. This counsel is embedded deep in our traditions. You only make things worse when you lay down a smoke screen of pious talk, saying, 'I'll pray for you,' and never doing it, or saying, 'God be with you,' and not meaning it. You don't make your words true by embellishing them with religious lace. In making your speech sound more religious, it becomes less true. Just say 'yes' and 'no.' When you manipulate words to get your own way, you go wrong."

READ

Read the passage aloud slowly.

THINK

Imagine yourself going to the mailbox today and finding in it a letter addressed to you, containing the words of this passage. Think of yourself opening the letter. Then read the passage aloud again, and as you do, see yourself walking back from the mailbox.

1. What meaning do the words have for you? What is Jesus getting at?
2. How do you "pretend this is easier than it really is" regarding having a pure thought life? Regarding really meaning what you say?
3. How do these commands speak to the deepest part of you, the part Jesus wants?

PRAY

Ask Jesus to show you situations in which you are likely to say something you don't mean. Ask him to help you discover what that's about — perhaps impressing people or pretending to be better than you are.

LIVE

Jesus understands how difficult his words are for us. Sense yourself being pulled along with love and grace by Jesus.

PRAY WITH SIMPLICITY

MATTHEW 6:5-13

5 "And when you come before God, don't turn that into a theatrical production either. All these people making a regular show out of their prayers, hoping for stardom! Do you think God sits in a box seat?

6 "Here's what I want you to do: Find a quiet, secluded place so you won't be tempted to role-play before God. Just be there as simply and honestly as you can manage. The focus will shift from you to God, and you will begin to sense his grace.

7-13 "The world is full of so-called prayer warriors who are prayer-ignorant. They're full of formulas and programs and advice, peddling techniques for getting what you want from God. Don't fall for that nonsense. This is your Father you are dealing with, and he knows better than you what you need. With a God like this loving you, you can pray very simply. Like this:

> Our Father in heaven,
> Reveal who you are.
> Set the world right;
> Do what's best —
>   as above, so below.
> Keep us alive with three square meals.
> Keep us forgiven with you and forgiving others.
> Keep us safe from ourselves and the Devil.
> You're in charge!
> You can do anything you want!
> You're ablaze in beauty!
>   Yes. Yes. Yes."

READ

Read the passage aloud slowly, noticing what it says about simple prayer versus complex, showy prayer. What is the most important issue for you listed below? Be honest.

Simple Prayer	Complex, Showy Prayer
finding a quiet, secluded place	turning prayer into a dramatic production
not role-playing before God	making a regular show of prayers
being with God as simply and honestly as you can	using formulas, programs, and advice
watching the focus shift from you to God	using techniques to get what you want from God

THINK

Read the passage again. This time, picture yourself sitting with other people about six feet from Jesus and listening as he says these words. When does Jesus look directly at you as he teaches? What words is he saying because he knows you need them? Why are those words meant for you?

PRAY

Paraphrase the Lord's Prayer (verses 9-13). In other words, add to or change each phrase in a way that makes the prayer specific to you.

LIVE

Sit quietly before God, praying the Lord's Prayer if you wish, or just being silent. Feel the focus shift from you to God. Enjoy that.

AN INVITATION

MATTHEW 9:9-13

9   Passing along, Jesus saw a man at his work collecting taxes. His name was Matthew. Jesus said, "Come along with me." Matthew stood up and followed him.

10-11   Later when Jesus was eating supper at Matthew's house with his close followers, a lot of disreputable characters came and joined them. When the Pharisees saw him keeping this kind of company, they had a fit, and lit into Jesus' followers. "What kind of example is this from your Teacher, acting cozy with crooks and riffraff?"

12-13   Jesus, overhearing, shot back, "Who needs a doctor: the healthy or the sick? Go figure out what this Scripture means: 'I'm after mercy, not religion.' I'm here to invite outsiders, not coddle insiders."

READ

Once you are in a quiet place, thank God for the gift of his Word. Then read the passage.

THINK

When have you felt like the outsider? When have people scrutinized and criticized you for the people you associated with? Do you think their judgment was fair? Why or why not?

Ponder these words from Jesus: "'I'm after mercy, not religion.' I'm here to invite outsiders, not coddle insiders." Where do you think Jesus was going with this statement?

If you were present that day, how might have you responded?

PRAY

Hold your hands open in front of you. Sit in silence for several moments, staring at them. Invite the Holy Spirit to guide your life today. Pray that your hands will be a physical representation of what you desire your heart to be. Acknowledge that you are a physical open invitation to the Holy Spirit for his guidance toward paths of mercy, not religiosity. Ask him to bring to mind outsiders to whom you can show mercy today.

LIVE

As you are reminded of God's mercy on your life, take the risk of showing mercy to outsiders.

JESUS THE HEALER

MATTHEW 9:18-26

18-19 As he finished saying this, a local official appeared, bowed politely, and said, "My daughter has just now died. If you come and touch her, she will live." Jesus got up and went with him, his disciples following along.

20-22 Just then a woman who had hemorrhaged for twelve years slipped in from behind and lightly touched his robe. She was thinking to herself, "If I can just put a finger on his robe, I'll get well." Jesus turned — caught her at it. Then he reassured her: "Courage, daughter. You took a risk of faith, and now you're well." The woman was well from then on.

23-26 By now they had arrived at the house of the town official, and pushed their way through the gossips looking for a story and the neighbors bringing in casseroles. Jesus was abrupt: "Clear out! This girl isn't dead. She's sleeping." They told him he didn't know what he was talking about. But when Jesus had gotten rid of the crowd, he went in, took the girl's hand, and pulled her to her feet — alive. The news was soon out, and traveled throughout the region.

READ

Read the passage.

THINK/PRAY

Pick the episode that is more striking to you — either the healing of the hemorrhaging woman or the raising of the official's daughter. (If you choose the first story, read Leviticus 15:25-30 now to better understand her situation.)

Read the passage again, carefully. Immerse yourself in the story as though you are a character in it — an observer or one named in the passage. Use every sense to enter the scene; take part in each moment. Where are you in relation to others? To Jesus? What is it like for you to be there? How are you feeling?

After you exit the scene, talk with Jesus about what you saw and experienced.

LIVE

Think about your experience in the scene, as well as your discussion with Jesus, and jot down anything you want to remember.

Put your pen aside and sit quietly for a few minutes. Listen to the sound of your own breathing and the silence.

End by saying the Lord's Prayer aloud: "Our Father in heaven, reveal who you are. Set the world right; do what's best — as above, so below. Keep us alive with three square meals. Keep us forgiven with you and forgiving others. Keep us safe from ourselves and the Devil. You're in charge! You can do anything you want! You're ablaze in beauty! Yes. Yes. Yes" (Matthew 6:9-13).

WALK WITH ME

MATTHEW 11:28-30

28-30 "Are you tired? Worn out? Burned out on religion? Come to me. Get away with me and you'll recover your life. I'll show you how to take a real rest. Walk with me and work with me — watch how I do it. Learn the unforced rhythms of grace. I won't lay anything heavy or ill-fitting on you. Keep company with me and you'll learn to live freely and lightly."

READ

Read the passage slowly.

THINK

Read the passage again, listening for the words or phrases that stand out to you, such as:

- "come to me"
- "recover your life"
- "real rest"
- "walk with me and work with me"
- "watch how I do it"
- "keep company with me"

Notice the many different ways Jesus says, "Hang out with me." Which one do you find most inviting? Why?

What would it feel like to walk with Jesus and work with him? It's okay to be honest; "freely and lightly" may not describe what you think it would really be like. Instead you might think it would be forced and difficult. If so, what would you *desire* for it to be like?

Have you feared that a walk with Jesus might require heavy or ill-fitting things? What are they?

PRAY

Jesus speaks very personally and conversationally in this passage, using phrases like "Come to me." In fact, *I* or *me* occurs eight times, and *you* occurs five times. So consider that Jesus has been talking to *you*. What is your reply? What do you need to discuss with Jesus today?

LIVE

Walk with Jesus, either in your mind or on an actual walk. As you do, turn these words from Jesus over in your mind: rest, unforced, keep company with me, freely, lightly.

EYES SCREWED SHUT

MATTHEW 13:10-17

10　　The disciples came up and asked, "Why do you tell stories?"

11-15　　He replied, "You've been given insight into God's kingdom. You know how it works. Not everybody has this gift, this insight; it hasn't been given to them. Whenever someone has a ready heart for this, the insights and understandings flow freely. But if there is no readiness, any trace of receptivity soon disappears. That's why I tell stories: to create readiness, to nudge the people toward receptive insight. In their present state they can stare till doomsday and not see it, listen till they're blue in the face and not get it. I don't want Isaiah's forecast repeated all over again:

> Your ears are open but you don't hear a thing.
> 　Your eyes are awake but you don't see a thing.
> The people are blockheads!
> They stick their fingers in their ears
> 　so they won't have to listen;
> They screw their eyes shut
> 　so they won't have to look,
> 　so they won't have to deal with me face-to-face
> 　and let me heal them.

16-17　　"But you have God-blessed eyes — eyes that see! And God-blessed ears — ears that hear! A lot of people, prophets and humble believers among them, would have given anything to see what you are seeing, to hear what you are hearing, but never had the chance."

READ

Read the passage carefully.

THINK

Notice what Jesus says about human hearts. What does he draw attention to about our receptivity to his message? How does he deal with our resistance? What does he want for us?

Now read Jesus' words again, and hear them as if he is saying them to you personally. Meditate on his words until the message becomes familiar. What stands out that relates to your life?

PRAY

Tell Jesus about your meditation — your thoughts and feelings. Listen for his response.

LIVE

Search your memory (or your journal) for any insights God has given you in recent weeks as you have interacted with his Message. What have those truths led you to do? Were there times when God invited you to act on or think about something, but you ignored the request or put it off? Why? Revisit that experience with Jesus. Remember that his greatest desire is not to get you to act a certain way but to engage with you in relationship.

DAY 210

GOD ENCOUNTERS

On this seventh day, review and reflect on all you have read this week. Take the time to revel in the ways you've encountered God in the past six days.

A MATTER OF THE HEART

MATTHEW 15:1-14

1-2　After that, Pharisees and religion scholars came to Jesus all the way from Jerusalem, criticizing, "Why do your disciples play fast and loose with the rules?"

3-9　But Jesus put it right back on them. "Why do you use your rules to play fast and loose with God's commands? God clearly says, 'Respect your father and mother,' and, 'Anyone denouncing father or mother should be killed.' But you weasel around that by saying, 'Whoever wants to, can say to father and mother, What I owed to you I've given to God.' That can hardly be called respecting a parent. You cancel God's command by your rules. Frauds! Isaiah's prophecy of you hit the bull's-eye:

These people make a big show of saying the right thing,
　but their heart isn't in it.
They act like they're worshiping me,
　but they don't mean it.
They just use me as a cover
　for teaching whatever suits their fancy."

10-11　He then called the crowd together and said, "Listen, and take this to heart. It's not what you swallow that pollutes your life, but what you vomit up."

12　Later his disciples came and told him, "Did you know how upset the Pharisees were when they heard what you said?"

13-14　Jesus shrugged it off. "Every tree that wasn't planted by my Father in heaven will be pulled up by its roots. Forget them. They are blind men leading blind men. When a blind man leads a blind man, they both end up in the ditch."

READ

Sit at a table with this devotional. Read this passage with your palms open as a way of communicating that you are open to hear from God.

THINK

Jesus seems to spend a lot of time provoking the Pharisees by speaking harshly to them. Of all the religious groups in Israel, Jesus rebukes the Pharisees the most. And yet, these are supposed to be the most devout leaders in the entire nation. Joining Jesus in bashing the Pharisees is tempting. Thinking *I'm glad I'm not like them* is easy. But we often resemble the Pharisees more than we'd like to admit.

Think back and identify a time when your heart responded to Jesus the way the Pharisees responded to him. What might help you identify the moments when your heart is more Pharisee-like than Jesus-like? Who can you invite to help keep your heart in check?

Ponder the words Matthew quotes from Isaiah (verses 8-9). Under what circumstances does this describe you? What do you think God wants you to do about it?

PRAY

Ask God to give you a Jesus-like heart, one that is humble, transparent, and genuine.

LIVE

Invite others to help you keep your heart in check by giving them permission to ask you tough heart questions.

THE SOFTENED HEART

MATTHEW 19:3-9

3   One day the Pharisees were badgering him: "Is it legal for a man to divorce his wife for any reason?"

4-6   He answered, "Haven't you read in your Bible that the Creator originally made man and woman for each other, male and female? And because of this, a man leaves father and mother and is firmly bonded to his wife, becoming one flesh—no longer two bodies but one. Because God created this organic union of the two sexes, no one should desecrate his art by cutting them apart."

7   They shot back in rebuttal, "If that's so, why did Moses give instructions for divorce papers and divorce procedures?"

8-9   Jesus said, "Moses provided for divorce as a concession to your hardheartedness, but it is not part of God's original plan. I'm holding you to the original plan, and holding you liable for adultery if you divorce your faithful wife and then marry someone else. I make an exception in cases where the spouse has committed adultery."

READ

Read the passage aloud slowly. Consider that this teaching is an example Jesus gave from a longer teaching about forgiveness.

THINK

Matthew recorded this to come just after Jesus tells the parable about the servant who is forgiven a great deal and cannot forgive someone who has harmed him only slightly.

Imagine that you are there as Jesus is teaching. You've heard his parable about the unforgiving servant, and now he speaks of people being hardhearted. As you read the passage again, consider that we divorce ourselves from people in many ways — leaving a church, leaving a project, leaving a friendship. (If you wish, read Matthew 18:23-35 or try to recall the parable of the unforgiving servant. Try to feel for yourself that servant's incredible hardheartedness.)

1. What is hardheartedness really about?
2. How does hardheartedness toward others violate God's will for all of us?
3. Where in your life is hardheartedness a problem?
4. What is God urging you to do to cultivate a softened heart?

PRAY

Ask God to bring to mind those who might want to plead with you, "Give me a chance" (see Matthew 18:26,29). Try to picture yourself having mercy on this person. If it seems impossible, ask God to pour out his love into your heart.

LIVE

Sit quietly before God. Become hardhearted — how does this feel in your body? Become softhearted — how does that feel in your body? Stay with the softheartedness for several minutes.

✚ JESUS THREW THEM OUT

MATTHEW 21:12-17

12-14   Jesus went straight to the Temple and threw out everyone who had set up shop, buying and selling. He kicked over the tables of loan sharks and the stalls of dove merchants. He quoted this text:

> My house was designated a house of prayer;
> You have made it a hangout for thieves.

Now there was room for the blind and crippled to get in. They came to Jesus and he healed them.

15-16   When the religious leaders saw the outrageous things he was doing, and heard all the children running and shouting through the Temple, "Hosanna to David's Son!" they were up in arms and took him to task. "Do you hear what these children are saying?"

Jesus said, "Yes, I hear them. And haven't you read in God's Word, 'From the mouths of children and babies I'll furnish a place of praise'?"

17   Fed up, Jesus turned on his heel and left the city for Bethany, where he spent the night.

READ

Read the passage aloud.

THINK/PRAY

Imagine you are there when Jesus comes in the temple and cleanses it. To get your imagination going, read the passage a second time, but then set this book aside, close your eyes, and see yourself as a part of the scene.

Who are you? Where are you? Smell the incense and the scent of burning, sacrificed animal flesh. Jump at the loud crash of the tables and the fury in Jesus' voice as the sounds echo in the stunned silence. What are the expressions on the faces around you?

Now let the blind and crippled come into your view. Watch Jesus healing them. Listen to the voices of the children as they play and shout, "Hosanna!" What's your reaction to them? To Jesus' interaction with the disabled? To the indignation of the religious leaders? (Include not only your mental reaction but your physical reaction too, if any.)

Now follow Jesus as he walks out of the city, still fuming. Picture him initiating a conversation with you about the events of the day. Imagine that he asks you what it was like. Tell him.

LIVE

In C. S. Lewis's *The Lion, the Witch and the Wardrobe,* the lion, Aslan, "isn't safe. But he's good."[13]

Consider this statement in light of what you've just read about Jesus. How does this view of Jesus — that he sometimes does things that are painful to us — alter your perception of who he is? In what ways does this affect how you relate to him?

OVERLOOKED AND IGNORED

MATTHEW 25:31-40

31-33 "When he finally arrives, blazing in beauty and all his angels with him, the Son of Man will take his place on his glorious throne. Then all the nations will be arranged before him and he will sort the people out, much as a shepherd sorts out sheep and goats, putting sheep to his right and goats to his left.

34-36 "Then the King will say to those on his right, 'Enter, you who are blessed by my Father! Take what's coming to you in this kingdom. It's been ready for you since the world's foundation. And here's why:

I was hungry and you fed me,
I was thirsty and you gave me a drink,
I was homeless and you gave me a room,
I was shivering and you gave me clothes,
I was sick and you stopped to visit,
I was in prison and you came to me.'

37-40 "Then those 'sheep' are going to say, 'Master, what are you talking about? When did we ever see you hungry and feed you, thirsty and give you a drink? And when did we ever see you sick or in prison and come to you?' Then the King will say, 'I'm telling the solemn truth: Whenever you did one of these things to someone overlooked or ignored, that was me — you did it to me.'"

READ

Read the passage aloud slowly. As you read it, understand that Jesus said these words aloud too. They are his words.

THINK

This is a part of an entire sermon (or thematic sermon series) on watchfulness (see Matthew 23–25). The people in this passage were watching for the needy, but they didn't know it was Jesus they were watching. Read the passage again silently and slowly.

1. What words or phrases stand out to you?
2. Who are the overlooked and ignored in your life?
3. Imagine yourself overlooked and ignored. What do you now have in common with Jesus?
4. In what ways is God asking you to give someone food, drink, a room, clothes; to stop and visit someone; to go to a person locked away physically, emotionally, or mentally?

PRAY

Ask Jesus how he exists in the overlooked and ignored. Ponder this mystery. Ask him to show you your next step in grasping some part of this.

LIVE

As you serve people who are overlooked and ignored, be mindful of the presence of Jesus. See if you can spot him.

MY GOD, WHY?

MATTHEW 27:45-54

45-46 From noon to three, the whole earth was dark. Around mid-afternoon Jesus groaned out of the depths, crying loudly, *"Eli, Eli, lama sabachthani?"* which means, "My God, my God, why have you abandoned me?"

47-49 Some bystanders who heard him said, "He's calling for Elijah." One of them ran and got a sponge soaked in sour wine and lifted it on a stick so he could drink. The others joked, "Don't be in such a hurry. Let's see if Elijah comes and saves him."

50 But Jesus, again crying out loudly, breathed his last.

51-53 At that moment, the Temple curtain was ripped in two, top to bottom. There was an earthquake, and rocks were split in pieces. What's more, tombs were opened up, and many bodies of believers asleep in their graves were raised. (After Jesus' resurrection, they left the tombs, entered the holy city, and appeared to many.)

54 The captain of the guard and those with him, when they saw the earthquake and everything else that was happening, were scared to death. They said, "This has to be the Son of God!"

READ

If you have time, read Matthew 26:31–27:56. If not, read the shorter passage.

THINK

Church historian Bruce Shelley wrote, "Christianity is the only major religion to have as its central event the humiliation of its God."[14] Consider not only that Jesus' humiliation is immense, but his anguish is deeper than we can imagine. His own people wildly demanded his death. His friends deserted him. And now even his intimately loving Father has turned away.

Spend time wrestling heart and mind with why the Almighty would choose such a path. Reread Jesus' own words a few times to get closer to his experience.

PRAY

What wells up inside you as you spend time with the paradox of Jesus' death? Wonder? Grief? Distractedness? Tell Jesus about what surfaces. Then gently pull your thoughts back to his sacrifice and death, reading the passage again if you need to. Allow yourself to sink into the event deeply, again being aware of your reaction and talking to Jesus about it.

LIVE

Find a new place to be silent. For example, walk in a quiet place or sit in an empty church sanctuary. Bring your wristwatch or PDA and set the alarm so you can forget the time until it reminds you. Meditate on Jesus' sacrifice for you, then wait for what he would have you receive from him.

PARALYZED AND DESPERATE

MARK 2:1-12

1-5 After a few days, Jesus returned to Capernaum, and word got around that he was back home. A crowd gathered, jamming the entrance so no one could get in or out. He was teaching the Word. They brought a paraplegic to him, carried by four men. When they weren't able to get in because of the crowd, they removed part of the roof and lowered the paraplegic on his stretcher. Impressed by their bold belief, Jesus said to the paraplegic, "Son, I forgive your sins."

6-7 Some religion scholars sitting there started whispering among themselves, "He can't talk that way! That's blasphemy! God and only God can forgive sins."

8-12 Jesus knew right away what they were thinking, and said, "Why are you so skeptical? Which is simpler: to say to the paraplegic, 'I forgive your sins,' or say, 'Get up, take your stretcher, and start walking'? Well, just so it's clear that I'm the Son of Man and authorized to do either, or both . . ." (he looked now at the paraplegic), "Get up. Pick up your stretcher and go home." And the man did it — got up, grabbed his stretcher, and walked out, with everyone there watching him. They rubbed their eyes, incredulous — and then praised God, saying, "We've never seen anything like this!"

READ

Ask a friend or family member to read the verses aloud to you. Close your eyes and listen intently.

THINK

Imagine yourself in the story, referring to the text again as much as you need to. For a few minutes each, place yourself in the skins of the different individuals. Consider yourself on the roof with the four friends and the paralytic. Become the crippled man on the mat. Think of yourself as one of the four friends. Imagine yourself as someone standing in the crowded room of the house, able to easily see and hear the Pharisees. And consider yourself the owner of the house.

With which person in the story do you identify the most? Why?

PRAY

Imagine yourself again as the paralytic lying on his stretcher. Jesus looks at you and says, "Son, I forgive your sins." What is the expression on his face? What is the tone of his voice? What are you feeling when you hear those words?

Talk to Jesus about his actions and your reactions — mental, emotional, physical, spiritual.

LIVE

Consider those people around you who need a life-altering interaction with Jesus. What might you need to do to bring them to the feet of Jesus, even if it means making a big sacrifice for them?

DAY 217

GOD ENCOUNTERS

On this seventh day, review and reflect on all you have read this week. Take the time to revel in the ways you've encountered God in the past six days.

TELLING YOUR WHOLE STORY

MARK 5:25-34

25-29 A woman who had suffered a condition of hemorrhaging for twelve years — a long succession of physicians had treated her, and treated her badly, taking all her money and leaving her worse off than before — had heard about Jesus. She slipped in from behind and touched his robe. She was thinking to herself, "If I can put a finger on his robe, I can get well." The moment she did it, the flow of blood dried up. She could feel the change and knew her plague was over and done with.

30 At the same moment, Jesus felt energy discharging from him. He turned around to the crowd and asked, "Who touched my robe?"

31 His disciples said, "What are you talking about? With this crowd pushing and jostling you, you're asking, 'Who touched me?' Dozens have touched you!"

32-33 But he went on asking, looking around to see who had done it. The woman, knowing what had happened, knowing she was the one, stepped up in fear and trembling, knelt before him, and gave him the whole story.

34 Jesus said to her, "Daughter, you took a risk of faith, and now you're healed and whole. Live well, live blessed! Be healed of your plague."

READ

Read the passage aloud slowly.

THINK

Read the passage again, putting yourself in the place of the woman. (If it helps to imagine yourself instead as a man with an oozing sore, that's fine.)

1. From where did you get the courage to come behind Jesus and touch his clothes?
2. When Jesus looks at you, how do you feel?
3. How does it feel for you to tell Jesus your story—and for him to listen so well? (Read in the expanded passage how he also listens well when he has a little girl to heal.)
4. How does it feel to be complimented publicly by this holy man?

PRAY

Tell Jesus the "whole story" about something that's troubling you. Kneel as the woman did. Let the eyes of Jesus rest on you and bless you.

LIVE

Get up from your kneeling position and then sit or stand. Close your eyes and sense that you are living well, living blessed.

TAKE YOUR TURN

MARK 7:24-30

24-26 From there Jesus set out for the vicinity of Tyre. He entered a house there where he didn't think he would be found, but he couldn't escape notice. He was barely inside when a woman who had a disturbed daughter heard where he was. She came and knelt at his feet, begging for help. The woman was Greek, Syro-Phoenician by birth. She asked him to cure her daughter.

27 He said, "Stand in line and take your turn. The children get fed first. If there's any left over, the dogs get it."

28 She said, "Of course, Master. But don't dogs under the table get scraps dropped by the children?"

29-30 Jesus was impressed. "You're right! On your way! Your daughter is no longer disturbed. The demonic affliction is gone." She went home and found her daughter relaxed on the bed, the torment gone for good.

READ

Read the expanded passage to get the big picture in which this incident occurs. As you do, identify with Jesus' disciples: Witness his amazing miracles. Feel the exhaustion of not even having time to eat. See the people constantly pressing in on all sides.

Now reread the shorter passage. What is your reaction to the Greek woman's request? How do you feel when Jesus initially turns her down? When he changes his mind?

THINK

Pause to allow the Holy Spirit to help you understand what your initial reactions tell you about your heart.

Then take a moment to look more closely at this woman. What tensions, concerns, and frustrations fill her daily life? What do you see in her face when she's told to "stand in line"? When she replies? What does she feel when she sees her healed daughter?

Maybe at the end of this meditation you see things in a new light. In what ways does your new perspective mingle with your first reaction?

PRAY/LIVE

Become aware of Jesus in the room with you now, inviting you to talk with him about what today's passage was like for you. Don't hide feelings and thoughts that have surfaced within you, but openly share with him any questions, frustrations, or concerns you have. What does Jesus want you to see today? What does he want you to know? Spend several minutes in silence considering what you've experienced.

HEARTSTRINGS

MARK 10:17-22

17 As he went out into the street, a man came running up, greeted him with great reverence, and asked, "Good Teacher, what must I do to get eternal life?"

18-19 Jesus said, "Why are you calling me good? No one is good, only God. You know the commandments: Don't murder, don't commit adultery, don't steal, don't lie, don't cheat, honor your father and mother."

20 He said, "Teacher, I have — from my youth — kept them all!"

21 Jesus looked him hard in the eye — and loved him! He said, "There's one thing left: Go sell whatever you own and give it to the poor. All your wealth will then be heavenly wealth. And come follow me."

22 The man's face clouded over. This was the last thing he expected to hear, and he walked off with a heavy heart. He was holding on tight to a lot of things, and not about to let go.

READ

Pick a pace and read this passage quickly. Read it again at a different pace. Did you notice anything different the second time?

THINK

Write down your thoughts about this story. How are you similar to the rich man? How are you different?

Jesus knows that, though the rich man is morally good, he still has strings attached to his heart that will keep him from being a devoted follower.

Take an internal inventory of your heart. What things are deeply attached to your heart that must be relinquished for you to be a whole-hearted follower of Jesus? They may be possessions, but they may also be thoughts, relationships, activities, and so on.

Later in the passage, Jesus says this about anyone's chance of getting into God's kingdom: "No chance at all if you think you can pull it off by yourself. Every chance in the world if you let God do it" (verse 27). Based on these words from Jesus, write in your own words a description of the grace God offers to each one of us.

PRAY

Reflect on God's grace. Thank God for the grace he extends to you. Confess the times when you have abused his grace. Offer God the strings of your heart, those that keep you from completely following Jesus. Ask God to help you sever those strings and replace them with fray-proof connections to him.

LIVE

Live in freedom and follow Jesus.

THE BIG PICTURE

MARK 12:28-34

28 One of the religion scholars came up. Hearing the lively exchanges of question and answer and seeing how sharp Jesus was in his answers, he put in his question: "Which is most important of all the commandments?"

29-31 Jesus said, "The first in importance is, 'Listen, Israel: The Lord your God is one; so love the Lord God with all your passion and prayer and intelligence and energy.' And here is the second: 'Love others as well as you love yourself.' There is no other commandment that ranks with these."

32-33 The religion scholar said, "A wonderful answer, Teacher! So lucid and accurate — that God is one and there is no other. And loving him with all passion and intelligence and energy, and loving others as well as you love yourself. Why, that's better than all offerings and sacrifices put together!"

34 When Jesus realized how insightful he was, he said, "You're almost there, right on the border of God's kingdom."

After that, no one else dared ask a question.

READ

Read the passage aloud slowly.

THINK

Put yourself in the place of the religion scholar. You have studied theology and can explain its intricate details. You are weary with how most scholars argue over minor issues. You've come to Jesus to ask him to give you the big picture. Read the passage again, letting Jesus answer you directly.

Be impressed with Jesus' answer: He has combined part of the often-repeated *Shema Israel* (see Deuteronomy 6:4-9) and the last part of a much less quoted command: "Don't seek revenge or carry a grudge against any of your people. Love your neighbor as yourself. I am God" (Leviticus 19:18).

Consider an issue you've been puzzling over, a decision you need to make, or an approach you need to take with a difficult person. How does Jesus' simple but majestic summary help you?

PRAY

Ask God to help you love him "with all your passion and prayer and intelligence and energy." Take one at a time, if you wish. Then consider someone you know. Ask God to help you love that person the way you already love yourself. (You feed yourself, you clothe yourself, you give yourself a place to live — that's love.)

LIVE

Picture Jesus saying to you, "Love the Lord God with all your passion and prayer and intelligence and energy. . . . Love others as well as you love yourself." Don't take this as a scolding but as the best, wisest thing any person could do.

221

PETER BLOWS IT

MARK 14:66-72

66-67 While all this was going on, Peter was down in the courtyard. One of the Chief Priest's servant girls came in and, seeing Peter warming himself there, looked hard at him and said, "You were with the Nazarene, Jesus."

68 He denied it: "I don't know what you're talking about." He went out on the porch. A rooster crowed.

69-70 The girl spotted him and began telling the people standing around, "He's one of them." He denied it again.

After a little while, the bystanders brought it up again. "You've *got* to be one of them. You've got 'Galilean' written all over you."

71-72 Now Peter got really nervous and swore, "I never laid eyes on this man you're talking about." Just then the rooster crowed a second time. Peter remembered how Jesus had said, "Before a rooster crows twice, you'll deny me three times." He collapsed in tears.

READ

As you read the passage, put yourself in Peter's sandals. To get a more vivid picture of what is happening, skim the expanded reading.

THINK

How does Peter feel to be in the courtyard? What has happened since his bold declaration of devotion to Jesus no matter what, earlier in the chapter? What thoughts shoot through Peter's mind that lead him to leave the fireside for the porch?

Now imagine that the rooster has crowed and reality is caving in on Peter. Sit beside him in his anguish. What is he experiencing? As he remembers Jesus' words, what does Jesus' face look like in his mind's eye? What are the tones of Jesus' voice?

PRAY/LIVE

Let your meditation on Peter's failure lead you to consider your own heart and life. Where have you blown it lately? Talk to Jesus about this. Bravely let yourself feel the depth of what you've done. You might speak a prayer of humility or thanksgiving, or a request for something you need. Notice what you expect Jesus to do or say in response.

Now read the passage again slowly. What is Jesus saying in response to you? Be open to how he may be reacting differently to you or to your failure than you expected. Write down what Jesus' response was and what experiencing that was like.

THE MAIN CHARACTER IN THIS DRAMA

LUKE 3:16-20

16-17 But John intervened: "I'm baptizing you here in the river. The main character in this drama, to whom I'm a mere stagehand, will ignite the kingdom life, a fire, the Holy Spirit within you, changing you from the inside out. He's going to clean house — make a clean sweep of your lives. He'll place everything true in its proper place before God; everything false he'll put out with the trash to be burned."

18-20 There was a lot more of this — words that gave strength to the people, words that put heart in them. The Message! But Herod, the ruler, stung by John's rebuke in the matter of Herodias, his brother Philip's wife, capped his long string of evil deeds with this outrage: He put John in jail.

READ

Read the passage aloud four times, each time reading it with a different volume.

THINK

These verses tell us about John the Baptist, a torchbearer for the coming of Jesus' ministry, calling people to repent.

Focus first on the words describing "the main character in this drama." In your life, what would it mean to be a "mere stagehand" where the main character is Jesus? What might be some areas of your life where the Holy Spirit will make a clean sweep, changing you?

Now think about John's responses in the first few verses of the passage, concerning generosity, justice, and honesty.

PRAY

What do you need to repent of in areas where you have failed to be generous, just, and honest in the past week? Invite the Holy Spirit to put everything false "out with the trash to be burned."

Ask God to help you grow in generosity — for example, with your money, time, gifts, passions, energy, and so on.

Ask God to help you grow as an advocate for justice — for example, in your neighborhood, in your city, for the poor, for the unborn, for other people in the world, and so on.

Ask God to reveal areas of dishonesty or deception in your life. Implore him to give you the grace and courage to live a life of honesty and integrity.

LIVE

Live generously, justly, and honestly today, as a mere stagehand to the main character in this drama: Jesus.

DAY 224

GOD ENCOUNTERS

On this seventh day, review and reflect on all you have read this week. Take the time to revel in the ways you've encountered God in the past six days.

NO RUN-OF-THE-MILL SINNER

LUKE 6:27-36

27-30 "To you who are ready for the truth, I say this: Love your enemies. Let them bring out the best in you, not the worst. When someone gives you a hard time, respond with the energies of prayer for that person. If someone slaps you in the face, stand there and take it. If someone grabs your shirt, giftwrap your best coat and make a present of it. If someone takes unfair advantage of you, use the occasion to practice the servant life. No more tit-for-tat stuff. Live generously.

31-34 "Here is a simple rule of thumb for behavior: Ask yourself what you want people to do for you; then grab the initiative and do it for *them*! If you only love the lovable, do you expect a pat on the back? Run-of-the-mill sinners do that. If you only help those who help you, do you expect a medal? Garden-variety sinners do that. If you only give for what you hope to get out of it, do you think that's charity? The stingiest of pawnbrokers does that.

35-36 "I tell you, love your enemies. Help and give without expecting a return. You'll never — I promise — regret it. Live out this God-created identity the way our Father lives toward us, generously and graciously, even when we're at our worst. Our Father is kind; you be kind."

READ

Read the passage aloud slowly.

THINK

Read the passage aloud a second time, but pretend you are Jesus. Get into it and read it like you mean it; say the words and phrases the way you think he would have. Perhaps gently? Perhaps warmly? Perhaps passionately?

Read the passage aloud one more time, but this time put yourself in the place of Jesus' listener; you're sitting in the front row as Jesus speaks and looks directly at you.

1. If Jesus spoke these words to you, what would they mean?
2. Which words would stand out to you?
3. What might Jesus be trying to get across to you?

PRAY

Thank our kind God that he loves his enemies. Thank God that he loves you when you act as if you barely know him. Take the words that stood out to you (see question 2) and paraphrase those back to God in prayer.

LIVE

Sit quietly and picture the kind of person you would be if you were to:

- let your enemies "bring out the best in you"
- respond with the energies of prayer for people
- "practice the servant life" when someone is unfair
- "live generously"
- give without expecting in return

225

DO YOU SEE THIS WOMAN?

LUKE 7:37-47

37-39 Just then a woman of the village, the town harlot, having learned that Jesus was a guest in the home of the Pharisee, came with a bottle of very expensive perfume and stood at his feet, weeping, raining tears on his feet. Letting down her hair, she dried his feet, kissed them, and anointed them with the perfume. When the Pharisee who had invited him saw this, he said to himself, "If this man was the prophet I thought he was, he would have known what kind of woman this is who is falling all over him."

40 Jesus said to him, "Simon, I have something to tell you."

"Oh? Tell me."

41-42 "Two men were in debt to a banker. One owed five hundred silver pieces, the other fifty. Neither of them could pay up, and so the banker canceled both debts. Which of the two would be more grateful?"

43-47 Simon answered, "I suppose the one who was forgiven the most."

"That's right," said Jesus. Then turning to the woman, but speaking to Simon, he said, "Do you see this woman? I came to your home; you provided no water for my feet, but she rained tears on my feet and dried them with her hair. You gave me no greeting, but from the time I arrived she hasn't quit kissing my feet. You provided nothing for freshening up, but she has soothed my feet with perfume. Impressive, isn't it? She was forgiven many, many sins, and so she is very, very grateful. If the forgiveness is minimal, the gratitude is minimal."

READ

Read the passage slowly, noticing the major players and actions in the story. Picture the setting's sounds, smells, and sights.

THINK

Now choose one person in the story with whom you identify most — the Pharisee, the town harlot, or an onlooker — and read the story again. Imaginatively enter the scene, experiencing everything from that person's perspective. Hear the conversations. Feel the silence in the room as Jesus' feet are tenderly washed. Now listen to Jesus' voice and watch his face as he speaks. What do you feel? What thoughts go through your head?

PRAY

Talk with Jesus about what this experience has stirred up in you.

LIVE

Oswald Chambers said, "If human love does not carry a man beyond himself, it is not love. If love is always discreet, always wise, always sensible and calculating, never carried beyond itself, it is not love at all. It may be affection, it may be warmth of feeling, but it has not the true nature of love in it."[15]

Think about the degree of restraint or abandon you show in your relationship with Jesus (and with others). Consider the conscious or unconscious decisions you are constantly making about the way you'll act in that relationship. When does emotional momentum stir you? What do you do when it does? Under what circumstances do you set limits or hold back? What expectations or fears underlie your decisions? Share these with Jesus. What is something you could do today that would have "the true nature of love in it"?

SITTING BEFORE THE MASTER

LUKE 10:38-42

38-40   As they continued their travel, Jesus entered a village. A woman by the name of Martha welcomed him and made him feel quite at home. She had a sister, Mary, who sat before the Master, hanging on every word he said. But Martha was pulled away by all she had to do in the kitchen. Later, she stepped in, interrupting them. "Master, don't you care that my sister has abandoned the kitchen to me? Tell her to lend me a hand."

41-42   The Master said, "Martha, dear Martha, you're fussing far too much and getting yourself worked up over nothing. One thing only is essential, and Mary has chosen it — it's the main course, and won't be taken from her."

READ

This passage might be very familiar to you. So before reading, pause and ask God to give you fresh eyes and an open heart to absorb it. Then read it carefully.

THINK

Prayerfully let your creativity loose as you engage with this text. First put yourself in the skin of Mary. On that day, what might you be doing? What's going on around you in the house? What are you thinking and feeling when Martha complains about you?

Now, put yourself in Martha's shoes. What are you preparing? What are your motivations? What are you feeling? What might you be thinking and feeling after Jesus says those words to you?

LIVE

The text says that Mary "sat before the Master." Now it's your turn. Take an empty chair and place it in the middle of the room. Sit or kneel in front of it, imagining Jesus seated there. Read the passage again. Stay in this posture, in the silence, and ponder who Jesus is.

PRAY

As you remain before the chair, whisper, "Jesus, who am I more like today: Mary or Martha?" Don't rush this experience. Even if an urge to get up comes, continue to be still and sit in silence. Anticipate that Jesus will communicate with you. Wait for him and allow him to speak words of promise, correction, or comfort into your life.

LIVING IN GOD-REALITY

LUKE 12:25-34

25-28 "Has anyone by fussing before the mirror ever gotten taller by so much as an inch? If fussing can't even do that, why fuss at all? Walk into the fields and look at the wildflowers. They don't fuss with their appearance — but have you ever seen color and design quite like it? The ten best-dressed men and women in the country look shabby alongside them. If God gives such attention to the wildflowers, most of them never even seen, don't you think he'll attend to you, take pride in you, do his best for you?

29-32 "What I'm trying to do here is get you to relax, not be so preoccupied with *getting* so you can respond to God's *giving*. People who don't know God and the way he works fuss over these things, but you know both God and how he works. Steep yourself in God-reality, God-initiative, God-provisions. You'll find all your everyday human concerns will be met. Don't be afraid of missing out. You're my dearest friends! The Father wants to give you the very kingdom itself.

33-34 "Be generous. Give to the poor. Get yourselves a bank that can't go bankrupt, a bank in heaven far from bankrobbers, safe from embezzlers, a bank you can bank on. It's obvious, isn't it? The place where your treasure is, is the place you will most want to be, and end up being."

READ

Read the passage aloud slowly. Pretend you and Jesus are sitting in Starbucks, and he's saying these words to you quietly.

THINK

Now pretend that you've come home, and you're going over in your mind what Jesus said to you. Read the passage again.

1. What words or phrases draw you the most?
2. What do you think Jesus is trying to say to you?
3. In order to do what Jesus said, what are you going to have to really trust for?

   ☐ that he'll "do his best for you"
   ☐ that by *giving* instead of *getting,* you'll still have everything you need
   ☐ that "God-reality, God-initiative, God-provisions" are really enough
   ☐ other:

4. How do you feel about this?

PRAY

Respond to God about truly trusting him for these practical, important matters. Be honest about what you are — and are not — ready to do.

LIVE

Sit quietly before God. Receive from him the idea that he is your treasure: "The place where your treasure is, is the place you will most want to be, and end up being."

LOST AND FOUND

LUKE 15:1-10

1-3   By this time a lot of men and women of doubtful reputation were hanging around Jesus, listening intently. The Pharisees and religion scholars were not pleased, not at all pleased. They growled, "He takes in sinners and eats meals with them, treating them like old friends." Their grumbling triggered this story.

4-7   "Suppose one of you had a hundred sheep and lost one. Wouldn't you leave the ninety-nine in the wilderness and go after the lost one until you found it? When found, you can be sure you would put it across your shoulders, rejoicing, and when you got home call in your friends and neighbors, saying, 'Celebrate with me! I've found my lost sheep!' Count on it — there's more joy in heaven over one sinner's rescued life than over ninety-nine good people in no need of rescue.

8-10   "Or imagine a woman who has ten coins and loses one. Won't she light a lamp and scour the house, looking in every nook and cranny until she finds it? And when she finds it you can be sure she'll call her friends and neighbors: 'Celebrate with me! I found my lost coin!' Count on it — that's the kind of party God's angels throw every time one lost soul turns to God."

READ

Open your hands with your palms facing up. Sit for a moment in stillness and ask your heavenly Father to tell you important words that you need to hear today. Communicate that you are open to his guidance. Now read the passage.

THINK

In this passage two things — a sheep and a coin — are lost and then found. And both are celebrated upon their return.

As you think about the two stories of the lost items, which story hits you the most right now? Contemplate why that story jumps out at you today. Read it again, and put yourself in it.

When have you felt lost? Why did you feel that way?

In both stories people — a shepherd, a woman — proactively went after the lost item. How does it feel to know that God himself is proactively pursuing you for the simple yet profound fact that he loves you deeply?

Notice the element of celebration in these stories. What does this celebration make you feel? What should you begin to celebrate in your life or in the lives of others?

PRAY

Listen for God in these areas: What might he be communicating to you regarding your lostness? Regarding the fact that he desires to find you? Regarding how he celebrates your life?

LIVE

Recognize what God is doing in the world today — in the spectacular and in the mundane — and then celebrate it.

RETURNING TO SAY THANK YOU

LUKE 17:11-19

11-13   It happened that as he made his way toward Jerusalem, he crossed over the border between Samaria and Galilee. As he entered a village, ten men, all lepers, met him. They kept their distance but raised their voices, calling out, "Jesus, Master, have mercy on us!"

14-16   Taking a good look at them, he said, "Go, show yourselves to the priests."

They went, and while still on their way, became clean. One of them, when he realized that he was healed, turned around and came back, shouting his gratitude, glorifying God. He kneeled at Jesus' feet, so grateful. He couldn't thank him enough — and he was a Samaritan.

17-19   Jesus said, "Were not ten healed? Where are the nine? Can none be found to come back and give glory to God except this outsider?" Then he said to him, "Get up. On your way. Your faith has healed and saved you."

READ

Read the passage, focusing especially on the questions Jesus asks.

THINK

Not only are lepers deformed by their disease, but Old Testament law also excludes them from community with others. Ten men come to Jesus with this horrific skin disease. These men are physical and relational outsiders. When Jesus heals them, he also helps restore them to their communities.

When have you felt like an outsider and then experienced God's restoring you to community with others or with himself? Do you tend to be like the nine, who asked for God's help and didn't return, or are you like the one who returned to say thank you? Why?

Think about your last several requests to God in prayer. Have you turned around and come back, shouting your gratitude for how he has answered your requests and blessed you in the process? Why or why not? What needs to happen in your life for you to remember to return when God answers your prayers?

PRAY

Make this prayer time one of intentional thankfulness. Consider your recent requests to God (being specific). Return now and thank him for answering those requests, big and small.

LIVE

Every time you make a request, turn around and shout your gratitude.

DAY 231

GOD ENCOUNTERS

On this seventh day, review and reflect on all you have read this week. Take the time to revel in the ways you've encountered God in the past six days.

HEALING THE ENEMY

LUKE 22:47-53

47-48 No sooner were the words out of his mouth than a crowd showed up, Judas, the one from the Twelve, in the lead. He came right up to Jesus to kiss him. Jesus said, "Judas, you would betray the Son of Man with a kiss?"

49-50 When those with him saw what was happening, they said, "Master, shall we fight?" One of them took a swing at the Chief Priest's servant and cut off his right ear.

51 Jesus said, "Let them be. Even in this." Then, touching the servant's ear, he healed him.

52-53 Jesus spoke to those who had come — high priests, Temple police, religion leaders: "What is this, jumping me with swords and clubs as if I were a dangerous criminal? Day after day I've been with you in the Temple and you've not so much as lifted a hand against me. But do it your way — it's a dark night, a dark hour."

READ

Read the passage aloud slowly. Keep in mind that this occurs in the Garden of Gethsemane. Jesus has just prayed, "Father, remove this cup from me. But please, not what I want. What do *you* want?" Then Jesus noted that his disciples were sleeping when he'd asked them to watch with him (see verses 42-46).

THINK

Read the passage again. This time place yourself in the scene as one of the disciples watching what is going on.

1. How do you feel when Judas arrives with soldiers?
2. How do you feel when one of you strikes the chief priest's servant?
3. How do you feel when Jesus heals this servant — one of his attackers?
4. How do you feel when Jesus points out how silly and dramatic his assailants are? (He has been accessible to them for days and is now *letting them* arrest him.)

Finally, put yourself in the place of the servant of the chief priest who is healed by Jesus. How do you feel? What do you want to say to Jesus?

PRAY

Consider Jesus' behavior in this scene. What baffles you? What is awakened within you? Fear? A sense of worship? If there is any way this scene might help you trust Jesus more, tell him.

LIVE

Sit quietly with your hand on one of your ears. See yourself as someone who is about to injure Jesus, but instead he heals you from your own injuries. Sit in that sense of being healed by God. Sit in that sense of finally being able to hear Jesus in your heart with your willing ears.

LOOKING FOR THE LIVING ONE IN A CEMETERY

LUKE 24:1-12

1-3 At the crack of dawn on Sunday, the women came to the tomb carrying the burial spices they had prepared. They found the entrance stone rolled back from the tomb, so they walked in. But once inside, they couldn't find the body of the Master Jesus.

4-8 They were puzzled, wondering what to make of this. Then, out of nowhere it seemed, two men, light cascading over them, stood there. The women were awestruck and bowed down in worship. The men said, "Why are you looking for the Living One in a cemetery? He is not here, but raised up. Remember how he told you when you were still back in Galilee that he had to be handed over to sinners, be killed on a cross, and in three days rise up?" Then they remembered Jesus' words.

9-11 They left the tomb and broke the news of all this to the Eleven and the rest. Mary Magdalene, Joanna, Mary the mother of James, and the other women with them kept telling these things to the apostles, but the apostles didn't believe a word of it, thought they were making it all up.

12 But Peter jumped to his feet and ran to the tomb. He stooped to look in and saw a few grave clothes, that's all. He walked away puzzled, shaking his head.

READ

Read the passage carefully, paying attention to the various characters and their responses to the events of the story.

THINK

Which disciple or follower of Jesus do you most identify with in this passage? What is it about that person that reminds you of yourself?

Read the passage again, this time putting yourself in that person's position. What are your thoughts and feelings as you hear that Jesus is alive again? What runs through your mind as you see others' responses? What do you wonder about? Where do you go when you hear the news? What questions do you have?

PRAY

Now picture the risen Jesus approaching you later that day, inviting you to spend time with him. How do you interact with him? What do you say? Talk to him about what all of this has been like for you.

LIVE

Reflect on your prayer time. You might again consider the person in the story you chose and why, or you could think about how your understanding of faithfulness and discipleship was deepened or changed. Write down anything that seems significant.

LIFE-LIGHT

JOHN 1:12-18

12-13   But whoever did want him,
        who believed he was who he claimed
        and would do what he said,
    He made to be their true selves,
        their child-of-God selves.
    These are the God-begotten,
        not blood-begotten,
        not flesh-begotten,
        not sex-begotten.

14   The Word became flesh and blood,
        and moved into the neighborhood.
    We saw the glory with our own eyes,
        the one-of-a-kind glory,
        like Father, like Son,
    Generous inside and out,
        true from start to finish.

15   John pointed him out and called, "This is the One! The One I told you was coming after me but in fact was ahead of me. He has always been ahead of me, has always had the first word."

16-18   We all live off his generous bounty,
        gift after gift after gift.
    We got the basics from Moses,
        and then this exuberant giving and receiving,
    This endless knowing and understanding—
        all this came through Jesus, the Messiah.
    No one has ever seen God,
        not so much as a glimpse.
    This one-of-a-kind God-Expression,
        who exists at the very heart of the Father,
        has made him plain as day.

READ

Read the passage slowly and repeatedly. Don't rush through it. Take your time. Ruminate on the passage. Let it sink into the well of your soul.

THINK

What sticks out to you the most in these verses? Why is the Word coming to Earth such a big deal in the great scope of human history?

"The Word became flesh and blood, and moved into the neighborhood." What might your life be like if God moved into the house or apartment or locker or dorm room next to yours?

How might the environment of your neighborhood be different if he were your next-door neighbor? How might your own life be different? Be specific.

LIVE

Get a candle (if you don't have one, buy or borrow one). At night, go into a dark room (turn off any lights and shut any curtains). Light the candle and stare at the flame. Consider Jesus, the Word, coming to Earth in flesh and blood, becoming the Life-Light for the world.

PRAY

Stand in the dark room, still looking at the small flame. Allow these words to guide your prayers: "What came into existence was Life, and the Life was Light to live by. The Life-Light blazed out of darkness; the darkness couldn't put it out" (John 1:4-5).

TRUSTING AND EXPECTANT

JOHN 3:9-11,14-15,17-21

9-11   Nicodemus asked, "What do you mean by this? How does this happen?"

Jesus said, "You're a respected teacher of Israel and you don't know these basics? Listen carefully. I'm speaking sober truth to you. I speak only of what I know by experience; I give witness only to what I have seen with my own eyes. There is nothing secondhand here, no hearsay. Yet instead of facing the evidence and accepting it, you procrastinate with questions." . . .

14-15   "In the same way that Moses lifted the serpent in the desert so people could have something to see and then believe, it is necessary for the Son of Man to be lifted up — and everyone who looks up to him, trusting and expectant, will gain a real life, eternal life. . . .

17-18   "God didn't go to all the trouble of sending his Son merely to point an accusing finger, telling the world how bad it was. He came to help, to put the world right again. Anyone who trusts in him is acquitted; anyone who refuses to trust him has long since been under the death sentence without knowing it. And why? Because of that person's failure to believe in the one-of-a-kind Son of God when introduced to him.

19-21   "This is the crisis we're in: God-light streamed into the world, but men and women everywhere ran for the darkness. They went for the darkness because they were not really interested in pleasing God. Everyone who makes a practice of doing evil, addicted to denial and illusion, hates God-light and won't come near it, fearing a painful exposure. But anyone working and living in truth and reality welcomes God-light so the work can be seen for the God-work it is."

READ

Before you read the passage, understand that Jesus has just told Nicodemus (a scholar and teacher) that he must be "'born from above' by the wind of God, the Spirit of God" (verse 8). But Nicodemus is confused! Now read the passage silently.

THINK

Read the passage again, aloud this time, putting yourself in the place of Nicodemus standing on the rooftop in the moonlight, receiving Jesus' words.

1. Which words or phrases stand out to you? Consider these:

   ☐ "Everyone who looks up to him, trusting and expectant, will gain a real life, eternal life."
   ☐ "God didn't go to all the trouble of sending his Son merely to point an accusing finger, . . . [the Son] came to help, to put the world right again."
   ☐ "Anyone who trusts in him is acquitted."
   ☐ "God-light streamed into the world."
   ☐ "Anyone working and living in truth and reality welcomes God-light so the work can be seen for the God-work it is."

2. Why?

PRAY

Talk to Jesus about any phrases that confused you. Talk to him about the phrases that captivated you.

LIVE

Sit quietly before God. Put yourself in the place of Nicodemus again — possibly lying in your bed each night, going over these words Jesus said to you. Which words will you drift off with tonight?

DO YOU WANT TO GET WELL?

JOHN 5:1-9

1-6 Soon another Feast came around and Jesus was back in Jerusalem. Near the Sheep Gate in Jerusalem there was a pool, in Hebrew called *Bethesda*, with five alcoves. Hundreds of sick people — blind, crippled, paralyzed — were in these alcoves. One man had been an invalid there for thirty-eight years. When Jesus saw him stretched out by the pool and knew how long he had been there, he said, "Do you want to get well?"

7 The sick man said, "Sir, when the water is stirred, I don't have anybody to put me in the pool. By the time I get there, somebody else is already in."

8-9 Jesus said, "Get up, take your bedroll, start walking." The man was healed on the spot. He picked up his bedroll and walked off.

That day happened to be the Sabbath.

READ

Read this passage, being especially aware of how it depicts sickness, lack of wholeness, and the process of healing. These details might remind you of a truth you've considered before, or they might reveal something altogether new.

THINK

Read the verses again. What stands out to you? Why might the Holy Spirit be bringing this to your attention? Perhaps you deeply desire to experience wholeness of mind or spirit because you have been experiencing your woundedness lately. Or perhaps you find yourself questioning whether Jesus really can heal a physical sickness — either your own or someone else's.

PRAY

Ask Jesus what he has specifically for you that calls for healing. Talk to him about what you hear.

These possibilities might help get you started: Allowing Jesus to bring healing might require you to let go of something that hurts too much to release, and you don't think you're ready for it right now. Or you desire freedom and wholeness, but you feel stuck, imprisoned, fragmented. Or in this moment you find yourself ready for your healing: Be open to the possibility of Jesus bringing healing when you least expect it, of being "healed on the spot." On the other hand, perhaps you feel ready and are frustrated that nothing seems to be happening.

LIVE

If your time with Jesus and God's Message today moved you the tiniest bit closer to wholeness, rejoice. If not, simply let things be. Continue talking to Jesus about your situation, being alert to what he has for you.

NO CONDEMNATION

JOHN 8:1-11

1-2   Jesus went across to Mount Olives, but he was soon back in the Temple again. Swarms of people came to him. He sat down and taught them.

3-6   The religion scholars and Pharisees led in a woman who had been caught in an act of adultery. They stood her in plain sight of everyone and said, "Teacher, this woman was caught red-handed in the act of adultery. Moses, in the Law, gives orders to stone such persons. What do you say?" They were trying to trap him into saying something incriminating so they could bring charges against him.

6-8   Jesus bent down and wrote with his finger in the dirt. They kept at him, badgering him. He straightened up and said, "The sinless one among you, go first: Throw the stone." Bending down again, he wrote some more in the dirt.

9-10   Hearing that, they walked away, one after another, beginning with the oldest. The woman was left alone. Jesus stood up and spoke to her. "Woman, where are they? Does no one condemn you?"

11   "No one, Master."

"Neither do I," said Jesus. "Go on your way. From now on, don't sin."

READ

Write out today's passage. Say each word aloud as you go.

THINK

Imagine yourself in the crowd the day these events unfold. Picture the embarrassed and shamed expression on the woman's face. Hear the condescending voices of the religious leaders. Feel the Middle Eastern dirt blowing against you as Jesus bends down and writes something in it.

Now imagine yourself in the same situation as this woman. You're caught in a horrendous sin, exposed. Imagine you and Jesus having the same conversation:

"Does no one condemn you?"

"No one, Master."

He looks you in the eyes. "Neither do I. Go on your way. From now on don't sin."

What are you feeling? Thinking?

PRAY

Confess those acts of spiritual adultery you've engaged in recently. Close your eyes and imagine Jesus standing before you. Hear him telling you that he doesn't condemn you but that he wants you to stop sinning from now on.

LIVE

Ask the Holy Spirit to give you wisdom and guidance not to condone other people's (or your own) sin and at the same time not to condemn those people (or yourself) either. Ask the Spirit to bring to your mind people you can love while avoiding condemning and condoning.

DAY 238

GOD ENCOUNTERS

On this seventh day, review and reflect on all you have read this week. Take the time to revel in the ways you've encountered God in the past six days.

KNOWING THE GOOD SHEPHERD

JOHN 10:2-5,14-18

2-5 "The shepherd walks right up to the gate. The gatekeeper opens the gate to him and the sheep recognize his voice. He calls his own sheep by name and leads them out. When he gets them all out, he leads them and they follow because they are familiar with his voice. They won't follow a stranger's voice but will scatter because they aren't used to the sound of it." . . .

14-18 "I am the Good Shepherd. I know my own sheep and my own sheep know me. In the same way, the Father knows me and I know the Father. I put the sheep before myself, sacrificing myself if necessary. You need to know that I have other sheep in addition to those in this pen. I need to gather and bring them, too. They'll also recognize my voice. Then it will be one flock, one Shepherd. This is why the Father loves me: because I freely lay down my life. And so I am free to take it up again. No one takes it from me. I lay it down of my own free will. I have the right to lay it down; I also have the right to take it up again. I received this authority personally from my Father."

READ

Read these words of Jesus aloud slowly. Notice the two sets of closeness expressed: between Jesus and the Father, and between Jesus and the sheep.

THINK

Read these words of Jesus again aloud, as if he were explaining this to you personally. Notice that the word *know* occurs five times. Jesus knows his sheep; they know Jesus. The Father knows Jesus; Jesus knows the Father.

1. What do you make of the centrality of knowing one another?
2. Jesus, the Good Shepherd, does the following for the sheep. Which of these do you most need for Jesus to do for you today?

   ☐ call his own sheep by name
   ☐ lead them out
   ☐ know his own sheep
   ☐ put the sheep before himself, sacrificing himself, if necessary
   ☐ gather and bring other sheep

3. The sheep recognize Jesus' voice and respond by following him and knowing him. How do you need to respond to Jesus today?
4. How are you growing in your capacity to recognize his voice, perhaps through your experiences in this book?

PRAY

Talk to Jesus about what you need from him. Especially talk about your capacity to recognize his voice. Ask for help with this.

LIVE

Sit quietly before God and practice alert waiting. Receive the assurance that such practice will help you be more alert to Jesus' voice when you hear it.

HOLDING ON TO LIFE

JOHN 12:20-26

20-21 There were some Greeks in town who had come up to worship at the Feast. They approached Philip, who was from Bethsaida in Galilee: "Sir, we want to see Jesus. Can you help us?"

22-23 Philip went and told Andrew. Andrew and Philip together told Jesus. Jesus answered, "Time's up. The time has come for the Son of Man to be glorified.

24-25 "Listen carefully: Unless a grain of wheat is buried in the ground, dead to the world, it is never any more than a grain of wheat. But if it is buried, it sprouts and reproduces itself many times over. In the same way, anyone who holds on to life just as it is destroys that life. But if you let it go, reckless in your love, you'll have it forever, real and eternal.

26 "If any of you wants to serve me, then follow me. Then you'll be where I am, ready to serve at a moment's notice. The Father will honor and reward anyone who serves me."

READ

If possible, read the expanded passage to see the full picture of what is happening here. Then read this excerpt three times meditatively.

THINK

Write in your own words what you think Jesus means when he talks about a grain of wheat dying and reproducing itself. Think about what you wrote.

Now wait for Jesus to show you an area of your life — a relationship, a decision to be made, and so on — in which you are "hold[ing] on to life just as it is," and not allowing him to bring growth or change. In what ways might your stance be destructive or suffocating?

Ponder Romans 12:2: "Fix your attention on God. You'll be changed from the inside out." What would this area of your life look like if you were to "fix your attention on God," and in so doing, let go?

PRAY

Sit down. Hold your hands in tight fists. Then relax them, open them, and turn your palms upward. Talk with Jesus about what a life of open hands would look like. Ask him to show you what it means to "be where [he is]."

LIVE

Think again about your tightly held part of life. Try being "reckless in your love": let go just a little bit, with Jesus' help. Serve Jesus today. Follow him today.

THE FRIEND

JOHN 14:15-17

15-17 "If you love me, show it by doing what I've told you. I will talk to the Father, and he'll provide you another Friend so that you will always have someone with you. This Friend is the Spirit of Truth. The godless world can't take him in because it doesn't have eyes to see him, doesn't know what to look for. But you know him already because he has been staying with you, and will even be *in* you!"

READ

Because this passage is about the Holy Spirit, ask him to guide you in a prayerful reading of it. Make your reading a prayer in itself.

THINK

The Holy Spirit is the most neglected personhood of God. We often treat the Spirit like a tagalong part of the Trinity. Yet Jesus promises to leave his disciples (and us as his followers) with this important Friend. Is it hard for you to imagine that the Holy Spirit is offered to you as a friend? Why or why not?

What does it mean to have the Holy Spirit in you and guiding you throughout your day, as this passage says: "But you know him already because he has been staying with you, and will even be *in* you"? Is it comforting? Discomforting? Frustrating? Hard to comprehend? Awe-inspiring? How can you grow today in awareness that the Friend lives in you?

PRAY

Ask the Holy Spirit, your Friend, to remind you of his presence. Pray the words of this Scripture, asking him to "make everything plain to you" (verse 26) and reminding you of all the things that Jesus told the disciples (and you).

LIVE

As you drive, walk, work, study, and interact with others today, call on your Friend for his guidance with the thoughts you think, the words you speak, and the decisions you make.

ONE HEART AND MIND

JOHN 17:20-23,26

20-23
I'm praying not only for them
But also for those who will believe in me
Because of them and their witness about me.
The goal is for all of them to become one heart and mind—
Just as you, Father, are in me and I in you,
So they might be one heart and mind with us.
Then the world might believe that you, in fact, sent me.
The same glory you gave me, I gave them,
So they'll be as unified and together as we are—
I in them and you in me.
Then they'll be mature in this oneness,
And give the godless world evidence
That you've sent me and loved them
In the same way you've loved me.

. . . .

26
I have made your very being known to them—
Who you are and what you do—
And continue to make it known,
So that your love for me
Might be in them
Exactly as I am in them.

READ

Read the passage aloud slowly, remembering that this is Jesus praying for you ("those who will believe in me").

THINK

Read it again slowly, but this time substitute your name (or your name and "all of them") when you read *them* or *they*.

If you need to, read the passage one more time before considering these questions.

1. What are you most excited about Jesus praying for you or saying about you?

   ☐ your witness for Jesus
   ☐ to be one heart and mind with other followers of Jesus
   ☐ to be one heart and mind with God and Jesus
   ☐ that Jesus has given you glory
   ☐ that Jesus is in you
   ☐ that you'll be mature in oneness
   ☐ that you'll give the world evidence that God sent Jesus
   ☐ that Jesus made the very being of God known to you
   ☐ that God's love for Jesus is in you
   ☐ that Jesus is in you

2. Why?

PRAY

Thank Jesus for praying for you. Talk to him about the prayer phrases you found most meaningful. Pray Jesus' prayer for his followers alive today in the world.

LIVE

Walk around today with the sense that Jesus is in you and that this was always his plan — to be in you.

242

TAKE YOUR FINGER AND EXAMINE MY HANDS

JOHN 20:19-29

19-20   Later on that day, the disciples had gathered together, but, fearful of the Jews, had locked all the doors in the house. Jesus entered, stood among them, and said, "Peace to you." Then he showed them his hands and side.

20-21   The disciples, seeing the Master with their own eyes, were exuberant. Jesus repeated his greeting: "Peace to you. Just as the Father sent me, I send you."

22-23   Then he took a deep breath and breathed into them. "Receive the Holy Spirit," he said. "If you forgive someone's sins, they're gone for good. If you don't forgive sins, what are you going to do with them?"

24-25   But Thomas, sometimes called the Twin, one of the Twelve, was not with them when Jesus came. The other disciples told him, "We saw the Master."

But he said, "Unless I see the nail holes in his hands, put my finger in the nail holes, and stick my hand in his side, I won't believe it."

26   Eight days later, his disciples were again in the room. This time Thomas was with them. Jesus came through the locked doors, stood among them, and said, "Peace to you."

27   Then he focused his attention on Thomas. "Take your finger and examine my hands. Take your hand and stick it in my side. Don't be unbelieving. Believe."

28   Thomas said, "My Master! My God!"

29   Jesus said, "So, you believe because you've seen with your own eyes. Even better blessings are in store for those who believe without seeing."

READ

Read John's description of the first time Jesus appeared to his disciples after his death and resurrection. Pay special attention to Jesus' words to them.

THINK

What does Thomas's response to Jesus' resurrection make you feel? How do you react to Thomas's disbelief? What about Jesus' response to him?

PRAY

Read the passage once more. This time pretend you are one of the disciples. Maybe you will be a believing disciple; maybe you will be Thomas. Pick a role that corresponds with where you actually are in your relationship with Jesus right now. Now play out the story. As you hear Jesus speak to you, respond to him from your heart. Let him engage you in conversation.

LIVE

If you're a Thomas, wonder what it would be like to "believe without seeing." If you're like the other disciples, remember to offer grace to others who need to see before believing. Thank God for the faith he has given you — either way.

GOD'S REDEMPTIVE PLAN

ACTS 1:1-11

1-5 Dear Theophilus, in the first volume of this book I wrote on everything that Jesus began to do and teach until the day he said good-bye to the apostles, the ones he had chosen through the Holy Spirit, and was taken up to heaven. After his death, he presented himself alive to them in many different settings over a period of forty days. In face-to-face meetings, he talked to them about things concerning the kingdom of God. As they met and ate meals together, he told them that they were on no account to leave Jerusalem but "must wait for what the Father promised: the promise you heard from me. John baptized in water; you will be baptized in the Holy Spirit. And soon."

6 When they were together for the last time they asked, "Master, are you going to restore the kingdom to Israel now? Is this the time?"

7-8 He told them, "You don't get to know the time. Timing is the Father's business. What you'll get is the Holy Spirit. And when the Holy Spirit comes on you, you will be able to be my witnesses in Jerusalem, all over Judea and Samaria, even to the ends of the world."

9-11 These were his last words. As they watched, he was taken up and disappeared in a cloud. They stood there, staring into the empty sky. Suddenly two men appeared — in white robes! They said, "You Galileans! — why do you just stand here looking up at an empty sky? This very Jesus who was taken up from among you to heaven will come as certainly — and mysteriously — as he left."

READ

Read the passage from the perspective of someone who has never read it before.

THINK

When are you tempted to be a spectator to the movements of God's redemptive plan rather than a participant involved in the action? Why? What are specific ways you can get off the bench and get up to bat for what God is up to in the world? What are some ways you can be a witness to others in your circle of influence?

You know that Jesus will come again in the future. What implications does that reality have on your life?

PRAY

Ask God to give you the courage to take the risk and get into the game, to participate in God's redemptive plan.

LIVE

Ask a close friend or family member to help pray, brainstorm, and discern the ways you can be a participant in God's redemptive plan for your life and the lives of those around you. Ask this person to keep you in check, reminding you that God wants his followers to act on what Jesus said and did.

DAY 245

GOD ENCOUNTERS

On this seventh day, review and reflect on all you have read this week. Take the time to revel in the ways you've encountered God in the past six days.

FEARLESS CONFIDENCE

ACTS 4:24-31

24-26   Hearing the report, they lifted their voices in a wonderful harmony in prayer: "Strong God, you made heaven and earth and sea and everything in them. By the Holy Spirit you spoke through the mouth of your servant and our father, David:

> Why the big noise, nations?
> Why the mean plots, peoples?
> Earth's leaders push for position,
> Potentates meet for summit talks,
> The God-deniers, the Messiah-defiers!

27-28   "For in fact they did meet — Herod and Pontius Pilate with nations and peoples, even Israel itself! — met in this very city to plot against your holy Son Jesus, the One you made Messiah, to carry out the plans you long ago set in motion.

29-30   "And now they're at it again! Take care of their threats and give your servants fearless confidence in preaching your Message, as you stretch out your hand to us in healings and miracles and wonders done in the name of your holy servant Jesus."

31   While they were praying, the place where they were meeting trembled and shook. They were all filled with the Holy Spirit and continued to speak God's Word with fearless confidence.

READ

Read the passage aloud slowly, keeping in mind that Peter and John were just released from police custody for preaching about Jesus. Most of this passage is their prayer.

THINK

Read the passage aloud again. What touches you most? How do you explain the "fearless confidence" of these men who have just suffered for Jesus?

Read the passage one more time, noting when a member of the Trinity is mentioned: God, Jesus (and his designation, Messiah), the Holy Spirit. Clearly, Peter and John, as well as these followers of Jesus, were living in the reality of the Trinity — active and living among them! What might it look like to live your life today immersed in the reality and power of the Trinity?

PRAY

Paraphrase the prayer of Peter, John, and Jesus' followers (verses 24-30) as it fits your life today, including what God has done in the past (verses 24-28), what is happening today (verse 29), and how you wish for God to work today (verse 30).

LIVE

Remind yourself throughout the day that a follower of Jesus is immersed in the Trinitarian reality — really!

JESUS, THE MASTER

ACTS 7:51–8:1

51-53 "And you continue, so bullheaded! Calluses on your hearts, flaps on your ears! Deliberately ignoring the Holy Spirit, you're just like your ancestors. Was there ever a prophet who didn't get the same treatment? Your ancestors killed anyone who dared talk about the coming of the Just One. And you've kept up the family tradition — traitors and murderers, all of you. You had God's Law handed to you by angels — gift-wrapped! — and you squandered it!"

54-56 At that point they went wild, a rioting mob of catcalls and whistles and invective. But Stephen, full of the Holy Spirit, hardly noticed — he only had eyes for God, whom he saw in all his glory with Jesus standing at his side. He said, "Oh! I see heaven wide open and the Son of Man standing at God's side!"

57-58 Yelling and hissing, the mob drowned him out. Now in full stampede, they dragged him out of town and pelted him with rocks. The ringleaders took off their coats and asked a young man named Saul to watch them.

59-60 As the rocks rained down, Stephen prayed, "Master Jesus, take my life." Then he knelt down, praying loud enough for everyone to hear, "Master, don't blame them for this sin" — his last words. Then he died.

1 Saul was right there, congratulating the killers.

READ

Read the passage aloud once. Then read it again silently and slowly, paying careful attention to your response.

THINK

Stephen calls Jesus "Master," and his actions agree. Have you ever read or heard stories of other martyrs like Stephen, people who died for Jesus' sake? What do these stories make you feel?

PRAY

Become aware of Jesus inviting you to share with him your thoughts and feelings. Perhaps stories of martyrdom make you angry, grieved, or afraid. Maybe you find yourself pulling away from such stories. You might have questions. Maybe you want only to sit silently with Jesus. As you open your heart's reaction to him, let that become your prayer.

LIVE

Read the passage again, this time prayerfully. Look for clues to help you discern Jesus' response to Stephen's martyrdom, as well as Jesus' response to you. Write down anything you want to remember or think about later.

THE MIRACULOUS RELEASE

ACTS 12:7-15

7-9 Suddenly there was an angel at his side and light flooding the room. The angel shook Peter and got him up: "Hurry!" The handcuffs fell off his wrists. The angel said, "Get dressed. Put on your shoes." Peter did it. Then, "Grab your coat and let's get out of here." Peter followed him, but didn't believe it was really an angel — he thought he was dreaming.

10-11 Past the first guard and then the second, they came to the iron gate that led into the city. It swung open before them on its own, and they were out on the street, free as the breeze. At the first intersection the angel left him, going his own way. That's when Peter realized it was no dream. "I can't believe it — this really happened! The Master sent his angel and rescued me from Herod's vicious little production and the spectacle the Jewish mob was looking forward to."

12-14 Still shaking his head, amazed, he went to Mary's house, the Mary who was John Mark's mother. The house was packed with praying friends. When he knocked on the door to the courtyard, a young woman named Rhoda came to see who it was. But when she recognized his voice — Peter's voice! — she was so excited and eager to tell everyone Peter was there that she forgot to open the door and left him standing in the street.

15 But they wouldn't believe her, dismissing her, dismissing her report. "You're crazy," they said. She stuck by her story, insisting. They still wouldn't believe her and said, "It must be his angel."

READ

Imagine you are in a roomful of your friends, and they have asked you to read them a story. With this scenario in mind, read the passage.

THINK

Good stories grab hold of us and won't let go. This story is no exception. Scripture sometimes "messes" with us in appropriate ways. How does this passage mess with you and your understanding of God?

The people praying for Peter's release from prison didn't believe it when he was standing at the door. They thought Rhoda was crazy or it must be someone else or an angel of Peter (but not Peter himself). Is it hard to believe that the Holy Spirit is powerful enough to perform such sensational acts? Why or why not? If this were to happen today, would you be skeptical or cynical? Why or why not?

How often do you pray for God to work and, when he does, react with shock or disbelief? What does this reveal about the faith behind your prayers?

PRAY

What can you pray that God will do — and *wholeheartedly believe* that he will answer? Pray for that with bold confidence and hope, knowing that God is powerful and is listening to your prayer.

LIVE

Be keenly aware today of how the Holy Spirit is working — in the sensational, in the mundane, or in both.

LIVE AS YOU WERE MEANT TO LIVE

ACTS 16:25-34

25-26 Along about midnight, Paul and Silas were at prayer and singing a robust hymn to God. The other prisoners couldn't believe their ears. Then, without warning, a huge earthquake! The jailhouse tottered, every door flew open, all the prisoners were loose.

27-28 Startled from sleep, the jailer saw all the doors swinging loose on their hinges. Assuming that all the prisoners had escaped, he pulled out his sword and was about to do himself in, figuring he was as good as dead anyway, when Paul stopped him: "Don't do that! We're all still here! Nobody's run away!"

29-31 The jailer got a torch and ran inside. Badly shaken, he collapsed in front of Paul and Silas. He led them out of the jail and asked, "Sirs, what do I have to do to be saved, to really live?" They said, "Put your entire trust in the Master Jesus. Then you'll live as you were meant to live — and everyone in your house included!"

32-34 They went on to spell out in detail the story of the Master — the entire family got in on this part. They never did get to bed that night. The jailer made them feel at home, dressed their wounds, and then — he couldn't wait till morning! — was baptized, he and everyone in his family. There in his home, he had food set out for a festive meal. It was a night to remember: He and his entire family had put their trust in God; everyone in the house was in on the celebration.

READ

Read the passage aloud slowly, keeping in mind that just before this, Paul and Silas (after doing good) are stripped by a crowd, beaten black-and-blue by officials, and put in jail.

THINK

Read the passage again, noticing that this Bible version translates the word *saved* in these ways: "to really live" (verse 30) and "live as you were meant to live" (verse 31). The Greek word for "salvation" has to do with deliverance for the future but also living a new kind of life in the here and now.

1 Why do you think the jailer is so dramatically affected by Paul's and Silas's behavior?

2. Why would the jailer have an idea of what it meant to "put [his] entire trust in the Master Jesus"?

3. Picture these scenes:

   • the jailer making his prisoners feel at home with his family
   • the jailer dressing the wounds his coworkers had inflicted
   • Paul and Silas baptizing the family
   • the group eating a festive meal together, not knowing what would happen to Paul and Silas the next day

PRAY

Talk to God about what touches you most in this passage. What does that tell you about what you need from God? Ask God for that.

LIVE

Ponder the next twenty-four hours. In what area might you rejoice even though circumstances might not be happy? Who might you love who isn't expecting it? Watch for unexpected events and celebrate them.

NOT A GAME

ACTS 19:11-17

11-12 God did powerful things through Paul, things quite out of the ordinary. The word got around and people started taking pieces of clothing — handkerchiefs and scarves and the like — that had touched Paul's skin and then touching the sick with them. The touch did it — they were healed and whole.

13-16 Some itinerant Jewish exorcists who happened to be in town at the time tried their hand at what they assumed to be Paul's "game." They pronounced the name of the Master Jesus over victims of evil spirits, saying, "I command you by the Jesus preached by Paul!" The seven sons of a certain Sceva, a Jewish high priest, were trying to do this on a man when the evil spirit talked back: "I know Jesus and I've heard of Paul, but who are you?" Then the possessed man went berserk — jumped the exorcists, beat them up, and tore off their clothes. Naked and bloody, they got away as best they could.

17 It was soon news all over Ephesus among both Jews and Greeks. The realization spread that God was in and behind this. Curiosity about Paul developed into reverence for the Master Jesus.

READ

Read the passage.

THINK

Often God allows us to experience unpleasant consequences of choices we make, sometimes so we realize how our choices affect our relationship with him and other people. For example, he might allow ugly parts of our character to be exposed, with embarrassing and painful results. Why do you think God uses consequences to draw people's attention to the thorny parts of their hearts? What do you think God wanted the sons of Sceva to learn about themselves through this experience?

PRAY

Recall a difficult experience that helped you see more of your weaknesses or faults. Ponder the state of your relationship with God before the experience. How did it change? Think about your relationships with others, both before and after the experience. What changed? In other words, in what ways did your newfound awareness impact how you relate to others?

LIVE

Mull over these words, written by Teresa of Avila in her *Interior Castle:* "We are fonder of consolations than we are of the cross. Test us, Lord — for You know the truth — so that we may know ourselves."[16] Can you identify with her confession? Can you identify with her request to be more fully exposed to God and to see herself more clearly? Sit and talk with Jesus about your reaction to testing from God, contrasting it with your reaction to feel-good experiences.

FAITH JOURNEY

ACTS 22:1-10

1-2 "My dear brothers and fathers, listen carefully to what I have to say before you jump to conclusions about me." When they heard him speaking Hebrew, they grew even quieter. No one wanted to miss a word of this.

2-3 He continued, "I am a good Jew, born in Tarsus in the province of Cilicia, but educated here in Jerusalem under the exacting eye of Rabbi Gamaliel, thoroughly instructed in our religious traditions. And I've always been passionately on God's side, just as you are right now.

4-5 "I went after anyone connected with this 'Way,' went at them hammer and tongs, ready to kill for God. I rounded up men and women right and left and had them thrown in prison. You can ask the Chief Priest or anyone in the High Council to verify this; they all knew me well. Then I went off to our brothers in Damascus, armed with official documents authorizing me to hunt down the followers of Jesus there, arrest them, and bring them back to Jerusalem for sentencing.

6-7 "As I arrived on the outskirts of Damascus about noon, a blinding light blazed out of the skies and I fell to the ground, dazed. I heard a voice: 'Saul, Saul, why are you out to get me?'

8-9 "'Who are you, Master?' I asked.

"He said, 'I am Jesus the Nazarene, the One you're hunting down.' My companions saw the light, but they didn't hear the conversation.

10 "Then I said, 'What do I do now, Master?'

"He said, 'Get to your feet and enter Damascus. There you'll be told everything that's been set out for you to do.'"

READ

Read the passage from the perspective of Paul's mother. What might she be thinking as she hears these words?

THINK

Paul's faith began in an amazing way on the road to Damascus (see the beginning of Acts 9 for more details). He was bold to share his story and ultimately The Story, the one of God and man. This passage gives us a thorough yet succinct explanation of the person Paul was before he met Christ, how he met Christ, and the person he became after he met Christ.

Reflect on your story—how you came to faith and how your faith journey is continuing today. Who were you before Christ? What was meeting Christ like? In what ways is your life different now as a result of meeting him? Are other people different today because of your interaction with Jesus?

LIVE

Think about how you might describe your life-altering encounter with the Living God and your faith journey. Now write or type your story of faith in just two or three paragraphs. Finally, ask someone you know to help you hone it to include the most appropriate details.

PRAY

Pray that God will provide you an opportunity to present your story and The Story (of God and man) with another person in the next week. When you sense the open door plainly before you, take the risk and share the stories.

DAY 252

GOD ENCOUNTERS

On this seventh day, review and reflect on all you have read this week. Take the time to revel in the ways you've encountered God in the past six days.

WHY ARE YOU OUT TO GET ME?

ACTS 26:12-18

12-14 "One day on my way to Damascus, armed as always with papers from the high priests authorizing my action, right in the middle of the day a blaze of light, light outshining the sun, poured out of the sky on me and my companions. Oh, King, it was so bright! We fell flat on our faces. Then I heard a voice in Hebrew: 'Saul, Saul, why are you out to get me? Why do you insist on going against the grain?'

15-16 "I said, 'Who are you, Master?'

"The voice answered, 'I am Jesus, the One you're hunting down like an animal. But now, up on your feet — I have a job for you. I've handpicked you to be a servant and witness to what's happened today, and to what I am going to show you.

17-18 "'I'm sending you off to open the eyes of the outsiders so they can see the difference between dark and light, and choose light, see the difference between Satan and God, and choose God. I'm sending you off to present my offer of sins forgiven, and a place in the family, inviting them into the company of those who begin real living by believing in me.'"

READ

Read the passage aloud slowly. This is Paul speaking before King Agrippa, telling about his conversion.

THINK

Read the passage aloud again, this time noting all the personal pronouns in this very personal conversation: *I, me, you.*

Read it a third time, noting how the conversation focuses on the past and the future.

1. Why do you think Jesus doesn't just say, "I'm the Son of God. Your doctrine is wrong. Change it"?
2. How do you respond to Jesus' giving Saul a job to do even though he's been murdering Christians? What does this tell you about Jesus?
3. Consider what Paul might have prayed next; there he is, blind, with his underlings leading him to safety.

PRAY

Have a conversation with Jesus similar to Paul's.

First, Jesus asks you, "Why are you . . . ?" How do you respond?

Next, Jesus tells you exactly who he is — a glimpse of him you have missed: "I am Jesus the One you're . . ."

Finally, Jesus says, "Up on your feet — I have a job for you." What is the job? How do you respond?

Live today asking Jesus this question: *Is there anything about you I'm missing out on? That I don't understand or accept? Show me.*

PRIDE COMES BEFORE A FALL

ROMANS 2:17-24

17-24 If you're brought up Jewish, don't assume that you can lean back in the arms of your religion and take it easy, feeling smug because you're an insider to God's revelation, a connoisseur of the best things of God, informed on the latest doctrines! I have a special word of caution for you who are sure that you have it all together yourselves and, because you know God's revealed Word inside and out, feel qualified to guide others through their blind alleys and dark nights and confused emotions to God. While you are guiding others, who is going to guide you? I'm quite serious. While preaching "Don't steal!" are you going to rob people blind? Who would suspect you? The same with adultery. The same with idolatry. You can get by with almost anything if you front it with eloquent talk about God and his law. The line from Scripture, "It's because of you Jews that the outsiders are down on God," shows it's an old problem that isn't going to go away.

READ

Whisper to yourself the words of this passage.

THINK

Paul, writing mostly to Gentiles (non-Jews) in the church in Rome, finds himself addressing Jews in this passage, and warns those who have become arrogant because of their ancestral heritage. He warns that their arrogance, laziness, and apathy do not sit well with God. It leads to all sorts of thoughts and behaviors that dishonor God, including saying one thing and actually doing another.

You may or may not have Jewish roots, but this passage is relevant to all of us. What areas of your own heart might be arrogant or apathetic because of your upbringing, your heritage, or what you have done (and not done) in the past?

What might your friends who are far from God think or feel about this? What can be done about it?

When was the last time you said or taught one thing yet acted quite differently? What emotions might God feel when he sees us thinking or acting contrary to his character?

PRAY

Sit for a few minutes in silence, asking God to help you know the feeling of true humility. Then call on him to forgive you where your life has not lived up to what you claim to believe. (Be specific.)

LIVE

Courageously invite others around you to help you remain humble. Give them permission to do what it takes to help your life match your words.

TRUSTING WHEN IT'S HOPELESS

ROMANS 4:16-21

16   This is why the fulfillment of God's promise depends entirely on trusting God and his way, and then simply embracing him and what he does. God's promise arrives as pure gift. That's the only way everyone can be sure to get in on it, those who keep the religious traditions *and* those who have never heard of them. For Abraham is father of us all. He is not our racial father — that's reading the story backward. He is our *faith* father.

17-18   We call Abraham "father" not because he got God's attention by living like a saint, but because God made something out of Abraham when he was a nobody. Isn't that what we've always read in Scripture, God saying to Abraham, "I set you up as father of many peoples"? Abraham was first named "father" and then *became* a father because he dared to trust God to do what only God could do: raise the dead to life, with a word make something out of nothing. When everything was hopeless, Abraham believed anyway, deciding to live not on the basis of what he saw he *couldn't* do but on what God said he *would* do. And so he was made father of a multitude of peoples. God himself said to him, "You're going to have a big family, Abraham!"

19-21   Abraham didn't focus on his own impotence and say, "It's hopeless. This hundred-year-old body could never father a child." Nor did he survey Sarah's decades of infertility and give up. He didn't tiptoe around God's promise asking cautiously skeptical questions. He plunged into the promise and came up strong, ready for God, sure that God would make good on what he had said.

READ

Read the passage aloud slowly.

THINK

Read the passage again, but silently.

1. What did God do for Abraham?
2. If you were Abraham, which of the following efforts would be most difficult for you?

   ☐ daring to trust God to do what only God can do
   ☐ believing in spite of hopeless circumstances
   ☐ living on the basis of what God says he will do
   ☐ not focusing on hopeless circumstances
   ☐ not asking cautiously skeptical questions
   ☐ plunging into God's promise and coming up strong and ready for God
   ☐ remaining sure that God will make good on what he says
   ☐ other:

Read the passage again. What words or phrases stand out to you?

PRAY

Thank God for Abraham, "our *faith* father." Ask God to help you trust him and his way. Ask God to help you simply embrace him and what he does.

LIVE

Sit quietly before God. Get used to the idea that you really can embrace him and what he does. Imagine one way your life might be different if you do this.

SO-CALLED FREEDOM

ROMANS 6:15-21

15-18　So, since we're out from under the old tyranny, does that mean we can live any old way we want? Since we're free in the freedom of God, can we do anything that comes to mind? Hardly. You know well enough from your own experience that there are some acts of so-called freedom that destroy freedom. Offer yourselves to sin, for instance, and it's your last free act. But offer yourselves to the ways of God and the freedom never quits. All your lives you've let sin tell you what to do. But thank God you've started listening to a new master, one whose commands set you free to live openly in *his* freedom!

19　I'm using this freedom language because it's easy to picture. You can readily recall, can't you, how at one time the more you did just what you felt like doing — not caring about others, not caring about God — the worse your life became and the less freedom you had? And how much different is it now as you live in God's freedom, your lives healed and expansive in holiness?

20-21　As long as you did what you felt like doing, ignoring God, you didn't have to bother with right thinking or right living, or right *anything* for that matter. But do you call that a free life? What did you get out of it? Nothing you're proud of now. Where did it get you? A dead end.

THINK

Search yourself for an area where you don't walk in freedom but continue to struggle with sin. When do you easily give in to temptation? Why? Are there times when you don't feel the pull so strongly? Why? What comfort, relief, or pleasure does the sin give you (no matter how short-lived or shallow)? What pain or discomfort does it bring? What do you fear you would lose if you gave up the sin?

READ

Read the passage with your specific sin in mind. Sift these verses through your life experience. How do they hold up? Do you find Paul's description of living "any old way we want" to be accurate? What about his perspective on "offer[ing] yourselves to the ways of God" — living in obedience to his commands? Take time to identify what you do and don't agree with.

PRAY

Talk to God about the things you've uncovered. If you have unanswered questions or problems you can't reconcile, share them. If you're frustrated, express it to him. Maybe you will challenge him to show you freedom, as you agree to take on the challenge of giving his ways a shot.

LIVE

"Offer yourselves to the ways of God and the freedom never quits." Rest in this freedom today.

NOTHING BETWEEN US AND GOD'S LOVE

ROMANS 8:31-39

31-39 So, what do you think? With God on our side like this, how can we lose? If God didn't hesitate to put everything on the line for us, embracing our condition and exposing himself to the worst by sending his own Son, is there anything else he wouldn't gladly and freely do for us? And who would dare tangle with God by messing with one of God's chosen? Who would dare even to point a finger? The One who died for us — who was raised to life for us! — is in the presence of God at this very moment sticking up for us. Do you think anyone is going to be able to drive a wedge between us and Christ's love for us? There is no way! Not trouble, not hard times, not hatred, not hunger, not homelessness, not bullying threats, not backstabbing, not even the worst sins listed in Scripture:

> They kill us in cold blood because they hate you.
> We're sitting ducks; they pick us off one by one.

None of this fazes us because Jesus loves us. I'm absolutely convinced that nothing — nothing living or dead, angelic or demonic, today or tomorrow, high or low, thinkable or unthinkable — absolutely *nothing* can get between us and God's love because of the way that Jesus our Master has embraced us.

READ

Read the passage four times very slowly.

THINK

Logically understanding that God loves us is fairly easy. But grasping this truth to its fullest extent in our hearts and souls — in every corner of our everyday existence — requires more. We think we know God loves us, but we don't often ponder this profound truth, this important element of our identity as God's children.

Read the passage again. This time underline the phrases that speak directly to you and encourage your heart. With each underline, say aloud, "Thank you, God, for how much you love me."

"Do you think anyone is going to be able to drive a wedge between [you] and Christ's love for [you]? . . . No way!" When you read Paul's words, what flows through your mind and heart?

PRAY

Sit in silence with one thought in mind: *I am loved by God.* If your mind begins to wander, simply whisper, "Thank you for loving me, Jesus." Claim the promises of this passage as your own.

LIVE

Live confidently knowing that "absolutely *nothing* can get between [you] and God's love." He loves you that much!

EMBRACE GOD, HEART AND SOUL

ROMANS 10:8-13

8-10 So what exactly was Moses saying?

> The word that saves is right here,
>> as near as the tongue in your mouth,
>> as close as the heart in your chest.

It's the word of faith that welcomes God to go to work and set things right for us. This is the core of our preaching. Say the welcoming word to God — "Jesus is my Master" — embracing, body and soul, God's work of doing in us what he did in raising Jesus from the dead. That's it. You're not "doing" anything; you're simply calling out to God, trusting him to do it for you. That's salvation. With your whole being you embrace God setting things right, and then you say it, right out loud: "God has set everything right between him and me!"

11-13 Scripture reassures us, "No one who trusts God like this — heart and soul — will ever regret it." It's exactly the same no matter what a person's religious background may be: the same God for all of us, acting the same incredibly generous way to everyone who calls out for help. "Everyone who calls, 'Help, God!' gets help."

READ

Read the passage aloud slowly.

THINK

Read the passage again silently.

1. Look at the rich phrases and see which one speaks to you most:

   ☐ "the word . . . as near as the tongue . . . as close as the heart"
   ☐ "the word of faith that welcomes God to go to work"
   ☐ "embracing, body and soul, God's work of doing in us what he did in raising Jesus"
   ☐ "calling out to God"
   ☐ "God has set everything right between him and me!"
   ☐ "No one who trusts God like this — heart and soul — will ever regret it."
   ☐ "Everyone who calls, 'Help, God!' gets help."

2. Why does this phrase touch you?
3. In what way would you like this phrase to become a stronger reality in your life?

PRAY

Thank God for his nearness, his willingness to be embraced, his willingness to hear us and set things right. Talk to God about your next step in trusting him heart and soul.

LIVE

Sit quietly before God, imagining what it feels like to live trusting him and embracing him — a life without regret.

DAY 259

GOD ENCOUNTERS

On this seventh day, review and reflect on all you have read this week. Take the time to revel in the ways you've encountered God in the past six days.

AN OFFERING

ROMANS 12:1-3

1-2 So here's what I want you to do, God helping you: Take your everyday, ordinary life — your sleeping, eating, going-to-work, and walking-around life — and place it before God as an offering. Embracing what God does for you is the best thing you can do for him. Don't become so well-adjusted to your culture that you fit into it without even thinking. Instead, fix your attention on God. You'll be changed from the inside out. Readily recognize what he wants from you, and quickly respond to it. Unlike the culture around you, always dragging you down to its level of immaturity, God brings the best out of you, develops well-formed maturity in you.

3 I'm speaking to you out of deep gratitude for all that God has given me, and especially as I have responsibilities in relation to you. Living then, as every one of you does, in pure grace, it's important that you not misinterpret yourselves as people who are bringing this goodness to God. No, God brings it all to you. The only accurate way to understand ourselves is by what God is and by what he does for us, not by what we are and what we do for him.

READ

Read the passage twice, aloud.

THINK

Choose a theme that speaks to you — perhaps the idea that God is the real source of goodness in your life or perhaps the contrast Paul makes between what your culture draws out in you and what God draws out in you. What does this passage say about that issue?

PRAY

Pick one phrase from the passage that pinpoints the theme that impacts you. Repeat that phrase to yourself slowly several times. Each time you say it, notice your internal response. What thoughts, memories, or feelings does it stir up?

Now bring these thoughts back to the passage, line by line, in a conversation with God: He speaks to you through the words in the passage, then you respond to what he said. (For example, if you feel the power of your culture is "dragging you down," you bring that feeling to each line of the passage and see how God replies.) When you're finished, repeat the phrase to yourself one last time, checking your heart's reaction. Is it different? Don't worry if this process leaves unanswered questions. Just be open to what God is showing you through your meditation.

LIVE

Consider one of the four "everyday, ordinary" parts of your life suggested in the passage: sleeping, eating, going to work, walking around. What would placing this activity before God as an offering look like? How would you think about this activity differently? Would the frequency, method, or other details of your activity change? Try it today.

GOVERNMENT AND GOD

ROMANS 13:1-7

1-3   Be a good citizen. All governments are under God. Insofar as there is peace and order, it's God's order. So live responsibly as a citizen. If you're irresponsible to the state, then you're irresponsible with God, and God will hold you responsible. Duly constituted authorities are only a threat if you're trying to get by with something. Decent citizens should have nothing to fear.

3-5   Do you want to be on good terms with the government? Be a responsible citizen and you'll get on just fine, the government working to your advantage. But if you're breaking the rules right and left, watch out. The police aren't there just to be admired in their uniforms. God also has an interest in keeping order, and he uses them to do it. That's why you must live responsibly — not just to avoid punishment but also because it's the right way to live.

6-7   That's also why you pay taxes — so that an orderly way of life can be maintained. Fulfill your obligations as a citizen. Pay your taxes, pay your bills, respect your leaders.

THINK

There are all sorts of opinions out there regarding how our government should be run. And people have a hard time talking about church and government in the same paragraphs. *Separation of church and state,* we think.

But when was the last time you thanked God for people in office or prayed for their leadership? Have you ever thought about the truth that God is powerful and in control of the world in such a way that he is not surprised by who is in office, regardless of that person's political views?

In this passage, Paul commands, "Fulfill your obligations as a citizen. Pay your taxes, pay your bills, respect your leaders." What is your obligation as a citizen to this country and to the kingdom of God? In what specific ways can you respect your leaders?

READ

Read the passage.

PRAY

Find a list of names of your local officials (mayor, city council members, county officials), as well as your state and federal officials (governor, congressmen and women, senators, Supreme Court justices, vice president, and president). Pray for each one of them by name. Pray that God would use them to lead wisely and justly.

LIVE

Consider writing a short note or letter of encouragement to one or two of the government officials you prayed for, telling them you are thankful for what they do.

DEBATABLE MATTERS

ROMANS 14:6-10,13

6-9 What's important in all this is that if you keep a holy day, keep it for *God's* sake; if you eat meat, eat it to the glory of God and thank God for prime rib; if you're a vegetarian, eat vegetables to the glory of God and thank God for broccoli. None of us are permitted to insist on our own way in these matters. It's *God* we are answerable to — all the way from life to death and everything in between — not each other. That's why Jesus lived and died and then lived again: so that he could be our Master across the entire range of life and death, and free us from the petty tyrannies of each other.

10 So where does that leave you when you criticize a brother? And where does that leave you when you condescend to a sister? I'd say it leaves you looking pretty silly — or worse. Eventually, we're all going to end up kneeling side by side in the place of judgment, facing God. Your critical and condescending ways aren't going to improve your position there one bit. . . .

13 Forget about deciding what's right for each other. Here's what you need to be concerned about: that you don't get in the way of someone else, making life more difficult than it already is.

READ

Read the passage aloud slowly, keeping in mind that Paul has been addressing a controversy about what foods are right to eat.

THINK

Read the passage aloud again, imagining that Paul, your brother in Christ, is sitting next to you in a window seat, saying these things to you.

1. Why do people insist on their own way about debatable matters?
2. When you're critical, what words and tone do you usually use? When you're being condescending, what facial expression and arm gestures do you use?
3. What does this passage say about why moral superiority is so silly?

Read the passage aloud again. Which phrase speaks most deeply to you?

PRAY

Take the phrase that spoke to you and talk to God about it. Ask him to let that truth sink into your deepest self. Ask him to guide you in that truth.

LIVE

When Mother Teresa was asked how someone might pray for her, she asked that person to pray that she would not get in the way of what God wanted to do. Move through life with that consciousness, acting with God's love but not getting in the way of what God wants to do.

STRENGTH IS FOR SERVICE

ROMANS 15:1-6

1-2 Those of us who are strong and able in the faith need to step in and lend a hand to those who falter, and not just do what is most convenient for us. Strength is for service, not status. Each one of us needs to look after the good of the people around us, asking ourselves, "How can I help?"

3-6 That's exactly what Jesus did. He didn't make it easy for himself by avoiding people's troubles, but waded right in and helped out. "I took on the troubles of the troubled," is the way Scripture puts it. Even if it was written in Scripture long ago, you can be sure it's written for *us*. God wants the combination of his steady, constant calling and warm, personal counsel in Scripture to come to characterize *us*, keeping us alert for whatever he will do next. May our dependably steady and warmly personal God develop maturity in you so that you get along with each other as well as Jesus gets along with us all. Then we'll be a choir — not our voices only, but our very lives singing in harmony in a stunning anthem to the God and Father of our Master Jesus!

THINK

Paul specifies that we are to help others in areas where we are "strong and able in the faith." What are some areas in which you have received training, direction, or guidance? What are some of your natural gifts and strengths?

READ

Read the passage with a heart of gratitude for those who, past and present, "step in and lend a hand" to you, even if you don't remember specific details.

PRAY

Ponder what this passage says about Jesus and how he dealt with people's troubles. Now think about his call to follow him (see Matthew 16:24). When you think about being like Jesus in this way, what questions, thoughts, and feelings come up? Share these with him.

LIVE

Contemplate the role that service to others plays in your daily life. There are a variety of forms this might take, for example, lending a listening ear or emotional support, doing manual labor or other chores for someone, or giving money, food, shelter, or clothing to a person in need. Has your service to others become another form of overwork? Or is it truly integrated into your life in a comfortable and valuable way? Have you been selfish in the use of your time? Should you be giving more of yourself to others than you currently do?[17]

CALLED INTO THIS LIFE

1 CORINTHIANS 1:26-31

26-31 Take a good look, friends, at who you were when you got called into this life. I don't see many of "the brightest and the best" among you, not many influential, not many from high-society families. Isn't it obvious that God deliberately chose men and women that the culture overlooks and exploits and abuses, chose these "nobodies" to expose the hollow pretensions of the "somebodies"? That makes it quite clear that none of you can get by with blowing your own horn before God. Everything that we have — right thinking and right living, a clean slate and a fresh start — comes from God by way of Jesus Christ. That's why we have the saying, "If you're going to blow a horn, blow a trumpet for God."

READ

Ruminate over these verses. Take your time and read them slowly.

THINK

What sticks out to you in this passage concerning God and your relationship with him?

When have you tried to "get by with blowing your own horn before God," either overtly or subtly?

Consider the entire story of Scripture, starting with Genesis. Think about the types of people God fights for and the types he uses to impact human history: Abraham, Moses, Gideon, Saul (later Paul), Peter, and so on. Many of them started out inadequate or less-than-qualified for the job. How does this make you feel about God's desire to use you in his grand plan for the world?

PRAY

Write down your thoughts and prayers in these two areas:

1. "Take a good look, friends, at who you were when you got called into this life." Think about what your life was like — specifically and generally — before meeting Christ. (If you don't remember because you let Christ in when you were really young, think about the person you were even five years ago.)
2. Reflect on the person you are today — the ways you are different due to God's involvement in your life.

Thank God for what he's done.

LIVE

Live confidently today, knowing that God wants to use you — yes, even you — for his ultimate purpose and plan. Live openly before him, realizing that you are an instrument in a world desperately in need of hope.

YOU ARE A TEMPLE

1 CORINTHIANS 3:11-17

11-15   Remember, there is only one foundation, the one already laid: Jesus Christ. Take particular care in picking out your building materials. Eventually there is going to be an inspection. If you use cheap or inferior materials, you'll be found out. The inspection will be thorough and rigorous. You won't get by with a thing. If your work passes inspection, fine; if it doesn't, your part of the building will be torn out and started over. But *you* won't be torn out; you'll survive — but just barely.

16-17   You realize, don't you, that you are the temple of God, and God himself is present in you? No one will get by with vandalizing God's temple, you can be sure of that. God's temple is sacred — and you, remember, *are* the temple.

READ

Read the passage aloud slowly.

THINK

Read it aloud again, imagining Paul speaking to you as a good father would speak to you (see 1 Corinthians 4:14-17).

In the metaphor where each of us is a building, Jesus is the foundation. What "cheap or inferior materials" might someone use for their foundation? (In general, this would be anything other than Jesus, but be specific for yourself and others like you.)

The sort of building that you are is a temple. A temple is where people go to pray. Not only is God himself present in the temple (you), but both the Holy Spirit and Jesus also live inside you and intercede for you (see Romans 8:26-27,34). What might you do to keep your temple a sacred space?

Read the passage again silently. What does it make you want to be or do or entrust to God?

PRAY

Talk to God about your being a temple for him — even celebrate it! Then ask what you need to know and do to make the Trinity feel at home inside you.

LIVE

Move through life today, musing to yourself about truly being a temple in which the Trinity dwells. Do something to celebrate that.

DAY 266

GOD ENCOUNTERS

On this seventh day, review and reflect on all you have read this week. Take the time to revel in the ways you've encountered God in the past six days.

✛ NO SMALL THING

1 CORINTHIANS 5:1-6

1-2   I also received a report of scandalous sex within your church family, a kind that wouldn't be tolerated even outside the church: One of your men is sleeping with his stepmother. And you're so above it all that it doesn't even faze you! Shouldn't this break your hearts? Shouldn't it bring you to your knees in tears? Shouldn't this person and his conduct be confronted and dealt with?

3-5   I'll tell you what I would do. Even though I'm not there in person, consider me right there with you, because I can fully see what's going on. I'm telling you that this is wrong. You must not simply look the other way and hope it goes away on its own. Bring it out in the open and deal with it in the authority of Jesus our Master. Assemble the community — I'll be present in spirit with you and our Master Jesus will be present in power. Hold this man's conduct up to public scrutiny. Let him defend it if he can! But if he can't, then out with him! It will be totally devastating to him, of course, and embarrassing to you. But better devastation and embarrassment than damnation. You want him on his feet and forgiven before the Master on the Day of Judgment.

6   Your flip and callous arrogance in these things bothers me. You pass it off as a small thing, but it's anything but that. Yeast, too, is a "small thing," but it works its way through a whole batch of bread dough pretty fast.

READ

Read the passage.

THINK

Have you ever observed the process of baking bread? By the work of a pinch of yeast, a small ball of dough doubles in size. Consider how this process is similar to what happens with sin and tolerance among Christians. In what way does "flip and callous arrogance" make the problem worse?

PRAY

Think of a particular experience you've had with sin lately — either your own or that of someone you're close to. How did you respond? Did the sin break your heart? Did you confront it? Did you avoid or ignore it?

Picture Jesus sitting with you. Talk to him about what happened. Explore your heart with him and ask him to uncover why you responded the way you did.

LIVE

Consider this statement by Julian of Norwich: "[God] comes down to the lowest part of our need. For he never despises that which he himself has made."[18] Do you believe it's true about you? About others you know? Write down what this touches in you and anything you sense God is inviting you to do in response.

RISKING SOMEONE'S ETERNAL RUIN

1 CORINTHIANS 8:7-9

7   In strict logic, then, nothing happened to the meat when it was offered up to an idol. It's just like any other meat. I know that, and you know that. But knowing isn't everything. If it becomes everything, some people end up as know-it-alls who treat others as know-nothings. Real knowledge isn't that insensitive.

We need to be sensitive to the fact that we're not all at the same level of understanding in this. Some of you have spent your entire lives eating "idol meat," and are sure that there's something bad in the meat that then becomes something bad inside of you. An imagination and conscience shaped under those conditions isn't going to change overnight.

8-9   But fortunately God doesn't grade us on our diet. We're neither commended when we clean our plate nor reprimanded when we just can't stomach it. But God *does* care when you use your freedom carelessly in a way that leads a fellow believer still vulnerable to those old associations to be thrown off track.

READ

This passage was part of an actual letter. Pretend you have just pulled this letter from your mailbox. Read the words as though they are handwritten by a friend.

THINK

Paul gives instruction here to the church in Corinth regarding meat sacrificed to idols. Translated to our current culture, this instruction would be similar to Christians who believe that people should never drink alcohol versus Christians who believe that people have the freedom to drink alcohol, depending on their maturity in their Christian walk. Paul says, "We need to be sensitive to the fact that we're not all at the same level of understanding in this."

Think of a situation when you could have been more sensitive to other believers who may have a different understanding than you. How can you grow to be more sensitive to others without becoming soft on the truth? What sacrifices in your own life need to be made to ensure you aren't tripping up other believers?

Where is the limit on our freedom in Christ?

PRAY

Ask God to search your heart in the area of sensitive interaction with other believers. Consider not only *what* you say or do but also *how* you say or do it. Ask the Holy Spirit to give you wisdom and compassion for healthy, God-honoring relationships with other believers.

Finally, ask God to show you if there is anyone you need to request forgiveness from due to an interaction that involved differing views on these types of issues.

LIVE

If applicable, boldly but humbly seek out those individuals and their forgiveness for your lack of sensitivity. Consider also talking with friends or family members in the near future about what freedom in Christ expressed appropriately might look like.

EXPERIENCING GOD'S WONDER AND GRACE

1 CORINTHIANS 10:1-10

1-5 Remember our history, friends, and be warned. All our ancestors were led by the providential Cloud and taken miraculously through the Sea. They went through the waters, in a baptism like ours, as Moses led them from enslaving death to salvation life. They all ate and drank identical food and drink, meals provided daily by God. They drank from the Rock, God's fountain for them that stayed with them wherever they were. And the Rock was Christ. But just experiencing God's wonder and grace didn't seem to mean much — most of them were defeated by temptation during the hard times in the desert, and God was not pleased.

6-10 The same thing could happen to us. We must be on guard so that we never get caught up in wanting our own way as they did. And we must not turn our religion into a circus as they did — "First the people partied, then they threw a dance." We must not be sexually promiscuous — they paid for that, remember, with 23,000 deaths in one day! We must never try to get Christ to serve us instead of us serving him; they tried it, and God launched an epidemic of poisonous snakes. We must be careful not to stir up discontent; discontent destroyed them.

READ

Read the passage aloud slowly, realizing that Paul is referring to how the Israelites exited Egypt, crossed the Red Sea, and journeyed to the Promised Land.

THINK

Read the passage again.

1. What miracles did the Israelites experience? (Note: Some people read verse 4 to mean that the same rock followed them or appeared at each of their resting places — and "the Rock was Christ." So Christ journeyed with them.)
2. "Just experiencing God's wonder and grace didn't seem to mean much" to the Israelites. Try to understand and explain how they could have developed this attitude.
3. Which of these ways that the Israelites wanted their own way captivates you most?

   ☐ turning religion into a circus — partying and dancing
   ☐ being sexually promiscuous
   ☐ trying to get Christ to serve us instead of serving him
   ☐ stirring up discontent (or maybe just not dealing with it)

PRAY

Read the passage one more time. Thank God that he draws you to experience his wonder and grace every day. Ask him to keep you away from temptation and to teach you how to deal with it.

LIVE

Be alert and expectant today, noticing God's wonder and grace, and thanking him for it. See yourself as learning from the Israelites' mistakes.

EXPANDED PASSAGE: 1 CORINTHIANS 11:17-34

MY BODY, BROKEN FOR YOU

1 CORINTHIANS 11:23-29

23-26 Let me go over with you again exactly what goes on in the Lord's Supper and why it is so centrally important. I received my instructions from the Master himself and passed them on to you. The Master, Jesus, on the night of his betrayal, took bread. Having given thanks, he broke it and said,

> This is my body, broken for you.
> Do this to remember me.

After supper, he did the same thing with the cup:
> This cup is my blood, my new covenant with you.
> Each time you drink this cup, remember me.

What you must solemnly realize is that every time you eat this bread and every time you drink this cup, you reenact in your words and actions the death of the Master. You will be drawn back to this meal again and again until the Master returns. You must never let familiarity breed contempt.

27-28 Anyone who eats the bread or drinks the cup of the Master irreverently is like part of the crowd that jeered and spit on him at his death. Is that the kind of "remembrance" you want to be part of? Examine your motives, test your heart, come to this meal in holy awe.

29 If you give no thought (or worse, don't care) about the broken body of the Master when you eat and drink, you're running the risk of serious consequences.

THINK

Briefly think back on the last time you took Communion. What was it like for you? Did it feel routine or special? In what ways? Who was there with you? Did the presence of that person(s) change the experience for you in any way? How did you prepare yourself?

READ

Read the passage, being especially aware of how you usually approach Communion.

PRAY

Be aware of the Holy Spirit's presence with you now. Meditate on what stands out to you in Paul's description of the communion experience. What is your reaction to his words? Do you resonate with his serious tone? Do you feel challenged by anything in particular? Invite the Holy Spirit to examine your heart and to filter out any junk he finds there — and make you clean.

LIVE

Take time to examine your heart now, as at Communion. What do you need to clear up with God? With another person? Meditate on this Anglican prayer from the *Book of Common Prayer* (1979): "We do not presume to come to this thy Table, O merciful Lord, trusting in our own righteousness, but in thy manifold and great mercies. We are not worthy so much as to gather up the crumbs under thy Table. But thou art the same Lord whose property is always to have mercy. Grant us therefore, gracious Lord, so to eat the flesh of thy dear Son Jesus Christ, and to drink his blood, that we may evermore dwell in him, and he in us. *Amen.*"[19]

270

Find out the next time your church plans to offer Communion, and set aside time on your calendar to revisit this prayer of examination before you participate.

BANKRUPT WITHOUT LOVE

1 CORINTHIANS 13:3-7

3-7 If I give everything I own to the poor and even go to the stake to be burned as a martyr, but I don't love, I've gotten nowhere. So, no matter what I say, what I believe, and what I do, I'm bankrupt without love.

> Love never gives up.
> Love cares more for others than for self.
> Love doesn't want what it doesn't have.
> Love doesn't strut,
> Doesn't have a swelled head,
> Doesn't force itself on others,
> Isn't always "me first,"
> Doesn't fly off the handle,
> Doesn't keep score of the sins of others,
> Doesn't revel when others grovel,
> Takes pleasure in the flowering of truth,
> Puts up with anything,
> Trusts God always,
> Always looks for the best,
> Never looks back,
> But keeps going to the end.

READ

Ask God to give you fresh insight into these familiar words, allowing you to learn things that you haven't before. Now read the passage.

THINK

Whether we know Scripture well or not, most of us have heard this passage read during a wedding ceremony. Its words are encouraging and uplifting, and we might hope the couple won't forget them (and us either). But as you know, reading the words is much easier than living by them.

Ponder this sentence: "So, no matter what I say, what I believe, and what I do, I'm bankrupt without love." What specifically does this mean in your own life?

Consider the list that defines love. Read line by line, asking yourself these two questions: In what ways am I living this out well? In what ways do I need to improve?

PRAY

Pick the one that needs more improvement, and communicate it to God. Ask him to remodel your life in such a way that you quickly see changes in this area. Ask for the ability to recognize when you're not exemplifying the godly love described in this passage.

LIVE

Someplace where you will see it often today — in your PDA, on your hand, or at the top of a notebook — write the one way you want to improve. When you see it, ask yourself how you might express that attribute to those around you.

DON'T HOLD BACK

1 CORINTHIANS 15:51-58

51-57 But let me tell you something wonderful, a mystery I'll probably never fully understand. We're not all going to die — *but* we are all going to be changed. You hear a blast to end all blasts from a trumpet, and in the time that you look up and blink your eyes — it's over. On signal from that trumpet from heaven, the dead will be up and out of their graves, beyond the reach of death, never to die again. At the same moment and in the same way, we'll all be changed. In the resurrection scheme of things, this has to happen: everything perishable taken off the shelves and replaced by the imperishable, this mortal replaced by the immortal. Then the saying will come true:

> Death swallowed by triumphant Life!
> Who got the last word, oh, Death?
> Oh, Death, who's afraid of you now?

It was sin that made death so frightening and law-code guilt that gave sin its leverage, its destructive power. But now in a single victorious stroke of Life, all three — sin, guilt, death — are gone, the gift of our Master, Jesus Christ. Thank God!

58 With all this going for us, my dear, dear friends, stand your ground. And don't hold back. Throw yourselves into the work of the Master, confident that nothing you do for him is a waste of time or effort.

READ

Read this passage a few times, slowly and meditatively.

THINK

What phrase or idea in this passage stands out to you? Perhaps you are drawn toward the "blast to end all blasts" or being free from the fear of death, or maybe you are more drawn to the concept of not holding back in your work. Allow this idea to unfold in your mind. What does it mean for your life today?

PRAY

Talk to the Master about how this makes you feel. If you have questions for him, don't hold on to them: Let Jesus hear them and then let them go. Trust that your questions will be answered at the right time.

Once you have shared your concerns with Jesus, sit with him in silence, being open to whatever he might say in response.

LIVE

Consider Paul's instruction to the Christians in Corinth to "throw [them]-selves into the work of the Master." Ponder: What is the "work" you have been made for? Consider your interests, abilities, skills, passions. When do you feel most alive? (The work you've been made for may or may not correspond to your current vocation.)

What holds you back from pursuing this work with your whole heart — however that might look at this stage in your life? Consider the legitimate reasons, as well as the reasons that might be illegitimate but are still preventing you from moving ahead. Talk to God about this. Ask him to show you what he would have you do, even if that's the simple step of waiting on him to slowly reveal your work over time.

272
273

DAY 273

GOD ENCOUNTERS

On this seventh day, review and reflect on all you have read this week. Take the time to revel in the ways you've encountered God in the past six days.

YES!

2 CORINTHIANS 1:17-22

17-19 Are you now going to accuse me of being flip with my promises because it didn't work out? Do you think I talk out of both sides of my mouth — a glib *yes* one moment, a glib *no* the next? Well, you're wrong. I try to be as true to my word as God is to his. Our word to you wasn't a careless yes canceled by an indifferent no. How could it be? When Silas and Timothy and I proclaimed the Son of God among you, did you pick up on any yes-and-no, on-again, off-again waffling? Wasn't it a clean, strong Yes?

20-22 Whatever God has promised gets stamped with the Yes of Jesus. In him, this is what we preach and pray, the great Amen, God's Yes and our Yes together, gloriously evident. God affirms us, making us a sure thing in Christ, putting his Yes within us. By his Spirit he has stamped us with his eternal pledge — a sure beginning of what he is destined to complete.

READ

Read the passage slowly, at least three times.

THINK

In these verses, Paul writes to the church in the city of Corinth about the promises of God through the fulfillment of Jesus. Read the passage again and circle the word *yes* each time it appears in the text.

So often we hear the word *no,* but this passage says, "God affirms us, making us a sure thing in Christ, putting his Yes with us." What does it mean to hear *yes* from God?

What would your life look like (specifically) if you allowed "God's Yes and [y]our Yes together, gloriously evident"?

PRAY

Allow God to affirm you as you simply sit with him.

Invite him to bring his promises of "yes" to your mind and heart. What specific promises has he given to you? Embrace those promises and ask him to place these stamps of "yes" on your heart so you can carry them with you.

LIVE

Write down one or two specific "yeses" God has given you. Carry that note around with you. Consider sharing these promises with a friend, roommate, family member, classmate, or coworker today.

EXPANDED PASSAGE: EXODUS 34:29-35; 2 CORINTHIANS 3:7-18

LIFTING THE VEIL

2 CORINTHIANS 3:12-18

12-15 With that kind of hope to excite us, nothing holds us back. Unlike Moses, we have nothing to hide. Everything is out in the open with us. He wore a veil so the children of Israel wouldn't notice that the glory was fading away — and they *didn't* notice. They didn't notice it then and they don't notice it now, don't notice that there's nothing left behind that veil. Even today when the proclamations of that old, bankrupt government are read out, they can't see through it. Only Christ can get rid of the veil so they can see for themselves that there's nothing there.

16-18 Whenever, though, they turn to face God as Moses did, God removes the veil and there they are — face-to-face! They suddenly recognize that God is a living, personal presence, not a piece of chiseled stone. And when God is personally present, a living Spirit, that old, constricting legislation is recognized as obsolete. We're free of it! All of us! Nothing between us and God, our faces shining with the brightness of his face. And so we are transfigured much like the Messiah, our lives gradually becoming brighter and more beautiful as God enters our lives and we become like him.

READ

Read the passage aloud slowly.

THINK

Again, slowly read verses 12-15 with a mood of despair. Then read verses 16-18 with a mood of joy, mystery, and surprise.

1. What words or phrases stand out to you? Why?
2. If you didn't choose words or phrases from verses 16-18, do that now. Read them again and note the frequency of these words: *face, personal, personally, bright, brighter, brightness.*

PRAY

Paraphrase verses 16-18 back to God, something like: Whenever I turn my face to you, O God, you remove the veil and there we are — face-to-face! I will suddenly recognize you as a living, personal presence, not [fill in, perhaps: a remote, unknown figure]. And when you are personally present, a living Spirit, that old, constricting legalism is recognized as obsolete. I'm free of it! All of us are! Nothing between me and you, my face shining with the brightness of your face. And so I am transfigured much like the Messiah. My life gradually becomes brighter and more beautiful as you enter my life and I become like you.

LIVE

Sit quietly before God, basking in one of these phrases:

- you are "a living, personal presence"
- nothing between you and me
- as you enter my life, it gradually becomes brighter and more beautiful

OUR ORDINARY LIVES

2 CORINTHIANS 4:5-13

5-6 Remember, our Message is not about ourselves; we're proclaiming Jesus Christ, the Master. All we are is messengers, errand runners from Jesus for you. It started when God said, "Light up the darkness!" and our lives filled up with light as we saw and understood God in the face of Christ, all bright and beautiful.

7-12 If you only look at *us*, you might well miss the brightness. We carry this precious Message around in the unadorned clay pots of our ordinary lives. That's to prevent anyone from confusing God's incomparable power with us. As it is, there's not much chance of that. You know for yourselves that we're not much to look at. We've been surrounded and battered by troubles, but we're not demoralized; we're not sure what to do, but we know that God knows what to do; we've been spiritually terrorized, but God hasn't left our side; we've been thrown down, but we haven't broken. What they did to Jesus, they do to us — trial and torture, mockery and murder; what Jesus did among them, he does in us — he lives! Our lives are at constant risk for Jesus' sake, which makes Jesus' life all the more evident in us. While we're going through the worst, you're getting in on the best!

13 We're not keeping this quiet, not on your life. Just like the psalmist who wrote, "I believed it, so I said it," we say what we believe.

READ

Read the passage aloud once. Read it a second time, and if a word catches your attention, stop and toss it around in your mind. Listen briefly for what your heart is saying in reply. Then keep reading.

THINK

In the silence that follows your reading, meditate on what you heard. How do you relate to the troubled, terrorized, and battered lifestyle Paul and other Christians in the first century led? If you can't relate, what other people around you might be run-down and struggling?

PRAY

Tell God what you've been thinking about. What is your response to the trouble and pain in or around you? If it's your own pain, share with God what you wish you could do in response. If it's the pain of another, notice your impulse to help, fix, or ignore. Be open to God's response to you. Let your sharing lead you into a silent prayer of thankfulness, humility, or request.

LIVE

In her book *Going on Retreat,* Margaret Silf describes what she calls a "retreat on the streets": Small groups of people meet to pray, then they go off into the city with only a few dollars to spend on food that day, taking opportunities to talk with the homeless, unemployed, disturbed, or addicted. At the end of the day, the group gathers to share thoughts and feelings, and to pray.[20]

While this kind of retreat may not be appropriate for you at this time, think about how you could intentionally seek to engage with the needs and feelings of disadvantaged people around you. What would your "ordinary life" look like if you let the light within you shine amid the darkness?

A FRESH START

2 CORINTHIANS 5:14-21

14-15   Our firm decision is to work from this focused center: One man died for everyone. That puts everyone in the same boat. He included everyone in his death so that everyone could also be included in his life, a resurrection life, a far better life than people ever lived on their own.

16-20   Because of this decision we don't evaluate people by what they have or how they look. We looked at the Messiah that way once and got it all wrong, as you know. We certainly don't look at him that way anymore. Now we look inside, and what we see is that anyone united with the Messiah gets a fresh start, is created new. The old life is gone; a new life burgeons! Look at it! All this comes from the God who settled the relationship between us and him, and then called us to settle our relationships with each other. God put the world square with himself through the Messiah, giving the world a fresh start by offering forgiveness of sins. God has given us the task of telling everyone what he is doing. We're Christ's representatives. God uses us to persuade men and women to drop their differences and enter into God's work of making things right between them. We're speaking for Christ himself now: Become friends with God; he's already a friend with you.

21   How? you ask. In Christ. God put the wrong on him who never did anything wrong, so we could be put right with God.

READ

Read the passage.

THINK

What implications does this passage have for your life right now?

Meditate on these words: "Now we look inside, and what we see is that anyone united with the Messiah gets a fresh start, is created new. The old life is gone; a new life burgeons!" (You might consider their radical inclusiveness.)

"Become friends with God; he's already a friend with you." How can you become a better friend to God? What would that entail? How does it feel to know that God is already a friend to you? Do you feel deserving of his friendship? Why or why not?

PRAY

Thank God that he gives you a fresh start with your life and a fresh start every single morning. Let your thankfulness spill over; tell God that you are grateful to have new life in him.

Ask God to help you become a better friend to him and to help you understand what a friend he is to you!

LIVE

"God has given us the task of telling everyone what he is doing. We're Christ's representatives." Who can you tell today about what God is doing in the world?

A WIDE-OPEN, SPACIOUS LIFE

2 CORINTHIANS 6:1-13

1-10   Companions as we are in this work with you, we beg you, please don't squander one bit of this marvelous life God has given us. God reminds us,

> I heard your call in the nick of time;
> The day you needed me, I was there to help.

Well, now is the right time to listen, the day to be helped. Don't put it off; don't frustrate God's work by showing up late, throwing a question mark over everything we're doing. Our work as God's servants gets validated — or not — in the details. People are watching us as we stay at our post, alertly, unswervingly . . . in hard times, tough times, bad times; when we're beaten up, jailed, and mobbed; working hard, working late, working without eating; with pure heart, clear head, steady hand; in gentleness, holiness, and honest love; when we're telling the truth, and when God's showing his power; when we're doing our best setting things right; when we're praised, and when we're blamed; slandered, and honored; true to our word, though distrusted; ignored by the world, but recognized by God; terrifically alive, though rumored to be dead; beaten within an inch of our lives, but refusing to die; immersed in tears, yet always filled with deep joy; living on handouts, yet enriching many; having nothing, having it all.

11-13   Dear, dear Corinthians, I can't tell you how much I long for you to enter this wide-open, spacious life. We didn't fence you in. The smallness you feel comes from within you. Your lives aren't small, but you're living them in a small way. I'm speaking as plainly as I can and with great affection. Open up your lives. Live openly and expansively!

READ

Read the passage aloud slowly.

THINK

Read the passage again, noting these words (and their various forms): *work, working; life, living, lives, alive.*

1. What does this passage have to say to someone who thinks life is boring?
2. What does it say to someone who thinks living for God is boring?
3. With what sort of heart did Paul and his friends do their work for God?

Read the passage one more time — very slowly.

4. What words or phrases are most meaningful to you?
5. How do they connect with your life right now?

PRAY

Talk to God about the opportunity to live a "wide-open, spacious life." Ask him to show you how to work hard with a heart of "gentleness, holiness, and honest love," and with a life of power and joy.

LIVE

Sit in the word *live*. Picture yourself fully alive, partnering with God in what he is doing (or wants to do) in you, and in the people and circumstances around you.

DISTRESS THAT DRIVES US TO GOD

2 CORINTHIANS 7:8-13

8-9   I know I distressed you greatly with my letter. Although I felt awful at the time, I don't feel at all bad now that I see how it turned out. The letter upset you, but only for a while. Now I'm glad — not that you were upset, but that you were jarred into turning things around. You let the distress bring you to God, not drive you from him. The result was all gain, no loss.

10   Distress that drives us to God does that. It turns us around. It gets us back in the way of salvation. We never regret that kind of pain. But those who let distress drive them away from God are full of regrets, end up on a deathbed of regrets.

11-13   And now, isn't it wonderful all the ways in which this distress has goaded you closer to God? You're more alive, more concerned, more sensitive, more reverent, more human, more passionate, more responsible. Looked at from any angle, you've come out of this with purity of heart. And that is what I was hoping for in the first place when I wrote the letter. My primary concern was not for the one who did the wrong or even the one wronged, but for you — that you would realize and act upon the deep, deep ties between us before God. That's what happened — and we felt just great.

13   And then, when we saw how Titus felt — his exuberance over your response — our joy doubled. It was wonderful to see how revived and refreshed he was by everything you did.

LIVE

Since we are spirits in bodies, tangible objects or physical activities can help us enter into prayer. If it's daytime, close the curtains or go into a room without windows. Light a candle and spend a few minutes watching the flame before you read and pray today. Let your awareness of the flame quiet your tendency to be aware only of yourself.

READ

Read the passage twice. According to Paul, what are God's reasons for using jarring things to bring us to repentance? How does Paul describe a life that's been turned around and brought back closer to God?

THINK

Now set the text aside and take a few moments to sit with your eyes closed and recall recent experiences you've had with sin. Did you repent? If so, how did God lead you to that? Did you resist? What turned you around? If you didn't repent, do you notice ways that God was reaching out to you that you refused? What were the thoughts that held you back?

PRAY

Go back to the passage again. Prayerfully reread Paul's perspective on repentance. How does his outlook interact with your current situation? Is there a message you sense God is speaking to you?

DAY 280

GOD ENCOUNTERS

On this seventh day, review and reflect on all you have read this week. Take the time to revel in the ways you've encountered God in the past six days.

DAY 281

EXPANDED PASSAGE: 2 CORINTHIANS 8–9

GENEROUS OFFERINGS

2 CORINTHIANS 9:8-15

8-11 God can pour on the blessings in astonishing ways so that you're ready for anything and everything, more than just ready to do what needs to be done. As one psalmist puts it,

> He throws caution to the winds,
>   giving to the needy in reckless abandon.
> His right-living, right-giving ways
>   never run out, never wear out.

This most generous God who gives seed to the farmer that becomes bread for your meals is more than extravagant with you. He gives you something you can then give away, which grows into full-formed lives, robust in God, wealthy in every way, so that you can be generous in every way, producing with us great praise to God.

12-15 Carrying out this social relief work involves far more than helping meet the bare needs of poor Christians. It also produces abundant and bountiful thanksgivings to God. This relief offering is a prod to live at your very best, showing your gratitude to God by being openly obedient to the plain meaning of the Message of Christ. You show your gratitude through your generous offerings to your needy brothers and sisters, and really toward everyone. Meanwhile, moved by the extravagance of God in your lives, they'll respond by praying for you in passionate intercession for whatever you need. Thank God for this gift, his gift. No language can praise it enough!

READ

Read the passage, imagining that Paul is speaking these words specifically to you.

THINK

Paul talks here about generosity as an important element of God's character. Taking care of the poor is close to the heart of God. Jesus spoke — and lived — generously, just like his Father.

Do you think followers of God are known as being generous people? Why or why not?

In what ways can you grow in your generosity with your time? Your love? Your money? Your abilities? Your possessions? Your life?

PRAY

Walk around inside and outside your home. Look at your possessions: clothes, electronic equipment, books, furniture, paintings on the walls, maybe even the car in your driveway, and so on. What does all this stuff make you think? (Even if most of it belongs to others, like your parents, what's running through your head and heart?) Use Paul's words as the foundation for your communication with God, praying as you are walking around.

Talk with God about your desire to be more generous with the objects you possess. Ask him to bring to mind the people you could be more generous with today and in what way. Ask God to make you more like him — a person of generosity.

LIVE

Go and live with generosity at the forefront of your mind.

EXPANDED PASSAGE: 2 CORINTHIANS 11

GOD'S HIDDEN SERVANTS

2 CORINTHIANS 11:21,23-30

21 I shouldn't admit it to you, but our stomachs aren't strong enough to tolerate that kind of stuff.

21,23 Since you admire the egomaniacs of the pulpit so much (remember, this is your old friend, the fool, talking), let me try my hand at it. . . . Are they servants of Christ? I can go them one better. (I can't believe I'm saying these things. It's crazy to talk this way! But I started, and I'm going to finish.)

23-27 I've worked much harder, been jailed more often, beaten up more times than I can count, and at death's door time after time. I've been flogged five times with the Jews' thirty-nine lashes, beaten by Roman rods three times, pummeled with rocks once. I've been shipwrecked three times, and immersed in the open sea for a night and a day. In hard traveling year in and year out, I've had to ford rivers, fend off robbers, struggle with friends, struggle with foes. I've been at risk in the city, at risk in the country, endangered by desert sun and sea storm, and betrayed by those I thought were my brothers. I've known drudgery and hard labor, many a long and lonely night without sleep, many a missed meal, blasted by the cold, naked to the weather.

28-29 And that's not the half of it, when you throw in the daily pressures and anxieties of all the churches. When someone gets to the end of his rope, I feel the desperation in my bones. When someone is duped into sin, an angry fire burns in my gut.

30 If I have to "brag" about myself, I'll brag about the humiliations that make me like Jesus.

READ

Read the passage aloud slowly, keeping in mind that the Corinthians were partial to slick preachers.

THINK

Which sort of teachers (of the Bible, of spiritual things) do you gravitate toward: the animated, joking, smooth servants of God or the hidden, suffering, unrecognized servants of God?

Paul was the second type. In those days, they didn't know him as we do — the great apostle Paul who wrote nearly half the New Testament. He may not have been all that popular a fellow.

Read the passage again silently. If you were to admire the apostle Paul, what in this passage describes what you would admire him for?

Keep in mind that Paul was also a person of joy. His joy was not in being well-known and appreciated. Instead he was one who encouraged his reader to "celebrate God all day, every day . . . *revel* in him!" (Philippians 4:4). When do you need Paul's sort of joy in your life?

PRAY

Ask God to give you discernment (not judgment) about his servants and which ones are best to follow. Ask God to give you great satisfaction in serving him regardless of how successful that service may look.

LIVE

Watch today for an opportunity to feel the desperation for another who is at the end of his or her rope, or to have an angry fire in your gut when someone is duped into sin. Make an effort to weep for those who weep and rejoice with those who rejoice.

RELATIONSHIPS ARE MESSY

2 CORINTHIANS 12:16-21

16-18 And why is it that I keep coming across these whiffs of gossip about how my self-support was a front behind which I worked an elaborate scam? Where's the evidence? Did I cheat or trick you through anyone I sent? I asked Titus to visit, and sent some brothers along. Did they swindle you out of anything? And haven't we always been just as aboveboard, just as honest?

19 I hope you don't think that all along we've been making our defense before you, the jury. You're not the jury; God is the jury — God revealed in Christ — and we make our case before him. And we've gone to all the trouble of supporting ourselves so that we won't be in the way or get in the way of your growing up.

20-21 I do admit that I have fears that when I come you'll disappoint me and I'll disappoint you, and in frustration with each other everything will fall to pieces — quarrels, jealousy, flaring tempers, taking sides, angry words, vicious rumors, swelled heads, and general bedlam. I don't look forward to a second humiliation by God among you, compounded by hot tears over that crowd that keeps sinning over and over in the same old ways, who refuse to turn away from the pigsty of evil, sexual disorder, and indecency in which they wallow.

READ

Read the passage aloud slowly.

THINK

Enter the scenes that Paul is describing. Envision the individual members of the Corinthian church he's writing to. Replay Paul's history with them — how he first came to the cosmopolitan city preaching the Message of Christ for the first time. Many believed and repented, and many formed new churches. Since then, those churches have helped support him financially, and he's acted as a spiritual mentor and father to them. Imagine what goes on in his mind as he anticipates visiting them again; think about what his last visit was like.

PRAY

Now read the passage again aloud. Notice the messiness of human relationships — misunderstandings, conflicts, and tensions. In the silence that follows your reading, consider your own relationships. Pick one in which you've felt the most recent tension or problems. Open up to God, asking him to show you what he wants you to know about it.

LIVE

Write down in a journal what God uncovered for you about your problematic relationship. Ask him to make clear anything he is asking you to notice or do about it, then sit quietly and attentively as you wait for his response. Don't assume that you should necessarily do anything; instead be open to how God leads you.

IN NEED OF CORRECTION

GALATIANS 1:6-12

6-9 I can't believe your fickleness — how easily you have turned traitor to him who called you by the grace of Christ by embracing a variant message! It is not a minor variation, you know; it is completely other, an alien message, a no-message, a lie about God. Those who are provoking this agitation among you are turning the Message of Christ on its head. Let me be blunt: If one of us — even if an angel from heaven! — were to preach something other than what we preached originally, let him be cursed. I said it once; I'll say it again: If anyone, regardless of reputation or credentials, preaches something other than what you received originally, let him be cursed.

10-12 Do you think I speak this strongly in order to manipulate crowds? Or curry favor with God? Or get popular applause? If my goal was popularity, I wouldn't bother being Christ's slave. Know this — I am most emphatic here, friends — this great Message I delivered to you is not mere human optimism. I didn't receive it through the traditions, and I wasn't taught it in some school. I got it straight from God, received the Message directly from Jesus Christ.

READ

Read the passage aloud. Reflect by writing your thoughts down in a journal or typing them into your computer.

THINK

This feels like a scathing lecture from Paul — and it certainly is. He is disgusted because the church in Galatia has turned from the true Message of the gospel to other slick teachers and optimistic (but empty) ways of thinking.

Consider carefully: What are the essentials of the gospel — the good news of Jesus Christ? What does it most certainly include? What does it most certainly not include?

Have you ever been tempted to turn from the Message of the gospel or to add to, delete, or alter portions of it to make it conveniently fit your life? Have you ever heard others add to, delete, or alter the Message of the gospel? What might be done about that? What are the consequences of doing such a thing?

What might Paul say to you if he were here today?

PRAY

Prayerfully reflect on the importance of the gospel Message. Ask God to give you a mind that discerns and carefully weighs the truth of the gospel and that knows how the gospel should be applied to your life.

LIVE

Spend a few minutes searching for and reading at least three key passages in your Bible that speak specifically to the meaning of the gospel.

NO LONGER TRYING TO BE GOOD

GALATIANS 2:16,19-21

16 We know very well that we are not set right with God by rule-keeping but only through personal faith in Jesus Christ. How do we know? We tried it—and we had the best system of rules the world has ever seen! Convinced that no human being can please God by self-improvement, we believed in Jesus as the Messiah so that we might be set right before God by trusting in the Messiah, not by trying to be good. . . .

19-21 What actually took place is this: I tried keeping rules and working my head off to please God, and it didn't work. So I quit being a "law man" so that I could be *God's* man. Christ's life showed me how, and enabled me to do it. I identified myself completely with him. Indeed, I have been crucified with Christ. My ego is no longer central. It is no longer important that I appear righteous before you or have your good opinion, and I am no longer driven to impress God. Christ lives in me. The life you see me living is not "mine," but it is lived by faith in the Son of God, who loved me and gave himself for me. I am not going to go back on that.

Is it not clear to you that to go back to that old rule-keeping, peer-pleasing religion would be an abandonment of everything personal and free in my relationship with God? I refuse to do that, to repudiate God's grace. If a living relationship with God could come by rule-keeping, then Christ died unnecessarily.

READ

Read the passage aloud slowly.

THINK

Read it again silently.

1. What did Paul find that was better than trying to be good?
2. Which of the following astonishing statements by Paul do you find most intriguing? (The first three are truer the more the last two come to pass.)

   ☐ "My ego is no longer central."
   ☐ "It is no longer important that I appear righteous before you or have your good opinion."
   ☐ "I am no longer driven to impress God."
   ☐ "Christ lives in me."
   ☐ "The life you see me living is not 'mine,' but it is lived by faith in the Son of God."

Read the passage one more time — very slowly — letting it sink into the innermost parts of you.

PRAY

Talk to God about Paul's amazing statements. Which of them do you want help in making true of yourself? To what degree do you really believe that "Christ lives in [you]"? If you need help believing this, tell God.

LIVE

Take something with you through your day to remind yourself that the life you now live is not yours, but is Christ's life in you. The item could be a cross, a piece of paper with this statement written on it, a stone on which you have written *LIFE,* or whatever will help remind you.

GROWTH: A RESULT OF HOW HARD YOU TRY?

GALATIANS 3:2-6

2-4   Let me put this question to you: How did your new life begin? Was it by working your heads off to please God? Or was it by responding to God's Message to you? Are you going to continue this craziness? For only crazy people would think they could complete by their own efforts what was begun by God. If you weren't smart enough or strong enough to begin it, how do you suppose you could perfect it? Did you go through this whole painful learning process for nothing? It is not yet a total loss, but it certainly will be if you keep this up!

5-6   Answer this question: Does the God who lavishly provides you with his own presence, his Holy Spirit, working things in your lives you could never do for yourselves, does he do these things because of your strenuous moral striving *or* because you trust him to do them in you? Don't these things happen among you just as they happened with Abraham? He believed God, and that act of belief was turned into a life that was right with God.

READ

As you read this passage, try not to identify yourself too firmly with the author's anger, but stay open to any similarities you recognize between yourself and his listeners.

THINK/PRAY

Pondering one question that particularly challenges you. For example, "Does God richly bless and change me because I try so hard to be good? Or because I trust him to do it?" Or ask yourself what "crazy" efforts you're making toward a transformational work that he's begun in you. Share your heart's response openly with the Father. Bring him your questions and concerns, and ask for his help in opening up to his model of growth.

LIVE

Take several minutes to try stepping outside your usual "craziness." Taste what it could be like to see growth as a process of letting God "complete . . . what was begun by God." Rest in the presence of his Holy Spirit, "lavishly provide[d to] you." Don't worry about how you'll grow spiritually; don't try to make a plan for how you'll change yourself. Use this time to practice simply being, finding out what it is to be yourself in the presence of Love.

DAY 287

GOD ENCOUNTERS

On this seventh day, review and reflect on all you have read this week. Take the time to revel in the ways you've encountered God in the past six days.

COMPLETE ACCESS TO THE INHERITANCE

GALATIANS 4:1-7

1-3   Let me show you the implications of this. As long as the heir is a minor, he has no advantage over the slave. Though legally he owns the entire inheritance, he is subject to tutors and administrators until whatever date the father has set for emancipation. That is the way it is with us: When we were minors, we were just like slaves ordered around by simple instructions (the tutors and administrators of this world), with no say in the conduct of our own lives.

4-7   But when the time arrived that was set by God the Father, God sent his Son, born among us of a woman, born under the conditions of the law so that he might redeem those of us who have been kidnapped by the law. Thus we have been set free to experience our rightful heritage. You can tell for sure that you are now fully adopted as his own children because God sent the Spirit of his Son into our lives crying out, "Papa! Father!" Doesn't that privilege of intimate conversation with God make it plain that you are not a slave, but a child? And if you are a child, you're also an heir, with complete access to the inheritance.

READ

Read the passage at least five times. Take your time. Slow down and reflect on what you read.

THINK

Paul is a master craftsman of metaphors. And so we find him here in the middle of another word picture, contrasting the difference between the rights and privileges of a slave and those of an heir. We were once slaves, but as believers we are now called sons and daughters — heirs — and God desires for us to live in freedom, not slavery: "Thus we have been set free to experience our rightful heritage."

What does it mean for you to experience your rightful heritage in Christ? What does it mean to have freedom in your relationship with him? How do you temper that freedom so as not to abuse God's grace?

In what ways does being an heir rather than a slave change your interaction with your Father? Be specific.

PRAY

Imagine yourself in the lap of your Father, remembering that you have the "privilege of intimate conversation with God" and "complete access to the inheritance." With the mind-set of a child, pray like a child. Begin your prayer with "Papa." Pray freely and without fear, knowing that this childlike and intimate language is not only permissible but desirable. Tell him your fears. Tell him your joys. Tell him your dreams.

LIVE

Pray frequently, creatively, and confidently, knowing that you have great freedom to approach your heavenly Papa, who is always accessible to you.

GETTING OUR WAY

GALATIANS 5:16-17,19-23

16-17   My counsel is this: Live freely, animated and motivated by God's Spirit. Then you won't feed the compulsions of selfishness. For there is a root of sinful self-interest in us that is at odds with a free spirit, just as the free spirit is incompatible with selfishness. These two ways of life are anti-thetical, so that you cannot live at times one way and at times another way according to how you feel on any given day. . . .

19-21   It is obvious what kind of life develops out of trying to get your own way all the time: repetitive, loveless, cheap sex; a stinking accumulation of mental and emotional garbage; frenzied and joyless grabs for happiness; trinket gods; magic-show religion; paranoid loneliness; cutthroat competition; all-consuming-yet-never-satisfied wants; a brutal temper; an impotence to love or be loved; divided homes and divided lives; small-minded and lopsided pursuits; the vicious habit of depersonalizing everyone into a rival; uncontrolled and uncontrollable addictions; ugly parodies of community. I could go on.

    This isn't the first time I have warned you, you know. If you use your freedom this way, you will not inherit God's kingdom.

22-23   But what happens when we live God's way? He brings gifts into our lives, much the same way that fruit appears in an orchard — things like affection for others, exuberance about life, serenity. We develop a will-ingness to stick with things, a sense of compassion in the heart, and a conviction that a basic holiness permeates things and people. We find ourselves involved in loyal commitments, not needing to force our way in life, able to marshal and direct our energies wisely.

23   Legalism is helpless in bringing this about; it only gets in the way.

READ

Read the passage aloud slowly. Read verses 16-17 and 19-21 again slowly. What words or phrases stand out to you? Why do you think they stand out? Read verses 22-23 again slowly. What words or phrases stand out to you? Why do you think they stand out?

THINK

These two ways of life — self-focus and God-focus — negate each other. To live the first way shuts out the second. To live the second way shuts out the first. The first is empowered by the idea that we must get what we want when we want it. The second is empowered by a faithful, fruitful love for God.

PRAY

Talk to God about the ideas that stood out to you in verses 22-23. Tell God why these are attractive to you. Tell God how they reflect his deep character.

LIVE

Hold one of the following words in front of you today: *exuberance, serenity, willingness, compassion, conviction.* Let that word permeate what you do.

FREE FROM PLEASING OTHERS

GALATIANS 6:11-16

11-13 Now, in these last sentences, I want to emphasize in the bold scrawls of my personal handwriting the immense importance of what I have written to you. These people who are attempting to force the ways of circumcision on you have only one motive: They want an easy way to look good before others, lacking the courage to live by a faith that shares Christ's suffering and death. All their talk about the law is gas. They *themselves* don't keep the law! And they are highly selective in the laws they *do* observe. They only want you to be circumcised so they can boast of their success in recruiting you to their side. That is contemptible!

14-16 For my part, I am going to boast about nothing but the Cross of our Master, Jesus Christ. Because of that Cross, I have been crucified in relation to the world, set free from the stifling atmosphere of pleasing others and fitting into the little patterns that they dictate. Can't you see the central issue in all this? It is not what you and I do — submit to circumcision, reject circumcision. It is what *God* is doing, and he is creating something totally new, a free life! All who walk by this standard are the true Israel of God — his chosen people. Peace and mercy on them!

READ

Carefully read the passage.

THINK

This passage is rebuking first-century Christians for believing that ceremonial Jewish acts like circumcision could alleviate all guilt before God. Consider how you relate to this message. Who are you interested in impressing? How much energy do you expend figuring out ways to be more accepted by others? Is your security rooted in others, or is it rooted in your total acceptance by God?

Do you ever imagine God taking sides — either with you against the world or with everyone else against you? How would your life look if you lived to please only him?

PRAY

Let your thoughts lead you into conversation with God. Interact with him on what you're thinking about, remembering that he loves and accepts you. You might write things down as they come to mind, but don't let your writing shrink your awareness so you forget God's presence. Confide in him why you do what you do, even if you know your reasons are selfish or foolish.

LIVE

Return to the question of how your life would look if you lived only to please him — "to boast about nothing but the Cross of our Master." What one thing, even if tiny and internal, could you do to start living this way? Maybe you begin by asking God to give you a whiff of the air that exists beyond the "stifling atmosphere of pleasing others."

WHO WE ARE

EPHESIANS 1:11-19

11-12   It's in Christ that we find out who we are and what we are living for. Long before we first heard of Christ and got our hopes up, he had his eye on us, had designs on us for glorious living, part of the overall purpose he is working out in everything and everyone.

13-14   It's in Christ that you, once you heard the truth and believed it (this Message of your salvation), found yourselves home free — signed, sealed, and delivered by the Holy Spirit. This signet from God is the first installment on what's coming, a reminder that we'll get everything God has planned for us, a praising and glorious life.

15-19   That's why, when I heard of the solid trust you have in the Master Jesus and your outpouring of love to all the followers of Jesus, I couldn't stop thanking God for you — every time I prayed, I'd think of you and give thanks. But I do more than thank. I ask — ask the God of our Master, Jesus Christ, the God of glory — to make you intelligent and discerning in knowing him personally, your eyes focused and clear, so that you can see exactly what it is he is calling you to do, grasp the immensity of this glorious way of life he has for his followers, oh, the utter extravagance of his work in us who trust him — endless energy, boundless strength!

THINK

Consider your identity. Who are you — *really*? In what do you find your true identity and sense of worth? In other words, what makes you, you? Are the sources of your self-worth healthy or unhealthy? Jot down a few notes about how you see your identity.

READ

Read the passage silently, but mouth the words of the verses as you read. What does this passage say about your identity? What is Christ's role in shaping your identity? Refer to your notes. How does this picture of your identity compare to those initial thoughts?

PRAY

Paul includes several elements in his prayers for the church at Ephesus. It is full of thanksgiving, petitions for intimacy with the Father, clarity for direction, knowledge of a life lived with Christ, and strength.

Make Paul's prayer in verses 15-19 your own. For example, *I ask you — the God of my Master, Jesus Christ, the God of glory — to make me intelligent and discerning in knowing you personally.* And so on.

Next, ask God to bring to mind an individual who needs prayer. Come before God and pray these verses for that person's current situation and overall life. Pray for his or her identity. Make your prayer specific by replacing the applicable words in today's passage with the individual's name.

Are there others for whom you could pray this prayer? Spend time interceding for them as well.

LIVE

If the Spirit nudges you to do so, tell the person that you prayed specifically for him or her. Read that person the prayer from Scripture.

REALLY ALIVE IN CHRIST

EPHESIANS 2:1-6

1-6   It wasn't so long ago that you were mired in that old stagnant life of sin. You let the world, which doesn't know the first thing about living, tell you how to live. You filled your lungs with polluted unbelief, and then exhaled disobedience. We all did it, all of us doing what we felt like doing, when we felt like doing it, all of us in the same boat. It's a wonder God didn't lose his temper and do away with the whole lot of us. Instead, immense in mercy and with an incredible love, he embraced us. He took our sin-dead lives and made us alive in Christ. He did all this on his own, with no help from us! Then he picked us up and set us down in highest heaven in company with Jesus, our Messiah.

READ

Read the passage aloud slowly.

THINK

Read the passage again, noting the "old stagnant life" as described in the first part of the paragraph and all that God has done in the second part.

1. How do you relate to the "old stagnant life" described in verses 1-3?
2. How difficult or easy is it for you to believe that the "old stagnant life" is not in sync with "the first thing about living"?
3. Repeat in your own words what God has done in verses 4-6. What does this tell you about what God is really like?
4. How difficult or easy is it for you to believe that God is like that?

PRAY

Ask God to help you more easily believe in the goodness of life with him (verses 1-3) and in the goodness of God's own self (verses 4-6). Respond to God about what it's like to be surrounded by such goodness.

LIVE

Be aware of having an interactive life with this God who is unendingly compassionate and who makes us really alive all day long.

CHRIST'S EXTRAVAGANT LOVE

EPHESIANS 3:10-20

10 Through followers of Jesus like yourselves gathered in churches, this extraordinary plan of God is becoming known and talked about even among the angels!

11-13 All this is proceeding along lines planned all along by God and then executed in Christ Jesus. When we trust in him, we're free to say whatever needs to be said, bold to go wherever we need to go. So don't let my present trouble on your behalf get you down. Be proud!

14-19 My response is to get down on my knees before the Father, this magnificent Father who parcels out all heaven and earth. I ask him to strengthen you by his Spirit — not a brute strength but a glorious inner strength — that Christ will live in you as you open the door and invite him in. And I ask him that with both feet planted firmly on love, you'll be able to take in with all followers of Jesus the extravagant dimensions of Christ's love. Reach out and experience the breadth! Test its length! Plumb the depths! Rise to the heights! Live full lives, full in the fullness of God.

20 God can do anything, you know — far more than you could ever imagine or guess or request in your wildest dreams! He does it not by pushing us around but by working within us, his Spirit deeply and gently within us.

READ

As you read this passage, look for a word or theme that refreshes you. Maybe this will be Paul's specific description of God's "magnificent" strength and power, or the picture of being "free to say whatever needs to be said, bold to go wherever we need to go."

THINK/PRAY

Think about the portion of the passage you chose. Why do you think it touches you today? Are you feeling tired? Trapped? Discouraged?

Now sit in silence, picturing yourself opening the door to Christ and letting him come inside to be with you in your troubles. Talk to him about what is bringing you down.

Look back at the passage, and read — a few times, slowly — the part that spoke to you. What message does Christ want you to hear today? Savor this message and let it speak to your need.

LIVE

Pick a word from the passage that symbolizes what uplifted you. Write it down or doodle a picture that represents its meaning to you. Now put it where you will often see it and reflect on it. Maybe you'll use a sticky note and put it on your steering wheel, your bathroom mirror, or your microwave door. When you see it throughout the day, pause to recall Christ's Message to you.

DAY 294

GOD ENCOUNTERS

On this seventh day, review and reflect on all you have read this week. Take the time to revel in the ways you've encountered God in the past six days.

PERMEATED WITH ONENESS

EPHESIANS 4:1-6

1-3   In light of all this, here's what I want you to do. While I'm locked up here, a prisoner for the Master, I want you to get out there and walk — better yet, run! — on the road God called you to travel. I don't want any of you sitting around on your hands. I don't want anyone strolling off, down some path that goes nowhere. And mark that you do this with humility and discipline — not in fits and starts, but steadily, pouring yourselves out for each other in acts of love, alert at noticing differences and quick at mending fences.

4-6   You were all called to travel on the same road and in the same direction, so stay together, both outwardly and inwardly. You have one Master, one faith, one baptism, one God and Father of all, who rules over all, works through all, and is present in all. Everything you are and think and do is permeated with Oneness.

READ

Read this passage with another believer, if possible.

THINK

If you can, take this book to a spot within viewing distance of a road (whether busy or seldom traveled). Consider the road. Watch the cars and people that pass by.

Now think about the metaphor of traveling on a road used in this passage. Ponder Paul's words: "You were all called to travel on the same road and in the same direction, so stay together, both outwardly and inwardly." What does inward unity look like? What does outward unity look like? Do you know other followers of Christ who are not traveling on the same road or in the same direction you are?

"Everything you are and think and do is permeated with Oneness." Does this describe your relationships? Your church community? The body of Christ around the world? What can be done to strengthen this oneness with other believers?

With another believer (or several), brainstorm ways — little and big — to help create greater oneness in Christ.

PRAY

When you drive on or walk beside roads today, use that as a trigger to pray for unity among other believers — in your personal circles, in your town, and around the world.

LIVE

Do what you can to live in unity with others.

✚ DRINKING THE SPIRIT OF GOD

EPHESIANS 5:15-20

15-16 So watch your step. Use your head. Make the most of every chance you get. These are desperate times!

17   Don't live carelessly, unthinkingly. Make sure you understand what the Master wants.

18-20   Don't drink too much wine. That cheapens your life. Drink the Spirit of God, huge draughts of him. Sing hymns instead of drinking songs! Sing songs from your heart to Christ. Sing praises over everything, any excuse for a song to God the Father in the name of our Master, Jesus Christ.

READ
Read the passage aloud slowly.

THINK
Read the passage again, picturing yourself in the crowd of people listening to this letter read aloud (as was done in those days). The writer, Paul, spent two years with your group and knows you well.

1. What does "live carelessly" mean to you?
2. How would you go about "drink[ing] the Spirit of God"? What would that look like for you?

Read the passage again and notice what words or phrases stand out to you. Why do you think they speak to you that way?

PRAY
Speak back to God the words that spoke to you. Tell God what they mean to you and what you would like to do about them. Talk to God about how well he knows you, that he would speak to you so personally.

LIVE
Each time you drink a liquid today, pause and picture yourself being filled with the liquid Spirit of God. Enjoy that.

EXPANDED PASSAGE: EPHESIANS 5:1-2,21–6:9

RELATIONSHIPS FOR LIVING WELL

EPHESIANS 6:1-9

1-3 Children, do what your parents tell you. This is only right. "Honor your father and mother" is the first commandment that has a promise attached to it, namely, "so you will live well and have a long life."

4 Fathers, don't exasperate your children by coming down hard on them. Take them by the hand and lead them in the way of the Master.

5-8 Servants, respectfully obey your earthly masters but always with an eye to obeying the *real* master, Christ. Don't just do what you have to do to get by, but work heartily, as Christ's servants doing what God wants you to do. And work with a smile on your face, always keeping in mind that no matter who happens to be giving the orders, you're really serving God. Good work will get you good pay from the Master, regardless of whether you are slave or free.

9 Masters, it's the same with you. No abuse, please, and no threats. You and your servants are both under the same Master in heaven. He makes no distinction between you and them.

READ

Read the passage, letting it call to mind the relevant relationships in your life.

THINK

Mull over what this passage is saying about whole and healthy relationships — children to parents, fathers to children, and employees to employers. What is your reaction to the description given of each relationship? Perhaps you feel longing or maybe sadness or annoyance? Explore your reaction.

PRAY

Pick one relationship this passage brought to mind and take a few minutes to observe what kind of child, parent, employee, or student you are. How does your fulfillment of this role compare to the standard Paul sets? Ponder the models in your life for that role. How were you parented? How do your role models relate to their employers? Talk to Jesus about this, and share with him any disappointment, gratitude, or frustration you feel about your own role and your role models.

LIVE

What is Jesus' invitation to you in the relationship you selected? Perhaps it is just to continue growing in your awareness of what kind of person you are in relationships. Or perhaps you sense Jesus leading you toward a specific action. Make a note of what you hear so you can refer to it.

THE POSTURE OF GRATEFULNESS

PHILIPPIANS 1:3-6

3-6 Every time you cross my mind, I break out in exclamations of thanks to God. Each exclamation is a trigger to prayer. I find myself praying for you with a glad heart. I am so pleased that you have continued on in this with us, believing and proclaiming God's Message, from the day you heard it right up to the present. There has never been the slightest doubt in my mind that the God who started this great work in you would keep at it and bring it to a flourishing finish on the very day Christ Jesus appears.

READ

Read the passage. After doing so, write out the entire passage. Then read it again.

THINK

The subject of thankfulness in prayer will come up many times in this devotional, but there's no way to offer too much gratitude when we communicate with God. Of course it seems to be in our nature to approach God only when times are tough, when we feel like venting, or when we have a need. God listens to all our prayers, but it's hard to pray heartfelt, God-honoring prayers with an ungrateful and complaining spirit. We should *always* be grateful for *something* in prayer.

Paul models a thankful heart for us here as he reflects on the church in Philippi. On a scale of one to ten — one being "frequently ungrateful" and ten being "always thankful" — what number would you give your prayers? What number would your friends give your prayers? What would it take for your prayers to move toward ten?

LIVE/PRAY

Find a small photo of an old friend or family member. Place it in a location where you will see it often. Every time you look at the photo, pause and thank God for who that person is, what that person means to you, and who God is forming that person to become. Be reminded that God, who started this great work in him or her, will "keep at it and bring it to a flourishing finish" one day.

SETTING ASIDE ADVANTAGES

PHILIPPIANS 2:2-11

2-4   Agree with each other, love each other, be deep-spirited friends. Don't push your way to the front; don't sweet-talk your way to the top. Put yourself aside, and help others get ahead. Don't be obsessed with getting your own advantage. Forget yourselves long enough to lend a helping hand.

5-8   Think of yourselves the way Christ Jesus thought of himself. He had equal status with God but didn't think so much of himself that he had to cling to the advantages of that status no matter what. Not at all. When the time came, he set aside the privileges of deity and took on the status of a slave, became *human*! Having become human, he stayed human. It was an incredibly humbling process. He didn't claim special privileges. Instead, he lived a selfless, obedient life and then died a selfless, obedient death — and the worst kind of death at that — a crucifixion.

9-11   Because of that obedience, God lifted him high and honored him far beyond anyone or anything, ever, so that all created beings in heaven and on earth — even those long ago dead and buried — will bow in worship before this Jesus Christ, and call out in praise that he is the Master of all, to the glorious honor of God the Father.

READ

Read the passage aloud slowly, noticing the recurring words, such as *advantage, privileges, selfless, obedient, obedience.*

THINK

1. Read verses 5-8 again and consider what amazes you about Jesus, perhaps that he:

   - "didn't think so much of himself"
   - "[didn't] cling to the advantages"
   - "set aside the privileges"
   - "took on the status of a slave"
   - "lived a selfless, obedient life and then died a selfless, obedient death"

2. Read verses 9-11 again and consider what amazes you about God, perhaps that he:

   - "lifted [Jesus] high and honored him" more than any other (including God himself)
   - is honored by how people bow to worship Jesus Christ

3. Now read verses 2-4 again and consider what God is calling you to be or do.
4. In what way does your admiration for Jesus' and God's radical behavior (verses 5-11) inspire you to the behavior described in verses 2-4?

PRAY

Tell Jesus what you admire about his willingness to come to earth and his way of being while here. Tell God what you admire about his humility. Ask them to help you do whatever came to you in question 3.

LIVE

Look for opportunities today to help someone get ahead. If and when you do, sense Jesus' companionship in your efforts.

NOTHING LESS THAN TOTAL COMMITMENT

PHILIPPIANS 3:15-21

15-16 So let's keep focused on that goal, those of us who want everything God has for us. If any of you have something else in mind, something less than total commitment, God will clear your blurred vision — you'll see it yet! Now that we're on the right track, let's stay on it.

17-19 Stick with me, friends. Keep track of those you see running this same course, headed for this same goal. There are many out there taking other paths, choosing other goals, and trying to get you to go along with them. I've warned you of them many times; sadly, I'm having to do it again. All they want is easy street. They hate Christ's Cross. But easy street is a dead-end street. Those who live there make their bellies their gods; belches are their praise; all they can think of is their appetites.

20-21 But there's far more to life for us. We're citizens of high heaven! We're waiting the arrival of the Savior, the Master, Jesus Christ, who will transform our earthy bodies into glorious bodies like his own. He'll make us beautiful and whole with the same powerful skill by which he is putting everything as it should be, under and around him.

READ

Read the passage two times slowly.

THINK

Read again what Paul says about "total commitment." Write down honestly what you feel and think about it, without judging your own reaction.

Now read again what Paul says about those who are "choosing other goals" in life rather than knowing Jesus. What thoughts, memories, or feelings do you have as you read this? Jot them down.

Finally, read again, paying special attention to what Christians have to look forward to. What does this make you feel? Note the promise that evokes the greatest response in you.

LIVE

Think about a circumstance in your life that frustrates you with its monotony or pointlessness. Once again become aware of the goal in this passage: a simple and trusting openness to God and total commitment to what he has for you.

Now consider the following statement by Oswald Chambers: "The spiritual saint never believes circumstances to be haphazard, or thinks of his life as secular and sacred; he sees everything he is dumped down in as the means of securing the knowledge of Jesus Christ."[21] Do you believe that the God who intends to make you "beautiful and whole" is the same God who has allowed your circumstance? Why or why not?

PRAY

Ask Jesus to help you become totally committed to wanting "everything God has for [you]." Ask him to help you recognize and avoid "taking other paths, choosing other goals." Thank him that "there's far more to life for [you]."

DAY 301

GOD ENCOUNTERS

On this seventh day, review and reflect on all you have read this week. Take the time to revel in the ways you've encountered God in the past six days.

SHAPING WORRIES INTO PRAYERS

PHILIPPIANS 4:6-9

6-7 Don't fret or worry. Instead of worrying, pray. Let petitions and praises shape your worries into prayers, letting God know your concerns. Before you know it, a sense of God's wholeness, everything coming together for good, will come and settle you down. It's wonderful what happens when Christ displaces worry at the center of your life.

8-9 Summing it all up, friends, I'd say you'll do best by filling your minds and meditating on things true, noble, reputable, authentic, compelling, gracious — the best, not the worst; the beautiful, not the ugly; things to praise, not things to curse. Put into practice what you learned from me, what you heard and saw and realized. Do that, and God, who makes everything work together, will work you into his most excellent harmonies.

READ

Read the passage, including the expanded passage, if possible.

THINK

How do you handle something that worries you? Do you ignore the problem so you can put off thinking about it for as long as possible? Do you feel depressed and pessimistic about it, pretty sure of negative results, no matter what? Do you spend a lot of energy identifying a solution and working toward it? Whatever your answer, pinpoint your primary way of reacting. See if you know why you handle worry the way you do.

Now consider one worry you have today and how you've been dealing (or not dealing) with it.

PRAY

Sit in silence for a few minutes with your eyes closed. Breathe deeply and let your mind quiet down. Become aware of God's presence.

Express to God your concern. Even though he knows the situation, tell him all about it, every detail. In what way has your anxiety affected other areas of your life, such as relationships, work, or school? What's the worst-case scenario you're afraid might happen? Whether rational or irrational, share with God what you fear.

LIVE

Recall the Person you've experienced God to be in the past weeks and months. Reflect on previous notes you've made about experiencing God through his Message and prayer. From that, focus on three of his attributes. How do these elements of his character relate to your situation? What do they indicate about his presence with you right now? Picture this God in your mind. Remember today that this is the God who has heard your concern, the God who "will work you into his most excellent harmonies."

HE IS SUPREME

COLOSSIANS 1:15-23

15-18 We look at this Son and see the God who cannot be seen. We look at this Son and see God's original purpose in everything created. For everything, absolutely everything, above and below, visible and invisible, rank after rank after rank of angels — *everything* got started in him and finds its purpose in him. He was there before any of it came into existence and holds it all together right up to this moment. And when it comes to the church, he organizes and holds it together, like a head does a body.

18-20 He was supreme in the beginning and — leading the resurrection parade — he is supreme in the end. From beginning to end he's there, towering far above everything, everyone. So spacious is he, so roomy, that everything of God finds its proper place in him without crowding. Not only that, but all the broken and dislocated pieces of the universe — people and things, animals and atoms — get properly fixed and fit together in vibrant harmonies, all because of his death, his blood that poured down from the cross.

21-23 You yourselves are a case study of what he does. At one time you all had your backs turned to God, thinking rebellious thoughts of him, giving him trouble every chance you got. But now, by giving himself completely at the Cross, actually *dying* for you, Christ brought you over to God's side and put your lives together, whole and holy in his presence. You don't walk away from a gift like that! You stay grounded and steady in that bond of trust, constantly tuned in to the Message, careful not to be distracted or diverted. There is no other Message — just this one. Every creature under heaven gets this same Message. I, Paul, am a messenger of this Message.

READ

Wherever you are, stand up and read the passage aloud. Stand prayer-fully in a posture that communicates to God respect and receptivity to his Word.

THINK

This passage speaks of the supremacy and power of God manifested through Jesus Christ. What specific attribute or characteristic of Jesus sticks out to you most in this passage? Why do you think it does?

"We look at this Son and see the God who cannot be seen. We look at this Son and see God's original purpose in everything created." What are specific, practical ways in which you can "look at this Son"?

What does the following mean? "He was supreme in the beginning and — leading the resurrection parade — he is supreme in the end." What implications does this have in your life today? Wonder about the suprem-acy of Christ.

PRAY

Reflect on the attribute of Christ that struck you (for example, maybe it was that everything "finds its purpose in him"). In what ways would the world be different if Christ did not possess that attribute? In what ways would your life be different? How and why?

LIVE

Live your day knowing that you serve — and are loved by — the God who holds the entire world together!

ALL-PURPOSE GARMENT

COLOSSIANS 3:3-5,12-17

3-4   Your old life is dead. Your new life, which is your *real* life — even though invisible to spectators — is with Christ in God. *He* is your life. When Christ (your real life, remember) shows up again on this earth, you'll show up, too — the real you, the glorious you. Meanwhile, be content with obscurity, like Christ.

5   And that means killing off everything connected with that way of death: sexual promiscuity, impurity, lust, doing whatever you feel like whenever you feel like it, and grabbing whatever attracts your fancy. That's a life shaped by things and feelings instead of by God. . . .

12-14   So, chosen by God for this new life of love, dress in the wardrobe God picked out for you: compassion, kindness, humility, quiet strength, discipline. Be even-tempered, content with second place, quick to forgive an offense. Forgive as quickly and completely as the Master forgave you. And regardless of what else you put on, wear love. It's your basic, all-purpose garment. Never be without it.

15-17   Let the peace of Christ keep you in tune with each other, in step with each other. None of this going off and doing your own thing. And cultivate thankfulness. Let the Word of Christ — the Message — have the run of the house. Give it plenty of room in your lives. Instruct and direct one another using good common sense. And sing, sing your hearts out to God! Let every detail in your lives — words, actions, whatever — be done in the name of the Master, Jesus, thanking God the Father every step of the way.

READ

Read the passage aloud slowly.

THINK

Read the passage again and consider these segments included in the process of stepping into the new life.

1. A new life is possible (verses 3-4).
2. We get rid of the old life (verse 5).
3. We put on the new life (verses 12-14).
4. We consider background thoughts and behavior needed to put on new life (verses 15-17).

Which segment of this process speaks to you most right now? Reread the verses that correspond to that segment. Now, what word or phrase in that segment speaks to you? Why do you think that is? How does that idea relate to the other segments? How does it relate to love, the "all-purpose garment"?

PRAY

Pray back to God the segment that speaks to you, personalizing it. For example, based on verse 15, *Please let the peace of Christ keep me in tune with others — show me that true peace of Christ!*

LIVE

Sit quietly in the idea that your old life really is dead. All the good, loving attitudes and behaviors of Jesus are open to you. Allow yourself to be invited to step into that today.

VIRTUE CHECKLIST

COLOSSIANS 4:2-6

2-4 Pray diligently. Stay alert, with your eyes wide open in gratitude. Don't forget to pray for us, that God will open doors for telling the mystery of Christ, even while I'm locked up in this jail. Pray that every time I open my mouth I'll be able to make Christ plain as day to them.

5-6 Use your heads as you live and work among outsiders. Don't miss a trick. Make the most of every opportunity. Be gracious in your speech. The goal is to bring out the best in others in a conversation, not put them down, not cut them out.

READ

Read this passage several times, each time narrowing your focus to the part that challenges you the most.

THINK

What did you focus on? Was it a virtuous action that is not part of your lifestyle? Or perhaps it was something you already do, but you noticed something different about the way or reason why Paul says to do it. What is your emotional response when you think of changing this area of your life? Do you feel eager? Overwhelmed? Threatened or protective? Unsure?

PRAY

Talk with Jesus about the item on Paul's list of virtues that challenged you most and about how you responded to it. Sit in silence to wait for what Jesus might have to say to you.

LIVE

As you read the following statement made by Saint Bernard of Clairvaux, also consider what Paul tells Christians to do in today's passage: "If then you are wise, you will show yourself rather as a reservoir than as a canal. For a canal spreads abroad water as it receives it, but a reservoir waits until it is filled before overflowing, and thus communicates, without loss to itself, its superabundant water. In the Church at the present day, we have many canals, few reservoirs."[22]

Are you more like a canal, a reservoir, or something else altogether? Would others who know you agree? Talk with Jesus about this and be open to what he is showing you about yourself. In what way is he inviting you to live differently?

ONLY GOD APPROVAL

1 THESSALONIANS 2:3-8

3-5   God tested us thoroughly to make sure we were qualified to be trusted with this Message. Be assured that when we speak to you we're not after crowd approval — only God approval. Since we've been put through that battery of tests, you're guaranteed that both we and the Message are free of error, mixed motives, or hidden agendas. We never used words to butter you up. No one knows that better than you. And God knows we never used words as a smoke screen to take advantage of you.

6-8   Even though we had some standing as Christ's apostles, we never threw our weight around or tried to come across as important, with you or anyone else. We weren't aloof with you. We took you just as you were. We were never patronizing, never condescending, but we cared for you the way a mother cares for her children. We loved you dearly. Not content to just pass on the Message, we wanted to give you our hearts. And we *did.*

READ

Read the passage, noting the word *approval.*

THINK

It's tempting to promote ourselves, to see ourselves more highly than we ought. If we examine ourselves honestly, we will have to admit that we are often trying to win the approval of the crowd.

Think back over the past week. What decisions did you make solely to look good in the eyes of others? What would it take for you to go through today without making decisions based on trying to make yourself look good? What would it take for you to live today for "only God approval"?

PRAY

Confess those recent circumstances when you were tempted to seek approval from other people. Ask God to help you be "free of error, mixed motives, [and] hidden agendas." Ask him to help you focus your desire for acceptance and approval entirely on him.

LIVE

Before every decision, before every comment, ask yourself, *What is my motive? Is it to get approval from the crowd or to get approval from God?* Let these questions make you aware today of how — and why — you make decisions.

SOMEONE ELSE'S FAITH AND LOVE

1 THESSALONIANS 3:6-13

6-8 But now that Timothy is back, bringing this terrific report on your faith and love, we feel a lot better. It's especially gratifying to know that you continue to think well of us, and that you want to see us as much as we want to see you! In the middle of our trouble and hard times here, just knowing how you're doing keeps us going. Knowing that your faith is alive keeps us alive.

9-10 What would be an adequate thanksgiving to offer God for all the joy we experience before him because of you? We do what we can, praying away, night and day, asking for the bonus of seeing your faces again and doing what we can to help when your faith falters.

11-13 May God our Father himself and our Master Jesus clear the road to you! And may the Master pour on the love so it fills your lives and splashes over on everyone around you, just as it does from us to you. May you be infused with strength and purity, filled with confidence in the presence of God our Father when our Master Jesus arrives with all his followers.

READ

Read the passage aloud slowly.

THINK

Ask God to bring to mind those you know who live their lives before God routinely showing "faith and love" (a really alive faith) and giving others joy. You may not know these people well or see them often (they may be missionaries from your church, friends of friends, or speakers you've listened to), but the way they live reassures you that this kind of life is possible. Read the passage again in light of these people.

PRAY

First, thank God for these people, that:

- their faith and love make you feel better
- they think well of you and you want to see them
- their faith is so alive it keeps you more alive
- you experience joy because of them

Second, pray for these people who, although they may seem so mature, still need your prayers. Pray that:

- if their faith falters, someone (maybe you) can help them
- God the Father and Jesus the Master will clear their roads
- Jesus will pour into their lives a love that fills them and "splashes over on everyone"
- they may be "infused with strength and purity"
- they may be "filled with confidence in the presence of God"

LIVE

Rejoice restfully that people who love God and live the Message really do exist in this world.

DAY 308

GOD ENCOUNTERS

On this seventh day, review and reflect on all you have read this week. Take the time to revel in the ways you've encountered God in the past six days.

NOT A SET-UP FOR REJECTION

1 THESSALONIANS 5:1-10

1-3   I don't think, friends, that I need to deal with the question of when all this is going to happen. You know as well as I that the day of the Master's coming can't be posted on our calendars. He won't call ahead and make an appointment any more than a burglar would. About the time everybody's walking around complacently, congratulating each other — "We've sure got it made! Now we can take it easy!" — suddenly everything will fall apart. It's going to come as suddenly and inescapably as birth pangs to a pregnant woman.

4-8   But friends, you're not in the dark, so how could you be taken off guard by any of this? You're sons of Light, daughters of Day. We live under wide open skies and know where we stand. So let's not sleepwalk through life like those others. Let's keep our eyes open and be smart. People sleep at night and get drunk at night. But not us! Since we're creatures of Day, let's act like it. Walk out into the daylight sober, dressed up in faith, love, and the hope of salvation.

9-10   God didn't set us up for an angry rejection but for salvation by our Master, Jesus Christ. He died for us, a death that triggered life. Whether we're awake with the living or asleep with the dead, we're *alive* with him!

READ

Read the passage twice.

THINK

When you think about the end of the world and Jesus' return to Earth, what do you feel? Nervous? Excited? Halfhearted interest? In everyday life, how often do you think, feel, act, or plan as though you really believe that Jesus will come back someday soon?

PRAY

Prayerfully think about Paul's statement: "We . . . know where we stand." What does it stir up in you? Do you feel confident or uncertain about where you stand with Jesus? Talk to him about your reaction to this phrase.

LIVE

Ruth Haley Barton voices the questions "Is God really good? If I trust myself to him, isn't there a good chance that I will wind up where I least want to be or that God will withhold what I want the most? Isn't God a little bit like Lucy in the Peanuts comic strip, who pulls the football away just as Charlie Brown gives himself completely to the kick, causing him to fall flat on his face?"[23]

Take a moment to absorb these questions and reconsider Paul's statement that "God didn't set us up for an angry rejection but for salvation." How do your deep-down-inside expectations of God correspond with Paul's perspective? With the perspective Barton describes? Share with God your honest beliefs about him and your expectations of how he'll treat you.

Suspend for a few minutes whatever disbelief you have, and imagine you truly believe God is trustworthy. How might you live differently?

309

WE GIVE THANKS

2 THESSALONIANS 1:3-4

3-4   You need to know, friends, that thanking God over and over for you is not only a pleasure; it's a must. We *have* to do it. Your faith is growing phenomenally; your love for each other is developing wonderfully. Why, it's only right that we give thanks. We're so proud of you; you're so steady and determined in your faith despite all the hard times that have come down on you. We tell everyone we meet in the churches all about you.

READ

Read this passage very slowly and cautiously. Imagine yourself as a surgeon carefully cutting and dissecting it. Give focused attention to each word.

THINK/PRAY

What or whom are you grateful for today? Why? Pause and give thanks to God for these now.

Who is growing in their faith, maturing into God's likeness, and loving others well? Thank God for them now, including names and details.

Who needs to grow more in their faith, needs to mature further into God's likeness, and could love others more appropriately and generously? Thank God for them and pray for them now, including names and details.

Which followers of Christ have fallen on hard times but are determined and are persevering? Thank God for them and pray for them now, including names and details. Pray also for the persecuted church — those Christ-followers around the globe who are being arrested and tortured and murdered simply because of what they believe. Thank God for their incredible passion and commitment to Jesus. Finally, ask God to give you the same courage, commitment, and love for Christ.

LIVE

Carry all these individuals in your thoughts today. Ask God to bring them to mind during the coming week. As you remember them, "thanking God over and over," pray for them.

LIFE IN THE SPIRIT

2 THESSALONIANS 2:13-17

13-14   Meanwhile, we've got our hands full continually thanking God for you, our good friends — so loved by God! God picked you out as his from the very start. Think of it: included in God's original plan of salvation by the bond of faith in the living truth. This is the life of the Spirit he invited you to through the Message we delivered, in which you get in on the glory of our Master, Jesus Christ.

15-17   So, friends, take a firm stand, feet on the ground and head high. Keep a tight grip on what you were taught, whether in personal conversation or by our letter. May Jesus himself and God our Father, who reached out in love and surprised you with gifts of unending help and confidence, put a fresh heart in you, invigorate your work, enliven your speech.

READ

Read the passage aloud slowly. Then recall the small, inconsequential things that have occupied your thoughts in the last few moments, hours, or days.

THINK

Read the passage again, noting how Paul viewed an average life as so spectacular because he was immersed in the Trinitarian reality (God, Jesus, and Holy Spirit in verses 13-14).

1. Which of these truths about God's unseen reality most captivate you?

    □ You are "so loved by God!"
    □ You have a "bond of faith in the living truth" with others.
    □ You're invited to life in the Spirit.
    □ "You get in on the glory of our Master, Jesus Christ."
    □ God reaches out to you in love.
    □ God surprises you "with gifts of unending help and confidence."
    □ God can "put a fresh heart in you."
    □ God can "invigorate your work."
    □ God can "enliven your speech."

2. Think about today's events — even mundane ones. Which of the truths mentioned in question 1 do you need to link with each event?

PRAY

Pray about each event, that you will live in this unseen reality, that you'll see how these truths are present. For example, pray about a conversation or a homework assignment or a work project, that you'll participate in it knowing you are loved and receiving God's gifts of unending help and confidence.

LIVE

Pick one of these truths about life in the Spirit and sense its reality. If you have trouble doing this, ask God to help you.

IF YOU DON'T WORK, YOU DON'T EAT

2 THESSALONIANS 3:6-15

6-9   Our orders — backed up by the Master, Jesus — are to refuse to have any-thing to do with those among you who are lazy and refuse to work the way we taught you. Don't permit them to freeload on the rest. We showed you how to pull your weight when we were with you, so get on with it. We didn't sit around on our hands expecting others to take care of us. In fact, we worked our fingers to the bone, up half the night moonlighting so you wouldn't be burdened with taking care of us. And it wasn't because we didn't have a right to your support; we did. We simply wanted to provide an example of diligence, hoping it would prove contagious.

10-13   Don't you remember the rule we had when we lived with you? "If you don't work, you don't eat." And now we're getting reports that a bunch of lazy good-for-nothings are taking advantage of you. This must not be tol-erated. We command them to get to work immediately — no excuses, no arguments — and earn their own keep. Friends, don't slack off in doing your duty.

14-15   If anyone refuses to obey our clear command written in this letter, don't let him get by with it. Point out such a person and refuse to subsi-dize his freeloading. Maybe then he'll think twice. But don't treat him as an enemy. Sit him down and talk about the problem as someone who cares.

READ

Read the passage carefully.

THINK

Why do you think Paul is making such a big deal out of Christians who freeload off others? Why is he encouraging those in Thessalonica to make a big deal out of it? In what ways do you think laziness and freeloading impact relationships?

PRAY

Read the passage again, this time listening for a word or phrase that stands out to you, such as "duty," "excuses," or "[not] as an enemy . . . [but as] someone who cares." Chew on this for a few minutes. Share with God what pops up in you as you consider it.

Now read again the part of the passage that contains the word or phrase. Why do you think this word is standing out to you today? Does it trigger a fear? Does it challenge you? What part of your life does it touch?

LIVE

Read the whole passage one last time. This time, listen for the action or attitude God is inviting you to take on this week. Maybe he's asking you to lovingly sit down with a friend and speak plainly about her freeloading. Maybe he wants you to start looking for a job or to stop "borrowing" or using stuff that isn't yours. Make a note of how you can take steps in the direction God is indicating. If you are especially aware of God's presence with you when you take these steps, what might the impact be?

UNCONTAMINATED BY SELF-INTEREST

1 TIMOTHY 1:3-7

3-4 On my way to the province of Macedonia, I advised you to stay in Ephesus. Well, I haven't changed my mind. Stay right there on top of things so that the teaching stays on track. Apparently some people have been introducing fantasy stories and fanciful family trees that digress into silliness instead of pulling the people back into the center, deepening faith and obedience.

5-7 The whole point of what we're urging is simply *love* — love uncontaminated by self-interest and counterfeit faith, a life open to God. Those who fail to keep to this point soon wander off into cul-de-sacs of gossip. They set themselves up as experts on religious issues, but haven't the remotest idea of what they're holding forth with such imposing eloquence.

THINK

Paul as mentor has sent carefully written instructions to his disciple Timothy. This is the first volume of his guidance for Timothy, urging him as a young leader to mature in Christ. Among the complexities of life, Paul boils the message down to one simple concept: love. Not just love, but "love uncontaminated by self-interest and counterfeit faith, a life open to God."

READ

With this background in mind, meditate on the passage.

PRAY

While remaining open to God, consider what love looks like when it's "uncontaminated by self-interest and counterfeit faith." Then ask God the following questions, pausing between each one to listen to the Holy Spirit's response:

God, what about my love is contaminated by self-interest? Ask God to help remove the contamination of selfishness in your life.

Father, what about my love is counterfeit or fake? Ask for courage to be authentic with God, others, and yourself.

Lord, what about my life and love is closed off, hidden, or resistant to you and your purposes? Ask God to give you the willingness and to help you be more open to his purposes, even if doing so feels uncertain and scary.

LIVE

Go live and love selflessly, authentically, and openly.

HUMBLE CONTEMPLATION

1 TIMOTHY 2:1-2,8-9

1-2   The first thing I want you to do is pray. Pray every way you know how, for everyone you know. Pray especially for rulers and their governments to rule well so we can be quietly about our business of living simply, in humble contemplation. . . .

8-9   Since prayer is at the bottom of all this, what I want mostly is for men to pray — not shaking angry fists at enemies but raising holy hands to God. And I want women to get in there with the men in humility before God, not primping before a mirror or chasing the latest fashions.

READ

Read the passage aloud slowly.

THINK

Read the passage again, noting what is said about prayer:

- how to pray: "every way you know how" and "raising holy hands"
- government-related prayer: good ruling so through simple, humble, contemplative living, the Message about Christ may spread
- tone of prayer: "humble contemplation" and women praying in humility
- pray for: "everyone you know" and "rulers"
- outcome of prayer: the Message will spread, women will do "something beautiful for God" (verse 10)

Read the passage one more time. What do you think God is telling you about how you need to pray?

PRAY

Lift holy hands as you ask God to lead you in praying that governments will "rule well so [Christians] can be quietly about [their] business of living simply, in humble contemplation."

LIVE

Sit quietly with your hands raised, outstretched, eager for God's Message to permeate the nations of our planet.

DAY 315

GOD ENCOUNTERS

On this seventh day, review and reflect on all you have read this week. Take the time to revel in the ways you've encountered God in the past six days.

PRECONDITIONS OF LEADERSHIP

1 TIMOTHY 3:1-13

1-7 If anyone wants to provide leadership in the church, good! But there are preconditions: A leader must be well-thought-of, committed to his wife, cool and collected, accessible, and hospitable. He must know what he's talking about, not be overfond of wine, not pushy but gentle, not thin-skinned, not money-hungry. He must handle his own affairs well, attentive to his own children and having their respect. For if someone is unable to handle his own affairs, how can he take care of God's church? He must not be a new believer, lest the position go to his head and the Devil trip him up. Outsiders must think well of him, or else the Devil will figure out a way to lure him into his trap.

8-13 The same goes for those who want to be servants in the church: serious, not deceitful, not too free with the bottle, not in it for what they can get out of it. They must be reverent before the mystery of the faith, not using their position to try to run things. Let them prove themselves first. If they show they can do it, take them on. No exceptions are to be made for women—same qualifications: serious, dependable, not sharp-tongued, not overfond of wine. Servants in the church are to be committed to their spouses, attentive to their own children, and diligent in looking after their own affairs. Those who do this servant work will come to be highly respected, a real credit to this Jesus-faith.

READ

Read this passage a few times slowly and carefully.

THINK

As you absorb the moral expectations presented in this passage, what is your reaction? Perhaps you desire to change, or perhaps you feel irritated. Maybe you feel shame or guilt. Maybe relief. Does reading this make you want to be a leader? If not, why not? Share your reaction with God.

PRAY

Take several minutes to read the text again slowly, letting each instruction direct you toward a new area of your heart to examine with the Holy Spirit. (Don't feel that you must work your way through the entire passage: The goal is to uncover content for prayer, not get through the entire list.) In which areas does your life look different from the model Paul is describing? For example, you've been more pushy than gentle with someone, or you've been more unreliable than dependable. Tell God about what you find.

LIVE

Ask God to show you what it would look like to embrace transformation in an area you've examined today, realizing that starting with baby steps might be just right for you. Take courage that "our personalities are transformed — not lost — in the furnace of God's love."[24] God's transformation will not obliterate your personality; instead, the process will make you more into the one-of-a-kind you who God made you to be.

GET THE WORD OUT

1 TIMOTHY 4:10-16

10 This is why we've thrown ourselves into this venture so totally. We're banking on the living God, Savior of all men and women, especially believers.

11-14 Get the word out. Teach all these things. And don't let anyone put you down because you're young. Teach believers with your life: by word, by demeanor, by love, by faith, by integrity. Stay at your post reading Scripture, giving counsel, teaching. And that special gift of ministry you were given when the leaders of the church laid hands on you and prayed — keep that dusted off and in use.

15-16 Cultivate these things. Immerse yourself in them. The people will all see you mature right before their eyes! Keep a firm grasp on both your character and your teaching. Don't be diverted. Just keep at it. Both you and those who hear you will experience salvation.

READ

Read the passage, focusing on the words *teach* and *keep*.

THINK

In these verses, Paul, as almost a father figure, passes on wise words to young Timothy — and to us — about modeling our faith.

How can we be a part of that, no matter how old we are?

On a scale of one to ten — one being spiritual flabbiness and ten being spiritually fit — how would you rate your spiritual fitness? Why did you give yourself that rating?

How well are you "teach[ing] believers with your life" in these five areas: "by word, by demeanor, by love, by faith, by integrity"? Very well? In which areas? Not so well? In which areas? How can you make your life a better teacher in all of these?

PRAY

See if you can open your life to God like you would open a book. Consider the areas (such as school, family, work, and other activities), and write them down if that helps. Acknowledge to God your openness, then invite him to do his work in your life — whatever that might be — encouraging you, challenging you, and shaping your words, your demeanor, your love, your faith, and your integrity.

LIVE

Write these five words on an index card: *word, demeanor, love, faith, integrity.* Ask God to help you teach with your life in these specific areas throughout your day.

THE SPECIAL MINISTRY

1 TIMOTHY 5:1-4,7-10

1-2 Don't be harsh or impatient with an older man. Talk to him as you would your own father, and to the younger men as your brothers. Reverently honor an older woman as you would your mother, and the younger women as sisters.

3-4,7-8 Take care of widows who are destitute. If a widow has family members to take care of her, let them learn that religion begins at their own doorstep and that they should pay back with gratitude some of what they have received. This pleases God immensely. . . . Tell these things to the people so that they will do the right thing in their extended family. Anyone who neglects to care for family members in need repudiates the faith. That's worse than refusing to believe in the first place.

9-10 Sign some widows up for the special ministry of offering assistance. They will in turn receive support from the church. They must be over sixty, married only once, and have a reputation for helping out with children, strangers, tired Christians, the hurt and troubled.

READ

Read the passage aloud slowly.

THINK

Before reading the passage again, consider the following cultural ideas. Which ones have you unconsciously accepted?

- ☐ Older people and younger people don't mix much.
- ☐ Older people are retired, so they don't do "special ministry." (You don't know many people who help out "with children, strangers, tired Christians, the hurt and troubled.")
- ☐ Older people are tired and don't want to do much at church anymore.
- ☐ Older people aren't generally the people you go to for advice.
- ☐ Older people have Social Security benefits and don't need anyone's help.
- ☐ Older people are people you feel sorry for, not "reverently honor."

Read the passage again. Envision the sort of older person Paul was talking about. What older person do you know who is like the one Paul describes? In what small ways might you "reverently honor" this person? Try to wrap your mind around the idea that you can *look forward* to being such an older person.

PRAY

Thank God for older people in your life who resemble Paul's description. Pray for those who need more of what Paul describes. Pray for yourself that you'll be this sort of older person.

318

LIVE

Sit quietly. Pretend your joints don't work as well as they used to. Ponder what it would be like to still be eager to get up every day to be with Jesus and partner with him in what he's doing in the world.

BEING YOURSELF BEFORE GOD

1 TIMOTHY 6:6-12

6-8   A devout life does bring wealth, but it's the rich simplicity of being your-self before God. Since we entered the world penniless and will leave it penniless, if we have bread on the table and shoes on our feet, that's enough.

9-10   But if it's only money these leaders are after, they'll self-destruct in no time. Lust for money brings trouble and nothing but trouble. Going down that path, some lose their footing in the faith completely and live to regret it bitterly ever after.

11-12   But you, Timothy, man of God: Run for your life from all this. Pursue a righteous life — a life of wonder, faith, love, steadiness, courtesy. Run hard and fast in the faith. Seize the eternal life, the life you were called to, the life you so fervently embraced in the presence of so many witnesses.

READ

Read the passage twice.

THINK

Mull over Paul's advice to Timothy. Do you agree with his statements and assumptions about material wealth? About the value of being yourself before God? Why or why not? Explore your thoughts and share them with God.

PRAY

Consider your belongings, including favorite things and stuff you don't usually think about. In what ways might some of these items get in the way of you being yourself, plain and simple, before God? In what way does your attachment to these possessions alter your view of who you are? (Don't be too quick to answer here.)

LIVE

Read the passage again, considering more carefully Paul's description of "a righteous life." Do you notice an especially strong desire for any of these qualities? Listen for what God may be saying to you through the text and through your desire. Is he inviting you to do anything — even something small — in response to this time today?

✚ RUN AFTER MATURE RIGHTEOUSNESS

2 TIMOTHY 2:22-26

22-26   Run away from infantile indulgence. Run after mature righteousness — faith, love, peace — joining those who are in honest and serious prayer before God. Refuse to get involved in inane discussions; they always end up in fights. God's servant must not be argumentative, but a gentle listener and a teacher who keeps cool, working firmly but patiently with those who refuse to obey. You never know how or when God might sober them up with a change of heart and a turning to the truth, enabling them to escape the Devil's trap, where they are caught and held captive, forced to run his errands.

READ

Slowly read these verses. Let their message saturate your heart and mind.

THINK

In Paul's second leadership letter to Timothy, he writes words of encouragement and challenge that we, too, need to take to heart in the coming week. Paul is talking about some aspects of a mature faith.

Imagine he is sitting beside you, speaking these words to you directly. How do you feel when you hear them? What part of the passage resonates most with you? Why? Maybe "infantile indulgence" seems a little patronizing. Perhaps "mature righteousness" seems impossible or defeating. Maybe with some people you've lost hope that "God might sober them up."

PRAY

Sit in a comfortable position, being silent and as still as you can. Ask God *why* he has given you this particular piece of instruction through Paul (the one that resonated most with you). Listen for the gentle whisper of God's voice in the midst of the silence. Maybe he will show you a spot of childishness or one of righteousness. Maybe he will offer you hope.

LIVE

As you continue to sit in silence, explore what God might want you to do with this piece of instruction. How are you to live it out today? This week? This month?

GOD-BREATHED AND USEFUL

2 TIMOTHY 3:1-5,15-17

1-5 Don't be naive. There are difficult times ahead. As the end approaches, people are going to be self-absorbed, money-hungry, self-promoting, stuck-up, profane, contemptuous of parents, crude, coarse, dog-eat-dog, unbending, slanderers, impulsively wild, savage, cynical, treacherous, ruthless, bloated windbags, addicted to lust, and allergic to God. They'll make a show of religion, but behind the scenes they're animals. Stay clear of these people. . . .

15-17 Why, you took in the sacred Scriptures with your mother's milk! There's nothing like the written Word of God for showing you the way to salvation through faith in Christ Jesus. Every part of Scripture is God-breathed and useful one way or another — showing us truth, exposing our rebellion, correcting our mistakes, training us to live God's way. Through the Word we are put together and shaped up for the tasks God has for us.

READ

Read the passage aloud slowly.

THINK

Before dismissing the first paragraph as a description of people other than yourself, consider that Western culture, in general (and our individual selves, in particular), tends to be self-absorbed, self-promoting, cynical, and addicted to lust.

Read the passage again. This time notice the enormous change from the first paragraph to the second.

1. How does the way Scripture moves us (verse 16) help us to be different from the general culture?
2. Scripture is God-breathed — words breathed to you from our relational God, not a bunch of rules. Picture God speaking to you, "showing [you] truth, exposing [y]our rebellion, correcting [y]our mistakes, training [you] to live [his] way."

Can you picture God doing these things in ways exactly right for you? In gentle yet firm ways? To rescue you before you blow it?

PRAY

Ask God to help you be open to his showing you truth, exposing your rebellion, correcting your mistakes, and training you to live his way. Ask him to show you specific details, if any, that you need to know at this moment.

LIVE

Imagine what living an interactive life with God would be like, one in which all day long you experience him gently showing you truth, exposing your rebellion, correcting your mistakes, and training you to live his way. Why would this be the best way to live?

321
322

DAY 322

GOD ENCOUNTERS

On this seventh day, review and reflect on all you have read this week. Take the time to revel in the ways you've encountered God in the past six days.

AN HONEST JUDGE

2 TIMOTHY 4:1-8

1-2   I can't impress this on you too strongly. God is looking over your shoulder. Christ himself is the Judge, with the final say on everyone, living and dead. He is about to break into the open with his rule, so proclaim the Message with intensity; keep on your watch. Challenge, warn, and urge your people. Don't ever quit. Just keep it simple.

3-5   You're going to find that there will be times when people will have no stomach for solid teaching, but will fill up on spiritual junk food — catchy opinions that tickle their fancy. They'll turn their backs on truth and chase mirages. But *you* — keep your eye on what you're doing; accept the hard times along with the good; keep the Message alive; do a thorough job as God's servant.

6-8   You take over. I'm about to die, my life an offering on God's altar. This is the only race worth running. I've run hard right to the finish, believed all the way. All that's left now is the shouting — God's applause! Depend on it, he's an honest judge. He'll do right not only by me, but by everyone eager for his coming.

READ

Read Paul's instructions to his apprentice Timothy, trying to identify the primary theme.

THINK

What common thread runs through all of Paul's statements and instructions here? Perhaps it's the tone of what he's saying (such as urgent or tender), or maybe it's that every statement somehow relates to a particular object or event (such as Christ's judgment of everyone, or people-pleasing versus God-pleasing). Write down the theme you see.

PRAY

Read the passage again with the theme in mind. Notice how each part of the passage unpacks the meaning even more. What especially stands out to you? Perhaps it's the reason that repentance and evangelism are so important or the anticipation of standing before God as he looks at your life. Think about what you discover, and be transparent with God about it.

LIVE

Now read the passage once more, this time listening for what you sense God, through the text, is saying to you personally. Maybe he's drawing your attention to your need to please people, or maybe you're relieved to understand more clearly that repentance isn't about being perfect (a mirage) but about living in accordance with reality. What will you do with what God is showing you? Sit in silence for a few minutes. Jot down your new intention.

AGENT OF CHRIST

TITUS 1:1-4

1-4   I, Paul, am God's slave and Christ's agent for promoting the faith among God's chosen people, getting out the accurate word on God and how to respond rightly to it. My aim is to raise hopes by pointing the way to life without end. This is the life God promised long ago — and he doesn't break promises! And then when the time was ripe, he went public with his truth. I've been entrusted to proclaim this Message by order of our Savior, God himself. Dear Titus, legitimate son in the faith: Receive everything God our Father and Jesus our Savior give you!

READ

Read the opening words of greeting from Paul to Titus in these verses.

THINK

Paul describes himself as "Christ's agent for promoting the faith among God's chosen people." Are you "God's slave and Christ's agent"? Do those terms accurately describe your life? Why or why not? How can your life be lived in such a way that you are "getting out the accurate word on God" to those around you? How can your life be "promoting the faith" among others by word and action? Take time to consider these questions, being specific.

Paul gives the purpose of his life to Titus by saying, "My aim is to raise hopes by pointing the way to life without end. This is the life God promised long ago — and he doesn't break promises!" In what way does God raise hopes? Has he raised your hopes?

PRAY

Ask Christ to help you be his agent. Invite him to reveal to you how you might best "respond rightly" to his Word.

LIVE

"Respond rightly" to what you hear from God, remembering that you go forth into this day as an agent of Christ.

A GOD-FILLED LIFE

TITUS 2:11-14

11-14   God's readiness to give and forgive is now public. Salvation's available for everyone! We're being shown how to turn our backs on a godless, indulgent life, and how to take on a God-filled, God-honoring life. This new life is starting right now, and is whetting our appetites for the glorious day when our great God and Savior, Jesus Christ, appears. He offered himself as a sacrifice to free us from a dark, rebellious life into this good, pure life, making us a people he can be proud of, energetic in goodness.

READ

Read the passage aloud slowly.

THINK

Read the passage aloud again, this time picturing the words being spoken by someone you look up to and admire. Which of these rich words or phrases stand out to you? Why do you need these words and ideas at this moment in your life?

Read it one more time, picturing yourself saying the words to someone you wish to encourage.

PRAY

Ask God to guide you in one or all of these movements of growth:

☐ turning your back on a "godless, indulgent life"
☐ taking on a "God-filled, God-honoring life"
☐ believing that "this new life is starting right now"
☐ being "energetic in goodness"
☐ other:

LIVE

Consider God, who is "energetic in goodness." Inhale that goodness. See how much God wishes to bring you along. Try on the belief that this new life starts right now.

WASHED INSIDE AND OUT

TITUS 3:1-11

1-2   Remind the people to respect the government and be law-abiding, always ready to lend a helping hand. No insults, no fights. God's people should be bighearted and courteous.

3-8   It wasn't so long ago that we ourselves were stupid and stubborn, dupes of sin, ordered every which way by our glands, going around with a chip on our shoulder, hated and hating back. But when God, our kind and loving Savior God, stepped in, he saved us from all that. It was all his doing; we had nothing to do with it. He gave us a good bath, and we came out of it new people, washed inside and out by the Holy Spirit. Our Savior Jesus poured out new life so generously. God's gift has restored our relationship with him and given us back our lives. And there's more life to come — an eternity of life! You can count on this.

8-11   I want you to put your foot down. Take a firm stand on these matters so that those who have put their trust in God will concentrate on the essentials that are good for everyone. Stay away from mindless, pointless quarreling over genealogies and fine print in the law code. That gets you nowhere. Warn a quarrelsome person once or twice, but then be done with him. It's obvious that such a person is out of line, rebellious against God. By persisting in divisiveness he cuts himself off.

READ

Read the passage.

PRAY

What parts of this passage do you react to more than others? Maybe an argument you've had comes to mind, or maybe you have trouble adopting the attitude toward authority described here. Perhaps you wish you could be given a "good bath" and made new. Try to summarize your primary thought. Express it to God.

THINK

Although being purified ("washed inside and out by the Holy Spirit") is good for us and brings wonderfully satisfying results, the process often involves humbling, which isn't easy. Richard Foster said, "Humility means to live as close to the truth as possible: the truth about ourselves, the truth about others, the truth about the world in which we live."[25]

Think about Foster's statement, considering yourself, others, and the world around you. What elements of God's truth in this passage did you have trouble receiving? Maybe you're too hard on yourself and won't believe God's acceptance of you. Maybe you're afraid that if you admit the limitations of someone you look up to, it will unravel everything good you believe about that person. Or maybe you realize you don't want to get close to the real needs and problems of the world. Be open with God about the grime that keeps you from being clean and living closer to the truth.

LIVE

Now, keeping in mind how near or far you live from the truth about yourself, others, and the world, picture God as he's described in this passage: stepping in and washing you inside and out, removing the grime that separates you from the truth. What do you think or feel about that? Whatever surfaces, share it openly with him.

A TRUE CHRISTIAN BROTHER

PHILEMON 8-20

8-9 In line with all this I have a favor to ask of you. As Christ's ambassador and now a prisoner for him, I wouldn't hesitate to command this if I thought it necessary, but I'd rather make it a personal request.

10-14 While here in jail, I've fathered a child, so to speak. And here he is, hand-carrying this letter — Onesimus! He was useless to you before; now he's useful to both of us. I'm sending him back to you, but it feels like I'm cutting off my right arm in doing so. I wanted in the worst way to keep him here as your stand-in to help out while I'm in jail for the Message. But I didn't want to do anything behind your back, make you do a good deed that you hadn't willingly agreed to.

15-16 Maybe it's all for the best that you lost him for a while. You're getting him back now for good — and no mere slave this time, but a true Christian brother! That's what he was to me — he'll be even more than that to you.

17-20 So if you still consider me a comrade-in-arms, welcome him back as you would me. If he damaged anything or owes you anything, chalk it up to my account. This is my personal signature — Paul — and I stand behind it. (I don't need to remind you, do I, that you owe your very life to me?) Do me this big favor, friend. You'll be doing it for Christ, but it will also do my heart good.

READ

Read the passage and, if possible, the entire book of Philemon. (Don't worry — it's only twenty-five verses long!)

THINK

Here Paul writes a letter to Philemon concerning a slave named Onesimus. Paul has grown to see this man as a friend and — more specifically and importantly — as a brother in Christ. So Paul encourages Philemon to accept Onesimus in the same way.

Paul is saying that the greatest label we can have for one another is "true Christian brother" or true Christian sister.

What Christians do you have a hard time accepting as brothers or sisters in Christ? Why is it hard to think of other believers this way? Explore your heart: Is it their backgrounds, ethnicities, behaviors, cultural differences, theological differences, or something else? What would need to change in you for you to accept these people, seeing them as Christian brothers and sisters?

PRAY

Talk to God about this. Tell him about your struggle to accept others. Thank him that he accepts you, and thank him that he sees you and other believers as no less than his very own children. Ask God to help you see others with the same eyes.

LIVE

As you encounter people who are different from you, be reminded that God sees them with the label "my children" — and that means you too.

HOLDING EVERYTHING TOGETHER

HEBREWS 1:3

3   This Son perfectly mirrors God, and is stamped with God's nature. He holds everything together by what he says — powerful words!

READ

Read this verse over and over again. Let it resonate in your heart. Become familiar with the words. Memorize it before moving to the next section.

THINK

Though the authorship of Hebrews is uncertain, we can be certain of the message of the book: God's plan to redeem history came in the form of his Son, Jesus.

Spend time meditating on the passage. First, consider the purpose of a mirror: to display in perfect clarity a faithful representation of an object or person. How incredible to realize that Jesus' role was to be a mirror of God to the world! Second, consider the monumental act of holding *everything* together. How amazing to know that Jesus does this, that he is vital to the vast scope of human history!

In what ways does the significance of Jesus in the world impact your view of him?

PRAY

Stand in front of a mirror and consider Jesus, who mirrors God. While looking at your reflection, ask God for the courage and guidance to help you mirror Jesus to the world, reflecting him as you go about every day.

LIVE

Consider how you might reflect Jesus today — and do it.

DAY 329

GOD ENCOUNTERS

On this seventh day, review and reflect on all you have read this week. Take the time to revel in the ways you've encountered God in the past six days.

RICHES OF GLORY

HEBREWS 2:6-10

6-9 It says in Scripture,

> What is man and woman that you bother with them;
> why take a second look their way?
> You made them not quite as high as angels,
> bright with Eden's dawn light;
> Then you put them in charge
> of your entire handcrafted world.

When God put them in charge of everything, nothing was excluded. But we don't see it yet, don't see everything under human jurisdiction. What we do see is Jesus, made "not quite as high as angels," and then, through the experience of death, crowned so much higher than any angel, with a glory "bright with Eden's dawn light." In that death, by God's grace, he fully experienced death in every person's place.

10 It makes good sense that the God who got everything started and keeps everything going now completes the work by making the Salvation Pioneer perfect through suffering as he leads all these people to glory.

READ

Read the passage aloud slowly.

THINK

Read the passage again, noting the diverse themes of death and suffering versus angels and glory. What words or phrases fascinate you most? Pause a moment and ask God to help you understand them and continue to be absorbed by them. Why do you think those words or phrases fascinate you? What is going on in your life right now — feelings, circumstances, decisions — that they might correspond to?

PRAY

Ask that you will be continually fascinated by God's glory, God's well-deserved honor and brightness.

LIVE

Sit in the quiet and reflect on how you would feel if God were degrading, dishonoring, and not at all beautiful. Why is it better to live and breathe on an earth created by such a magnificent God?

SHARP AS A SURGEON'S SCALPEL

HEBREWS 4:12-13

12-13 God means what he says. What he says goes. His powerful Word is sharp as a surgeon's scalpel, cutting through everything, whether doubt or defense, laying us open to listen and obey. Nothing and no one is impervious to God's Word. We can't get away from it — no matter what.

READ

Read these two verses. Then read verse 13 first (beginning with "Nothing") and verse 12 next. Finally, read the verses in their proper order again.

THINK

Most of us believe that God's Message, his Word, is important. In fact, you probably wouldn't be reading these words right now if you didn't believe God's Word is significant. But if you're like many people, reading it sometimes feels like a chore — less than enjoyable.

Most Jewish children in the first century would memorize the first five books of the Bible (the Pentateuch) before their thirteenth birthdays.[26] They were taught to believe that the words were a love letter to them from God himself.

Think now about how important Scripture is to *you*. What if you were unable to read or hear anything from the Bible for twelve months? Would you miss it? Why or why not? What do you think "no one is impervious to God's Word" means? In what ways have you experienced God's Word to be precise and powerful, "sharp as a surgeon's scalpel"?

PRAY

Start praying by thanking God for the gift of his Word. Ask him to give you more passion and desire for it. Give God permission to let his Word "[lay you] open to listen and obey" in the days and weeks ahead.

LIVE

Memorize these verses, and pray them regularly as a way of asking God to make Scripture increasingly important in your life.

SPIRITUAL LIFELINE

HEBREWS 6:13-19

13-18　When God made his promise to Abraham, he backed it to the hilt, putting his own reputation on the line. He said, "I promise that I'll bless you with everything I have — bless and bless and bless!" Abraham stuck it out and got everything that had been promised to him. When people make promises, they guarantee them by appeal to some authority above them so that if there is any question that they'll make good on the promise, the authority will back them up. When God wanted to guarantee his promises, he gave his word, a rock-solid guarantee — God *can't* break his word. And because his word cannot change, the promise is likewise unchangeable.

18-19　We who have run for our very lives to God have every reason to grab the promised hope with both hands and never let go. It's an unbreakable spiritual lifeline, reaching past all appearances right to the very presence of God.

READ

Read the passage aloud slowly.

THINK

Read the passage aloud again, noting the emphasis on promises and hope. Consider what part hope has played in your life. Its opposites are despair, suspicion, doubt, and cynicism. What does this passage tell you about hope?

Read the passage aloud one more time. What words or phrases stand out to you? Why are those words or phrases important for you today?

PRAY

Pick out phrases that you'd like to pray and converse with God about, such as:

- ☐ "make good on the promise"
- ☐ "his word cannot change"
- ☐ "grab the promised hope"
- ☐ "never let go"

LIVE

Walk through this day trying on an attitude of greater hope — expectancy, anticipation, trust. This is what everyday life in the kingdom of God looks like.

THROWING OUT THE OLD PLAN

HEBREWS 8:1-2,6-12

1-2   In essence, we have just such a high priest: authoritative right alongside God, conducting worship in the one true sanctuary built by God. . . .

6-12   But Jesus' priestly work far surpasses what these other priests do, since he's working from a far better plan. If the first plan — the old covenant — had worked out, a second wouldn't have been needed. But we know the first was found wanting, because God said,

> Heads up! The days are coming
> > when I'll set up a new plan
> > for dealing with Israel and Judah.
> I'll throw out the old plan
> > I set up with their ancestors
> > when I led them by the hand out of Egypt.
> They didn't keep their part of the bargain,
> > so I looked away and let it go.
> This new plan I'm making with Israel
> > isn't going to be written on paper,
> > isn't going to be chiseled in stone;
> This time I'm writing out the plan *in* them,
> > carving it on the lining of their hearts.
> I'll be their God,
> > they'll be my people.
> They won't go to school to learn about me,
> > or buy a book called *God in Five Easy Lessons*.
> They'll all get to know me firsthand,
> > the little and the big, the small and the great.
> They'll get to know me by being kindly forgiven,
> > with the slate of their sins forever wiped clean.

READ

Read the passage from the perspective of someone living in Old Testament times, hearing the promise of a "new plan" that has no form yet. What would life be like without Jesus? Sit and take in this picture of life. Let yourself imagine what it would be like to sin in that context and to relate to God.

THINK

Read the passage again, this time from your present-day perspective, noting contrasts with the Old Testament perspective. What does it mean to you to hear God say he'll "throw out the old plan" that expects you to perfectly obey Old Testament laws? How does this reality make you see Jesus differently? What's it like to have such an approachable high priest to make sure your sins are "wiped clean," to "kindly" forgive you, and to show you what God is like?

PRAY/LIVE

Talk with Jesus about what stands out to you from this time of meditation. Perhaps a new desire to be obedient arises in contrast to previous discouragement over trying to change. Maybe you want to thank Jesus for being near you, or maybe you feel like singing a song of praise to him. Maybe you just want to sit in quiet gratitude because God threw out the "old plan" and wrote out the new plan, "carving it on the lining of [your] heart."

WHAT WE CAN'T SEE

HEBREWS 11:1-3,39-40

1-2   The fundamental fact of existence is that this trust in God, this faith, is the firm foundation under everything that makes life worth living. It's our handle on what we can't see. The act of faith is what distinguished our ancestors, set them above the crowd.

3   By faith, we see the world called into existence by God's word, what we see created by what we don't see. . . .

39-40   Not one of these people, even though their lives of faith were exemplary, got their hands on what was promised. God had a better plan for us: that their faith and our faith would come together to make one completed whole, their lives of faith not complete apart from ours.

READ

If possible, read all of Hebrews 11, but focus on verses 1-3 and 39-40.

THINK

This familiar passage of Scripture is often called the Faith Hall of Fame. It lists people of the Bible who exhibited the faith — sometimes at extreme personal cost — that made God famous. Talking about faith is much easier than living it out every day, but we can turn to these people's lives for inspiration.

You've heard, and possibly even uttered, the saying "Seeing is believing." The writer of Hebrews begins with a definition of faith that he connects to eyesight. Faith, he writes, is "our handle on what we can't see. . . . By faith, we see the world called into existence by God's word, what we see created by what we don't see." So, really, *not* seeing is believing.

What do you have a hard time believing because you can't prove it by seeing or touching it yourself? Would faith be easier if you could physically see the object of your faith? (Would faith still be faith if you could see the object, or would faith cease to be faith and become fact?)

PRAY

Thank God for godly people who inspire you to the kind of faith described in this chapter of the Bible.

LIVE

Sometime today, choose one of the people mentioned in the Faith Hall of Fame and read his or her story in Scripture. (Use a concordance to find the story, if you need to.)

WELL-TRAINED

HEBREWS 12:7-11

7-11   God is educating you; that's why you must never drop out. He's treating you as dear children. This trouble you're in isn't punishment; it's *training*, the normal experience of children. Only irresponsible parents leave children to fend for themselves. Would you prefer an irresponsible God? We respect our own parents for training and not spoiling us, so why not embrace God's training so we can truly *live*? While we were children, our parents did what *seemed* best to them. But God is doing what *is* best for us, training us to live God's holy best. At the time, discipline isn't much fun. It always feels like it's going against the grain. Later, of course, it pays off handsomely, for it's the well-trained who find themselves mature in their relationship with God.

READ

Read the passage aloud slowly.

THINK

Read the passage again.

How might God use the "trouble you're in" to *train* you? Don't jump on the first thing that comes to mind. Sit quietly for a while and see what God brings to you.

How might you cooperate better in this training? Once again, the first thing that comes to mind might not be God, but an old tape from the past. So take time to listen.

PRAY

Tell God what sort of well-trained person you'd like to be. What would you look like? Express confidence that this picture would be a much better life for you.

LIVE

Try to crawl into the persona of the well-trained person you'd like to become. How would your burdens in life be lighter?

DAY 336

GOD ENCOUNTERS

On this seventh day, review and reflect on all you have read this week. Take the time to revel in the ways you've encountered God in the past six days.

BE RELAXED WITH WHAT YOU HAVE

HEBREWS 13:5-9

5-6   Don't be obsessed with getting more material things. Be relaxed with what you have. Since God assured us, "I'll never let you down, never walk off and leave you," we can boldly quote,

> God is there, ready to help;
> I'm fearless no matter what.
> Who or what can get to me?

7-8   Appreciate your pastoral leaders who gave you the Word of God. Take a good look at the way they live, and let their faithfulness instruct you, as well as their truthfulness. There should be a consistency that runs through us all. For Jesus doesn't change — yesterday, today, tomorrow, he's always totally himself.

9   Don't be lured away from him by the latest speculations about him. The grace of Christ is the only good ground for life. Products named after Christ don't seem to do much for those who buy them.

READ

Read the passage aloud.

THINK

Spend time pondering the connection the writer is making between obsession with material possessions and the belief that God might leave us or let us down. What do you make of this? How are the two ideas related to each other?

PRAY

Take several minutes to explore your life in light of this instruction. How do you relate to material things? Do you often wish you had more? Do you feel that nothing can harm you because of what you have? What fears do you have about God letting you down? What would it be like to "be relaxed with what you have"? Talk with him about this subject. Attentively listen for his input.

LIVE

Continue praying by personalizing the verses, pausing frequently to notice your internal reaction to what you're saying. For example, *God, help me avoid being obsessed with getting more material things. I want to be relaxed with what I have, since you assured me . . ."*

When you're finished, look through the passage one more time, honestly confessing the contrary reactions, if any, you experienced when praying. With each, become aware of the possibility that your contrary feeling or belief could change. (Don't try to force that change; just be aware of the possibility.) For example, you could repeat to your soul that "God is there, ready to help," or you could ask God to increase your belief that he'll "never walk off and leave you."

337

✚ ACT ON WHAT YOU HEAR

JAMES 1:19-27

19-21   Post this at all the intersections, dear friends: Lead with your ears, follow up with your tongue, and let anger straggle along in the rear. God's righteousness doesn't grow from human anger. So throw all spoiled virtue and cancerous evil in the garbage. In simple humility, let our gardener, God, landscape you with the Word, making a salvation-garden of your life.

22-24   Don't fool yourself into thinking that you are a listener when you are anything but, letting the Word go in one ear and out the other. *Act* on what you hear! Those who hear and don't act are like those who glance in the mirror, walk away, and two minutes later have no idea who they are, what they look like.

25   But whoever catches a glimpse of the revealed counsel of God — the free life! — even out of the corner of his eye, and sticks with it, is no distracted scatterbrain but a man or woman of action. That person will find delight and affirmation in the action.

26-27   Anyone who sets himself up as "religious" by talking a good game is self-deceived. This kind of religion is hot air and only hot air. Real religion, the kind that passes muster before God the Father, is this: Reach out to the homeless and loveless in their plight, and guard against corruption from the godless world.

READ

Meditate on this passage. Underline words or phrases that stick out to you. Circle repeated words.

THINK

Consider what roles specific body parts have in your spiritual formation. James says here that our lives as followers of Jesus can be shaped by how we choose to use (or refrain from using) our ears and our tongue.

How have your ears and tongue been beneficial or damaging to your interactions with others recently? Be specific. When have you said one thing and done the other? Think about what James says about that.

PRAY

Start your time of communication with God by putting your hands on your ears and saying aloud, "God, I desire to listen to what you want me to hear."

Remain in the silence. (You can lower your hands.)

Now put your hands over your mouth and say aloud, "God, I desire to use my tongue to speak words that are helpful and to refrain from speaking words that are hurtful."

Remain in the silence.

Confess those times when you have not listened and when you have spoken unnecessary and harmful words.

Remain in the silence.

LIVE

In conversations today, be mindful of the percentage of time you are speaking compared to the time you are listening to others. Then ask yourself whether the percentage is healthy.

SO-CALLED IMPORTANT PEOPLE

JAMES 2:1-9

1-4   My dear friends, don't let public opinion influence how you live out our glorious, Christ-originated faith. If a man enters your church wearing an expensive suit, and a street person wearing rags comes in right after him, and you say to the man in the suit, "Sit here, sir; this is the best seat in the house!" and either ignore the street person or say, "Better sit here in the back row," haven't you segregated God's children and proved that you are judges who can't be trusted?

5-7   Listen, dear friends. Isn't it clear by now that God operates quite differently? He chose the world's down-and-out as the kingdom's first citizens, with full rights and privileges. This kingdom is promised to anyone who loves God. And here you are abusing these same citizens! Isn't it the high and mighty who exploit you, who use the courts to rob you blind? Aren't they the ones who scorn the new name — "Christian" — used in your baptisms?

8-9   You do well when you complete the Royal Rule of the Scriptures: "Love others as you love yourself." But if you play up to these so-called important people, you go against the Rule and stand convicted by it.

READ

Read the passage aloud slowly. Who are the "so-called important people" in your life? (They don't have to be wealthy, but just people you want to impress or want to think highly of you.)

THINK

Read the passage again, noticing these words: *ignore, segregate, exploit, scorn*. James is urging us to love people and use things (as opposed to loving things and using people).

1. Whom do you "use" to entertain you? To help you? To make you feel better?
2. What does it look like to love others as you love yourself? To give others the same amount of time, energy, and attention you give yourself?

Set aside these thoughts and read the passage one more time. What comes to you from this passage? What might God be saying to you today?

PRAY

Pray for those in your life you are tempted to use. Ask God to show you how to care for them the way you already care for yourself.

LIVE

Sit quietly, picturing Jesus greeting people he encountered with great love (he never used anyone). What feeling did each person have in his presence? Feel that. You are in his presence now.

WISE LIVING

JAMES 3:13-18

13-16   Do you want to be counted wise, to build a reputation for wisdom? Here's what you do: Live well, live wisely, live humbly. It's the way you live, not the way you talk, that counts. Mean-spirited ambition isn't wisdom. Boasting that you are wise isn't wisdom. Twisting the truth to make yourselves sound wise isn't wisdom. It's the furthest thing from wisdom — it's animal cunning, devilish conniving. Whenever you're trying to look better than others or get the better of others, things fall apart and everyone ends up at the others' throats.

17-18   Real wisdom, God's wisdom, begins with a holy life and is characterized by getting along with others. It is gentle and reasonable, overflowing with mercy and blessings, not hot one day and cold the next, not two-faced. You can develop a healthy, robust community that lives right with God and enjoy its results *only* if you do the hard work of getting along with each other, treating each other with dignity and honor.

READ

Stand up and read the passage. Then read it a second time.

THINK

Defining something accurately involves stating what it is and what it is not. James does just that, telling us what wisdom is and is not. Review the passage again. Make two columns on a piece of paper, and in your own words write in one column what James says wisdom is not. Then in the other column write what James says wisdom is.

How do these characteristics of wisdom (and the lack thereof) line up with your actions recently? If James followed you around and observed your life for a week, what comments might he make about the presence — or absence — of wisdom? James says that wisdom is hard work. In what ways do you see it as hard work?

PRAY

Tell God your desire to become wise, to "do the hard work of getting along with each other." Ask him to help you.

LIVE

Ask a friend or family member you trust to give you honest feedback for the next few weeks about wisdom in your life. Give them permission to affirm wise areas of your life and wise decisions you make, as well as to point out unwise areas of your life and unwise decisions you make.

A LOUD NO . . .
A QUIET YES

JAMES 4:7-10

7-10 So let God work his will in you. Yell a loud *no* to the Devil and watch him scamper. Say a quiet *yes* to God and he'll be there in no time. Quit dabbling in sin. Purify your inner life. Quit playing the field. Hit bottom, and cry your eyes out. The fun and games are over. Get serious, really serious. Get down on your knees before the Master; it's the only way you'll get on your feet.

READ

This is a short passage of contrasts. Read the entire thing aloud. Read it again, this time reading every other sentence aloud. Read it again, this time reading the other sentences aloud. Then read it again in its entirety.

THINK

Someone has said that we usually think of Satan in one of two ways: We either give him too much credit for his work in the world or we don't give him any credit at all. Neither view is right. James tells us that we are to "yell a loud *no* to the Devil and watch him scamper." So this means the Devil is active, but it also means that yelling no at him by Jesus' power in us is enough to scare him away.

In what ways have you seen Satan work destructively in your life, in the lives of others around you, and in the world? What do you think your practical response should be to the Devil's work?

James also tells us to "say a quiet *yes* to God and he'll be there in no time." Think about the times you need to say that "quiet *yes*" for God to come to you.

PRAY

Are you tempted to sin? Shout a loud *no* to Satan and be assured that he will leave you alone.

Are you in need of God's comfort and promises in your life? Whisper that you need him and be assured that he is at your side.

Rest in God's promises in Scripture.

LIVE

Remember the power that God has in your life and over the Devil. Live confidently that in Christ we always win, which means we don't have to be afraid. Utilize the tools of "a loud *no*" and "a quiet *yes*" in your walk with Jesus.

✚ HEALED INSIDE AND OUT

JAMES 5:13-18

13-15   Are you hurting? Pray. Do you feel great? Sing. Are you sick? Call the church leaders together to pray and anoint you with oil in the name of the Master. Believing-prayer will heal you, and Jesus will put you on your feet. And if you've sinned, you'll be forgiven — healed inside and out.

16-18   Make this your common practice: Confess your sins to each other and pray for each other so that you can live together whole and healed. The prayer of a person living right with God is something powerful to be reckoned with. Elijah, for instance, human just like us, prayed hard that it wouldn't rain, and it didn't — not a drop for three and a half years. Then he prayed that it would rain, and it did. The showers came and everything started growing again.

READ

Read the passage aloud slowly.

THINK

Read the passage aloud again. What is God inviting you to do or be in this passage? How does this invitation resonate with what's going on in your life right now? Where are you hurting or sick or in need of forgiveness? Where do you need to sing?

PRAY

Offer a "believing-prayer"—one that trusts God. Confess your sins to God, and ask him if there is someone you could confess to so "you can live together whole and healed." If there is, ask God for the courage to speak to the person about it.

LIVE

Try to live in the reality that you are freshly confessed—whole and healed inside and out. What does that look like in your life today?

DAY 343

GOD ENCOUNTERS

On this seventh day, review and reflect on all you have read this week. Take the time to revel in the ways you've encountered God in the past six days.

A DEEP CONSCIOUSNESS OF GOD

1 PETER 1:13-22

13-16 So roll up your sleeves, put your mind in gear, be totally ready to receive the gift that's coming when Jesus arrives. Don't lazily slip back into those old grooves of evil, doing just what you feel like doing. You didn't know any better then; you do now. As obedient children, let yourselves be pulled into a way of life shaped by God's life, a life energetic and blazing with holiness. God said, "I am holy; you be holy."

17 You call out to God for help and he helps — he's a good Father that way. But don't forget, he's also a responsible Father, and won't let you get by with sloppy living.

18-21 Your life is a journey you must travel with a deep consciousness of God. It cost God plenty to get you out of that dead-end, empty-headed life you grew up in. He paid with Christ's sacred blood, you know. He died like an unblemished, sacrificial lamb. And this was no afterthought. Even though it has only lately — at the end of the ages — become public knowledge, God always knew he was going to do this for you. It's because of this sacrificed Messiah, whom God then raised from the dead and glorified, that you trust God, that you know you have a future in God.

22 Now that you've cleaned up your lives by following the truth, love one another as if your lives depended on it.

READ

Read this passage, and the expanded passage, if possible.

THINK

Peter, the young apostle who denied Jesus during the last hours of Jesus' life, is now a grown man and mature Christ-follower. Here he writes words of encouragement and wisdom to other followers of Jesus.

Peter talks about being holy, meaning different, separate, set apart. He encourages followers to live differently from how the world lives — with "a deep consciousness of God." What would it mean for your life's journey to travel through it with that "deep consciousness"?

What does "let yourselves be pulled into a way of life shaped by God's life" mean, practically? It sounds good, but what would it mean to really live that way?

Peter instructs, "Love one another as if your lives depended on it." What would loving others this way require of you?

PRAY

Let these phrases guide your prayer life right now:

- "I am holy; you be holy."
- "You must travel with a deep consciousness of God."
- "Let [yourself] be pulled into a way of life shaped by God's life."
- "Love one another as if your [life] depended on it."

LIVE

Ask God for a way to live separately, differently, and uniquely from the way the world lives.

344

THE KIND OF LIFE CHRIST LIVED

1 PETER 2:11-17,21

11-12 Friends, this world is not your home, so don't make yourselves cozy in it. Don't indulge your ego at the expense of your soul. Live an exemplary life among the natives so that your actions will refute their prejudices. Then they'll be won over to God's side and be there to join in the celebration when he arrives.

13-17 Make the Master proud of you by being good citizens. Respect the authorities, whatever their level; they are God's emissaries for keeping order. It is God's will that by doing good, you might cure the ignorance of the fools who think you're a danger to society. Exercise your freedom by serving God, not by breaking the rules. Treat everyone you meet with dignity. Love your spiritual family. Revere God. Respect the government. . . .

21 This is the kind of life you've been invited into, the kind of life Christ lived. He suffered everything that came his way so you would know that it could be done, and also know how to do it, step-by-step.

READ

Read the passage aloud slowly.

THINK

Read the passage again aloud, noting what "the kind of life you've been invited into, the kind of life Christ lived" looks like.

1. What, if anything, in this description of "the kind of life Christ lived" surprises you?
2. What, if anything, in this description fits with what you've been doing lately?
3. What, if anything, in this description challenges you?
4. Consider the day you have in front of you. How might the ideas of respect, celebration, and living Christ's life fit into it?

PRAY

Thank God for the rich "kind of life Christ lived." Ask God to draw you more deeply into that ongoing, vibrant life of Christ. Add anything else that came to you during today's meditation.

LIVE

Rest and delight in living "the kind of life Christ lived" today. Consider that you won't be bored; rather, it will be an adventure.

IN ADORATION

1 PETER 3:13-18

13-18 If with heart and soul you're doing good, do you think you can be stopped? Even if you suffer for it, you're still better off. Don't give the opposition a second thought. Through thick and thin, keep your hearts at attention, in adoration before Christ, your Master. Be ready to speak up and tell anyone who asks why you're living the way you are, and always with the utmost courtesy. Keep a clear conscience before God so that when people throw mud at you, none of it will stick. They'll end up realizing that *they're* the ones who need a bath. It's better to suffer for doing good, if that's what God wants, than to be punished for doing bad. That's what Christ did definitively: suffered because of others' sins, the Righteous One for the unrighteous ones. He went through it all — was put to death and then made alive — to bring us to God.

READ

Read this passage a few times, slowly and meditatively.

THINK

Mull over Peter's exhortation to adore Christ in every kind of circumstance. Do you agree with the link he makes between adoring Christ and doing good to others? When you're relating to others, what kinds of things do you give your attention to, if not to adoring Christ? Do you have other goals, like giving the person a good impression of you or making useful connections? In what ways does this approach to relationships leave you satisfied or dissatisfied?

PRAY

Share with Jesus what has surfaced for you, remembering that he, "the Righteous One," already knows the unrighteousness in you, and "went through it all" for you anyway: He loves you.

Sit with him in silence. Even if you don't sense him saying anything, that's okay. Just stay there, open to him. If you are led to genuine adoration of him, go ahead and take time to tell him what you think of him. If not, just receive his acceptance of you.

LIVE

Douglas Steere, a leading Quaker of the twentieth century, once said, "In the school of adoration the soul learns why the approach to every other goal has left it restless."[27] Think back to how you relate to others and notice any dissatisfaction or restlessness in that. What would it look like for you to give Peter's idea a shot: to walk through today "in adoration before Christ"? Try it.

346

NO LONGER TYRANNIZED

1 PETER 4:1-2,14,19

1-2   Since Jesus went through everything you're going through and more, learn to think like him. Think of your sufferings as a weaning from that old sinful habit of always expecting to get your own way. Then you'll be able to live out your days free to pursue what God wants instead of being tyrannized by what you want. . . .

14   If you're abused because of Christ, count yourself fortunate. It's the Spirit of God and his glory in you that brought you to the notice of others. . . .

19   So if you find life difficult because you're doing what God said, take it in stride. Trust him. He knows what he's doing, and he'll keep on doing it.

READ

Read the passage aloud slowly.

THINK

Read verses 1-2 again slowly. How does any suffering (which may be more like disappointment or frustration) you're going through relate to "being tyrannized by what you want," for example, wanting your own way but not getting it? In what ways does your "wanter" (the part of you that decides what you want) need to be invited to change?

Read verses 14 and 19 again slowly. Are you being discounted or badly treated because you're living a selfless, Christlike life? If so, in what ways? If not, how might that happen to you at some point?

PRAY

Ask the Holy Spirit to fill you and help you change the deep desires inside you. If you're being mistreated because of Christ, ask the Holy Spirit to help you absorb the truth that the Spirit and his glory is what brought you to the notice of others.

LIVE

Picture yourself as one who has "the Spirit of God and his glory in you" so you will come "to the notice of others." Consider that such a suffering life is intimately linked with God and provides the companionship of the Spirit.

BUILDING ON WHAT YOU'VE BEEN GIVEN

2 PETER 1:3-9

3-4 Everything that goes into a life of pleasing God has been miraculously given to us by getting to know, personally and intimately, the One who invited us to God. The best invitation we ever received! We were also given absolutely terrific promises to pass on to you — your tickets to participation in the life of God after you turned your back on a world corrupted by lust.

5-9 So don't lose a minute in building on what you've been given, complementing your basic faith with good character, spiritual understanding, alert discipline, passionate patience, reverent wonder, warm friendliness, and generous love, each dimension fitting into and developing the others. With these qualities active and growing in your lives, no grass will grow under your feet, no day will pass without its reward as you mature in your experience of our Master Jesus. Without these qualities you can't see what's right before you, oblivious that your old sinful life has been wiped off the books.

READ

Go into a room by yourself and close the door behind you, then read the passage aloud.

THINK

A God-pleasing life has been given to us by an intimate relationship with Christ himself. And Peter reminds us of our "best invitation" to participate in God's amazing, all-encompassing plan to redeem the world! Peter says we should complement our "basic faith" with the following:

- "good character"
- "spiritual understanding"
- "alert discipline"
- "passionate patience"
- "reverent wonder"
- "warm friendliness"
- "generous love"

Take your time to ponder each character trait. Then think about those you are doing well in. Think about those you need to grow in.

PRAY

Admit your need for God's guidance and help in your growth in him. Ask him to help you grow in those areas where you recognize you need the most improvement.

LIVE

On a small sheet of paper, write down the character traits you desire to develop. Review often what you wrote.

Ask the Holy Spirit for encouragement — to illuminate and reveal areas of your life that show these character traits when they become evident.

DESTRUCTIVE DIVISIONS

2 PETER 2:1-3

1-2 But there were also *lying* prophets among the people then, just as there will be lying religious teachers among you. They'll smuggle in destructive divisions, pitting you against each other — biting the hand of the One who gave them a chance to have their lives back! They've put themselves on a fast downhill slide to destruction, but not before they recruit a crowd of mixed-up followers who can't tell right from wrong.

2-3 They give the way of truth a bad name. They're only out for themselves. They'll say anything, *anything*, that sounds good to exploit you. They won't, of course, get by with it. They'll come to a bad end, for God has never just stood by and let that kind of thing go on.

READ

Read the passage aloud slowly.

THINK

Read the passage again slowly, noticing what causes destructive divisions. Keep in mind that the people who cause divisions rarely realize they're doing it. They may have good intentions (or *think* they have them) because they believe they're right about something.

1. Where have you witnessed destructive divisions within the body of Christ lately?
2. How might you grieve over having witnessed people:

   - pitting other people against one another
   - biting the hand that helped them
   - looking out for only themselves (even if unconsciously)
   - exploiting other people for their own cause

3. In what ways do such destructive divisions *lie* (see verse 1) to the world about who God is and what God is like?
4. What might God be leading you to pray? What sort of person might God be leading you to *be*?

PRAY

Thank God for doing what he promises in this passage: never standing by and letting destructive divisions go on. Ask God to show you how you are not to stand by, but to be one who prays for the injured as well as the "*lying* prophets" — for both to grasp truth and love and to find healing.

LIVE

Grieve with God over people's willingness to create divisions within the church, which embodies the noncompetitive unity of the Trinity.

DAY 350

GOD ENCOUNTERS

On this seventh day, review and reflect on all you have read this week. Take the time to revel in the ways you've encountered God in the past six days.

IF ANYONE DOES SIN

1 JOHN 1:6–2:2

6-7　If we claim that we experience a shared life with him and continue to stumble around in the dark, we're obviously lying through our teeth — we're not *living* what we claim. But if we walk in the light, God himself being the light, we also experience a shared life with one another, as the sacrificed blood of Jesus, God's Son, purges all our sin.

8-10　If we claim that we're free of sin, we're only fooling ourselves. A claim like that is errant nonsense. On the other hand, if we admit our sins — make a clean breast of them — he won't let us down; he'll be true to himself. He'll forgive our sins and purge us of all wrongdoing. If we claim that we've never sinned, we out-and-out contradict God — make a liar out of him. A claim like that only shows off our ignorance of God.

1-2　I write this, dear children, to guide you out of sin. But if anyone does sin, we have a Priest-Friend in the presence of the Father: Jesus Christ, righteous Jesus. When he served as a sacrifice for our sins, he solved the sin problem for good — not only ours, but the whole world's.

READ

Read the passage.

THINK

Truth. Grace. The two sides of a fence we often fall off of when responding to sin. In going to one extreme, we might rebuke sin but leave the sinner feeling condemned or rejected. In going to the other extreme, we might communicate acceptance to the sinner but minimize the sin, leaving the sinner in its bondage. John's perspective is different.

Look at the two halves of the problem presented in this passage: our attitude toward sin and our expectations of how God views sin. Notice what John points out about the role the Father and Jesus each play in the situation and the choice we have in how we view ourselves. Take a few moments to let John's statements about these things sink into you.

PRAY

What is your attitude toward the sins with which you struggle? What deeper desire lies beneath the draw that particular sin has on you? Does your guilt hold you back from Jesus? Talk to him about this.

Now sit silently, listening for Jesus' response to you. What is his desire for you?

LIVE

Consider a situation that holds temptation for you. Ask Jesus to remind you of his presence as Priest-Friend the next time you're faced with that temptation.

LET'S NOT JUST TALK ABOUT LOVE

1 JOHN 3:16-24

16-17   This is how we've come to understand and experience love: Christ sacrificed his life for us. This is why we ought to live sacrificially for our fellow believers, and not just be out for ourselves. If you see some brother or sister in need and have the means to do something about it but turn a cold shoulder and do nothing, what happens to God's love? It disappears. And you made it disappear.

18-20   My dear children, let's not just talk about love; let's practice real love. This is the only way we'll know we're living truly, living in God's reality. It's also the way to shut down debilitating self-criticism, even when there is something to it. For God is greater than our worried hearts and knows more about us than we do ourselves.

21-24   And friends, once that's taken care of and we're no longer accusing or condemning ourselves, we're bold and free before God! We're able to stretch our hands out and receive what we asked for because we're doing what he said, doing what pleases him. Again, this is God's command: to believe in his personally named Son, Jesus Christ. He told us to love each other, in line with the original command. As we keep his commands, we live deeply and surely in him, and he lives in us. And this is how we experience his deep and abiding presence in us: by the Spirit he gave us.

READ

Read the passage slowly and carefully until you understand the crux of John's argument: that we can cease to be controlled by the internal voice of self-criticism when we love others.

PRAY

What role does self-criticism play in your life? Maybe there's that voice in your head constantly telling you what you *should* have done. Maybe you can instantly think of six aspects of yourself that you'd change if you could. Maybe receiving compliments or affirmation from others is hard for you. Explore this with God, and talk with him about what you find. Be open to what he might want to show you about yourself.

THINK

Why do you think John so firmly ties together loving other people and freedom from self-criticism? Ponder this connection. In what ways are the two related?

Become aware of how much you do and do not believe John's argument. Be honest with yourself and with God, remembering that it's okay to admit that, while you think something sounds true, you aren't sure you believe it.

LIVE

Pay special attention today to how much you criticize yourself or minimize praise given by others. Notice what runs through your head when you look in the mirror or if you beat yourself up over mistakes at work. Jot these things down if you need help remembering. Then, sometime later in the day, talk to God for a few minutes about what you are noticing. Recall what John says about loving others and self-criticism, and ponder it some more.

GOD'S INDWELLING LOVE

1 JOHN 4:7,11-13,16-18

7   My beloved friends, let us continue to love each other since love comes from God. Everyone who loves is born of God and experiences a relationship with God. . . .

11-12   My dear, dear friends, if God loved us like this, we certainly ought to love each other. No one has seen God, ever. But if we love one another, God dwells deeply within us, and his love becomes complete in us — perfect love!

13,16   This is how we know we're living steadily and deeply in him, and he in us: He's given us life from his life, from his very own Spirit. . . . We know it so well, we've embraced it heart and soul, this love that comes from God.

17-18   God is love. When we take up permanent residence in a life of love, we live in God and God lives in us. This way, love has the run of the house, becomes at home and mature in us, so that we're free of worry on Judgment Day — our standing in the world is identical with Christ's. There is no room in love for fear. Well-formed love banishes fear. Since fear is crippling, a fearful life — fear of death, fear of judgment — is one not yet fully formed in love.

READ

Read the passage aloud slowly.

THINK

Read the passage again slowly, pausing after the word *love* each time you read it aloud. While the command to love one another can be difficult, consider also these things that empower people to love one another:

- "Love comes from God."
- We experience a relationship with God.
- We receive love from God, so we're turning that love around to others.
- "God dwells deeply within us."
- God gives us his life.
- God gives us the Spirit.
- God lives in us and we live in God.
- The love we've already experienced is chasing away fear, which often keeps us from loving others.

1. Which of the above ideas is the easiest for you to grasp? Why?
2. Which one is the most difficult for you to grasp? Why?

Draw a little stick figure of yourself as the recipient of what is being given (love or relationship or God's own life or the Spirit).

3. How does it feel to receive like this?

PRAY

Thank God for pouring into you such things (your answers to 1 and 2, the entire list, or other phrases in the passage). Express your desire to be saturated with God's love so it overflows in you and pours out to others. (Or express the desire to have that desire.)

LIVE

Contemplate yourself as an absorber and container of God's love, as one who is taking up permanent residence in a life of love.

PROOF THAT WE LOVE GOD

1 JOHN 5:1-3

1-3 Every person who believes that Jesus is, in fact, the Messiah, is God-begotten. If we love the One who conceives the child, we'll surely love the child who was conceived. The reality test on whether or not we love God's children is this: Do we love God? Do we keep his commands? The proof that we love God comes when we keep his commandments and they are not at all troublesome.

READ

Read the passage three times slowly.

THINK

What do you think of this connection between loving God and loving others? Does one or the other feel more difficult for you? Which one? What about it is difficult?

PRAY

Talk to God about the difficulties you experience in this area. Openly share with him your feelings about your struggle. Listen for what he might have to say.

LIVE

C. S. Lewis wrote, "It may be possible for each of us to think too much of his own potential glory hereafter; it is hardly possible for him to think too often or too deeply about that of his neighbor. . . . The dullest and most uninteresting person you talk to may one day be a creature which, if you saw it now, you would be strongly tempted to worship. . . . There are no ordinary people."[28] How does this suggestion alter the way you view others you know? How does it alter the way you view yourself? As you go through your day, ponder these ideas more, but also be ready to ponder-in-practice: As you come across "God's children" during the day, look for small ways to love them.

LIVING OUT THE TRUTH

2 JOHN 4-6

4-6 I can't tell you how happy I am to learn that many members of your congregation are diligent in living out the Truth, exactly as commanded by the Father. But permit me a reminder, friends, and this is not a new commandment but simply a repetition of our original and basic charter: that we love each other. Love means following his commandments, and his unifying commandment is that you conduct your lives in love. This is the first thing you heard, and nothing has changed.

READ

Focus on these verses, but read all of 2 John, if possible.

THINK

If you grew up in the church, you know that love is a critical ingredient in the life of a follower of Jesus. This ingredient may seem elementary, and believers often talk about love. But that's for good reason: Love is the very nature of God! John reminds us: "Love means following his commandments, and his unifying commandment is that you conduct your lives in love. This is the first thing you heard, and nothing has changed."

On a scale of one to ten (with one being the lowest and ten being the highest), how would you rank your "love quotient"? How might your friends rank your love quotient? What is needed for you to grow in your understanding and expression of love to others?

What would your life look like if you were "diligent in living out the Truth"?

PRAY

Ask God to help you see the direct correlation between love and following his commands.

LIVE

Love God. Study his commands. Follow them.

EXPANDED PASSAGE: 3 JOHN

HOSPITALITY WORTHY OF GOD HIMSELF

3 JOHN 5-11

5-8   Dear friend, when you extend hospitality to Christian brothers and sisters, even when they are strangers, you make the faith visible. They've made a full report back to the church here, a message about your love. It's good work you're doing, helping these travelers on their way, hospitality worthy of God himself! They set out under the banner of the Name, and get no help from unbelievers. So they deserve any support we can give them. In providing meals and a bed, we become their companions in spreading the Truth.

9-10   Earlier I wrote something along this line to the church, but Diotrephes, who loves being in charge, denigrates my counsel. If I come, you can be sure I'll hold him to account for spreading vicious rumors about us.

As if that weren't bad enough, he not only refuses hospitality to traveling Christians but tries to stop others from welcoming them. Worse yet, instead of inviting them in he throws them out.

11   Friend, don't go along with evil. Model the good. The person who does good does God's work. The person who does evil falsifies God, doesn't know the first thing about God.

READ

Read the passage carefully, imagining that John is writing specifically to you.

THINK

What opportunity have you had recently to show someone hospitality or in some way help someone who is trying to do good? How did you respond to that opportunity? What do you notice about the motives and priorities behind your action (or nonaction)?

PRAY

Lay before God what you have remembered about that opportunity and what you have discovered in your heart. Maybe you will rejoice with him about the victory you experienced in overcoming a temptation to be greedy or mean-spirited, or perhaps you will feel sadness at a missed opportunity.

LIVE

Brainstorm with God what it might look like for you to take steps toward being more hospitable to others. Think about some gifts you have to offer to others (such as your good cooking, your listening ear, your encouragement). Perhaps some of your gifts you are glad to share, while others you're hesitant to offer to others. Regardless of how you feel about each gift, write down what you have that could be helpful to someone.

Now think of a specific person who would be helped by your hospitality. Offer your list to God, and ask him what he would have you offer to this person. Don't force yourself to give something you can give only grudgingly; remember, "God loves it when the giver delights in the giving" (2 Corinthians 9:7). Be open to take this small step toward hospitality, and be open to how God may change your heart as you do it.

DAY 357

GOD ENCOUNTERS

On this seventh day, review and reflect on all you have read this week. Take the time to revel in the ways you've encountered God in the past six days.

GRACE VERSUS LICENSE

JUDE 3-8

3-4   Dear friends, I've dropped everything to write you about this life of salvation that we have in common. I have to write insisting — begging! — that you fight with everything you have in you for this faith entrusted to us as a gift to guard and cherish. What has happened is that some people have infiltrated our ranks (our Scriptures warned us this would happen), who beneath their pious skin are shameless scoundrels. Their design is to replace the sheer grace of our God with sheer license — which means doing away with Jesus Christ, our one and only Master.

5-7   I'm laying this out as clearly as I can, even though you once knew all this well enough and shouldn't need reminding. Here it is in brief: The Master saved a people out of the land of Egypt. Later he destroyed those who defected. And you know the story of the angels who didn't stick to their post, abandoning it for other, darker missions. But they are now chained and jailed in a black hole until the great Judgment Day. Sodom and Gomorrah, which went to sexual rack and ruin along with the surrounding cities that acted just like them, are another example. Burning and burning and never burning up, they serve still as a stock warning.

8   This is exactly the same program of these latest infiltrators: dirty sex, rule and rulers thrown out, glory dragged in the mud.

READ

Read these verses aloud, including all the passion you sense from Jude.

THINK

Think about the meaning of *license,* or *lawlessness.* Now compare that to what you know *grace* to be. What differences do you see between them?

PRAY

Sit in silence and think back on experiences you've had with license — times you've done whatever you felt like, turning your back on what was right. Now consider experiences you've had with grace. Ask God to show you one of these experiences to focus on. Recall the details: What was it like for you? What was going on around you? What were you feeling about what you'd done wrong?

If you focus on an experience of grace, recall how God made that grace known to you — maybe through another person or through something you read. What did it feel like to be presented with that option? What was it like to take God up on his grace?

If you focus on an experience of license (when you did not open up to God's grace), were you aware of any other options at the time? What motivated you to choose the route you took? What did you feel later, after the dust had settled?

LIVE

Ask God what he wants you to take away from this time with him and his Word. Be assured that "every detail in our lives of love for God is worked into something good" (Romans 8:28). This doesn't mean that we'll feel happy right away or all the time but that God does want to see us restored. Walk through today pondering the grace of this reality.

THE SOVEREIGN-STRONG

REVELATION 1:4-8

4-7   I, John, am writing this to the seven churches in Asia province: All the best to you from THE GOD WHO IS, THE GOD WHO WAS, AND THE GOD ABOUT TO ARRIVE, and from the Seven Spirits assembled before his throne, and from Jesus Christ — Loyal Witness, Firstborn from the dead, Ruler of all earthly kings.

> Glory and strength to Christ, who loves us,
> > who blood-washed our sins from our lives,
> Who made us a Kingdom, Priests for his Father,
> > forever — and yes, he's on his way!
> Riding the clouds, he'll be seen by every eye,
> > those who mocked and killed him will see him,
> People from all nations and all times
> > will tear their clothes in lament.
> > > Oh, Yes.

8   The Master declares, "I'm A to Z. I'm THE GOD WHO IS, THE GOD WHO WAS, AND THE GOD ABOUT TO ARRIVE. I'm the Sovereign-Strong."

THINK

Revelation is a surreal book, full of visions and events that usually stir up more questions than answers. But from one perspective, the book is not as complex as it seems. Revelation displays the final piece of God's magnificent and victorious story for people. In short, the book could be summarized with two words: God wins. And because of this, it propels us into overwhelming gratitude. Revelation is about worship.

READ

Read the passage aloud, noting the characteristics and actions of God.

PRAY

Lie on your back in stillness (outside, if possible, where you can see the sky). Focus on the magnificence of God's character and how he brings victory to humanity. As you think about who God is, whisper these words to him:

> God, you are A to Z.
> God, you are The God Who Is.
> God, you are The God Who Was.
> God, you are The God About to Arrive.
> God, you are the Sovereign-Strong.

Express your gratitude to God in whatever heartfelt way you wish.

LIVE

Live your life today in complete and total thankfulness for who God is and for the plan he's had in mind all along. Use your life as a palette to display your grateful response to him as the victorious Sovereign-Strong.

LISTEN

REVELATION 2:7,10-11,17

7   "Are your ears awake? Listen. Listen to the Wind Words, the Spirit blowing through the churches. I'm about to call each conqueror to dinner. I'm spreading a banquet of Tree-of-Life fruit, a supper plucked from God's orchard." ...

10   "Fear nothing in the things you're about to suffer — but stay on guard! Fear nothing! The Devil is about to throw you in jail for a time of testing — ten days. It won't last forever.

"Don't quit, even if it costs you your life. Stay there believing. I have a Life-Crown sized and ready for you.

11   "Are your ears awake? Listen. Listen to the Wind Words, the Spirit blowing through the churches. Christ-conquerors are safe from Devil-death." ...

17   "Are your ears awake? Listen. Listen to the Wind Words, the Spirit blowing through the churches. I'll give the sacred manna to every conqueror; I'll also give a clear, smooth stone inscribed with your new name, your secret new name."

READ

Read the passage aloud slowly.

THINK

Sit down (if you aren't already sitting). Read the passage aloud again, standing up each time you read, "Are your ears awake? Listen. Listen to the Wind Words, the Spirit blowing through the churches."

When you're finished, stand up again and ponder what God might have been trying to say to you recently about your life with him, about your behavior toward others, about your deepest self, about how you could be salt and light in the world. What recurring themes have you noticed in Scripture? Among friends? From wise Christians you've read about? At church gatherings?

Now lie down on the floor with your arms outstretched above you, if you can. Ask God what he wants to say to you today. Wait expectantly. Don't be bothered if nothing specific comes to you. Consider this practice as one of the most important things you'll ever do: listening to God and inviting him to speak to you.

PRAY

Talk to God about learning to listen to him. Ask God to show you how he speaks to you most frequently.

LIVE

Sit in the quiet, and lavish yourself with the thought that God seeks you out to speak to you. You get to live an interactive relationship with God.

BEFORE THE THRONE

REVELATION 4:2-8

2-6   I was caught up at once in deep worship and, oh! — a Throne set in Heaven with One Seated on the Throne, suffused in gem hues of amber and flame with a nimbus of emerald. Twenty-four thrones circled the Throne, with Twenty-four Elders seated, white-robed, gold-crowned. Lightning flash and thunder crash pulsed from the Throne. Seven fire-blazing torches fronted the Throne (these are the Sevenfold Spirit of God). Before the Throne it was like a clear crystal sea.

6-8   Prowling around the Throne were Four Animals, all eyes. Eyes to look ahead, eyes to look behind. The first Animal like a lion, the second like an ox, the third with a human face, the fourth like an eagle in flight. The Four Animals were winged, each with six wings. They were all eyes, seeing around and within. And they chanted night and day, never taking a break:

> Holy, holy, holy
> Is God our Master, Sovereign-Strong,
> THE WAS, THE IS, THE COMING.

READ

Read the passage once aloud, and get a feel for what is happening. As you read it a second time, do you notice a common theme? Write it down.

THINK/PRAY

Close your eyes and imagine what's described here: the amber and the emerald, the thunder and the lightning, the torches and the sea. See if you can sense the awe of the place. What does it feel like to be there?

Listen as the Four Animals begin to chant, "Holy, holy, holy." Speak these words to God a few times. Share with him what they express for you. Think about what holiness means to you, but not for long. Return your attention to The Was, The Is, The Coming. Join the Four Animals in their worship again: "Holy, holy, holy."

LIVE

What is one way you could worship God today? Perhaps you know a poem or song that puts words and emotion to your love for him today; read it, play it, sing it. Perhaps you have a special skill like dancing, surfing, or art; perform that for him today. Maybe there is a specific action you could take that would honor him. Do it. Maybe you'll want simply to tell him what you like about him.

BEFORE THE THRONE

REVELATION 7:9-12

9-12 I looked again. I saw a huge crowd, too huge to count. Everyone was there — all nations and tribes, all races and languages. And they were *standing*, dressed in white robes and waving palm branches, standing before the Throne and the Lamb and heartily singing:

> Salvation to our God on his Throne!
> Salvation to the Lamb!

All who were standing around the Throne — Angels, Elders, Animals — fell on their faces before the Throne and worshiped God, singing:

> Oh, Yes!
> The blessing and glory and wisdom and thanksgiving,
> The honor and power and strength,
> To our God forever and ever and ever!
> Oh, Yes!

READ

Stand up and read this passage aloud in a loud and excited tone of voice, imagining yourself before the throne of God.

THINK

Have you heard it said that our sole purpose in life is to worship God? Read again the words that the worshipers sing in this scene. How does this relate to your worship of God?

"Salvation to our God." What has God saved you from, specifically?

"The blessing and glory and wisdom and thanksgiving, the honor and power and strength." What comes to mind when you think about these words? What are you feeling about the God described by them? Why?

What might this passage have to do with shared worship in church each week?

PRAY

Why is God worthy of your worship? Consider lying down on your face before him as you tell him (with specifics), just as the angels, elders, and animals do in this passage.

Go on to worship God as you communicate with him. Respond to him with thankfulness, authenticity, honesty, and passion.

LIVE

Take out a piece of paper or your journal. Write down a few sentences or paragraphs telling God how grateful you are for him and for what he has done, is doing, and will do. Include gratitude directed to the Lamb of God. Start and end with the phrase "Oh, yes!"

Then read your writing aloud to God as an act of worship.

DEATH GONE FOR GOOD

REVELATION 21:1-11

1   I saw Heaven and earth new-created. Gone the first Heaven, gone the first earth, gone the sea.

2   I saw Holy Jerusalem, new-created, descending resplendent out of Heaven, as ready for God as a bride for her husband.

3-5   I heard a voice thunder from the Throne: "Look! Look! God has moved into the neighborhood, making his home with men and women! They're his people, he's their God. He'll wipe every tear from their eyes. Death is gone for good — tears gone, crying gone, pain gone — all the first order of things gone." The Enthroned continued, "Look! I'm making everything new. Write it all down — each word dependable and accurate."

6-8   Then he said, "It's happened. I'm A to Z. I'm the Beginning, I'm the Conclusion. From Water-of-Life Well I give freely to the thirsty. Conquerors inherit all this. I'll be God to them, they'll be sons and daughters to me. But for the rest — the feckless and faithless, degenerates and murderers, sex peddlers and sorcerers, idolaters and all liars — for them it's Lake Fire and Brimstone. Second death!"

9-11   One of the Seven Angels who had carried the bowls filled with the seven final disasters spoke to me: "Come here. I'll show you the Bride, the Wife of the Lamb." He took me away in the Spirit to an enormous, high mountain and showed me Holy Jerusalem descending out of Heaven from God, resplendent in the bright glory of God.

The City shimmered like a precious gem, light-filled, pulsing light.

READ

If you can, skim the expanded passage once quickly to get a broader perspective on the context of these verses. Then read this excerpt three times slowly.

THINK

Among all the images and names given in this passage — for the believers, for God, for the way life will be then and what will happen — which stands out to you? Consider God "mov[ing] into the neighborhood" or God "wip[ing] every tear from [our] eyes." Can you believe that this will someday be reality?

PRAY

Offer God your belief or disbelief in the promise of his coming kingdom. Thank him for the promise of it, even if you struggle to believe. Ask him to help you hope in it. Sit in silence for a bit, and be aware of him hearing you and looking at it all with you.

LIVE

What might be different in you (even if it's just the tiniest shift in perspective), knowing that a place "resplendent in the bright glory of God" waits for you?

DAY 364

GOD ENCOUNTERS

On this seventh day, review and reflect on all you have read this week. Take the time to revel in the ways you've encountered God in the past six days.

LIVING DAILY FOR GOD

One year. Perhaps the beginning of a life lived for him. What was it like? What did you discover that made you stop and really think about this almighty, all-knowing, paradoxical God? What fired your curiosity? What frightened you?

And as he revealed himself to you, how did God work in your life? Where has he led you in this past year? Through the valleys or to the peaks of the mountains? A little of both? On the way, what did you discover about him? About yourself? How has he changed who you are to make you more the person he wants you to be?

Take the things you have learned and put into practice this year and let them become part of the life God has planned for you. Don't let the discipline of reading and studying his Word languish. You're on a roll! Keep up the good work, because God is with you. In the words of the Message, "God, who got you started in this spiritual adventure, shares with us the life of his Son and our Master Jesus. He will never give up on you. Never forget that" (1 Corinthians 1:9).

NOTES

1. *The Book of Common Prayer* (San Francisco: HarperSanFrancisco, 1983), 55.
2. Henri Nouwen, *The Inner Voice of Love* (New York: Image, 1999), 98.
3. C. S. Lewis, *Mere Christianity* (New York: Touchstone, 1996), 87.
4. *The Book of Common Prayer*, 81.
5. Nouwen, 101.
6. Peter Kreeft, *Three Philosophies of Life* (San Francisco: Ignatius, 1989), 89.
7. Summarized from Richard Foster, *Prayer* (San Francisco: Harper Collins, 1992), 87–90.
8. William Johnston, ed., *The Cloud of Unknowing* (New York: Doubleday, 1973), 47.
9. W. E.Vine, *An Expository Dictionary of Biblical Words*, eds. Merrill F. Unger and William White (Nashville: Thomas Nelson, 1985), 18.
10. C. S. Lewis, *The Problem of Pain* (San Francisco: HarperSanFrancisco, 2001), 91.
11. David Jacobsen, *Clarity in Prayer* (Mills Valley, CA: Omega, 1979), 93.
12. Jan Karon, *These High, Green Hills* (New York: Penguin, 1996), 301.
13. C. S. Lewis, *The Lion, the Witch and the Wardrobe* (London: HarperCollins, 1998), 75.
14. Bruce L. Shelley, *Church History in Plain Language* (Nashville: Thomas Nelson, 1995), 3.
15. Oswald Chambers, *My Utmost for His Highest* (Uhrichsville, OH: Barbour, 2006), 52.
16. Teresa of Avila, *Interior Castles: The Collected Works of St. Teresa of Avila,* trans. Kieran Kavanaugh, OCD and Otilio Rodriguez, OCD (Washington, DC: ICS Publications, 1980), 2:309.
17. These questions adapted closely from Emilie Griffin, *Wilderness Time* (San Francisco: HarperSanFrancisco, 1997), 47.

18. Julian of Norwich, *Revelation of Love*, ed. and trans. John Skinner (New York: Doubleday, 1996), 13.
19. *The Book of Common Prayer*, 1983), 337.
20. Margaret Silf, *Going on Retreat* (Chicago: Loyola, 2002), 40–41.
21. Chambers, 193.
22. Bernard of Clairvaux, as quoted in *Prayer: Finding the Heart's True Home* by Richard Foster (San Francisco: HarperSanFrancisco, 1992), 168.
23. Ruth Haley Barton, *Sacred Rhythms* (Downers Grove, IL: InterVarsity, 2006), 117.
24. John Dalrymple, *Simple Prayer* (Wilmington, DE: Michael Glazier, 1984), 109–110.
25. Richard J. Foster, *Prayer: Finding the Heart's True Home* (San Francisco: HarperSanFrancisco, 1992), 61.
26. That the World May Know Ministries "Rabbi and Talmidim," *Follow the Rabbi*, March 7, 2007, http://community.gospelcom.net/Brix?pageID=2753.
27. Douglas V. Steere, *Prayer and Worship* (New York: Edward W. Hazen Foundation, 1938), 34.
28. C. S. Lewis, *The Weight of Glory* (Grand Rapids: Eerdmans, 1965), 14–15.

BEGINNER DEVOTIONS

INDEX

The Message//REMIX: Solo is intended to immerse you in the beauty and depth of the Bible through lectio divina. It is not a topical Bible or a concordance. However, if you are looking for a reading on a specific subject, the following index of topics and day numbers may be of assistance. It is not meant to be an exhaustive list of the topics covered by the Scripture passages discussed in this book. If you find that you want to delve deeper into a particular topic, see *The Message Three-Way Concordance* (Colorado Springs: NavPress, 2006).

ABOUT THE AUTHORS

Eugene H. Peterson is a pastor, scholar, writer, and poet. After teaching at a seminary and then giving nearly thirty years to church ministry in the Baltimore area, he created *The Message* — a vibrant translation of the Bible from the original Greek and Hebrew.

Eugene and his wife, Jan, now live in his native Montana. They are the parents of three and the grandparents of six.

Jan Johnson is a retreat leader and spiritual director and has written more than fifteen books, including *Enjoying the Presence of God* (NavPress), *Savoring God's Word* (NavPress), and *When the Soul Listens* (NavPress).

J.R. Briggs is the pastor and cultural cultivator of *resonate* at Calvary Church in the greater Philadelphia area. He is the author of *When God Says Jump* (TH1NK) and *Redefining Life for Men* (TH1NK). He loves to read, skydive, play basketball, camp, hike, ski, and blog. He and his wife, Megan, live in Perkasie, PA, with their son, Carter.

Katie Peckham has an MA in spiritual formation and soul care from Talbot Seminary and works as a spiritual director in Orange County, CA. She enjoys swimming, running marathons, and teaming up with her husband, Daniel, to serve the Christian missions community by using photojournalism to connect the American church with what God is doing overseas.

Learn what God says through
The Message

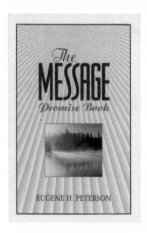

The Message Promise Book
Eugene H. Peterson
978-1-57683-015-4

The Message Promise Book arranges verses by topic, making it easy to discover the Bible's wisdom about a wide range of issues. *The Message Promise Book* will help you see your situation from God's perspective, expressed in everyday language that you can easily understand and apply to your life.

To order copies, call NavPress at 1-800-366-7788 or log on to www.navpress.com.

Give The Message of Hope

The Message of Hope
Eugene H. Peterson
978-1-57683-293-6

God offers eternal hope that runs
much deeper than any other. In
The Message of Hope, selected
passages from *The Message*
show how the life, death, and
resurrection of Jesus demonstrate
God's awesome love for us.

- Ideal for people suffering loss or facing discouraging
  times in their lives
- Perfect for evangelizing an unsaved community or as
  a gift to congregational members
- Small size makes it easy to carry for one's own
  inspiration or to give away at a moment's notice

To order copies, call NavPress at 1-800-366-7788
or log on to www.navpress.com.